'An extraordinarily frank account'
The Age

'Van Raay's compelling memoir, written simply
but with deep insight and a passion for life, comes in
three parts... Van Raay ties these three phases together
with her search for the middle road, and her painful,
joyful journey to self-acceptance'
Herald Sun

'*God's Call Girl*, a journey starkly recounted by van Raay
in this study of a lost life recovered by bizarre chance'
Courier-Mail

'[A] turbulent story, a frank and often shocking book'
New Idea

CARLA VAN RAAY was born into the Catholic south of Holland and came to Melbourne, Australia, with her family in 1950, when she was twelve. She was a radiant child until the age of six, when trauma changed her. Her choice to enter a convent at the age of eighteen was part of her inability to face life. In 1969, when she was almost thirty-one, she found the courage to leave.

Carla adjusted to the world without guidance from anyone. She fell in love for the first time in her life more than two years after her marriage. Alone and with a daughter to support, the idea of prostitution came to her. She worked for pimps as an escort to learn the ropes, then struck out on her own. Loving her work at first, the nasty sides of the business gradually asserted themselves. Carla realised that she was being driven by dark forces. The truth eventually became clear and she was able to start healing the abuses of her childhood.

Carla has been celibate for the last twelve years and now lives in Perth, Western Australia. She is currently working on a series of booklets to accompany her interactive seminars on Radical Innocence. Her website is located at www.carlavanraay.com

God's Callgirl

ONE WOMAN'S INCREDIBLE JOURNEY FROM
THE CONVENT TO THE MASSAGE PARLOUR

God's Callgirl

CARLA VAN RAAY

EBURY
PRESS

First published by HarperCollins*Publishers*, Australia 2004

First published in Great Britain by Ebury Press 2006

14 16 18 20 19 17 15 13

Text © Carla van Raay 2004

Ebury Press, an imprint of Ebury Publishing.
Random House, 20 Vauxhall Bridge Road, London SW1V 2SA

Random House Australia (Pty) Limited
20 Alfred Street, Milsons Point, Sydney, New South Wales 2061, Australia

Random House New Zealand Limited
18 Poland Road, Glenfield, Auckland 10, New Zealand

Random House (Pty) Limited
Isle of Houghton, Corner of Boundary Road and Carse O'Gowrie,
Houghton, 2198, South Africa

Random House Publishers India Private Limited
301 World Trade Tower, Hotel Intercontinental Grand Complex,
Barakhamba Lane, New Delhi 110 001, India

The Random House Group Limited Reg. No. 954009

www.randomhouse.co.uk

A CIP catalogue record for this book is available from the British Library.

Cover design by Two Associates
Typeset by Kirby Jones Design

Every effort has been made to trace and contact the copyright holders of photographs featured in
the book. If notified, the publisher will rectify any errors or omissions in subsequent editions.

ISBN 9780091913687 (after Jan 2007)
ISBN 0091913683

Printed and bound in Great Britain by Bookmarque Ltd, Croydon, Surrey

DEDICATED TO THE INNOCENCE

WITHIN US ALL

The grace is always there. Let the dis-grace, the idea that you don't have grace, leave you.

PAPAJI (HLW POONJA), BOMBAY, 1975

CONTENTS

FOREWORD

IN *GOD'S CALLGIRL*, Carla van Raay writes with blinding honesty about her extraordinary life. I was facilitating a women's group during 1987, and during the weeks we all spent together heartfelt feelings were shared, problems were solved and eventually our stories were told — some short, some long, with fear and embarrassment, tears and laughter. All these stories were real and moving, and releasing for the storyteller.

However, a tall, thin, shy woman with a nervous laugh held us spellbound with her tales of convent life and her subsequent, wildly improbable efforts to make some sense out of her existence. I don't think that anyone who attended that group will ever forget Carla. We all loved her — for her honesty, for her courage, for her zany sense of humour and, most of all, for her innocence. Somehow, through the abuse, the fear, the conditioning, the wild life choices she made, Carla achieved the impossible — she remained innocent. It is a rare quality these days. Without exception, every woman in that group begged her to write this book.

As I read through these pages, I was touched again by this moving and almost unbelievable story. Then again, if you knew Carla, it would not seem unbelievable at all.

Persephone Arbour, Perth, Western Australia

PREFACE

THIS STORY WAS bitter and angry when I began to write it many years ago, a dreadful soap opera intending to expose 'the awful nuns'. I meant to tell the world what I had suffered in a convent for twelve and a half years and whip up some anger against the Catholic Church and everything these institutions stand for.

That motivation disappeared as my anger subsided, and in 1986 I approached the then Councillor Joan Watters, a woman with influence in the city of Perth in Western Australia, whom I figured could help me with my quest to find a publisher. Armed with the proposed book's introduction, first chapter, an outline of the other chapters and a photograph of myself as a postulant in the order of the Faithful Companions of Jesus, I had no trouble convincing her of the merit of getting my story published. At my request she made contact with the press. In spite of our best efforts to vet the piece, a sensational headline appeared in every Sunday newspaper around the country: WHY I CHANGED FROM CONVENT TO BROTHEL. EX-NUN SPEAKS OUT ON NEW ROLE.

This immediately aroused the concern of my four brothers and sister in Melbourne, who pleaded with me not to publish my story out of consideration for our parents. Not only would it hurt them deeply to read the details of their once respected and now wayward daughter's life, but it would upset their dependent relationship with the nuns. Retired, they were still living in a house provided by the FCJs. I agreed, and let slip an opportunity when a publisher approached me.

Both my parents have since died and all ties, except friendly ones, have been severed with the FCJs. Many of the nuns involved in this story are now very old or deceased. The characters in this story are to me like roses on a bush: they bloomed brilliantly once and now many are faded and dead. This story is not about dishonouring the memory of their blooming, but about distilling the lessons provided by their actions and my own. Isn't that what life is all about? God breathes, and there we are: rosy, alive characters, full of blood and self-importance, on a stage with narrow confines. Then God breathes again — or perhaps he sighs at the spectacle — and we are all gone, returned to the place where everything comes from.

God bless all the old roses, and me too — a rose nearing an age usually not mentioned unless unavoidable. *God's Callgirl* is an honest autobiographical account and also, inevitably, a purely personal interpretation of events. Emotionally I have grown up and my story is in no way intended to hurt anyone at all. For this reason I have changed names to avoid coincidental identification of someone who is still living, and have also transposed some details. Members of my family, former members of my religious community, as well as my ex-clients in the sex industry, might well call my story fiction and that's unavoidable.

If anyone mentioned in this story is still alive and thinks they are being unduly criticised, or feels that I'm not doing them justice, I want to make it clear that this story is first of all an exposé of myself, warts and all.

Over the years, as I wrote the story of Carla — the girl who grew up in the Catholic south of Holland and came to Australia at the age of twelve, then chose at the virginal age of eighteen to enter a convent, and leave it at a virginal thirty-one — understanding began to dawn on me that it had been *my inevitable choice* to become a nun, then a prostitute. These were roles that I played which expressed my neurosis rather than my true self. I needed to experience who I was *not* in order to find out who I *am*. Maybe that is how life works; in any case, that is how it worked for me.

'What we resist, persists' is a well-known phrase. I did not understand sex, was afraid of it, suppressed it, and so it was on my mind all the time. Then, in order to understand it, I experimented in glorious and inglorious ways. This book describes the highlights as well as the lows of life as a prostitute, and the suffering caused by extreme indulgence.

The grace of the time I live in, and the help of many friends, has allowed me to become aware of my patterns and transcend them. It might not be good to indulge in memories, but it is dangerous to ignore them. So I am going to tell my story and be done with it, for I do not ever want to live this tale again!

HIERARCHY WITHIN THE ORDER OF THE FAITHFUL COMPANIONS OF JESUS

(in order of importance and authority)

Reverend Mother General

Head of the order; resides in the Mother House in England.

Reverend Mother Vicar

Presides over a region; for example, Australia (where there were four convents).

Reverend Mother/Mother Superior

Governs a convent.

Fully professed nuns

Those who have made final vows after a period of eight and a half years. Seniority among the fully professed also bestowed status.

Professed nuns

Those who have made their first vows upon graduating from the novitiate; or have renewed them three years after graduating.

Novices

Those undergoing the two-year probation period, after postulancy, before making their first vows.

Postulants

Those undergoing the first six months of probation or trial period.

Lay sisters

The main physical workers who supported the teaching sisters by cooking, cleaning and doing laundry work. They often received assistance from the postulants and novices. Lay sisters completed a similar probationary period to fully professed nuns, but never became eligible for a position in authority.

PART ONE

IT'S A CATHOLIC GIRL

I WAS BORN A Catholic girl child on 28 October 1938, at seven minutes past four in the afternoon, in a little Dutch town called Tilburg. It was my mother's first experience of giving birth, and her most terrible. It was my first experience of original sin, meaning I was too evil to be kissed until after baptism.

It was a whimsical time to be born. Draughts of cold air mingled with warm. Leaves floated from plane, oak and chestnut trees and were shuffled noisily along pavements and into porches. Roses lingered; their perfume mingled with that of pungent chrysanthemums and the dark smell of earth on misty mornings. Summer was leaving and people's thoughts turned to the inevitability of winter.

The house where I was born stood in a row of terraces. Each had an upstairs with a croft window set into a steep roof. There was a tiny garden in front, just big enough to grow bushes of blue hydrangeas and surrounded by a low wall finished with nicely rounded-off bricks — a perfect perch when mild weather drew people outside to talk to one another. The backyard was too small for growing vegetables, which was one of the reasons we moved after the war.

The street had the provocative name of Malsenhof, meaning 'garden of delights' or 'lush garden'. It did not live up to its name, however, and is no longer there today, gone to make way for rows of undelightful flats.

Mothers had their babies at home in those days; the doctor was only summoned in cases of clear defeat. My extreme reluctance to be born was finally overcome by the doctor's forceps of steel yanking me through a dry passage.

My beautiful mother was twenty-five, my handsome father twenty-four, but they had little idea of what they were doing, having babies. One thing they did seem to know was this: I was going to be the wonder child neither of them had ever been. Their plan was to grow me into a showpiece to impress all the family members and neighbours. It was a bigger issue for my mother, since her family had been against the wedding because she had married far below her social status.

After my first mandatory screech I was wiped clean by the midwife and given to my trembling mother for a drink at the breast. She was proud of me, no doubt about that, and proud of her achievement now that the pain was almost forgotten and the mess as good as out of the way. And I was sweet, which helped a lot. Her next thought was to get me baptised.

The Catholic culture into which I was born had a simple and totally sinister premise: human nature, it asserted, was basically evil. That meant evil from the very beginning and at the kernel of one's existence. Religion permeated the bones and marrow of the people in the southern part of Holland where I was born. It was a staunch belief that without Christian baptism souls would go to hell.

For innocent babies there was a special place called limbo, the catechism said, where they would mercifully not suffer hellfire but they would never 'see the face of God' either. This fact was created by a bull promulgated by the sages of the Catholic church in some century or other, and scrapped in the late twentieth century by another bull, but in 1938 there was no doubt about limbo's existence. So after a birth there was usually a scramble to get to church with the newborn to minimise its chance of going to that forlorn place. The baby's mother was rarely present at the baptismal ceremony, not having recovered sufficiently from the ordeal of bringing another bundle of sin into the world. Instead, an aunt would parade down the street with the baby in her arms, surrounded by a bevy of female relatives and friends, the baby on a pillow and covered by a white shroud of satin and lace. Walking was the only way to get to church, unless you happened to own a horse and carriage or that rare thing, a motor car, and we owned neither. If it rained, the shroud would protect the baby.

My mother's younger sister hurried me off to church and duly had me baptised and given Latin names as tradition required. My parents must have felt I needed at least three saints to ward off the devil: I was named Carolina Johanna Maria.

The names also represented my forebears. My first name was after my father's German-born mother, Carola. I was never called this particular derivative of Carolina, because my brave mother, who disliked, no, *hated* all Germans (barring my father) and snubbed her nose at her husband's family, said, 'Carola over my dead body!' She saved the day by making a minor change in the spelling, and a big change in its implication, and named me Carla.

Carla meant 'strong woman', which was just as well, given the karma that awaited me. My mother loved to call me Kareltje when she was in a good mood; a diminutive of the male Karel, from the Dutch word, *kerel*, meaning 'strong man'.

Being a Catholic baby generally wasn't too bad, if you were breastfed like I was. I was breastfed until my sister came along fifteen months later. But times were about to change. Holland would soon go to war. More significantly, there were also family wars looming, those private battles that happen within the walls of houses where children are growing up.

My mother was a buxom but not overweight woman with rich auburn, kinky hair swathed in waves around her head, gracing her smooth forehead and fair face. Her brown eyes were slightly hooded, her eyebrows a perfect arch and her lips full. She had been brought up by devout and genteel parents, and had studied and gained diplomas in sewing, tailoring and teaching. During the war her work as a seamstress on the black market helped to keep us all alive. As a teenager it worried my mother that her family was well off while others around her were so poor. It was a problem easily fixed: she married a man who didn't have much more than a violin and a handsome face.

My father's good looks were of the breathtaking kind: he was tall, muscular and perfectly proportioned. His face was remarkably regular. He had a fine, straight nose and grey eyes set in a face without lines. His jaw was chiselled square, his mouth — well, determined might be the best way to describe it. He had a practical mind and knew a lot about how to make things, how to grow plants in a garden and how to mend shoes.

My father was one of many children; by the time he was born his parents no longer bothered with a crib or cot — they kept him in the bottom drawer of a chest of drawers. He used to tell this story with a touch of wry humour, but the experience seemed to have left him with a never-ending sense of shock and grief.

His birthplace was Kranenburg, a town so close to the Dutch–German border that the inhabitants spoke the language of both countries, although his family preferred German. They were able to settle in Holland without any trouble when my father was seventeen and claim Dutch nationality.

When war threatened to break out my father was twenty-five. He was conscripted into the Dutch army, where his loyalty was briefly questioned. He had no qualms about fighting for Holland: after all, this was the country that now gave him his bread and living. My father translated his gratitude into enthusiasm for defending the country he now truly considered his own.

His extended family, unfortunately, did not feel the same way. The relatives in Germany, in particular, saw my father's unreserved allegiance to his new country as an unforgivable betrayal. His own younger brother, Anton, enlisted in the Dutch army but became an informer for the Germans. My father was heartbroken at his brother's attitude, but unflinching in his loyalty.

World War II broke out less than a year after I was born. My mother became a bundle of nerves, but gradually eased off as the occupation of Holland became an accepted way of life and my father came home from work again in the evenings. The war was just something that happened to people and little children.

AN INHERITANCE FROM both my parents' families was guilt about sex — nothing unusual in the guilt-ridden Catholicism of that time, but worth a mention.

My mother's family line went back to French nobility who had escaped the guillotine during the French Revolution by fleeing the country. In status-conscious Holland they had set themselves high above the assumed looser morals of the hoi polloi, so when passion overtook my courting grandparents, resulting in a pregnancy, they married in a hurry. My mother told me this when I was about to get married myself (though I was not in the least pregnant), but there was more. My grandmother was walking alone in the fields one day when a thunderstorm rumbled up. She had started on her way home when a terrible thing happened: a bolt of lightning came down right beside her, split a tree and scorched it as black as soot. That was the last thing my grandmother ever saw. She became blind, either because the lightning flash had scorched her retinas, or from shock, or both. Whatever it was, she never recovered and gave birth to her daughter (and later to three more children) as a stone-blind woman.

It isn't difficult to imagine what they said to themselves: it was God who had punished my grandmother. God had made her blind because her child had been conceived in *lust*. This was against their fine Catholic sensibilities, which dictated that sexual intercourse was not for pleasure but for the sole purpose of procreation. Yes, God had punished my grandmother in this mortal life so that she would be spared hell hereafter. Her husband, an earnest man, shared the guilt bravely, without having to be struck by lightning. Instead, he had to pay dearly for the nannies to help bring up their children.

My mother, therefore, considered herself 'a child of lust' and never felt good about her own sexuality. The uncanny thing is that she too ended up having premarital sex — a repeated act of damnable lust! She confessed all this to me as she grew older and longed for a confidant other than the local priest. *The feeling of guilt*, an insightful friend wrote to me recently, *looks for a way to justify itself.* She married my father, a healthy, handsome, poor and lustful man. Her faith and vows of holy matrimony told her to obey him — and to obey him meant to submit to his lust. In all other things, it seemed, *he* obeyed *her*, and so they had their trade-off, the basis for many a successful marriage.

This was my legacy. I was guilty from birth by being born a Catholic, naturally evil even before I inherited my mother's guilt, and later my father's, in the sexual drive he could not contain. Within a few years I would be in the grip of a guilt so fierce that I would call upon the devil to help me.

SHE'S NOT PERFECT AFTER ALL

 MY MOTHER SCREAMED and my father bellowed as they tried to save the wedding presents. A wonderful tumult of amber and china came falling down around me from the dining table, along with the tablecloth, when all of a sudden my father's hard hands gripped me, lifting me from the shards. What a shocking feeling! My father's focus was the loss of the irreplaceable — our future income would never allow for such beautiful and frivolous things again.

I was a most disappointing child. For a start, I ate coal. They wanted to hide this from our relatives and tried to stop me with smacks and terrible looks. But whenever they couldn't find me, I was in the cupboard near the fireplace, blackening my clothes, the floor and every exposed bit of my body. There were other deeds which made them shout and scream. I loved tearing big strips of peeling wallpaper, just to hear that wonderful *rrrripp*! In spite of likely distressing consequences, I was determined to see what was inside soft toys, especially the teddy bear that made a noise when you tipped it. The list of my disappointing acts was almost as long as each day.

It was scary when my papa grumbled in that big voice of his and said 'Tch, tch!' like a hissing train, or words that my mama didn't want him to say. '*Hou je mond*, Jan!' she would admonish. 'Don't speak like that in front of a child!' He told me often I was a bad girl. Sometimes when he picked me up I didn't know if he was going to hug me or hit me. I had a nice papa sometimes, and at other times a papa who made me feel scared. I wanted to be good for him. I loved him so much.

I wasn't a year old when my father went off to prepare for war in those few months before Holland fell to the Germans. He came back on leave, but was often away. Visiting friends and relatives made up for the lack of his company. My mother loved visitors. The Dutch way of life is a great social institution: everyone is geared up for visiting as if life depended on the custom. For children, visitors were no fun at all. Children suddenly had to become invisible unless they were still small enough to be admired in a cradle or pram.

I was two when a woman visitor arrived. It was summer and the magnificent hydrangeas in our tiny front garden were in full bloom. I loved their wondrous blue colour; the countless small florets that made up their large round heads. I sat under their long stems, watching the sparrows and finches as they hopped among the litter, looking for invisible things to eat. I had been sent there by my mother, who had told me that I'd be able to catch a bird if I put salt on its tail.

'Would it be mine for *ever*?' I'd asked. 'Of course, once you catch it,' she assured me with lots of nods of her head.

So off I had gone to fetch a handful of salt from the open wooden container in the kitchen and had crept under the hydrangeas to catch myself a bird, which would be mine for ever. I sat hunched and very still, with the crunchy salt in my right hand. Sparrows came and went — they flew by so fast! *Whirr!* Off they went as soon as they saw me. But there was one that stayed to peck at the sand. It didn't notice me. It was so close . . . I dropped the salt on its tail and reached over to grab it, but it flew away on very fast wings. No, no! It wasn't supposed to fly away!

I ran to my mother and screamed, 'Mama! The birdie flew away!'

I knew I was interrupting her visitor, but she had to fix up this shocking event! My lips trembled and tears started to roll down my cheeks. My mother was taken totally by surprise. Then the unbelievable happened: she began to laugh! She had duped me and now she was laughing at me for having believed her. My mother turned to her visitor and together they enjoyed the huge joke.

Mama! How could you do this to me? But I didn't say a word; I just stood there with a big pain in my heart and my breathing going hick, hickety-bump.

The woman left and still my mother ignored me. It was time for her to clear the tea table, then attend to my baby sister, and my disappointment was forgotten. It wasn't that she didn't love me or didn't care about my feelings — in those days, the feelings of children were just not taken into account. She had been treated that way when *she* was a child. I would grow up and treat my children in much the same way.

MY MOTHER, A trained teacher, appreciated the then innovative Montessori method of teaching, and although I was only two and a half she decided to walk me to the local Montessori school. Yes, the nuns said, I could begin tomorrow.

The next day I insisted on going there by myself. 'No, Mama, leave me alone! I know the way!' I talked the way she talked to my papa, with a very firm voice and a straight back, and she relented. She followed me from a discreet distance, hiding in the porches of the houses along the way to make certain I didn't get lost. I surefooted it to the right address and the happiest two and a half years of my young life began on that day.

It is the smells I recall best from that haven for children: a comforting lavender and talcum powder smell, the scent of oranges — very rare in wartime Holland — and of plasticine and glue, and flowers in vases. There were happy, bright colours, nice clean toilets with basins the right size for little people, and fish in tanks. I thrived there, in spite of the school being run by nuns whose debilitating vow of poverty allowed only the smallest pieces of paper for drawing. Paper was expensive during the German occupation. What could I draw on a piece of paper no bigger than my hand? It was scary to make a mistake and spoil it. The nuns told us that Jesus was poor and that poverty was a 'virtue'. For me, it was just a relief when art class was over at last.

For the poor people in our district it was a solace to be told that God had a soft spot for the luckless, the struggling, the deprived and the needy. We were poor because my virtuous mother obeyed her husband's will in bed, which produced more and more offspring to feed and clothe during and after the war. In twenty years she produced ten children in all, with two miscarriages as well.

Sunday being a very special day, a day of no work or chores for anyone, not even my mother (except she would still cook meals), I would make a beeline after lunch for the large wooden box protecting the bakelite radio, and sit on it. It stood next to the front-room window, just where the brown velvet curtains draped to the floor. How wonderfully cosy to wrap that soft warm curtain around myself! And to feel the music going right through my whole body! I was in heaven on the days when it rained outside or was blowing a gale, spending hours wrapped up and unnoticed on the classical music box. That's how I absorbed rhythm and harmony, passion and beauty.

It was also on Sundays that my father would take out his violin and play the few tunes that he knew. His musical education had been interrupted when his children arrived and he had to work hard to support his family. Going to war also did nothing to further his musical knowledge. So he played the same tunes over and over again but with the greatest pleasure, and I admired my father from the bottom of my heart. Paganini's *Carnival of Venice*, which gave him leeway for some creative variations, was one of his favourites.

It was my mother who eventually became annoyed by his playing. She hated him showing off, and the fact that he never seemed to tire of being pleased with himself, playing the same tunes over and over. My mother had a thing about the evils of pride.

My father was also fond of his mouth harmonica. I was in awe of his expertise, but my mother considered it a vulgar thing. She said his repertoire was boring. Poor Dad; for him, it would have been enough if she had never said out loud that she hated it.

It was an inviolable custom to visit one of my two sets of grandparents after Mass on Sundays, except when there was a bombing alert. However, when it came to my father's parents, Oma and Opa Koekeroe (so called because Opa kept pigeons that crooned '*koekeroe, koekeroe*'), they had to drag me there screaming. My father put on his determined face, and my mother — well, she secretly agreed with me, so I wasn't smacked for dragging my weight along the pavement all the way.

Most of my father's family appalled me. Except for Oma, they were thin and looking like sticks, as if they were starved of food or love or both, and there were a lot of them, aunts in bobby socks and uncles with clothes that smelled. I couldn't help but feel dirty in their house. The ever-present smell of pigeon poo didn't help. Oma waddled and wheezed; Opa was thin and bent and grew a wiry moustache. He wore the same clothes for too long and always had a pipe dangling from his lips or his gnarled fingers. He wheezed as well.

I much preferred going to my mother's parents' house, where the furniture was made of leather, where everything gleamed and there were even flowers in vases. There were shrubs growing in front of the bay windows facing the wide tree-lined pavement and the park over the road.

My relationship with my maternal grandfather was rather formal. Although we liked each other, I can't remember him saying anything to me that made a particular impact. He was altogether a solemn sort of man. My grandfather ran an importing business and was always first in the town to acquire the latest technology: the first gramophone, the first car on our cobblestone roads, the first telephone.

The men would play cards after church, for real money. As they concentrated on their game and drank draughts of whisky, the rich aroma of their expensive cigars filled the room. I delighted in being a part of the intellectual and sensual excitement, going around the table and making tidy heaps of the gambling coins. In this way I was able to participate vicariously in the air of secrecy and luxurious indulgence that pervaded the room. My grandfather liked me being there, my mother objected only weakly, and it meant that I had very little to do with my blind grandmother, who seemed to be for ever in bed due to complications later in life. She looked very pale and old. I climbed onto her big lace-covered bed once. Her eyes were the colour of some of my marbles, but she couldn't see me at all. Her mouth did not have many teeth. How did she feel? She didn't give much away, so my interest faded and I soon left the room again.

In spite of her disability and her illnesses, my grandmother had produced three girls then my Uncle Kees, whom I adored. Grandmother was only fifty-four when she died. She was laid in a casket of exquisite white satin, with madonna lilies all around her. The dining room was temporarily transformed into a funeral parlour, with black drapes on the walls, black curtains and screens. Tall wax candles were placed at either side of her head. She looked so beautiful and peaceful that I went up to her fearlessly, to gaze at her face close up. She had a lace collar under her chin and wore a new-looking black dress. Her hands were folded as if she was praying. I thought she looked better than ever before, if a little paler.

I was shocked when an adult noticed me so close to the corpse and whispered loudly and urgently for me to 'Come back here'. 'Here' was where all the adults stood at a respectful distance from the foot of the coffin, talking softly to each other. I scurried into my mother's skirts.

Everyone was worried about my grandfather, who was beside himself with constant grief. He followed her five years later.

THE OCCUPATION OF Holland continued and life went on in its adapted way. I got used to the sight of German soldiers patrolling the streets with threatening guns held tight, ready for use. They were usually young men dreaming of home, who didn't relish the vilification thrown at them by daring and outspoken people.

My Aunt Rita screamed at two of them one day, in a fit of fury, when she accompanied my mother and me to the shops down the street. Her husband was Jewish, and she knew many Jews who had been deported by the Germans and never been heard of since. Aunt Rita had to be dragged away smartly by my suddenly forceful mother. We were all glad to reach the alley behind our house and so avoid coming face to face with the men she had insulted from a distance. Aunt Rita ended up sobbing. Her husband, a carpet salesman, was lucky enough to escape deportation and after the war they lived in Amsterdam.

People sometimes became hungry during the war. The occupying forces would commandeer the pig from your backyard if they got to hear about it, and your vegetables as well. And before them, it was the government who wanted your food to feed the army. Food in the shops was rationed. Each household received coupons dictating how much we could buy of any one thing. Prices were outrageous and black marketeering was rife. I grew up in an atmosphere where children witnessed the importance of subterfuge; where people felt free to talk among themselves in hushed tones, but appeared to know nothing when asked a direct question. The cheerful butcher with round red cheeks brought us pieces of meat that would get him hanged if anyone found out about it, but he went away with shoes that my father had mended for him and a dress for his wife that my mother had sewn the night before.

War made some people enterprising, including me. We all participated in knocking coal off the back of the coal truck. Stealing turnips from the farmers was not allowed, but if you weren't caught you didn't get into trouble. Many a day we children sat in a row on the brick walls of our houses, chomping raw turnips and swedes originally destined for the cows. Things would not really improve until several years after the war was over.

Four children were born to our family during that anxious time; 'God's blessing' did not stop coming just because a war was on. In fact, God didn't seem to notice in the slightest.

My papa was so very handsome, especially in his military uniform, and my mama had a romantic heart. She sang Richard Tauber's songs along with him when he came on the radio. She sang that he was her heart's delight. And where he was, she longed to be. She was always breathless with joy to sing songs like that. There is a family photograph taken by a professional photographer of my father wearing his uniform. I have never seen anything more dashing.

In one family photo of my gorgeously handsome dad, my proud prim mother, my younger sister Liesbet and my little baby brother Adrian, the camera catches me as I do a fake whistle. My father taught me how to whistle but I had learned to be careful. Once, when we were sheltering in the cellar under the stairs, I had whistled a perfect imitation of the bomb that seemed to be coming straight for us. I was only four and not afraid of what I could not imagine — unlike my parents, who were holding their breath. My father had lunged at me and closed his hands over my throat — a very effective silencer.

Towards the end of the war my father donned his uniform once more to join the Allied Forces, returning regularly on leave, complete with a truck and a rifle. In those months he was the hero of the neighbourhood. He never had to go to the front line, not only because he was a family man, but because it was understood how difficult it was for him, having all but his immediate family in Germany.

My father brought the truck home whenever he could, sometimes against the rules, because he was an adventurous man who loved to surprise his wife and children. There wasn't enough room in our narrow cobbled street to properly accommodate it, so he used the vehicle to topple a couple of the myrtle trees in the way.

After lunch one day, he invited all the neighbourhood children for a ride in the back of the khaki-covered truck. This was an experience that nobody passed over and the truck was full with children. I was holding on to the wooden half-door at the back. Deciding to make the most of the fame that was rubbing off on me from my father's tremendous popularity, I took out a cigar I had recently bought and lit it, to the huge delight of all onlookers, who, of course, all wanted a puff.

My father drove us out of town and into the countryside as far as the little forest where we would often go for a walk and gather wood. When the road dwindled into a path through the trees, he had to stop and turn around. He needed to make a three-point turn to do so, leaning the back of the truck way over a culvert. My face went pale, paler than when I'd felt sick from the cigar, as the truck rumbled slowly away from solid ground and seemed about to plunge into the deep channel. But my father did not let himself or any of us down; he manoeuvred that truck flawlessly and delivered the noisy mob safely home to their parents, who were waiting in the street like a guard of honour.

My father took me on his knee later that day because my mother had heard of the cigar business and told him that I should be reprimanded. Unbelievably, he wasn't furious. For that one time, at least, he recognised something of his own enterprising self in me, and I became my father's daughter, not just the little person who crossed him in ways that he called sinfully disobedient. Perhaps the war had made him a bit softer.

It was my father's gruesome job to retrieve dead bodies from the fields and trenches. That was what the truck was for. He had to identify the bodies if he could. Sometimes they were decomposing, and the copper identity disc on its metal chain had sunk into the dead man's rotting chest. It was enough to shake any man.

TO ME, THE German soldiers were an enigma — for a long time I could not understand why people hated them. I was not frightened by them, because my father spoke to them when he met them in the street and made them laugh. His fluency in German saved him on several occasions.

Two German soldiers probably saved my life one day when I accompanied my father on one of his wood-collecting trips to the forest. My father had loaded me onto the cart which he had borrowed from a neighbour. It had two bicycle wheels and handles like a wheelbarrow's for pushing when you weren't pulling. He lifted me onto some potato sacks to ease the bumpiness of the ride. Later, the sacks would cover our firewood, so as not to attract the attention of any German soldiers who might commandeer the wood for themselves.

The forest was just in sight when the sound of sirens filled the air, warning people to take shelter. The Allies frequently flew over Holland to bomb the Germans out of their complacency. The sound of planes came nearer: there we were, in the open, far away from any shelter, and the bombs would fall at any moment! I was five, old enough to associate panic with these sirens, but still felt calm: my big, strong, wise papa would surely know how to protect us both. He was not about to turn tail on account of a siren.

My father walked doggedly on for a while, then made a decision. 'You wait here for me,' he said, as he lifted me off the cart and deposited me at the side of the track. 'I'll be back soon with the wood.'

My papa was going to leave me there by myself? I might be bombed to death and my papa was leaving me? Oh, no, Papa, no, no, no! I sank to my knees and stretched my arms out to him, screaming with absolute terror, refusing to grasp that he could leave me there. My father, the daredevil, laughed and threw me a few potato bags. 'Cover yourself with these!' he shouted.

My panic grew even wilder — how could a couple of jute bags protect me? But he was off already and looked back only once. 'Get the hell under those bags!' he yelled. I proceeded to worm myself right inside one of them, sobbing with terror, when I heard a sound from the other side of the track, a soft whistle. When I looked around I saw two soldiers in German uniform hiding under the bushes in a ditch. I recognised them by their helmets. The soldiers, both very young with good intentions obvious in their eyes, were urgently beckoning me to come to them. I did not hesitate, but ran into their arms.

I must have fainted, for the next thing I remember is waking up in my bed at home to the excited voices of my father, mother and the neighbours. I came groggily down the stairs and saw my father displaying a bandage around his thigh from where a bullet had just been extracted. He had been spotted in the forest by an American pilot who thought he was German and had circled until he scored a hit. I sat down bewildered on the lower steps of the stairs, listening to the hullabaloo.

Such incidents were typical of my father. On home leave from his soldiering duties one day, he dared the Germans to do their worst when once again the sirens were blowing. He lit his pipe and stood outside the back door, leaning against the brick wall. He had just inhaled a deep draught when a piece of shrapnel penetrated the bricks right by his left ear, shattering them and leaving a jagged hole in the wall. When he came inside he laughed at my distraught mother, whom he had successfully defied, and who was now weeping from a mixture of anger and relief. I was nearly six when the most shocking event of the war touched our neighbourhood, one which cowed everyone. I tried to make sense of their agitated gestures and hoarsely whispered words. Ten men had been rounded up and made to stand against the brick wall of the cotton mill, just on the edge of town, where they were shot in reprisal for the death of a German patrol soldier. One of the victims belonged to a family in our street. They had dragged his body home, leaving a trail of blood. Fierce hatred flared against the Germans.

PRIMARY INSULTS

BY THE TIME I left the Montessori school at the age of five I was able to read fluently and calculate in thousands. I was a rotund and beamingly happy child. Despite a worryingly prolonged case of whooping cough when I was three, I had come through. There were distressing things in my life that happened at night, but when I woke up these nightmares seemed to vanish. A young child lives in the present moment whenever possible, and I was no exception.

And then came primary school. It was also run by nuns, with the help of a few lay teachers, in a two-storey red-brick building next door to the Montessori school. By the adjoining wall was a mossy grotto sheltering a chipped and faded statue of the Virgin Mary standing on ancient slimy-green rocks. Oh, the terrible boredom of this new school! I could already read fluently so they put me up a grade, but it made hardly any difference. The only new and exciting thing was musical notation. The toilets in this school were horribly dirty, full of nasty words and awfulness. And for the first time in my life I started to seriously live in fear.

The nuns at my primary school in Tilburg were probably typical of teaching nuns in the 1940s worldwide. They preyed on the vulnerability of children. Fear is still used as a motivator in our education systems, but the nuns had it particularly easy. They could use the threats of eternal punishment in hell or being burned alive in purgatory on top of punishment and humiliation in the here-and-now. Sarcasm, ear-pulling, pinching of cheeks and slaps with the ruler were quite enough to intimidate us without us running the added risk of the disapproval of Almighty God. The nuns had God on their side, and they were against us, so we had it tough. Even touching a nun's habit was a sin punishable in purgatory. We would still furtively lift up the veil or hem of an unsuspecting nun, knowing we were clocking up time in the burning flames. Somehow it was worth it.

The greatest weapon in the nuns' armoury was the doctrine of God's omniscience: that is, he knew everything that went on. A huge eye hung on the wall of every classroom, peering into our most private thoughts. If this was designed to make us feel perpetually uncomfortable, it certainly succeeded as far as I was concerned. On hundreds of occasions I wondered what had prevented God from striking me dead. Maybe he would surprise me one day and the school's brick wall would fall on me as I walked by. From the classroom window I watched the wall of the nuns' living quarters across the schoolyard; my expectation that it would collapse was compounded by the Biblical story of the end of the world. Yes, God would destroy everything one day, and call his good children to sit on his right side and sort out the others for eternal damnation.

In the heat of a summer afternoon, the wall seemed to shimmer and quake; the end of the world was nearly here and I wasn't sure if I would be considered good enough to sit at God's right hand. Did God ever make mistakes? Maybe he would look at me and *think* I was good, like Saint Nicholas did last December when he brought me toys. Would God get confused, having to sort out everyone on the same crowded day?

Sinful Catholics in my childhood days had three ways of making up for wrongdoing and avoiding punishment. This was just as well, as the negative account would otherwise have been irredeemable.

Firstly there was confession, where — until my grand mis-understanding said otherwise — any sin could be forgiven. Secondly, there were the self-imposed punishments — literally 'beating God to it'; and thirdly, there were ejaculations. One *said* ejaculations. They were short prayers, we were told, so short that they went like little arrows (from the Latin, *jacula*) straight up to heaven and into God's ear. I saw an image of God's ears stuck full of little arrows, but I pushed the irreverent picture out of my mind.

Each ejaculation was worth many days' remission from purgatory — about three hundred days on average. Simply saying 'Praise be to God', for instance, could save hundreds of days from the flames! We were told that this was thanks to the accumulated credits earned by Jesus and the saints, which Catholics could draw on, as if on a bank account. The size of this account, and the expected length of purgatory for unconfessed and unatoned sins, was always fuzzy. How many days would you get for a swearword, or for disobedience — not to mention the bad *thoughts* we had all the time?

My thoughts were so elusive! I squirmed with shame at them. Common ones were wishing people dead, calling them horrible names in my head, and maiming them for life. 'God sees you' didn't just mean that we didn't have privacy in the toilet, or in our bedroom, or anywhere in the whole wide world; it meant God could read all our thoughts all the time and never miss a single one. I tried transferring my bad thoughts onto my dolls, making them my substitutes. That was no good, I soon realised: God could see through all that. It was invasion complete.

THE SCHOOL GOT partly damaged by a wartime bomb. The students were redirected to makeshift classrooms in the next parish, which was down the street. It was draughty there and cold, but that was par for the course in those days. Sometimes we gathered the still-warm shrapnel from the streets after a bombing raid, out of curiosity, not quite realising how it got there.

A new priest arrived in the parish and began to teach in some classes and walk around the playground. He was young and had a natural affinity with children. I gravitated towards him, and he took to me, which made some of my classmates say that I was his favourite. I liked the way he was full of good humour; he wasn't crusty and frowning like the old pastor. Sometimes I put my hand in his, and he would swing it or just hold it.

Stutteringly I begged him to enrol me in a junior pathfinder club called the Cubs. The Cubs' meeting place was at the Montessori school; they had polka-dot mushrooms for seats. Sadly, he refused. I remember him saying that it was only for children from families who did not have both parents, or something like that. But now I looked forward to school to be with Pater Janus at playtime. I felt so safe around him. He really loved children.

After school, it would be a lucky day if my Oome (Uncle) Kees had come to visit. He would lift me onto his big strong knee and talk to me in his gentle sweet voice. He was never cruel, not even to be funny, as adults often were. His eyes were beautiful — warm and shiny — and it felt wonderfully good to lean against his big chest and feel his arm around me. He took no notice of my mother's scandalised tone whenever she said, 'You're spoiling her, Kees!', which was often. To my constant wondrous surprise, he just smiled at me and jiggled me on his knee. He dared to ignore my mama! He wouldn't even put me down when my father scoffed, 'You don't know much about children, do you, Kees? They need to be disciplined!'

Oome Kees gave me a little doll dressed in traditional Dutch Volendam costume which I treasured for many years after he suddenly disappeared out of my six-year-old life. I thought he had died when he did not come around any more, but discovered only a few years ago that he suffered a brain injury after an accident when he was a sailor, and thereafter began a life of struggle and sad vagrancy until his death at fifty-seven. His true gift had been his undisguised love for me, his first niece. My life would have been different if I had not had an uncle like him. It might also have been different had he not disappeared. As it happened, after that the lights gradually went out in all directions.

I had assumed that my uncle was dead at just about the time when my pet rabbit died. My father had brought home a fluffy white rabbit. It was put in a cage and it was my job to look after him. We didn't have a cat or a dog, so this rabbit was really special; it wasn't just pretty and white, but oh so soft. I gave him vegetables from our big garden at the back of our new house, and leaves and weeds from my own little garden. I gathered the choicest treats for the rabbit.

How was I to know that he was being fattened for the pot? One day he was gone, although the cage door was still shut. 'Mama!' I cried, and ran to my mother. 'The rabbit has gone! He's not in his cage any more!' But she paid me no attention and the horrible feeling came over me that I was stupid to love this rabbit. What was worse — much worse — was that he was served up for dinner. No one said it was the white rabbit, of course. I watched everyone put some on their plate and some was put on mine.

Years later, when I watched a German war movie about a boy who unwittingly ate his parents in some soup he had found in their deserted house, the memory of that dinner came back. I couldn't protest at the time — I would have been belted for refusing to eat, and for stirring up feelings no one wanted to know about. Still, when I ate the rabbit — my murdered pet rabbit — somehow I joined that conspiracy, even though I felt sick. I joined in the lie that the feelings of children didn't matter, that *my* feelings didn't matter.

Yet my parents weren't monsters — far from it. My father and mother were sincere and talented people, with a saving sense of humour. I happened to be one of those children whose sense of justice was easily outraged and who hated having her judgment challenged. This was probably inherited, for my father hated having his judgment challenged too, especially by a little child. Perhaps it was on account of the helpless anger he felt at being criticised and belittled by his perfectionist wife, that he took his frustration out on his children.

It was sinfully wilful for a child to know its own mind, especially a girl child, although nowhere in the Catholic teachings can I find a justification for this. The whole church was, and is, a living example of male domination; the inferiority of women and girls its unspoken message.

As I grew older, we children couldn't argue without our words being met with indignant outrage. If this didn't shut us up, a belting from hard hands or worse would follow. Eventually my father dispensed with the time lag and belted us in a rage he was less and less able to control.

As it turned out, my deplored wilfulness was eroded — along with the brimming confidence that went with it — rather suddenly. One day my father decided he'd had more than enough. He made sure I would submit, or die.

LEAF OF A WEED

I WAS ONLY A few months into primary school, when suddenly I lost weight.

'She's growing too fast,' they all said, 'maybe that's why she's become so skinny, and so shy, as well.' They might have added, 'So shy that she is scared to look at you, and wants no one to even notice her.'

It wasn't a growth spurt; it was the terrible secret I now carried. I couldn't share it with anyone, this dark and sad burden on my soul.

What was it that I could no longer tell anyone, not even the priest, *especially* not Pater Janus? It wasn't just the recurrent nightmare, the awful, disgusting nightmare I had been suffering for about three years and could not escape, in which my papa, clad in his nightclothes, would creep to my bed like a thin ghost in the dead of night. While I was groggy with sleep, he would turn the bedclothes back and kiss me and trail his rough hands over my body. My papa would never kiss his little girl in the daytime, with everybody looking, but he put his big wet mouth smelling of tobacco to my face in the night, with hot bad air coming from his nose, and the kiss was hard, and his stubbly face hurt my skin.

It was so confusing! He smelled so horrible that I couldn't bear it, but I could not escape as he rubbed a smelly slimy thing over my face, and then — oh, horror of horrors — he put the dirty thing in my mouth.

Was it his tongue? I couldn't tell. No, I didn't think so, but what was it? I longed for total insensibility. I couldn't turn away; his hand kept my face to his, and anyway, I wouldn't dare. It was so hard to breathe. My papa panted and groaned, and then a warm thick stream gushed down my throat. Awful stickiness in my mouth. I longed for clean water, but there was none; there was only the merciful mindlessness of instant sleep.

In the mornings, the taste of it was still in my mouth. I thought I'd had an awful dream. In the beginning, when I was only three, I wanted to retch, vomit, get rid of it; then, out of the blue, I developed whooping cough. I coughed and coughed for weeks and months but couldn't get rid of what was choking me; could never wash my throat clean. But gradually, because I was a tough child and loved my father unquestioningly, I adjusted. A sort of unspoken conspiracy grew between us; I felt an inexplicable bond with him.

My mother might have expected that something had to give when she said no to him and meant it; or when she had a bad period, and he couldn't sleep because all his attention was on his penis and away from his heart. He left his bed when he thought she was asleep. She needed her reprieve. She had her bad dreams too, and often they turned into another pregnancy. My mother didn't allow herself to come out of her own fog, to see what was happening and stop it. When I developed cystitis she sewed me a pair of warm trousers to wear to school instead of a skirt, special permission from the principal.

At about this time, we schoolchildren were told the story of how Jesus died. Our teacher described in detail how Jesus was flogged and sweated blood, and how a crown of thorns was pressed into his head.

All these images were so new and vivid and brutal. It was the horror story of all time and I could feel myself starting to faint. 'After Jesus had suffered this way, he was nailed to a cross. A soldier hammered a big nail through each of his hands and each of his feet.' *Bang, bang, bang!* went the hammer in my head. 'Then they lifted the cross upright and, after a while, another soldier took a spear and drove it through Jesus's heart to make sure that he was dead.' I felt a stab in my chest, wanted to vomit.

It was impossible to understand these things. My head slumped to the desk, unable to look at the teacher any more. Then the teacher added, almost casually, that Jesus had suffered all that for *our sins*. We children had caused his death! *I* had caused his death!

The thick, hot, dark, heavy shame of my sins hit my soul. I felt that I, more than anyone else, had hurt Jesus. Why was this? Because of the dreadful thing that had happened in our coal shed at home.

The coal shed was attached to the kitchen and accessible from the tiny enclosed courtyard which also housed the toilet, called the WC, though there was no water in the closet. I had to pass the coal shed to get to the toilet.

Our toilet was a simple thunderbox, which was emptied into the backyard, which in turn grew magnificent vegetables. The smell of the box was so offensive that I learned to defecate in a big hurry, to get the job over and done with before I had to breathe. When my father was on the toilet it was unbearable even to be out in the open courtyard. Maybe it was his cigar-smoking, or his meat-eating, or the beginnings of the cancer in his bowels — or his frequent bad temper. Whatever the cause, the stench was overwhelming.

The coal shed doubled as a workplace for my father, who made and mended our shoes and created toys for Christmas and birthdays. My father was so good at toy-making; that was his Dr Jekyll side. He made me a go-cart, a wonderful doll's house and a rocking horse, and he painted them in bright colours. We were told that Black Pete, Saint Nicholas's helper, also hid in the coal shed, to find out if we were being good children or not. He was only there in the few weeks before 6 December, which is the children's feast of Saint Nicholas in Holland. But most of the time I felt safe in the coal shed, visiting my papa occasionally to watch him at work.

One day he called me in there and shut the door quickly without turning on the light, so that the only light that came through was between the uneven planks at the bottom of the door. His hand was rough on my shoulder and I could feel it shaking as he pulled me further inside, his fear transferring itself in a sickening rush to my body. I had never seen him like this before.

My father's face was contorted in a terrible way and he could barely get his words out. His hands found their way first around my shoulders, shaking them violently, and then suddenly around my neck as he began to strangle me. His tone was ugly, reminding me of the kind of talking that was not allowed in our house. Oh, the intense sorrow at this sudden rejection, with no idea of the reason. Couldn't he see my face? I adored him! My papa! *Please don't do this, Papa! I'm your little girl! Don't hurt me! I love you!* But my father was very afraid. He could not see his six-year-old daughter suffocating in his hands; all he wanted was to make himself feel safe.

'Don't talk to anyone about this . . .' he panted, poking a finger into my mouth to indicate what he meant, unable to say what had never been admitted to in daylight. The words came thickly from his twisted mouth, reverting to the dialect he had learned on the streets. 'Don't talk about it! Especially not to the priest! Understand? Nobody!' The veins in his forehead were standing out and his eyes were wild. He was grinding his teeth. Suddenly, he let me drop to the sooty floor. I fell in a bundle at his feet, unable to answer, pulsing one moment with the hopeless desire to plead, the next with the desire to die, until finally I was overcome by fear of actually dying.

He couldn't see me in the dark, didn't know whether I had understood, so he kicked at me, demanding an answer. He kicked me low on the spine and I sat up somehow. All this happened very quickly. He bent over me, and he was the devil and the dearest person in the world all rolled into one. I nodded soundlessly, not knowing how to breathe, utterly confused, not understanding what it was about my father's doings with me that was so very bad of me. Not for a moment could I imagine that my *papa* was bad. No, for him to treat me the way he did, I must have been a very bad girl indeed.

I lay down again in the dark shed, exhausted. He strode out and let the door fall shut. In this moment of complete distress, I could not call my mother. I closed my eyes and passed out.

When I came to, a panic rose from deep down in my stomach, a primal fear of ever being discovered. I could never confess my guilt, for I understood quite well that I was not to talk to the priest. I was a bad girl who could not be forgiven. All I could do was cover up my badness somehow from all the people around me. Even if I succeeded in convincing people that I was all right, I couldn't win in the end because *God* knew my blackness. I was terrified of death, because I believed I would go straight to hell. I was only six and knew no better.

I walked around as if in a fog. More than half of my waking awareness was busy trying to handle the wild feelings in my body. My life became more and more dream-like as this turmoil enveloped me. It became difficult to tell whether I was dreaming or not. I would wonder in terror whether I had really done the chore, my homework or any other task, or had I only dreamt it? I would do things twice because I couldn't make out what was real.

Oh, the terrible noise inside my head, my ears, my soul! I was haunted, imprisoned. Father Janus had become my friend. I had started to trust him and talk to him, but now there could be no more talking! I could not turn to him or to any other priest, could not confess, could not turn to God.

There was still my mother. Maybe *she* would do something to make it better. But she was too busy to sit down with any of her children to ask how we were feeling. There was never an intimate chat. She just didn't have that kind of time.

So I came up with my own desperate solution after the horror of the coal shed. Someone bad like me could turn to the devil and make a deal with him. With a fervent wish to buy time and avoid the flames of hell, I prayed to the evil one because I needed to rely on someone bigger than myself. 'Lucifer,' I began hesitantly, terrified of offending God still further by this switch in allegiance, 'I need your help. I am a very bad girl. I am so bad that God is not my friend any more. I want you to be my friend. Please help me not to die.'

My heinous prayer to the devil came out of the deepest desolation and abandonment. After a while, I felt that my prayers had been answered. *I survived*. But the guilt at my betrayal of God was terrible. It stopped me from breathing and eating, and I started to get things wrong, which in turn meant being derided by my father and the children at school. 'The idiot! That homework she handed in was four days late!' I arrived back late from lunch one day, after getting stuck in my baby brother's high chair. Why did I ever try to sit in it anyway? I couldn't get out of it and my mother's amusement at my expense had made me more desperate. I slunk back to school, to be faced by the locked steel gates. There was now only one way to get back in: I had to knock on the convent door and ask a nun to lead me through to the adjacent playground. She took me through in silence. I noticed that the nuns were making communion wafers; so that was where they came from, those white wafers that became the body of Christ!

Back in class, I couldn't explain clearly to the teacher what had happened. I stuttered my story several times over: 'I-I-I was stuck in the *kakkestoel*!' In my confusion, I used the colloquial for high chair; literally, the chair for shitting in, since it had a hole in the seat for a baby's potty. The other children understood, and they couldn't stop laughing. The more they laughed, the more I got it wrong.

My father did not know that his six-year-old daughter had gone to the devil. In my despair, I thought the devil to be a better ally than a punishing God. Every time my papa came to me at night, I thought I would die from suffocation. I wasn't able to face a hell worse than the one I was already in.

The recurring nightmare which I had begun to tell to Pater Janus was now strangled in my throat. I felt that the best course of action was to be as inconspicuous as possible, preferably invisible. More than ever, I felt obliged to get up very early in the morning and go to Mass (I never missed Mass unless I was seriously ill and couldn't walk). I had to eat, and go to school, and do my chores, but it was too dangerous and stressful to interact with anybody. I felt like a trembling weed, tolerated in the garden of life if nobody noticed me.

I could no longer bring myself to play with other children in the playground. I watched with agony, longing to join them when they skipped in teams, or hop-scotched, or sledded along the icy paths they had made with buckets of water on the frozen ground.

When I was a few years older, I did sometimes join in, especially sliding on the ice. You had to take a run-up, then launch yourself onto the thin strip of ice and try to make it to the end. At these times I glowed with contentment. But for two winters, while I suffered from cystitis caused by contact with my father's unwashed penis (though, for reasons clear only to himself, my father never penetrated me), I couldn't play outside for fear that the infection would get worse. I watched my classmates play from the corridor windows on the first floor, sipping warm milk from a thermos flask.

MY GROWING THINNESS was eventually noticed. My mother could see that there was something seriously changed in her daughter, but if she ever suspected the cause (because she did know her husband), she did nothing. My father, who watched his sturdy girl wilt and grow woefully thin, hid his terrible knowledge from himself. And so his eldest daughter, once so wickedly wilful, was brought to the doctor because she was inexplicably listless, underweight and wan. I was sent away to a health resort a few months after the war ended, to recover alongside emaciated war orphans and shell-shocked children.

I spent six miserable weeks in an institution run by nuns in an incongruously military style. They were harder, it seemed, than the nuns at my school. I was so homesick, so ill with pain in the whole of my gut, that I couldn't eat. In the refectory, the voice of an invisible all-seeing nun would boom out from a hidden loudspeaker, paralysing me with, 'Carla, eat that up! Don't try to pass it to your neighbour!'

We were searched for head lice, and for the first time in my life I felt the shame of having DDT powder poured all over my long blonde hair and the taste of it in my mouth. Back home, we were used to the almost daily ritual of picking out the nits. This was a serious business for my mother, the head baboon. From her we learned how to squash the tiny eggs, and the occasional runaway louse, between our fingernails. We never had to use poisons to control the lice we brought home from school because of our proud vigilance. Now I had to endure the nauseating smell of the white powder which was impossible not to inhale.

The nuns even checked how we lay in bed, arms crossed over our chests, not daring to move all night. 'Don't pull the fluff off the blankets, Carla! And all of you, children, sleep on your right side, not on your heart.'

I wrote away for some lollies, inspired by a girl who had some sent to her for her birthday. Unbelievably, my parents sent me a box of chocolates, and I put them under my mattress. They were promptly stolen and I felt unutterably cheated.

There was a wall that ran the length of the courtyard, dividing the boys from the girls. Mysterious rambunctious boys' voices came over the wall. Boys I'd never met before. My world had been extremely small; even at primary school the girls were segregated from the boys. These were *strange* boys, and curiosity got the better of me, so one day I looked through a crack in the wall. Oh, horror! A boy's eye was looking straight at *me* through the same crack. I ran away around a corner, panting, while my heart galloped like an untamed horse. I was not yet seven, too young to know the word 'sex', but sexual guilt could not have lain more heavily on any soul.

I felt so bad that day on the playground that I couldn't bring myself to receive holy communion the next morning. Every day we were ushered into the nuns' chapel to attend Mass, and for almost a week I stayed in my seat while everyone else filed to the communion rails. I squirmed in agony lest anyone should question my singular behaviour. The staff were seated in rows at right angles to me, in a good position to watch the children. I was in such a wretched state that I think I would have screamed or fainted if anyone had asked me why I was not taking communion.

Relief came at the end of the week, on confession day. Although the great sin that sat at the bottom of my soul could never be forgiven, I went into the confessional as all the other children did, and owned up to everything else. As a Catholic schoolchild, you couldn't *not* go to confession: you were herded there like sheep and just had to comply.

The priest seemed not to hear anything I said. 'I had bad thoughts about boys,' I told him in a faltering voice. Why didn't he pick up on my anxiety? Why didn't just one priest in all my life's weekly confessions pick it up? Were they preoccupied with themselves? Who can know what goes through the mind of a priest listening to children's confessions.

Needless to say, I gained no weight while I was in this place of military indifference. The phrase 'cold as charity' has a special significance for me. Before we were weighed for the last time, I ate as much as I could and didn't go to the toilet. I was anxious to please my well-meaning parents. The scales showed that my weight was still the same. I panicked and begged them to say I had gained two pounds. Naturally they obliged, eager to boost the statistics of their government project.

And so I was put on the train to go home. I was beside myself with joyful expectation. When the train entered Tilburg and I caught sight of my papa from my carriage, I yelled involuntarily with wild excitement.

The train stopped. Looking around, frowning, he couldn't see me. I ran up and stood in front of him, out of breath, suppressing a sob of love and joy. I so wanted to hug him and for him to hug me! But I didn't dare risk rejection, and I could not initiate any affection that might invite the wrong sort of advance, the sort that was worse than being ignored.

I still don't know whether my father deliberately resisted hugging his trembling little girl, or if he was simply oblivious to the moment and his own feelings. He led me to his bicycle; I was to go home riding on the back.

The station wasn't all that far from our house, but now I was faced with another dilemma: on the back of my papa's bike I had to hold on to something so as not to fall off. If only he had said, 'Hold on tight!', I would have had permission to put my arms around him as we went home, but he didn't, and I didn't want to risk being told brusquely to take my arms away. I found something at the back of the saddle to grip with both hands, and managed to stay on, my heart thumping all the way. This was a special occasion! I had been away and had been so lonely. I was so glad to be home again with my mama and papa. For them, my return was a disappointment. Nothing had changed. I was as thin as ever.

I NEVER STOPPED longing for my mama's understanding, for her to know how I felt. She was like a mirage, close but impossibly far away, and I became convinced that I had lost the battle to be loved and approved of in the way I wanted.

I developed scarlet fever. My mama didn't know what it was that made me so feverish. She kept me home from school, putting me on the couch in the living room for convenience, because my bed upstairs was too far away. This room, next to the kitchen, was unheated. The couch was filled with horsehair and very hard. The kitchen had wood and gas stoves which warmed up the whole room, and there was a big table to sit at for meals, to do homework on, and for Dad to cut out patterns for leather shoes after dinner. The horsehair couch was next to a draughty window and the cold winter wind pushed itself through the cracks under the sill like an unwelcome visitor. The cuckoo clock on the wall hammered its merciless ticking into my head. The autumn-leaf-patterned wallpaper made my head and stomach spin every time I opened my eyes and tried to focus.

Next door in the kitchen, my mama was busy all day with her three pre-school children. It was towards evening that she noticed I was delirious, became alarmed and called the doctor. When my papa came home from work in the dark of the evening, I heard my mama's anxious words, telling him about me. In a touching, gentle voice she asked, 'Shall we carry her up to her own bed?' She was clearly aware of the cold hardness of the horsehair sofa I was on. There was a discussion about how difficult that would be, as my bed was upstairs. The discussion ended with, 'It's best not to be too soft on her, that'll ruin her.' My papa's voice. I cried inside. There was nothing to show on the outside except the fever.

The doctor came in through the front door, bringing a gust of fresh air with him. He was dressed in black and carried a case. He was not an unusual sight, but to me it was remarkable because a doctor hardly ever visited us; we always went to visit *him*. I had only been to his surgery once, to have him look at the great number of warts covering my thighs. He had asked me to lift up my skirt so he could see them. This request put me into a panic of shame, because it reminded me of Papa, so I lifted my skirt reluctantly to just above knee level, blushing heavily and breathing very shallowly, studying the doctor's face intently. He seemed nonplussed about my hesitation; the doctor seemed to have no idea that the disgusting trail of warts on my thighs might have been the legacy of a penis leaving disgusting trails; that a small wart, stable on adult genitals, can go rampant on the tender skin of a child. The doctor said he couldn't do anything about the warts, and eventually they went away by themselves.

Now the doctor had come to see me. I knew everything that went on because my conscious self was out of my body; it sat on the end of the sofa and watched what the doctor did to my body. He took my temperature and looked into my throat. Then he turned a reproachful face to my mama, who was standing there with her hands twisted inside one another, biting her bottom lip, which was her habit when she didn't know what to do.

When he said, 'You should have called me earlier; it's scarlet fever, you know,' and added, 'She could have died,' I watched her intently. I could choose to die, if I wanted to. I would die, even risk hell, if she did not show she loved me. I saw the sudden blush of guilt that came over her face at the doctor's words. She seemed close to tears. I decided it was enough. She had shown such concern! Yes, my mama loved me.

I knew that then. And surely she would show it more now? She would notice me more, after I'd come so close to death to test her.

The doctor recommended I be moved to my own bed. My mama took in a quick embarrassed breath at this. Another signal of love: she was sorry she had neglected me and now she wanted me to be well. I returned to my body and responded to the medicines and the warmth of the cosy bed upstairs. My mother brought me hot soup and fed it to me. It was all worth the crisis. I felt nurtured and got better.

WAR AND WEEKENDS

WAR ACTIVITIES RESUMED in 1944 in an all-out effort to oust the Germans from occupying Holland. On many a night, with our papa gone out with his truck, Mama kept me and my little sister Liesbet up, sitting with her in the dimly-lit kitchen. There was only one candle, alight in its holder on the floor. She knitted non-stop on those nights, her head down, not looking at us as she mopped up the tears that rolled down her cheeks with a big hanky. I was so little when the war started, and only six when it ended. I felt helpless to see her in such distress. But we were kept busy. In the soft dimness of the candlelight, we made balls from skeins of wool and cotton. We wrapped the skeins around the back of a chair, walking around it as we wound each ball. We would soon learn how to knit, so we could add to her stock of knitted cotton socks, underpants and singlets.

Sunday was a special day of the week, war or no war. We were not allowed to do any work on a Sunday and the dishes piled up beside the sink. Sunday really was a day of rest and relaxation, and the specialness of that day is with me still — a pleasure for which I thank my Catholic upbringing.

During the week we worked very hard. I grew up in the days before washing machines and my hands were in hot sudsy water made soft by washing soda from as soon as I was old enough to stand on a chair to reach a washboard. My mama was house-proud, which meant that every week the windows had to be cleaned. That was my job too, and whether it froze or snowed or rained didn't seem to matter to her. When my hands turned blue and stiff in the winter cold, she would add some hot water to the vinegar bucket.

It was during wartime, with money still short, that I began to desperately want a rubber ball. I had seen one in a shop window in the square where I walked to deliver my completed crossword puzzles from the weekly newspaper. There was a cake to be won for the first correct entry, but mine was never drawn, worse luck. The ball cost much more than a few weeks' pocket money and my requests for it met with steady refusals.

It was then that I asked my papa whether the toys he had made for me were all mine, *really mine*? 'Yes,' he said. 'And can I do what I want with them?' I didn't tell him my intention, and he said yes again, almost absent-mindedly. He should have known better, but it wasn't until almost all of the toys had been sold to the neighbourhood children that he noticed and became very angry, demanding that I get them all back.

Get them back? Weren't the toys mine to do with as I pleased? He wasn't in a mood to reason. I was to go to all the children and tell them that I was not allowed to sell those toys and they had to give them back. The indignity of it! That day, I had the first and worst headache of my life, burning with humiliation and anger at the knowledge that *my* toys belonged to my papa and not to me at all. The children were unimpressed, but gave me back every one of my toys. Some of them had expressed great surprise at the unbelievably low prices I'd been asking for them anyway. I didn't know the value of things, and hadn't wanted to quote a price that might get a rejection.

I did get that rubber ball all the same. I used my savings from every possible source, including gifts from my beloved Uncle Kees, and the occasional leftover coins that were supposed to be dropped dutifully into my tin on the mantelpiece above the kitchen stove, for important purchases such as books. My mama and papa were not amused when they found out that my tin no longer rattled — they merely looked at each other when they noticed me playing with my ball, as if to say, 'What have we got here?!'

I continued to eat charcoal into the seventh year of my life, no matter the threats. Then I overheard a conversation I was meant to hear, which stopped my breath for a while and my coal-eating habit for ever.

'Is she a child of the devil, since she loves that black stuff so much?' my mama asked my papa peevishly. 'Tch!' he responded derisively, 'she sure looks like she could be.'

Child of the devil! As it was nearing Christmas, my parents simultaneously hit upon the idea of telling me that Black Pete reported naughty behaviour such as coal-eating to Saint Nicholas. Thankfully, my Uncle Kees came to visit just then, making light of the whole thing, but I was cured of the addiction for ever.

Our diet improved when an American soldier was billeted with us. We had been warned to expect billeting. My mama and I came home from shopping one day and found that a big man had fallen asleep in my bed. His boot-laced feet stuck out over the low white-painted wooden end of the slatted bed and kapok mattress. I remember it well, because it produced a rare moment of intimacy with my mama. She was as surprised as I was and, as our eyes met briefly, I read curiosity and amusement there too, not to mention her concern that the house was wide open to strangers just walking in. My mama didn't say a word to wake up the soldier and I marvelled at her self-control. Her breath came in quick shallow spurts, her mouth was sort of twisted out of shape, and she bit her bottom lip as she contemplated this new addition to her busy life. She smiled at me, and the delicious conspiracy of mama and daughter beholding an unsuspecting sleeping soldier was a heart-warming moment for me.

Ted, the soldier, turned out to be a good guy and stayed our friend for years after the war, until we left Holland in 1950 and lost contact. 'Here,' said Ted, 'try this!' and so we were introduced to chewing gum.

He brought food back from the mess, where he had his meals. We were particularly rich in oats for porridge while he lived with us. I pleaded with him, 'Ted, can you bring us butter, *please*?', but that was always chronically short. When I complained, 'Pa, these sandwiches are too dry to eat!', instead of scolding me, my papa made a promise that after the war I'd have butter a whole centimetre thick on my bread. I reminded him after the war, but alas he didn't keep his promise. He wasn't to know that for three years I had clung to his word, imagining the slabs of butter as I dipped my bread into my tea or milk.

ZEELAND, THE PROVINCE to the west of us, had been mercilessly and cruelly bombarded. It was time for our little town to accept the possibility that we too could be in the firing line. The neighbourhood decided to construct an underground shelter, big enough for everyone to huddle in during an air raid.

Every day after school I made a beeline for the dig, where a fantastic hole was forming under the ground. The entrance was only big enough for people to go down one at a time, or for chairs to be handed down singly. The earth was taken elsewhere so that the shelter's position would not be given away. You could never be sure of who would bomb you; many a Dutch person died from Allied action.

I went down into the shelter by myself one day, when all the diggers were huddled outside in an animated discussion. They'd had a gutful of this hard digging work. Most of them were older people, not fit to go to war. Naturally, it was very dark in the shelter, and rather damp. The light fell on a corner and I saw to my horror that a puddle of water had gathered there. I had just learned at school that the planet was composed of a thin layer of earth, and underneath that thin layer was a great depth of water, and under that there was fire and molten rocks.

My chest heaved in panic. The men had dug down to the water level and it was already seeping through! Suddenly, I felt that the earth had become very insecure under my feet, like the time when I was standing on melting ice in the canal last winter and people on the shore warned me to inch myself back carefully.

Luckily we never used that shelter. During air raids people fled to their cellars — sturdy structures deep under their houses, usually covered by a staircase, which was also a resistive structure. 'If there's a direct hit, the earth shelter would be useless anyway,' argued a wise old man. The shelter was used as a store for vegetables, and after the war it was filled in again.

As I grew up, new children kept arriving, as they did in all the Catholic families in the south of Holland. You were talked about if no children arrived for a while: *Why is God not blessing that marriage?*

The oldest girl in the family was expected to become a surrogate mother, and this was a role that I accepted without a murmur. It was my job to take the children off my mama's hands, especially after school and in the holidays. It was my special favour to take them for long walks, particularly to the railway overpass, which was through the town square, past all the houses and little shops in-between, past a farm and the church.

Churches and chapels held a fascination for me, and on our walks I would urge my little brood to come with me to investigate the places we never visited otherwise. One such place may not have been intended for such small visitors: it was an exquisitely gentle and intimate chapel dedicated to the Virgin Mary. At her feet knelt huge statues of angels, with wings wide open, bowing in adoration. Small candles lit up twin blue glass bulbs on either side of the tiny space.

We knelt at the communion rail right at the front, to be close to the wonder of the beautiful statues and the smell of the madonna lilies in large crystal vases. In tiny vases near her feet there were blue forget-me-nots and white wispy flowers, so sweet that they filled our hearts with devotion to the Mother of Jesus, who deserved this beauty around her.

Right there on the railing was a small angel on a heavy wooden box with a slot for donations. The angel's head bobbed in thanks when you dropped a coin in. Fascinating! My brothers and sisters all wanted to have my few coins to drop in, and there was a bit of hushed commotion until we suddenly noticed a smiling nun nearby. To our complete surprise, she held out a plate of biscuits and little cakes for us to eat! She didn't speak, but it wasn't necessary — we felt welcomed and appreciated, and decided that this chapel was definitely on our permanent list of places to visit!

If there was time we would go on to the railway overpass, little hands dragging along on both my arms until we finally got there. It was a wooden structure spanning four lines of rail, and every few minutes a train would pass underneath. Traffic — mostly horse-drawn except for the odd car, and people on bicycles — was stopped at the wooden gates operated by the keeper of the crossing who spent all day in the box at the side of the rails. We clambered up the two broad sets of wooden steps, keeping pace with bicycle-riders who didn't want to wait and instead pushed their machines up the narrow track near the railing. Once on top it was a matter of guessing not only which direction the next train would be coming from, but of judging exactly where we needed to be on the bridge so that the steam would hit our faces full on, wetting them with a delicious hot stream of sooty mystery, and threatening to engulf us in its wild confusion and carry us off. We had the solid wooden rails to hang on to and always survived wonderfully. We all returned home hours later with blackened faces. We were never scolded for that, because Saturday was bath day when everyone had a turn in the tub.

When we told our mama about the nun with biscuits and cakes in the chapel, she said it wasn't right for us to go there because it was the nuns' chapel and not meant for anybody else. The nun who gave us cookies must have liked children and was therefore a great enigma to us — not a bit like the nuns who taught us at school. Mama guessed she might have been a contemplative nun. She didn't want us disturbing her or the other sisters in the order. We were forbidden to go there again, and I am sad to say that we obeyed her command.

AFTER SEVERAL MONTHS of Allied fighting in the area, the liberators' tanks rolled in on 5 May 1945. They made the most fearsome rumbling racket over our cobblestones. The crowds waved to the victorious American soldiers, who threw cigarettes from their awesome metal towers. People scrambled to gather the precious booty before they were crushed by many feet. A little boy lost his small fistful when an old man ripped the cigarettes out of his hands without even a thank you. The little chap stood there, looking at his empty fist.

The whole neighbourhood went for a walk to see what the countryside looked like after the war had ended. A bridge over the canal had been destroyed, temporarily replaced by a span of ropes and planks. I was pushing a pram and brought up the rear. People chatted animatedly as they ambled; no one seemed anxious about crossing the canal on the swaying make-believe bridge, so I set foot on it bravely, but was overcome by a fear so great that I froze with my mouth wide open, unable to call out for help. A woman who had made it to the other side happened to look back, and ran back to guide me and the pram across.

All sorts of bullets and bombshells were salvaged from the war by our papa. Eventually, my mama put the large polished brass shells of bombs on the mantelpiece, to hold dried flower arrangements. But she was never quite sure of them; they were a constant reminder of the horror that bombs brought to people. On Sunday afternoons, my papa would sometimes make a show for us by burning the acrid powder from the bullets he had brought home. My mama didn't agree, it was dangerous, she said, and would also put bad ideas into our heads, but he loved to make us wonder at his cleverness.

A WEED GROWS UP

IT WAS ADVENT, the four weeks of penance and prayer before our first Christmas after the liberation, and we knelt to pray in front of the nativity crib set up in the living room. It was freezing cold in the room because the fire was lit only on Sundays, but the heavenly smell of the pine tree and the fresh straw near the crib made me feel ecstatic. Even the small candles that lit up the oxen, the donkey and the sheep, the three kings, the adoring Mary and the stunned Joseph released a cosy enticing smell.

We knelt on the seats of dining chairs and leaned against their backs, each with a rosary in our hands. I was seven, the eldest, and was expected to lead the prayers by reciting the first part of the Hail Mary. The rest of the family would come in with the second half. With each Hail Mary our fingers slipped to the next bead, and this did the counting for us. It should have been easy, but with my papa kneeling behind me, leaning heavily over the back of his chair and breathing impatiently, I just couldn't get it right. I would rather have been in the stable with the statues, lying in the straw and bathed by the soft light of the candles, than droning out Hail Marys.

I had intoned far too many Hail Marys, when my papa burst irreverently into my pious fantasy. 'What do you think you're doing, Carla?!'

There was a sudden panic in my heart, in anticipation of being shaken by the hands behind me. Thankfully, my mama took over, heading off a confrontation. We rose from our chairs and my papa scoffed at his somnambulant daughter, hissing disapproval coming from between his teeth: 'Tch, how can you be so stupid?!'

I turned down my eyes to ward off the crushing weight of his derision. Tears gathered inside; lately my insides had become a catchment of silent grief. The pain of not being respected by my papa seeped into my stomach and right down into my shoes.

The fear of making a mistake cowed me at every turn. But even greater than the fear of doing things wrong was the dread of being discovered for the evil girl I was. The terror was made worse by the feeling that everyone could see through me.

My seven-year-old mind burned. Sex obsessed me relentlessly; it seemed to surround me everywhere. I drew a surreptitious stick figure in the dust of a window pane, furtively adding a thing hanging between his legs (without knowing what it was, just that it was wicked — I had seen other naughty children do it), then hastily wiped it out, looking around to check whether anyone had noticed me. Worse, I felt like abducting little children and doing them terrible harm.

Walking to my aunt's house one day, along the familiar cobbled and tree-lined streets, I spotted a naked little girl in her front garden. The gardens were all very small in our area, barely three metres from the street to the front door. I was struck dumb by the sight of her genitals, so clearly visible on her tiny body. The feeling rushed through me that I wanted to shake that girl child, maul her viciously with my hands, throw her to the ground and stab her with a knife, hit her with a stick, a brick — anything. Kill her, but firstly maim her sexual parts. The compelling desire grew and grew in me. I was entranced, a force inside pushing me ever closer to the point of taking action. Suddenly, I became aware of the way my chest was heaving, and that my face was red and distorted, and I hurried off in case anyone saw me. The guilt I felt then was hot, sticky and terrible. *Never talk to anyone about it!*

When my papa touched me with his hands, or with his penis, or his mouth, he was telling me I was nice, that he liked me, and also that I was the worst, most sordid girl in the world. He told me this by his furtive actions, his compelling body. No words were ever spoken during our night-time encounters. Understanding all this was beyond me; there was no way I could work it out. My solution was to hide, and pretend that I did not have bad feelings. *Become invisible, Carla, hide who you really are.* This was difficult, because I felt as if I did not have a private self.

And so, at the end of term in grade three, when it was time to sing solo in class in front of thirty classmates, I fell into a serious panic. Everyone was going to receive a mark for singing and we all had to come up and sing a song of our own choice. For most of the children this was a bit of a treat: it was a rare thing to get out of your seat at any time and the general feeling was that this was an opportunity to show off. I merely felt huge distress at the thought of the eyes of others aimed at me. I heaved and squirmed, blushed and turned pale, hot and cold, and felt sick to my heart and stomach.

At last I was the only one left and there was no escape. The teacher motioned for me to come to the front. Inexorably, I found myself leaving my desk to face the silent group of expectant children. I opened my mouth and out came what I thought sounded like a suppressed scream, but it was the first bar of the banal song I'd chosen: '*Daar bij die molen*' ('Over by the windmill'). My performance held a total lack of finesse; I wasn't trying to be entertaining, just trying to get through the ordeal. Most of my vocal cords were out of action and a raw, scraping sound filled the attentive room. The teacher was kind. 'You have a voice like a bell,' she said, and gave me a 6 out of 10.

THE SOLDIERS WERE returning home after the war. They filled the trains that criss-crossed the countryside, including the carriage that brought me, my sister and aunt home from a stay in Amsterdam. While we were gone, our mama had been brought another baby by the stork. It was a boy, her fifth gift from God. We could see the storks up on the rooftops, standing on large untidy legs, looking out over the neighbourhood. Plenty of room for babies in their nests. Storks delivered babies hanging in nappies from their beaks.

The soldiers looked tired, but were filled with the excitement of going home. They were surely dreaming of the welcome that awaited them. The carriage was crammed full and the smell of woollen khaki uniforms was not unpleasant. I was enjoying sitting in the middle of this welter of male energy. It was when one of the soldiers caught my eye that I began to falter. He gave me an affectionate look, no doubt thinking that here was a Dutch child for whom he had fought the war; in seeing me he found a reason to justify the awfulness he had been through. I could feel his friendliness and good intentions, but I couldn't stop the blush, as livid as the shame that lived in my innermost being, from spreading across my cheeks and face. I was wretched. I couldn't bear to look around and longed to get off the train.

I HAD A Jekyll-and-Hyde father, but my mother had several sides to her also and her moods generally set the feeling of the house. What especially redeemed her in our eyes was her sporadic sense of humour, dispelling darkness as suddenly as the sun lights up the countryside. Then, her quirky, unexpected way of putting things sent us into fits of laughter. The house seemed transformed and evil an impossible reality.

Her wittiness attracted visitors to our house. Even when she was in her eighties and considered senile, she could suddenly throw off forty years and quip about life in the nursing home as if she were out on a picnic. Even though she was mostly sedated to relieve the pain of severe rheumatoid arthritis and the effects of syphilis, visitors were often delighted by her unexpected and funny remarks.

Mama loved music and often switched the wireless on. Classical music made her happy, and when I was little I watched her laugh as she worked, making the most of her day when her husband was away at work and she had the house to herself. She sang children's songs, war ditties, arias even, and at those times her brightness lifted our spirits.

A very special treat was to go shopping with my mama when I grew tall enough to walk arm in arm with her, as was the custom for women in Holland. It was a delicious closeness for both of us, and she would talk animatedly and cheerfully as we walked and shopped. Life became light again for me too, when I experienced the temporary happiness of forgetting myself.

Mother consulted the priest because she didn't want so many pregnancies. The priest told her that she had no right to refuse the husband she had promised to honour and obey in holy matrimony. So my mother had to cave in to my father's sexual demands; but she, the clever vixen, knew how to get back at him, the uneducated one. She had the ability to taunt him with words. He had only brute muscle against the power of her cutting derisive intellect.

My mama rarely approved of anything my papa did. She taunted him so much about playing his beloved violin that in the end he threw it against the wall and broke it. It could only be fixed at great cost, so he sold it to the repair man for a paltry twenty-five guilders — the violin that had been his personal Stradivarius. Did he gnash his teeth then, and weep when no one saw him, for letting his woman get the better of him? Or did revenge find its way through violence?

One day, during a more serious spat than usual, they both forgot that the neighbours would be listening through the walls. My mother mocked him in a loud jeering voice and dared him to kill her. This was something new. The insults had been flying for some time, and now the two of them were spinning in a vortex of bitter reprisal. We six children were crying out loud, sitting forlornly in a row on the kitchen table. Our parents were in full view through the kitchen door into the living room. Papa had the large carving knife in his hands and Mama was saying breathlessly, 'Go on then, do it! Kill me!' while she dared him with her eyes. She said it so many times that the only way he could save face was to actually stab her. She let go a scream and we children wailed the more loudly. The tribal bond with our parents was temporarily broken; we were abandoned, floating loose, drifting like flotsam on a churning murky ocean.

The blood brought my papa to his senses. He grabbed a towel and stemmed the flow from her neck. In time, the scar mended very well and was forgotten. I only noticed it again years later, in a photo of her lying in a nursing home bed, looking affectionately at my father, who was holding her hand. That's how it was between my parents — they truly loved each other and would never part. And yet they could not stand each other. When the stuff of passion can't be positive, let it be there anyway.

WHEN LIFE WAS not light but heavy, I escaped into daydreams. I had friends who lived with me from day to day — my dolls. I had several and they became alive for me. I talked to them, made clothes for them, put them to bed, gave them flowers and showered affection on them. My clever papa had made me a wooden doll's house painted a beautiful red. Even though the soft little carpets were the remnants of my pet rabbit, I kept them to decorate the floor. They gave me an eerie feeling of pure clean softness.

Only my dolls saw anything like the real me. I related to them as I would have preferred to relate to the people around me, if I had dared. With my dolls I was an untiringly tender mother, a sister, a child asking for help, a nurse, and a creative problem-solver. The dolls were alive for me until I was ten. When I was eleven, they were sometimes alive and sometimes not — curiously, it depended on how I chose to look at them.

I kept my doll's house in an open flat space halfway up the staircase, close to the ceiling. The area was big enough for a mattress and one day I persuaded my parents to let me sleep there with my family of dolls. However, a nocturnal visit from my papa, or maybe the nightmare of it happening again, made me wet the bed. I never mentioned it, and nothing was ever said to me about it. This was both a relief and a disturbance, because it must have been noticed by my mama, who washed my sheet and put a clean one on the bed. Why didn't she say something? Was she suffering from having to square things in her own confused mind? Didn't she know what was happening? Did she choose not to know? Instead of protecting me, she grew bitter and as I grew older began to regard me as a rival, calling me degrading names like *vuile dweil*, filthy rag.

MY MOTHER HAD to find some way to absorb the roughness she sometimes received at the hands of the man who demanded his marriage rights. One day she was nursing a mysteriously sore foot. It was never explained to us children why it was bandaged, or why she couldn't move from her chair. She whimpered whenever anyone came near her foot, and cried and rolled her eyes, sucking in her lips in pain when I accidentally bumped it. I felt the pain as much as she did: it went up my legs like knives of fire and I cried for her. But not far away was a bitch, growing and feeding on suppressed anger at my mother.

There were times when this bitch came out to bite everyone in her vicinity. I was eleven going on twelve, when my mother realised she was unable to stop me. There was to be a photo session — there were seven children by now — and a real live photographer was coming to our house. I knew instinctively that this would be an opportunity for my mother to show off her favourite son, Markus, the fourth child and her second boy. He had golden curls that were not cut off until he went to school, and both my mother and father adored him. Markus could do no wrong, but I knew how to wrong him and I knew how to destroy this special occasion for my mama, who had a much greater investment in how the family looked in photographs than my father did.

Mother was busy with the littlies and couldn't be everywhere at once, which gave me the perfect opportunity to repeatedly pinch my seven-year-old brother until he cried. With venom that would do a spider justice, copying the way a teacher had treated *me*, I nipped his pretty cheeks, sinking my fingernails in again and again, until finally the red marks didn't go away. My idea was to mar his good looks and make him cry so much that it would show on the photos.

The strategy worked, but didn't go unnoticed by my mother who was furious. She was helpless to undo the situation, but for the rest of that day she slapped my face and cursed me whenever we came within reach of one another. I did not attempt to get out of her way, somehow realising that every slap proved I had won. In the end it was my father who uncharacteristically took command and ordered her to stop, for God's sake, because the whole house was feeling unbearable.

She now often had to contend with the cold stubbornness of her eldest daughter, who pitted her will against her own when she had the courage. 'Bullheaded', she called me. 'I'm not a bull,' I would say quasi-innocently, and she fell for the bait to argue the point, saying that I knew what she meant. It was only my constant fear of dying and going to hell that made me repress the worst bouts of rebelliousness that boiled up inside me as if in a fast-heating cauldron, making my heart race and contorting my face as sweat broke out everywhere.

I was hotly tempted to kill both of my parents. I dreamed up elaborate murder schemes, and once almost convinced myself that I'd be able to do it and get away with it. Then I hesitated, and couldn't believe how bad I was. The 'real me' was this hideous person, who would be discovered when the outer layer of niceness was removed. The core of my being, I was convinced, was rotten. Everything in my religion confirmed it. I couldn't think any better of myself when I bought a box of chocolates for my mother's birthday with my scant pocket money, ate one to try them out, and then ate the lot, because it wouldn't do to give her a box that had been tampered with.

Nevertheless, in spite of everything I still was in love with God. This was not the God of fear and punishment, but a natural feeling in my heart that would assert itself when it got the chance. It might have been God the loving parent, the father in heaven whom a child could imagine to be kind and loving. Some adults in my life were kind and loving — my Uncle Kees, and Pater Janus, and even my own parents and teachers sometimes. When I felt God in my heart, I thrilled with joy to receive holy communion.

As the memory of the coal shed receded, I felt the lightness and cleanliness of confession once more. At my confirmation, I was proud to be a soldier of Christ. I felt able to please God in a way I had been unable to please my father. I imagined myself armed with light and swords made of fire, ready to cut the devil and evil to pieces, marching with fists on flailing arms through the alleyway behind our house, singing, '*Soldiers of Christ, we march to vindicate Thee*'. The German blood in me delighted in the marching rhythm of the confirmation hymns.

By then, I was no longer consciously aware of my alliance with the devil, but it lay there in my subconscious. Two strong opposing beliefs swayed me like a birch tree in a storm, first one way and then the other. I was good, brave and lovable; and it was just as clear at other times that I was the worst girl alive. By the end of my childhood I couldn't make sense of my own identity: the idea of my goodness was constantly invaded by shameful feelings, proving to me that this was my real self. I had no control over the terrible thoughts of harming and murdering others. It was exhausting, like trying to outrun a bad dream.

Being stupid was somehow the worst. I *hated* being thought of as stupid, but couldn't stop acting like a dunce sometimes. The curious thing was that somehow I stopped myself from becoming *completely* stupid. In class I was frequently caught staring out of the window, apparently not listening, unable to answer a question suddenly directed at me, unable to do a classroom task, but I had an uncanny ability to reproduce class lessons absolutely perfectly at exam time. This puzzled the teacher so much that she related it to the parish priest in charge of religious knowledge, who had noticed the same phenomenon. I had developed the capacity to tune in with part of my brain, while most of the rest of me was somewhere else — even I couldn't say where that was. Part of my brain was strictly programmed to remember what we had learned in class, at least until the tests. Tests over, I could let it all slip again and wipe the slate clean.

After I'd delivered another perfect score, the parish priest and my teacher stood on the landing leading to the upstairs classrooms, having a discussion. With the instinct of someone used to hearing the creaking of steps in the middle of the night, even when sound asleep, I was able to overhear their conversation, in spite of being out of earshot, by reading their body language and their curious looks. They were amazed by my behaviour and the odd results.

It turned out that they had run out of new prizes and I was about to receive a leather-bound missal for the second time. It was deeply satisfying for me to have this proof and recognition. Although I was apparently good for very little, I had not taken leave of all my senses, nor of my intelligence. Somehow it felt good to understate myself, for my true potential not to be recognised.

Nevertheless, I would often shake in terror of 'doing it wrong' — and doing things the wrong way seemed gradually to take on a life of its own. It was as if I had sold part of my brain to the devil — and of course I *had*. Slowly, I lost control. I felt compelled by a frightening, mysterious force to do the opposite of what was expected of me.

At the end of school on a freezing cold day, the senior parish priest approached me. He had a big bundle of papers in his hands and seemed anxious about them. He explained to me that he had an urgent message for the parishioners of Broekhoven One, my home parish, and would I be so kind as to drop a notice in everyone's letterbox?

I studied the pastor's face. Why had he approached me and not someone else? Ah! He probably thought I was very intelligent, because he had been discussing my hundred per cent success in the religious test with my teacher.

The priest standing before me would take it badly if I baulked. He was, after all, one of God's ministers and mouthpieces. As soon as he had recovered from the shock, my parents would then be informed about it. This is what went through my freezing brain as I stood there submissively in the sub-zero temperature of the playground. I gathered from what he was saying that there was some kind of one-upmanship going on between Broekhoven One and the neighbouring parish, Broekhoven Two.

'On no account,' said the scheming priest earnestly, 'must you put any of these leaflets into the letterboxes of the parishioners of Broekhoven Two.' He went on to explain where the boundaries were between the two parishes. Some of the street names I had never heard of before. How did he expect me to know streets I'd never been to? He was anxious and nervous, and I didn't tell him I didn't know what he was talking about because I didn't want to lose the image of being a clever girl so soon. A bundle of papers was transferred to my hands and I set off immediately, feeling confused and shaking with embarrassment. Even with the best will in the world, I had no chance of getting this one right. All the same, most children probably wouldn't have got it as badly wrong as I did that afternoon. Dutifully, I went to all the streets and letterboxes that were strange to me — which, I discovered later, were almost all in the wrong zone. I had inadvertently wreaked vengeance on a power-mongering priest who was all too happy to use a naive child. At the same time I had ruined his opinion of me, and disgraced myself further in my father's eyes. The terror of 'doing it wrong' became synonymous with the terror of never managing to be good enough to deserve respect.

GETTING OLDER AND A
LITTLE WISER

QUESTIONS ABOUT RELIGION and the soul plagued me. I had to know what my chances were of making it to heaven. I asked the priest in the confessional about the punishments for various sins, but he would sigh, or get impatient and tell me to ask someone else. I would go to confession again and ask why God put a tree in the garden of Eden if he didn't want it touched? Couldn't he have put it somewhere else? And what was so bad about learning the difference between good and evil from the forbidden apple? And what was limbo again? What did the souls do there? And purgatory — was it really the same as hell, except that one day you got out of there?

I asked my parents similar questions. Why did God punish people if he loved them and forgave them? Why did good people suffer? How many days would you get in purgatory for being rude? They tried to give me answers carefully, looking at each other to see if the other agreed or had a better idea. I would check up on them a few days later by asking the same question, watching them closely for signs of slipping up.

Alas, though it was my intention to finally get things straight in my head, I had inadvertently set a trap for my parents' uncertainties, and I gave up on adults at the tender age of eight. I decided that adults didn't *have* answers, so there was no point in asking them any questions. I started on the dangerous path of figuring things out by myself, reasoning with the information that I had gleaned and intuited. Given that most of this was superstition at best and a bastardisation of the truth at worst, I was bound to arrive at some bizarre conclusions. I am a water sign, a Scorpio, and given to arriving at immutable conclusions, a tendency aided and abetted by the Germanic blood in me.

MY PAPA HAD wanted a son as his first-born. He must have said this to someone in my presence, because I caught on pretty early and tried hard to be a boy for him. I carried things that were far too heavy for me, to show him how strong I was. My heart was soft, but I couldn't show it. Instead, I would have to be stronger than any boy around my own age and prove it by fighting him! An innocent newcomer to the street would be brought to my house by the neighbourhood kids, eager to see a contest. It always ended with me triumphantly standing with my foot on the poor fellow's quivering back, while the kids cheered in awe and reminded themselves not to mess with this crazy girl.

I had three brothers before we left Holland to come to Australia. Adrian was the eldest; he was strong but not assertive. He came running up to me one day with terror in his eyes because Henk, who was fourteen and the biggest kid around, a fellow with a meaner and more calculating streak than any of us, was chasing him. Adrian ran up and buried his head in my chest. I promptly put my arm around him and waited for the tall bully to round the corner. When he did he ran into my fist. It hurt, but it did the trick: Henk went sprawling and ran away with a bleeding nose. That evening his parents came around to abuse my parents.

The only problem with this sort of superiority was that I had no real friends. I wasn't exactly feared — I never went out of my way to pick a fight — but inside I felt like a cripple, believing that no one would bother to make me their friend if they really knew me. All I had was a doubtful prestige.

I regularly won the annual running races organised by parents for the local kids. We ran around the block. It was a very big block, including a farm and several shops. Sometimes I strained so hard that I felt close to apoplexy, but not to win was unthinkable while my papa was watching. I just had to win for him, and the whole neighbourhood seemed to know this too and cheered me on. Afterwards I would look up at him breathlessly, showing him the bottle of sherry or whatever that I'd chosen as a prize. I was white with anxiety and exhaustion: *Now, Papa, will you think I'm good enough? Now will you respect me?* I didn't care that the prizes I'd chosen were things I couldn't use myself — my papa could use them; that's what mattered to my love-starved soul. He laughed, my papa did; he was proud of me. I was fainting with pleasure and with an inexplicable pain in my heart.

For years, until I lost the drive for it, I was also good at playing competitive marble games. Pre-television, Tilburg children played outdoors a lot: ball games, skipping, hopscotch and marbles. We played on the smooth hard sand of the laneway behind our houses, or on the flagstones of the broad footpath that flanked the cobblestoned road. Marbles were made of either glass or clay. The glass ones were often marvellously whorled, opaque, translucent or smoky, ranging from small to quite large. They all had their respective values, just as paper money has different sizes and colours.

I was ambitious and in a few months had collected what might be the marbles equivalent of the district bank — a whole heavy-denier nylon stockingful of them, bulging obscenely. I didn't think it was obscene, however; not until I held up the loot for my mama to see. I was brimming with pride. Her eyes bulged with matching pride, or so I thought for one fleeting second. But no, it was with horror.

'Carla!' she said hoarsely, suddenly short of breath. 'That is pride! God punishes people who are full of pride. Pride is a sin!'

My mind was as wide open as my eyes at that moment, defenceless against the deeply hypnotic suggestion my mama planted there. I received this Catholic morality as the truth, and it threatened to for ever disconnect me from the will to compete.

My reaction was immediate and heroic. I walked to the middle of the street and, while everyone was watching, emptied the sinfully won marbles onto the cobblestones. The neighbourhood kids had no qualms about pushing each other aside to pick up the marbles and stuff them away, I noticed. Something inside me felt betrayed and the self-righteousness was galling. Now I was really confused. I was already struggling with so much; I added this new neurosis to the growing heap and changed course. I would value poverty, just like Jesus, who didn't even have a pillow to sleep on, as my mama and teachers told me. They forgot to add that in those days people had adequate substitutes for pillows, and in any case, Jesus hardly needed money when he had a group of adoring women to minister unto him wherever he went. The women simply picked up the tab. But no one taught me that *this* was the holiest of lifestyles.

MY PAPA WAS an outdoors man, a lover of nature, a grower of plants. He showed me the cobwebs glistening with a thousand diamonds in the early-morning summer sun. He took me for long walks through a forest on a huge private property not far away, to see the magic mushrooms — the ones with the polka dots — and taught me to listen to the wind and the birds as if he were an old American Indian.

Life outdoors was simply good. In our spacious backyard he taught me about worms, compost, the nasty beetles that eat potatoes, and friendly beetles like the ladybird. He showed me how to grow marigolds, pansies and sweet william, and how to collect their seeds. I wasn't so interested in the vegetables, except for the potatoes, because they were grown in the large communal plot a brisk walk away from our house. It was a large patch of earth next to the fields of barley, oats, turnips and kale that the farmers grew mainly for their cattle.

Potato-planting with my papa in the communal field meant a day in the wind and fresh air. Together, Papa and I made a furrow with our spades, paced out the distance between each spud, thudded in the all-important seed potato, heeled it down and then made the next furrow by covering the first one with soil. His Virgo nature was always full of the wonder of growing things. Plants to him were the miracles that sustained his faith in the existence of God. Science was no explanation at all; God had endowed the seed with the intelligence of what it would become. It was God, he said, who had given tiny seeds the wonderful power to recognise seasons and respond to temperature, water, nutrients and sunlight. My papa could make shoes, tables, toys, anything he put his mind to. But only God, he said, could make a flower.

Potato-planting day usually included the excitement of kite-flying. There was plenty of wind in this part of Holland, flat and unbroken by trees and houses. My papa was a supremely practical and inventive man with a boyish sense of fun. Until the day he died he took pleasure in the wind-vanes he made for himself and for countless others. In the early days, the vanes would whirr cheerfully and noisily as they strained in the wind. Later, he used plastic components that were quieter and increased the lifespan of the vanes. He made numerous kites — big ones that would stay up in the sky for days and nights on end, and little ones that we could learn to make ourselves, decorating the tails with all sorts of ribbons and ties.

An aunt on my mama's side once made the mistake of asking me who I liked better, my mama or my papa? This was a hard question and I screwed up my face. My aunt watched me closely; why was she staring so hard at me? I felt uncomfortable, but I asked myself who had been more fun that morning and said, 'Papa!' She scowled and left me suddenly, and it was plain that I had given the wrong answer. But my papa was always fun when he was out of the house. I even forgave him — though he never asked my forgiveness — for throwing me into the canal one summer's day to force me to learn how to swim. Before I went under, he dived in and told me to hang onto his shoulders as we headed for shore. I never did become a brilliant swimmer.

Life was pretty good, except for the underlying dreadfulness that came whenever Dr Jekyll became Mr Hyde. It was the way my papa flew off the handle. Once he threw a hammer at my youngest brother, barely missing his head. He pummelled his hands on my head if I contradicted or challenged him. He wouldn't stop until I threatened to black out, or somebody called for Mama.

It was the way he was so suspicious of my brother Adrian when he came home with some paper money in his hand, claiming he had found it. My papa did not believe him. He took his eight-year-old son into the living room and beat him with a leather belt every time he maintained that he had found the money. The angry questioning and the belting went on for hours.

My two front teeth were broken by my father in an accident that need never have happened. One day, when I was ten, I didn't want to eat my porridge. Normally I was fond of the stiff mixture my father almost invariably made for breakfast, which we covered with hot milk and brown sugar. But that day I had no appetite and declined, immediately causing a confrontation with him. He took it as a personal insult to his cooking and a challenge to his authority. Hotly, he ordered me to eat it. I still refused, trying to be polite. 'I don't feel like it today, Pa.' I was constipated and knew instinctively that I needed to fast.

'Eat it or I'll put your face in it!' he threatened even more furiously.

Like an idiot I warmed to this unjust, ridiculous challenge. With the plate of porridge in front of me on the table, I called his bluff. My father then proved that he was able to carry out his threat. He grabbed my neck from behind and, with his terrible strength, pushed my face so hard into the porridge that the thick white plate broke, and my two front teeth with it. Blood from my ruptured lips and gums mixed with the porridge. My mother moaned, 'Oh, John!' and was on the verge of tears. Then they both wiped my face and hair and clothes and sent me off to school.

IT MIGHT HAVE been my guardian angels who saved me from myself over the years. At times when I couldn't have cared less, or was too far removed to be aware, I believe that they stepped in firmly. It was probably due to them that I was saved from a foolish action when I was eleven, after attracting a sexually marauding man in the park we often visited. At the entrance there was a cement statue of Our Lady, seated with her child on her lap. She always had flowers on her knee or in her arms, clandestinely picked from the park and placed there by children whose legs were strong enough to climb up onto her lap. There was also a lake in the park where I went on my bicycle to catch tadpoles. The lake was popular with families.

I first sensed the presence of the man when I felt his gaze on me like an invading energy. I had grown attuned to lustful energy and his attention felt familiar; it frightened, yet excited me with its mystery. Instead of running away I was drawn to it like a moth to a flame. I turned around and smiled at the man lounging on the grass. He invited me to sit next to him, to show him the tadpoles, tell him my name. All the while I smelled him, smelled danger, saw the glint in his eyes, and yet took no notice. He asked me to come back the next day at mid-morning (when the likelihood of other people being there would be very small, I vaguely realised) and I agreed.

I turned up the next morning, not so much because I wanted to but because I felt that I had to keep my word. He wasn't there at the agreed time. I was stood up and felt ridiculous, not realising how lucky I really was. I hurried back home, feeling relieved and let down at the same time — and, of course, ashamed. The man had come to his senses, I thought, but I had not. I hardly ever had a kind thought for myself, not in those days, not in those years; not for decades.

LIFE IN A NEW COUNTRY

WE WERE ABOUT to leave the whole Dutch scene, the snow and ice flowers, Saint Nicholas and the coal shed — and all my dolls. My mother had inherited some money after her father's death, and she was going to spend it on getting us out of there.

In the summer of 1950 my father made the wooden boxes that would carry our furniture and possessions over the ocean. Regulations allocated us a certain size and some things had to be sacrificed. My parents did not have the heart to tell me that none of my dolls were going to be included. After all, I was nearly twelve.

We boasted to our friends about the adventures to come, and promised to write. Our friends were impressed. I had no idea then of the homesickness I would endure in the first year of my arrival in a country so far away, yearning for the places I would never return to. In my dreams, I would haunt the familiar streets and alleyways, smell the pussy willow and the daffodils so dear to me, scent the snow in the keen air, see the lush green leaves of the plane trees, and gaze at the wondrous candles of the horse chestnut's flowers. I would even hover over the house with the tar-roof coal shed that had been our home, and the place of so much sorrow. My heart ached to be there again; I had left it all too blithely.

A lumbering old troopship took six glorious weeks to carry us to Sydney. I had never seen the ocean before, and my pre-pubescent soul blossomed with the romance that ships are renowned for. It was in the air all around us.

We docked at Port Said, in Egypt. There, below the porthole of the cabin I shared with several other girls, I happened to spot a bronzed Egyptian god, stripped to the waist, who was working rather listlessly in the midday heat on the deck of the oil supply tanker that had bunkered next to our ship. The unsuspecting god was surprised by a piece of paper attached to a length of white sewing thread fluttering about his head. He looked up and smiled, and risked his life (I thought) in retrieving it.

'I like you,' said the ingenuous message, in my best English. The bronzed idol with the pitch-black hair and matching eyes flashed a beautiful smile. He searched for a pencil and, wonder of wonders, wrote a reply on the back of my tiny missive. I pulled up my little piece of windblown romance and read the heart-stopping message: 'I love you too.' For a girl who was used to being clipped over the ears for wanting to stay up to watch the movies, that was a glorious moment, a sort of vindication. I thought I must be at least a little bit attractive for such a magnificent human being to accept my message of admiration, and return it with such unhesitating kindness. I hunched over the edge of the porthole and smiled my thanks. He seemed pleased, and went back to work.

The ship's lunch bell rang. Romantic feelings struggled briefly with my tummy's desire for a fill of the ship's delicious food. I ran back fifteen minutes later, but my Egyptian and the tanker had left, as if it had all been a dream. But I had the piece of paper as proof and kept it as a treasure, showing it to no one.

That friendly exchange was the highlight of my journey, more memorable than my twelfth birthday on board ship, or even the moment we first alighted on Australian soil.

Our ship docked at Fremantle on a Sunday morning and stayed in port for the day. It was November and the flies were out in force.

We had known flies in Holland but they didn't come in persistent pesky hordes like this!

Stepping onto Australian land had a certain magical feel; it was so new, so different — alien, but friendly. A sweetness hung in the air, in spite of the heat. The streets of Fremantle were deserted; there wasn't one Australian in sight. Empty paper bags drifted and shuffled along the dusty and heat-shimmering bitumen streets — a sight I had never seen in my clean, cobblestoned country.

We returned to our boat and travelled on to Sydney as planned. After a long wait at the station, caused by a train workers' strike, we boarded a steam train that was to take us to the migrant camp beyond the Blue Mountains.

The train strained its way up the mountain ranges, and as it curved its long body around the steel tracks, I caught sight of its chimney stack. It was on fire! Flames shot out into the sky. I looked around my cabin to see if anyone else had spotted this and might be ready, like myself, to jump. I was used to the trains of home, feeling my face warm-wetted and sooted from the steam. Never had a chimney stack spewed flames! But no one seemed to care in the slightest and at last I flopped back on the seat, glad that I hadn't made the awful mistake of giving the alarm.

We spent six weeks in the migrant camp while our father looked for work. Life there had its hardships, especially for the adults, totally unused as they were to bare floorboards that had to be wet-mopped daily to keep off the dust; tin roofs with no insulation; rows of thunderboxes separated by jute curtains; public shower areas; and flies in the communal kitchen. We children, however, took most things in our stride, even as first-class adventures, except for the appalling smell of the toilets and the accompanying flies, and the open showers, which we were told to avoid if there were any adults there. Only once did I catch sight of a naked woman in the showers. Her breasts were most interesting and shocking to me, having none as yet myself — though I was aware of a strange stirring in my nipples that made them feel electric when I pressed them against cool glass. Needless to say, I felt wicked doing that and guilt-flustered by my furtive sensuality.

I went to six o'clock Mass every morning, catching the silhouettes of the magnificent Australian grasses in the gentle early light as I walked the distance up a hill. I was stunned by the beauty of what I saw, and heard, and felt. Great spiderwebs glistened in the morning sun. Magpies carolled — the song made me so happy. I had come to a place that was naturally bright. It was distinctly different from the dark reeking centuries of pain and awfulness that belonged to Europe. I felt light, like an angel in heaven. I picked bunches of pale straw-coloured grasses as if they were precious flowers, for my mother to put in the hut. Somebody laughed at me for picking the weeds, but thankfully my mother did not. She put them in an empty jam jar for a vase.

My very first day at school was grim. The schoolroom was makeshift, like everything else. The wooden walls had open spaces gaping between them and the roof. On that first day, a football kept coming into our room through the high windowless holes, and kept getting lobbed back out. Our male teacher was very young and couldn't easily control his class. Half the children had their back turned to him, since we sat on benches at long trestle tables arranged in rows like desks. To make it even more difficult for him, the room was L-shaped and his charges were of varying ages.

We were given plenty of free time to draw pictures while the teacher thought up something better to do. He consulted a colleague near the door as the football kept appearing and disappearing, causing a constant commotion. I lost interest in all of it and completely immersed myself in my drawing.

I was fond of pictures of ballerinas. To achieve their mesmerisingly sensuous poses, I had to try to get the curves and the proportions right, especially the curve of the foot as it balanced on the big toe — so unnatural, so feminine and so elegant. It didn't matter to me that bedlam reigned all around; I was used to concentrating while doing homework in a kitchen where my parents might be entertaining a visitor, or where younger sisters or brothers yelled and carried on, and occasionally the radio added to the cacophony. In such an environment I had learned to completely ignore whatever went on around me.

In this classroom it was no different, and so I didn't notice that while I was intently drawing and colouring, the class had been bullied into a deathly silence. The teacher had finally had enough and was beside himself with indignation. The class sat in absolute stillness, while the teacher dared anyone to speak again without putting up their hand first. It was in that perfect silence, charged with the teacher's fury and the children's fear of retribution, that I spoke softly but clearly to the girl sitting opposite me. 'Can I borrow your red colouring pencil?'

Her big eyes grew bigger with incredulous fear, looking first at me, then up at the teacher behind me. I had no time to figure out what was wrong: hands of steel gripped my shoulders and shook them mercilessly. The outraged teacher vented his helpless anger and frustration in a furious attack on my body. I was on the bench directly in front of him, so I was an easy target. The energy of his anger was familiar to me — just like my father's, and just as explosive. I was a trembling mess. Holding back the tears, I tried to keep my body rigid, in case it should slump and receive worse treatment.

Our classes were reorganised and, on the whole, school in the camp turned out to be more fun than it had been in Holland, on account of a few in our rag-tag unhomogeneous group who dared to be rude, inspiring the more timid. It took two teachers at a time to control us and instruct us in rudimentary English. We stuck our tongues out at them with a sneer when they tried to show us how to pronounce 'th'.

ON THE VERY first weekend, we went swimming with people from an Australian church. They offered to drive the children to Bathurst (the closest town) to 'the baths', as the pool was called, for a treat and we all accepted with a great deal of gusto. We spent hours at the baths, frolicking in the sun's generous heat, and nobody realised, until it was too late, that we were getting horribly burned. My back came up in blisters; the camp doctor came but couldn't help. This was learning about Australia first-hand.

The authorities in Holland had told us to cut our hair short, and sell our furs and blankets 'because it's so hot in Australia'. Since we eventually decided to settle in Melbourne, it was just as well that we did, at least, keep our woollen blankets. Even in the Bathurst camp, much further north than Melbourne but high on a plateau, the nights were as cold as the days were hot. We piled on six army-issue blankets at night. And the mysterious natives we were told about — the kangaroos, that is — were nowhere to be seen.

Cultures from different countries became apparent in rich and unexpected ways in the camp. Although most of us were Dutch, there were Italian and even Russian migrants. Each evening at sunset, a sonorous haunting Russian song would rise from the nearby hills. The time of day lent a quality of stillness to the air, allowing the sound to gently roll down from the hills into our astonished ears. The singing delighted us even as it made us shiver. We never saw the man who owned the voice and never knew what it was that made him sing like that. People surmised that he was singing his homesickness, or had a broken heart.

The Dutch Catholic priest from Victoria, Father Maas, came to visit our family. 'There's a head gardener's job going at a convent in Melbourne, and it might be that God is giving this one to you, John.' My father listened with eyes all intent. An outdoors job! This was not what he expected. 'It comes complete with a cottage for the family.'

My father and the priest went together to check it out. The 'garden' was about eighteen acres of grounds, neglected for years, surrounding a massive convent. Its name was Genazzano and it was also a college for girls from well-to-do families.

The cottage was in the convent grounds and still occupied by the previous gardener, who had been there for twenty years and refused to accept the sack or move on but had abandoned his job. Tall weeds surrounded the cottage, providing a fine home for snakes and rabbits. Undaunted by any of this, our whole family lived in large tents erected right outside the gardener's house by the desperate nuns while he was on holidays with his family. We were allowed to use the house's toilet facilities. This camping adventure was followed by a more dignified stay in a gracious house in the convent grounds called Grange Hill. Only when it became obvious that we were there to stay, and that my father had taken on the job he had so long neglected, did the old man and his family decide to leave.

The grateful nuns cooked dinner for us on the first day we moved into the cottage. The Reverend Mother came down and we all shook hands. She was a constantly smiling congenial nun, the one my mother would take to because of her unfailing kindness. She turned out to be often ingenuous and impractical, but was forgiven for her shortcomings, being an angel of light and soft-spoken roundness. She was accompanied by her impressive second-in-command — tall and straight and square-looking, who carried herself with an air of impeccable breeding but not a hint of snobbery.

Our English was broken, but we understood enough. My father was to have free run of the place to do whatever he could to improve matters, with a sizeable budget that had been put aside for the rehabilitation of the convent gardens. We children would attend the local parish primary school, run by the same nuns, free of charge. The cottage was free of rent and there was no charge for electricity. Paint would be provided to make the cottage a better home, and some other materials too, like plasterboard to fix a large hole in one of the walls.

We looked around the wooden house and couldn't believe our eyes. 'Look at that! Wooden planks on the inside walls, not even nailed on straight, caked with grease, and the grease is full of dust!' The planks were weatherboard, usually meant for outside walls. The floors were either scuffed wood or worn linoleum. The bedroom walls carried ugly smudges; the windows had apparently not been cleaned for months, or even years. My mother, my sister Liesbet and I would be doing most of the work to put things in order. We surveyed the scene together, staring incredulously and sighing. 'It'll scrub up into something decent,' we philosophised. It would just take some women's work and a bit of women's imagination; nothing new.

Some furniture had been left behind, and under the old couch in the living room we found a large Bible with a brass clip and gilded edges, and sensational nude figures of Adam and Eve and other vivid half-clad characters from Jewish history. Bethsheba was there, and the Sabine women being carried off to be raped. The Bible, to the Catholics of the Dutch south at least, was almost a heretical thing, something read only by vile Protestants. Alas, because of our prejudices, the precious book was not recognised for its historical or artistic value. It was promptly burned in the backyard incinerator, a 44-gallon metal drum.

The longed-for boxes of furniture and other belongings finally arrived from the waterfront, but they had been broken into. Heartless Australian wharfies must have taken our silverware. Most of my mother's precious embroidery, sewn in her younger days before she had children, was also missing. It was so sad, but we could only accept the situation, as most migrants were treated in the same way. 'Melbourne wharfie' was synonymous with 'thief' in those days.

There were no dolls for me; they weren't stolen, they'd never been packed. 'There wasn't enough room,' my parents said in soft voices, conspirators who had decided that enough was enough. My tears were huge, not only at the loss but at this betrayal. 'I'll buy you another doll sometime,' my father said, feeling sorry for me. Still, he must have hoped that I would forget, for one day when we were window shopping he told me sadly that the dolls were really too expensive and I had to wait. 'Till when?' I was trying to pin him down to a date, to an event, or a tangible time. But I already knew it was time to resign myself to a life without dolls.

My mother, sister and I set to with a tremendous will and made that greasy gardener's cottage spotless within a week. The three older boys — stocky Adrian, nine; curly-headed Markus, seven; and little five-year-old Willem — gathered wood for the chip heater and helped our father. We all minded the littlies — brown-haired and brown-eyed Berta, aged two, and blonde toddler, Teresa, who was only one.

Brother Leo, from the Redemptorist monastery up the street, stopped by a lot. Leaning his bicycle against our backyard fence, he would watch us climb the enormous pine tree in the yard. He told us about *The Age* newspaper. 'The red map of Australia, printed on the top left corner of the front page, proves that *The Age* is owned by Communists, and it's best not to buy it.' It was the time of Bob Santamaria, when the Catholics versus the Communists issue occupied political and Catholic minds.

In a few weeks the whole house was renovated; a shed was built for mending shoes and making windvanes; then a garage was built for the Chevrolet; and later still, a granny flat to house my three Australian-born brothers. They arrived over the next seven years, and would do as they pleased, rejecting their parents' old-fashioned and other-world discipline. The weedy paddock near the house was transformed into an extremely productive vegetable garden, and trees were planted as well. The best was a willow tree, which soon grew big enough to support a swing.

As for the grounds at Genazzano, my hardworking father gradually made a showpiece out of them. He was not only caretaker of the gardens, but the convent's electrician, plumber and carpenter too. He was the man-about-the-convent for about thirty nuns, who called themselves Faithful Companions of Jesus and lived in a fine three-storeyed house with a slate roof. The nuns were appreciative, and my father responded to being appreciated and being entrusted with responsibility. He could let his imagination run riot on a project while trying to save the nuns as much expense as possible. He established a nursery to save them from having to buy seedlings. And he grew flowers especially for the chapel in a designated bed in a bid to have the rest of the flowers left alone in the garden.

My father was happier than he had ever been. His volatile anger diminished for a while, and he no longer approached me at night. I had turned twelve, we were in a sunny if small house with paper walls, and Dad had been introduced to a new culture by crusty George, the assistant gardener. This was the culture of the 'men's room'. Nuns and girls were prohibited. The walls were hung not with holy pictures but photographs from risqué calendars. All sorts of glossy magazines lay in drawers, filled with advertisements from Melbourne establishments offering satisfaction to those who needed to be satisfied.

My father was eventually initiated into a more sophisticated — and more expensive — way of releasing his constant sexual drive than he had ever known. In his naivety he must have imagined that it was a safer way, and something that he could easily keep a secret. Never did he suspect that after many years of growing carelessness he would bring syphilis home to his wife one day, or that she, after suffering great mystification and confusion about her condition (he never said anything until she nailed him) would take a taxi to an address in Lygon Street and loudly and tearfully accuse the prostitute she found there. In spite of her pitiful condition, it was decided between my parents that it should be kept a family secret. But the secret was too heavy for my mother to bear alone. She eventually confided it to my sister Liesbet, who was grown-up by then. Eventually Liesbet confided it to all her sisters.

IT WAS OUR Dutch custom to visit people on a Sunday, and since there were no grandparents to go to now, we visited other Dutch families. Ten months or so after our arrival at Genazzano, we all boarded a train to visit a large family who had travelled with us on the transit ship, to find out how they were doing. The conversation was about the go-slow unions who threatened hardworking newcomers for showing up their lax attitudes; or the lack of choice in delicatessens and the food of home that we were all missing. It was about teenage daughters and sons, and how they disapproved of their friendships with those unreliable Australians.

We children were left to play with each other. We formed a sizeable bunch and, as usual, I felt nervous about being accepted by the others, even though I was one of the eldest at almost thirteen. To join in, I would have to speak up and be aggressive, and I wasn't in the mood that day. There was a tree in the yard. I was wearing a dress, but that didn't deter me from climbing to the very top. In spite of this feat, I went unnoticed. A heavy sadness came over me; there I was, alone at the top of the tree, desperately wanting to be like the other children, but separated from them and feeling so strangely lonely. I started to cry. Sobs welled up and, suddenly and unexpectedly, I felt free to let loose a deep, unnamed distress.

Everyone must have heard, including the adults inside the house. I glimpsed my mother's head at the back door briefly. She must have gone straight inside again. I imagined her announcing that Carla had thrown a tantrum and it was best to ignore her. The hot humiliation brought on by that assumption made me truly desolate. I had no clear idea why I was crying. My father's touch in the night had ceased since coming to Australia and I had been freed of a horror I had grown used to. The night-time visitor never returned — I had been used and discarded, and now I felt empty. I had lost my father's attention and so I wasn't his special girl any more. Even though I retained no waking consciousness of his nocturnal visits, my body missed his closeness and I felt strangely abandoned. I wailed even more loudly. The other children took no notice whatsoever. What could they do anyway? They could see that if I wanted to come down it would be not very difficult for me. The mystery was too much for them to handle.

The upshot was that my parents, understandably, felt humiliated in front of the other family by their queer child who wailed for attention instead of having a good time like all the other kids.

My emotional state was all too difficult for my parents, who were going through their own adjustments as best they could. I would soon be a teenager, their first one. What were they going to do with me?

NEW WINE IN OLD SKINS

OUR LADY OF Good Counsel, that was the name of our parish church in Holland. Its side wall held a magnificent Byzantine mosaic picture of the mother of Jesus with her child snuggled up against her, and hopeful little candles constantly burned there in her honour. People prayed to her, and then they went away and did what they wanted.

We had travelled for six weeks across the world and, by some uncanny karmic coincidence, ended up in a parish of the same name 12,000 miles later. We were in a strange land, in a different culture, but, incredibly, the picture of Our Lady of Good Counsel was the same, though not in genuine mosaic. It gave me the feeling that in some strange way nothing had changed. She had followed us to Australia, Our Lady, who was supposed to give us good advice. Why didn't I find the omen particularly comforting?

On our first day at the parish school, our mother dressed us up the way she had always done in Holland: she put big satin bows in our hair, and we wore the shiny lace-up shoes our father had made. The bows made us look conspicuous but it wouldn't have mattered what we wore: the Australian schoolchildren, Catholic or not, despised the newcomers simply because we were different. They couldn't understand us, so they ridiculed us.

They had derogatory names for migrant people. Dagos was reserved for the Italians who arrived in droves after 1950. We were called Clogs, quite a benign word compared with the one they used for their own indigenous people, who were also different. If we wanted to be cheeky, we would ask them what their grandfather's prison number was. After all, these children were nearly all descendants of the English and Irish sent to the penal colony for their misdeeds only two or three generations ago. The insult was lost on most of our classmates until our English improved.

I was eager to learn this new language and found it surprisingly easy. The roots of English, like Dutch, are in Latin, so guesswork paid off many times. As for trying to speak it, I listened to the broad accents of the local children, compared them to the educated newsreaders from the ABC and decided that I would never speak 'strine' but would opt for the King's English. My speech ended up a peculiar mongrel version of the official language, but I thought that at least it had class.

The nun in charge of our class taught three grades at the same time in the same room. Her name was Mother Mary Luke, FCJ. (FCJ was short for Faithful Companion of Jesus; all the nuns had these initials after their names.) Mother Mary Luke had seen a thing or two in her life, which had given her some sense of reality. She read out our written work and praised our unusual ways of putting things as imaginative.

The words of Keats' poem, written in huge calligraphy on a yellowing poster on the classroom wall, delighted me: 'Season of mists and mellow fruitfulness! Close bosom-friend of the maturing sun . . .' It was this piece of poetry that invited me to appreciate the dreaded English language. It often perplexed me; why, for example, pronounce ascer*tained* as ascer*tained* when certain rhymed with curtain?

All of us excelled in maths that first year, because the levels in Australia were way below what we were used to in Holland. Mother Mary Luke made shining examples of us by inviting us to do sums on the blackboard. The prestige helped — we began to be respected. Within a few months, we would join in reviling new migrants from other countries, and so we became part of the fabric of school society.

In the classroom next door my brothers did not fare quite so well at the hands of Sister Bartholomew. She always carried a long wooden ruler with a metal edge to it, and beat her pupils' hands and legs until big welts appeared. Sister Bartholomew was the boss of her classroom and children had to know it; she was a woman born in the bush and had a strong hand. When all the boys — Markus, Adrian and Willem — came home with welts on their hands and legs, our mother decided to march up to the school to remonstrate with Sister Bartholomew, in spite of her broken English. Nobody could make out her words, but everybody knew what she meant.

Sister Bartholomew was loud in her own defence. In those days, it was next to a sin to disagree with a nun and my mother was brave indeed to risk both ridicule and the nun's self-righteousness. We were all ashamed of our mother's poor command of English, but proud of her pluck. Our 'us and them' attitude now included our mother in 'us' and Sister Bartholomew in 'them'. The stakes were higher and life had become more exciting.

Mother Mary Luke, who had a conciliatory streak, assigned my sister and me tasks with a certain amount of responsibility, like looking after the flowers for the altar in the church. Our classroom was separated from the church by a wooden concertina room-divider; on Sundays, the concertina wall was shoved aside to accommodate the large number of parishioners, who sat on our desks. It was a cosy sort of feeling, being so close to Jesus in the tabernacle. I was promoted to the great responsibility of preparing the altar for next morning's Mass, which had to be done after school. I also had to make everything ready for the priest in the sacristy, where he got dressed up. I learned the words chasuble, alb, maniple, cincture, amice and stole — the essential wardrobe for the priest-craft.

Every single morning I attended Mass, and even acted as altar boy when the official one did not turn up. More and more frequently he failed to turn up, knowing I'd be there to take his place. I felt privileged to be so closely involved with the rites of the Mass. My devotion to Jesus grew.

My classmates were not so devotional, especially Jill, my sister Liesbet's best friend. She and my sister burst in one afternoon and caused mayhem by knocking over the box of white hosts kept for the communion rites. Once on the floor, the wafers could no longer be used and had to be disposed of, so Liesbet and Jill filled their mouths with them, laughing loudly and being very naughty. Then Jill decided to try the wine as well. She got hold of the wine bottle and a chalice, and declared the stuff very good indeed. Curiosity got the better of me and I tried some too. It was a special kind of port, truly delicious, and it made us feel very happy and bold. After lifting every cassock and examining every drawer, the irreverent whirlwind disappeared out the sacristy door.

I was amused but also aghast; after all, I had participated and had got a surprising lift from sipping the port. After that, it was never quite the same for me in the sacristy: temptation was always with me, and from time to time I quietly indulged it. After all, there was confession to make it all right again — only this type of thing you confessed in another parish.

Mother Mary Luke was a good sort, if a bit old for her job and a bit cranky because of her constant migraines. She appeared to have lost all her own teeth, but her thinnish smile was nevertheless genuine. Mother Mary Luke had a wisdom born of considerable teaching experience and dealing with parents and children. She was always in a hurry, never walking but always running, shoulders high and veil flapping as she covered the distance between the classroom and the staffroom several times a day. It was on one of those lightning runs that she flashed me a smile and said: 'When are you going to wake up, Carla?'

I was stunned. Something about the question stopped me in my mental tracks. She hadn't said, 'When are you going to *grow* up?' but 'When are you going to *wake* up?' My English was good enough for me to notice the difference. The implication was that I was asleep; that there was something to be woken up *to*. What could it be? I didn't know what the world looked like to people who were awake.

Her words haunted me, but there wasn't much time to indulge in pondering this conundrum, as the next two years of school were to be interrupted.

WE CAME HOME from school one day to find my mother in bed. She was lying in a pool of blood, moaning and delirious. We knew what to do and ran to the convent for Sister Victoire, the infirmarian, a trained nurse. The title 'Sister' distinguished worker sisters from the 'Mothers', who were teachers. Sister Victoire dropped everything and hurried over. She wasted no time and called an ambulance, which arrived promptly and took Mother away to hospital. On her way out, she opened blurry eyes and told us not to cry. She was weak with loss of blood from a miscarriage at a late stage of pregnancy, but so concerned that we should not worry about her. It broke my heart to see her so weak, so vulnerable and so thoughtful.

Sister Victoire didn't seem to think the situation was all that serious. She was a thin able woman with a heart of absolute gold and a steady bright nature that was healing in itself. Her smile made us feel less tragic. Sister removed the bloodied sheets from the bed, as if she did this every day, and talked animatedly to us while she bundled them up and took them away with her. That evening, dinner arrived for the family, cooked by the considerate nuns.

For several weeks I had to look after the family while my mother slowly recovered. She had been given a transfusion of the wrong kind of blood, which had nearly killed her. Being 'mother' at the age of thirteen for six children, and looking after our father as well, was no mean feat. My cooking skills were minimal, so I bought a cookbook and some new utensils and started to experiment on our Kookaburra gas stove. Someone could have warned me that it wouldn't work as the door of the stove didn't quite shut. There was no temperature gauge either, so I was up against it. But I was determined and didn't give up for a very long time.

My brothers didn't seem to mind at all and ate whatever came out of the oven, no matter how burned it was. I loved them for that, but I still developed a complex about my cooking. I fell back on staples: pancakes with slices of apple and covered in treacle, soups, and boiled vegies from the garden.

My father cooked all the meat, as I had no idea whatsoever and still don't. I can make meatballs in celery soup, though, which was my mother's speciality. She showed us girls how to make it with great pride, but somehow she always made that soup better than I, or anyone else, ever could. She just had a special knack for celery soup with meatballs.

I wanted to educate my brothers — who slept in bunk beds in a lino-floored room — to make their beds in the morning and go to bed clean at night so that their sheets wouldn't get dirty straight after being washed. But it was hopeless. They were used to doing the male chores, like getting the wood ready for the chip heater, and making beds wasn't one. As for washing their feet before bed — well, they might have done that once, but with no shower in the house it was asking too much. All we had was a weekly bath and a daily wash by hand at the sink. There would be no unmade beds in 'my' house, however, so I kept up a rigorous routine. If my emotional self was in constant chaos, at least I could bring order into my immediate environment!

At night, I put the little ones to bed. Often I would read stories to my two youngest sisters, who were nine and ten years my junior, or I would just make them up. I frightened them to death with stories of Bluebeard — the same stories that horrified me when I first read them — but when thunder shook the skies, I reassured my little sisters, telling them it was a display of the power of God and our angels were there to protect us.

Eventually my mother returned, but I continued to stay home from school while she convalesced. School didn't seem to matter an awful lot to me because I had already gone beyond the level we were being taught, and I continued to learn English from books and avid listening to the radio.

LIVING IN A cottage in the convent grounds, we were fairly isolated from normal contact with the neighbours. The convent, set in one of Melbourne's most exclusive suburbs, was flanked by large mansions mostly occupied by older people whose children had left home.

Directly opposite our humble gate onto the side street was a modest house with only a few bedrooms but lots of stained glass and high ceilings. In it, there lived a very old lady and her comparatively younger daughter. They had no family whatsoever and were very lonely. Their husbands had died, there were no children from the younger woman's marriage, and no family left in England, their country of origin. But Mrs Greig and Mrs Taylor had class and a little bit of money, and it was they who gave me my first taste of English elegance and sensibility. My sister and I were invited to go over for afternoon tea and hear the marvellous stories the two women delighted to tell. We were introduced to Winnie the Pooh, to Beatrix Potter, to Alice in Wonderland, and to cup cakes. We were even invited to stay over a few times, and slept in large comfortable beds, a radical change from having to share a bed with my sister, which I did until I left home.

On Sundays we sometimes accompanied them on rides in their shiny old black Ford, chauffeured by the faithful Bertie. Upon the ladies' return home Bertie had to inspect every room and look under all the beds to check for intruders before they would enter the house themselves. Then they would make him tea, pay him and let him go.

Having no immediate family, the two old ladies confided in their accountant, and it was he who eventually inherited their fortune. The first thing this villain did after the younger woman died was to demolish the house against the express and earnest wishes of both women. Then he built a number of villas on the site.

Mrs Greig crocheted a rug for me with many squares, edged in black. I treasured it, and luckily my mother kept it for me while I was 'out of this world' and later gave it back to me. I have it still, a reminder of the graciousness of two English ladies who made up for the absence of younger friends in my immediate neighbourhood.

I went back to school, but only occasionally, as my mother had difficulty coping with the three children who were still at home. It was on my way to school that I came across love-in-the-mist, a very delicate, blue, star-like flower surrounded by a mist of fine green tendrils accentuating the flower's blue tenderness. My romantic heart melted when I saw this miracle. If I hadn't seen it with my own eyes — if I'd first seen it in a drawing — I wouldn't have believed it could be real. English cottage flowers, which grew so well in Melbourne, were new to me.

The woman owner of the garden picked a sprig for me and told me its incredible name. I held the flower to my heart, and wished it could be right inside it. Then I thought of giving it to my overworked teacher, Mother Mary John, whom I hadn't seen for a while.

Mother Mary John was wearing her black-rimmed round glasses and her face was very pale when I caught her before assembly, in the middle of a run between the classroom and the lunchroom. I offered her the flower with the lovely name. She had the grace to slow down for a moment, then put the magnificent blue flower back in my hands. I could get a vase if I wanted and put it in front of the statue of Our Lady in the classroom.

I was wounded by her matter-of-factness and tears came. I was a child-mother hoping for some mothering myself; I had hoped to trade my gift of a special flower for some special love from my teacher. I felt so tired. But, I realised I shouldn't expect too much from people.

And so I turned my thoughts to Jesus, who was present in the tabernacle of the church in his mystical way, locked up there in the round white communion wafers and the bigger wafer of the monstrance. Yes, I knew that love existed. The only trouble was that humans were short of it.

I transferred my need for love to Jesus when I was thirteen, and entering puberty. I started to feel romantic love for him. I poured out my heart to him in the church at playtime and lunchtime. Jesus must love me, even if no one else did, and so my imaginary relationship flourished. It was my version of a relationship with the Divine: I loved Jesus even though I had never met him, couldn't possibly know what he looked like, and had no idea of who he really was.

This relationship saved my heart from closing up. It was the joy of all my romantic teenage years. It kept me alive. And when those sickly holy pictures were circulated with Jesus pointing straight at me with the words, 'You, yes, *you*, I *want* you!' my heart melted for being wanted and said, 'Yes! Yes, Jesus! I will forsake my mother and my father and brothers and sisters and all the world and follow you!' I pinned the picture up on the side of my wardrobe and prayed on my knees before it every day, my heart often leaping with the ever-growing certainty that I would become a nun one day, an ultimate lover of Jesus.

IN ALL, I SPENT more time at home than at Our Lady of Good Counsel primary school. My presence at home was probably a safety net for my mother; it helped her avoid her husband's sexual advances when he came home for lunch every day. She was too accessible, and so afraid of going through all that pain again. Nevertheless, he could not leave her alone and she became pregnant again and miscarried once more in the fifth month. After that, my mother underwent an operation to mend the parts that had stretched too wide. Oh, the bittersweetness of being relatively well again! There was no excuse now and she proceeded to have three more boy children; the last child was conceived after I left home.

In spite of all the busy happenings at home, my sister Liesbet and I did the ironing for Sister Kevin on Saturday afternoons, to earn extra pocket money. To give Saturday afternoons away was a big sacrifice and, much to Sister Kevin's annoyance, we didn't always make it. Upstairs from the convent laundry, we ironed table and bed linen and the nuns' strange-looking underwear, and put aside anything that needed mending. Sister Kevin caught us dressing up one afternoon. In a fit of giggles, we hadn't heard her climb up the long set of stairs and she gave us a shock. The inevitable lecture followed. We blushed and promised never to do it again, but laughed all the harder after she left. Sister Kevin was good at heart and always treated us to tea and cake.

Sister Kevin was well known to the boys because they gave her a hard time over her chook pen. The chicken run was next to our backyard, just behind the cyprus hedge, and its roof was too easy a target. Sticks, stones and rubbish were regularly thrown at it from the heights of the hedge, frightening any unlucky chook on her way to lay an egg. Really, it was all done to see Sister Kevin get into one of her prodigious tempers. The boys sniggered at the spectacle of this indignant nun 'off her rocker', as they would say.

AND SO PASSED my first two years in Australia. Hormones had already started their work on my sister who, despite being younger, experienced her first period at least six months before me. She found blood on her knickers and went to my mother in alarm, to be told matter-of-factly that this was a sign that she would be able to have babies later on. She was introduced to wearing cotton rags — old, thin but absorbent nappy material — which she had to pin to the inside of her knickers. I felt inferior to my sister and often ducked into the thickness of the cyprus hedge near the house to check my own underpants. My sister was much more sexually aware than I and attracted plenty of attention as a stunningly beautiful teenager. I would never be like her. I suppressed my sexuality as hard as I could, feeling awkward in the presence of boys and men.

It was during the summer after my thirteenth birthday that my periods started, in rather inauspicious circumstances. A large Dutch family well known to my parents lived on a farm not far from the sea, and they agreed to have me stay with them for a week or so. The woman of the house was a sturdy worker of few words, with a warm gruff sort of voice and a good heart. We went to the beach several times, and one day I decided to go there by bicycle, taking her youngest child, a boy of three, on the back. She packed us a lunch and off we went. We spent a couple of sunny hours at the beach and then it was time to go back. However, I was not quite sure which way to turn when I faced the highway. Both sides seemed familiar. I chose to turn right and set off with trepidation, knowing my propensity for getting things wrong. It wasn't until I reached the very end of the peninsula, the end of the road, that I was sure I was on the wrong track. Now I knew the way back, but it was an appallingly long distance! The afternoon was hot, the traffic dangerous to ride in, and my legs were ready to give way under me. But I had to press on, heart beating overtime, legs on fire, and my eyes burning from exhaustion, heat and shame.

Finally, there she was, the mother of my little charge — who had silently clung to the back of my bicycle all this time — ready to catch her boy in her arms and set him down. Then she noticed something else: the back of my dress was soaked in blood. She told me to take it off while she fetched me one of her daughter's dresses. She didn't scold me or tell me to go and clean myself up, but simply rinsed my dress, petticoat and pants in cold water and then plunged them into the soapy tub in her backyard, where she had been working when we arrived.

Sensing her motherliness, I soon recovered. Although she said very little, it was her attitude and her actions that counted. I was horrified at the sight of my feminine blood, but her natural acceptance of the situation confirmed our femaleness as good. The only thing she did not guess was that this was my first time. She gave me a clean strip of folded rag and two safety pins to fix to a pair of bloomers, and I relaxed in my borrowed dress while my own dried on the line.

My first menstrual bleeding could have been better, but it could also have been worse if it had occurred in my mother's presence. My mother was apt to call her daughters 'sluts' when they bled, or, at any other time our womanhood was obvious. Perhaps our youthfulness reminded her of the 'bad girl' she had been herself. Even my leaning idly against a doorway to watch a plumber do some work in our house one day exasperated her sense of decency.

'You filthy rag,' she said with venom in her suddenly husky voice, 'Stop standing like that, showing off to the plumber!'

She had spoken in Dutch, her insult passing over the head of the plumber. I looked down at myself in surprise, became conscious of my stance, and caught the energy of her guilt. Tears welled up, and anger, but the damage was done. I needed a mother during adolescence, one I could run to for protection, but she was doing the attacking herself.

KISSING MAKES YOU PREGNANT

 NEXT TO AN impressive church on the biggest hill in Richmond's Church Street stood the gracious Vaucluse convent and its Ladies' College. Also run by the FCJ nuns, Vaucluse catered for migrants and the less well off, offering them a rather lower standard of education than Genazzano.

If Jesus, who was supposed to be poor, had ever had children they would not have been accepted into Genazzano. And it wouldn't do for the gardener's daughters to go there either. Nuns make a vow of poverty, while keeping strictly to the class system that helps to perpetuate it. However, this system did allow the nuns to cater for the poor, and we girls received our education free of charge, as the children of the caretaker of Genazzano. The six boys went to the Christian Brothers after primary school.

That first morning at Vaucluse, the nuns didn't know where to place the migrant girls, Carla and Liesbet. They put their heads together for a few minutes, then Mother Eleanor made an announcement in her best English accent. 'You, Carla and Liesbet, will both go to Year 8 (the first year of secondary school) because we know that you must be behind, on account of your mother language not being English, and because you, Carla, have missed so much school over the past two years.' The words were spoken as from a pulpit. 'You will be able to give each other encouragement in a new and strange environment by being together in the same class,' said the other nun.

The well-intentioned nuns never thought of interviewing either of us to make a reasoned decision. The normal age for Year 8 was twelve. I was fourteen. My heart sank heavily, but I didn't have it in me to say anything.

We slept in the same bed, my dark-haired sister and I, not always the best of friends because we were ... well, so different. Our double bed was at the end of a long narrow room with a second double bed at the other end, where my two youngest sisters slept. My only claims to personal space were the wall over our bed, where I hung a neon cross I had been given for my birthday, and one side of the wardrobe, which I filled with holy pictures, the bigger the better, and the text of the prayers I recited every day. To be thrown together in the same class felt like an extension of sharing a bed, a forced mixing of our identities. I smarted from the humiliation of being put in the same class as my younger sister, and from not having been consulted. And so, for four long years I submitted to almost total boredom, feeling too old, too tall — in other words, a misfit.

Before we were admitted into our upstairs classroom, we all lined up on the broad covered verandah with its green-painted wooden railing. 'Lift up your skirts, girls, so we can inspect your bloomers.' Our bloomers were to guard against possible exposure during netball games or when going up and down stairs, and the hems of our skirts had to be just below knee-height. We wore stockings of thick brown lisle, lace-up shoes, a white blouse with a crisp white round starched collar and the college tie. 'You know, of course, that you are to wear college gloves and hats whenever you are in uniform off the premises.' Inspections by nuns and prefects continued until there was complete conformity.

Mother Eleanor was a good teacher, relying heavily on charts that she had made herself. The classroom was festooned with them, giving it an air of accomplishment. She always repeated what she said at least three times, knowing the principles of repetition and summary. But I was bored out of my mind. I stared out of the windows, which started above head height to shut out the world and reached to the ceiling. I wanted to scream, or jump out of those windows. Instead, I kept my frustrations bottled up, clenched my teeth and got easy high marks. High marks were a cinch; I could never be proud of them.

WE WERE FORBIDDEN to enter a non-Catholic church of any kind. Sometimes, rather than waiting in a long queue for a tram, I would walk to the next stop a short distance away, passing a Greek Orthodox church. The church, sandwiched tightly between old buildings serving as offices, was just a building until one afternoon it emanated strange haunting music which stirred something very deep in my soul.

'Maria,' I said to my Italian girlfriend, with whom I often sauntered a block or so, 'let's go in.'

To my delight she agreed; her wicked spirit of adventure was temporarily stronger than her superstitious fears. It wasn't her conscience that bothered Maria — church directives and school rules were totally amenable to her and her Italian family and friends (one followed them if they were convenient) — but superstition about the dangers of strange religions was another thing entirely.

Together we pushed open the large doors, stepped into the vestibule and entered another realm. It was a mystical place, where a swaying, chanting congregation was enacting a ritual of high seriousness. The great candlesticks, the larger-than-life book that was being waved about, the embroidered standards, the foreign chant that seemed to stir memories of lifetimes long gone by, and the longing expressed by the music — all of this felt much more potent, passionate and real to me than the devotions in my own church and the silly words of the songs we sang. The grass is always greener on the other side, they say.

This was almost certainly not an ordinary ceremony, but a special one because of the presence of an old patriarch that day. The old man came slowly down the aisle on his way out of the church. He smiled as he went, stopping to speak to members of his congregation. Maria and I stood near the door, ready to bolt if necessary — if, for instance, it became obvious that the devil was trying to subvert us for going into a 'heathen' church. The old man advanced closer and finally spotted us. He walked over and grasped both my hands. 'What is your name?' he asked earnestly, looking into my eyes. 'Carla,' I replied, overcome by his manner, which didn't seem at all devilish. The old man, whose language was that of his native Greece and who was probably hard of hearing as well, seemed very pleased with my name and held my hands firmly. 'Ah,' he said intently, 'that means *good*!'

I was astonished. A flood of delicious relief filled my body, flushing my cheeks and eyes. This man had recognised me as good! How was that possible? But it was true, I was good! Otherwise I wouldn't be *feeling* so good! That wise holy man had given me his blessing. It seemed he had realised the essential goodness of himself, and therefore that of everyone. He conveyed this to me with his touch and look. It was only temporary, because the pattern of unworthiness was strong in me and would reassert itself.

He greeted Maria cordially, and we left in a daze, not laughing, not snorting, not scoffing, but deeply impressed. I never went to the church again, although I passed it many times. I did not want to risk the doors being locked, or the place being empty of the magic that was there that day.

AT SCHOOL THE learning of facts went on relentlessly. Girls with good marks were invited to learn Latin, so for three years I crammed my head with declensions and whatnots. I hated it so much that my mother came to the convent on my behalf. 'Is there perhaps something better for her to do?' Why on earth didn't I ask to go up to another class? I was too used to submitting, too doubtful now of the worth of my own opinion, and too entrenched in the status quo.

'Latin,' enthused Mother Eleanor, 'is the basis of several languages, and Carla will be able to understand even the English language better if she continues.' My mother was convinced, and so I plodded on — until the day of the exam in Year 10, when I lost all memory of any Latin that I had ever learned.

The exam proceeded as per normal that day: the desks were separated from one another to prevent cheating; I was seated near the back as usual, on account of being tall. It was a lovely sunny day; through the high windows I could see little clouds drifting in a blue sky. The exam papers were distributed in silence and, after a briefly barked order to begin, we commenced.

I looked at the questions. They made no sense to me whatsoever. Nothing at all came to my brain. I was curiously undisturbed by this and decided to use the time to write a letter to a boy I knew in Holland, to whom everything I recounted would surely be riveting news. I wrote busily, head down, page after page.

The person in charge that day had been called in especially to invigilate. She probably knew no Latin at all. She walked up and down the rows and noticed nothing unusual. I didn't hand in anything at the end, but this wasn't noticed. In fact, it was presumed that my paper had been mislaid! I could feel the questioning eyes of Mother Francesca, mistress of Year 10, on the back of my head as I read the result sheets posted on the classroom wall. I had received a score of eighty per cent! No questions were asked of me, and they were not willing to risk being liable. The collusion was a delicious subterfuge and the high mark a tribute to my usual performance in Latin. I was only sorry it could not have been higher.

ONE OF THE greatest delights of my teenage years was the treasure called the library. Within it were the ultimate great escapes into imagination in pre-television Melbourne. There were books by G K Chesterton, favoured by the nuns because he had become a convert to Catholicism. I delighted in all the Father Brown series, conceived well before the age of drugs when even the worst crook had some redeeming grace. Then there was the unforgettable Scarlet Pimpernel and all the Madame Orczy books, which I read twice, and in my last year the wonderfully descriptive works of Thomas Hardy.

The library was a mysterious, dark, oak-panelled room, where the books were mostly kept in cabinets behind locked glass doors, safe from the casual touch. It was run by Mother Xavier, a gentle and refined nun whom I seldom saw because she was the mistress of Year 12. She had a genuine smile, which broke over rather prominent teeth in a sharply intelligent face, the twinkle in her eyes enhanced by the narrow-rimmed glasses she wore. It was the smell of her I liked. Maybe they all used the same soap, but they smelled different! Mother Xavier carried her relationship with God deep in a heart that had been broken once by a great human love. This made a distinct difference in her, and one for the better.

No Catholic schooling is complete without sex education. I say this with my tongue way up my cheek, because sex wasn't talked about at school, and yet, even as it was ignored, it was central to Catholicism. The word 'sex' was never once mentioned in the classroom; we were educated by example and by omission. There is a saying that silence can speak louder than words, and we were surrounded by women who had renounced sex for the love of God. Where did that put sex and sexual relationships on the scale of values?

But what could those nuns have told us about sex? Their sanctimonious ignorance paraded as wisdom. I was surely not the only one to be utterly bewildered by what they told us.

The most explicit reference to sex I ever heard was by Mother Anthony, who taught us maths. Mother Anthony was a bony, swarthy and sultry woman, most likely of Irish descent, who should have known better. Her knuckly hands were constantly under her apron, fingering her rosary beads. She told an attentive class of girls facing the summer in 1956: 'Kissing makes you pregnant.'

In the ensuing silence, Mother Anthony surveyed the impact of her sinister statement. We waited for more, and when nothing else came we giggled, squirmed and studied her face in an effort to read what was apparently obvious to her. Mother Anthony had a strange sense of humour, one more suited to cynical adults than young girls. But no, she wasn't joking this time. Her words created an image in my head of a boy's semen travelling from his mouth, down my throat, into my womb.

As for Mother Mary Paul, our class mistress in Year 11, all she had to say after her inspection of our ballgowns for the annual ball was that we should cover up our cleavage to prevent boys from falling into temptation. Inadvertently she told us exactly what to do if we ever (wickedly, wantonly and sinfully) *did* want to lead a boy into temptation. Not that *I* would have dared!

When I met Keith later that summer, three months before I was due to go into the convent, we developed a quasi-relationship during which he became entranced by the unattainable. Poor Keith. I never allowed him to kiss me on the mouth because of my fear of pregnancy.

APART FROM MY Italian girlfriend Maria, I made friends with Barbara. She wasn't tall, had bandy legs and well-developed breasts that already drooped by the age of fourteen. She had black curly hair, and a masculine style in the way she threw the ball with her left hand in the fast team game we called tagball. We wrote poems to one another on those languid summer days when blowflies hung about the open windows on the shady verandah called the ambulacrum. Our poems were sweet and passionate and very floral.

'Come to my place, Barb,' I'd say, and she did a couple of times, but it was difficult because the trams didn't run frequently at weekends. I went to her place once, when I insisted. There I met her mother, who disliked sunlight so intensely that she always kept the house as dark as possible, and her ungainly older brother, who immediately fell in love with me. It wasn't possible to carry on a conversation with Barbara's mother, who seemed to think that conversing meant being interrogated. Her husband was not around, I gathered. The house, though, was filled with exquisite flowers: madonna and tiger lilies and larkspur. These flowers had been grown by Barb, and the cookies that were served were baked by her too. Barb was a capable girl.

Poor Barb. Her dark eyes would flash with joy to see me, but I grew wary of her strangeness and the way black hairs grew on her hook-nosed face. Like everyone else, I deserted her. Barb never married but became a successful businesswoman, using the stenography skills she learned at college and her intelligence, which made her ever practical and reliable. I met her again many years later, when she made contact with me. I promised to ring her, but never did. It was cruel, but I was unable to accept my own strangeness, never mind hers.

Part of my strangeness came from the fact that my father was the head gardener at the other convent. He felt it was his duty to publicly show gratitude to the nuns at Vaucluse for educating his daughters and he did this by making us his envoys. Liesbet and I had to carry huge bunches of flowers, or plants in large pots, for the Reverend Mother. The trouble was that the Reverend Mother usually only appeared at morning assembly. To catch her meant placing ourselves between the hall and the door through which she would disappear. After the first time, however, she swept past us regally, veil flying, pretending not to see us. We left the plants outside the door, feeling awkward and dejected. The message was that we were no different from the others who dutifully attended her oratories. It was respect for her voice and wishes that was appreciated, not our attempts to show it with plants and flowers.

Feeling strange can be generated by simple things. Like not having a bra when you're fifteen. As I half skipped, half trod down the wooden stairs from the upstairs classrooms, I could feel my breasts bounce up and down under my singlet, shirt and tunic. Hadn't my mother noticed I was growing up? Clothes had always been her arena: what was in our wardrobe was always and only Mother's choice; she made practically everything herself. But not bras. Would I have to ask her for one, or save up for one myself with the pocket money that usually went on dances every week? Tears stung me. I was sure that all the other girls' mothers knew their daughters had breasts and bought them bras.

Meanwhile, regular periods confirmed that I was on my way to adulthood. Not long into this phase, I couldn't locate the large safety pins needed to hold the absorbing rag in place inside my pants. I solved the dilemma by wearing an extra pair of bloomers, hoping that the elastic would keep everything in that was supposed to be in. All day, I needed to make little adjustments, and finally it was time to go home.

I made it to the first tram, then headed for the second, but had to wait at the traffic lights. The lights turned green — and so did I, when the rag fell from under my skirt. Before I had time to pick it up, a gentleman — a real gentleman, that is, one trained to respond as quick as a flash to the needs of damsels in distress — bent down to retrieve it before he realised what it was. Somewhere in the middle of this gallant act, subtle signs of shocked recognition shook his frame, but he swung around with panache and offered the blood-streaked thing to me as if he hadn't seen what it looked like.

I stuffed the stained rag into my schoolbag, thanked him with what I hoped was convincing lack of guile, and swung around to run — but the lights had turned red, and so did I. This incident did absolutely nothing for my advancement into womanhood. I felt ashamed that I had made a gentleman come face to face with the bloody evidence of a woman's messiness — with what was her business alone, and not his.

My mother finally felt obliged to tell me about the birds and the bees. 'Come into the parlour,' she said. Taking me into the parlour for privacy indicated the seriousness .of her intent, but all she did was shove a little booklet into my hands and leave the room in a hurry, biting her lower lip. *Reproduction* it said on the cover, or some similar title. I was so angry at my mother for fobbing me off like this that I threw the booklet into a corner and left it there. And so I never got any the wiser for at least another fourteen years.

I GREW UP to be a not unattractive teenager — tall, with perfectly shaped legs and thick kinking blonde hair, and a marvellously clear complexion — but I didn't think of myself as good-looking. The worst thing about me was the size of my shoes. I was too old for my class, too skinny, my feet were too big and — wait for it — I felt I had too much space between my legs at the crotch. Apart from those glaring imperfections, I had two black front teeth, a legacy from that day I refused to eat my breakfast. My teeth had slowly blackened as the nerves died and smiling, alas, had become a terrible hazard.

There were other hazards. First was wearing a bathing suit, due to the unwanted gap between my legs, and the varicose veins that had begun to appear after I turned sixteen. Going dancing was a hazard, as the hankies stuffed down the bra my mother finally had bought me could easily slip. I felt cringingly inadequate. The beauty of my face might make someone look twice (I hoped and imagined this during my long trips on the trams) but as soon as anyone saw my feet, or saw me stand up to tower above most other people on the tram, he would surely sigh and turn away.

Deportment was another thing. Our mother showed us how to walk with a book on our heads, to keep our spines straight. She had been to modelling school and passed on some of her knowledge, like how to exercise our tummy muscles and keep them flat, but she never tried to make us feel good about our femaleness. On schooldays, our tummies were encased in elasticised girdles, the kind that rolled up in the sweaty heat and smelled as if the rubber was melting.

It was during my eighteenth year that romantic feelings overcame me in a new and stormy way. I fell in love with a boarder at the convent who played tennis regularly on the courts next to our house. She had a Russian surname and that alone fired my imagination, but it was also the way she moved and laughed. Without my being able to put it this way then, she represented the self I longed to be: confident, classy, at ease with friends, well off, intelligent and properly educated to be a true woman ... not at all straight-laced.

Alana was her name, and she was no snob. She was aware of my attention, because I came out to the courts and waved to her now and then. I was able to see the tennis courts from my bedroom window if I strained my neck, and so I looked out for her. One afternoon I strained so hard that the wooden-framed flyscreen fell out of the window with a crash, which made her turn around and laugh. She knew what was going on.

Alana was kind enough not to ridicule me, and even kinder to invite me for a couple of days' holiday with her parents at Lakes Entrance. I was beside myself with happiness. In her company I felt at ease because she was not superior or sarcastic. She was only a year older than I, but so much more sophisticated and mature. On parting she gave me a ceramic memento of the beautiful place we had been to, complete with real moss, shells and coral. The ardour I felt for Alana soon matured into a sane appreciation, and after that I waved to her occasionally and that was all.

When I returned home from Lakes Entrance, my mother took me aside. 'You know the neon cross I gave you for your birthday, Carla? Well, it got broken.' It was the cross on the wall of my bedroom which lit up softly at night. She didn't tell me who had done it, but I knew it was my sister. Even though she had many boyfriends, Liesbet had become jealous of my friendship with Alana, and had found her way of wreaking vengeance. She was jealous of my friendship with Barbara as well, and tried to pry her away from me. She also damaged Alana's memento. The sister I thought had it all, because she was so popular and somehow didn't have to do half of the housework I did, thought I was better off than her. Given that we had the same upbringing, where self-esteem was almost a sin, it wasn't surprising. Our mother deliberately fostered rifts between her daughters; for what reason, I'm not sure. To prevent us ganging up on her? Who knows? We talk of the past sometimes, my sister Liesbet and I. We love each other dearly and she is one of my best friends now, the sister who once refused to let me share a pilfered lipstick. 'No, you can't use this; you haven't even *got* lips!'

MUSIC AND SINGING were the highlights of the week at college. I had a good voice, true to pitch. Our music mistress was Mother Margaret Mary, a small nun with large glasses, who had to stand on the podium next to the piano to make herself visible to the class. The most remarkable thing about her was her sensitive mouth. Her upper lip was larger than the lower, and sat upon it as if waiting to be kissed. I envied those lips and tried to shape mine like hers.

Mother Margaret Mary gave us an assignment. We were to write our impressions of 'Prelude to the Afternoon of a Faun', a lyrical piece by Claude Debussy. I was so overcome with emotion at hearing the music that I couldn't write a thing about it for days. When I finally found words — ever so poetic and delicate they were — it was too late; she would not accept late work. Through her, we were introduced to 'Where is Sylvia?', 'Hark, Hark the Lark' and all the songs that become young ladies. It was sheer delight.

In those four years of college, I learned to feel connected to my classmates. Even so, I couldn't share their animated secret conversations about boys. Not only did I dismiss this stuff as something that didn't concern me because I was going to be a nun, I was genuinely turned off. I didn't know what the girls were talking about; couldn't even imagine it. Sex was awful, as far as my subconscious knew, and I prevented myself from finding out about the real facts of life. Yet I frequently dreamed of Bing Crosby, a much older daddy-type film star, whose crooning voice had captivated my soul. I would be swimming across the ocean and appear somehow in his swimming pool, where he would be sitting on the terrace and would graciously help me out of the water. The imagined touch of his hand and the sound of his voice thrilled my dreaming soul.

Apart from Barb, only two girls ever came to my place. They were overwhelmed to discover that I slept with my sister, and were not impressed that there were no cakes or biscuits for tea. My mother was not the kind to make sweets, and those were the days before my three youngest brothers grew up and junk food entered the place.

The one great hit I made with the in-crowd was the day I pretended to put an aspirin in a bottle of Coke I had brought to school. I had overheard them saying that aspirin in Coke could make you lose your normal senses, feel drunk or something like that. You had to shake the bottle and make the aspirin dissolve. None of them was game to try, but I announced that I would do it. They watched as I put the tablet in, then shook the bottle hard. They stared fascinated as I slowly drank the fizz and began to stagger about and slur my speech. I did a superb job of faking it — because the stuff really did nothing to me — and right up until the end of lunch break I managed to stay the hilarious centre of wonderful attention. The bell helped me to regain fairly instant composure.

WORK WAS THE order of the day both after school and at weekends, except on Sundays. There was always so much to do. We didn't have a washing machine, so we rubbed clothes and sheets on a wash-board with bare hands after they came out of the boiling copper. When the chores were done at home, I would go across the main road to Doctor Billings' house, to bathe the three children — which became five after twins were born, and six when they adopted a child with a disability.

Both parents were doctors, Catholic, and devoted to each other. It was an excruciating sight for me to see them embrace one another when they came home from work; my parents never did such a thing. It tied my belly in terrible knots to witness their affection. Shyness and tears would well up at the same time. I was paid ten shillings at the end of each week, and handed the lot over to my mother. It was up to her to graciously give me two shillings back, so I could go to a dance or the movies.

Dances were the thing that saved us during those teenage years. Liesbet and I went dancing every Saturday and most Wednesday evenings. We had to travel quite a distance to get to the Box Hill town hall two suburbs away. There was a tram to catch and a bus, but we often chose to walk to save our pocket money.

There were two bands at the town hall: ballroom dancing upstairs and rock'n'roll downstairs: two completely different worlds. All the folks who couldn't dance went downstairs, I told myself. I went there occasionally, out of curiosity, and was driven away by the raucousness of the music and the chaos on the dance floor.

Upstairs was much more graceful and predictable. My Italian friends preferred foxtrots and waltzes, and they had good rhythm. I was too tall for many of the shy Australian boys to ask me to dance, but the Italians were different and never minded the *papare e papaveri* — the tall poppy and the small one — dancing together, and neither did I. I danced with them every week and they became my friends.

I learned their songs, they gave us espresso coffee that made our spines run, and they saw us off on the last bus out. No one made advances, not even Luciano, the taxi driver. He became my mother's friend, and she would ring for him whenever she needed a taxi, for she never learned to drive herself. Luciano, so handsome with his blond wavy hair and perfect teeth, was particularly polite to young girls. He realised that teenage girls needed to be romanced, and then left alone. God bless Luciano — at first much maligned by my mother, as all Italians were, until he proved himself to her.

On Wednesdays we went to Manresa Hall, which was near the Jesuit college for boys. Mostly Catholic people went there, and a different set of Italians.

With my Italian friends I could be at ease, extroverted and saucy. I was friends with all of them but had no boyfriend, something that made them suspicious towards the end, before I was due to leave for good.

Mariano, a rather lonely Italian guy, started giving me chocolates and flowers, which I accepted, but I never took up his invitation to go out with him. They huddled in a circle one evening, speaking heated Italian, before facing me with their question: 'Do you live in Lygon Street?' I said no, I lived in Kew, but they wouldn't believe me. One of them was sure I was a whore he'd seen in Lygon Street, and they turned their backs on me. Mariano looked at me sadly, but there was nothing I could do. To him, it explained everything. I wanted to tell him and his friends that I was going into a convent and that was why I didn't encourage any boyfriends. As I was leaving I mentioned this to one Italian who stood away from the group. They never saw me again, as the time for going in was now so close, and whether my name was eventually redeemed or not I don't know. Italians! If only they weren't all suspicious Catholics!

I TURNED EIGHTEEN and started having nightmares about school, dreaming that I'd never be able to leave. At the end of Year 11, I still wore those dreadfully heavy lace-ups that made my big feet look even bigger. That year was to be my last, but before leaving I was to play the lead role in the annual school play.

Les Cloches de Corneville was a hackneyed production which wasn't expected to tax the imagination of the producer, the seemingly ubiquitous Mother Eleanor, to an inordinate degree. I was both appalled and flattered to be chosen for the role of the count, dressed in satin hose and frilly jacket. The female lead was Ann Hathaway, a small dainty girl with a voice that made her a professional later in life. This was before the time of PA systems on stage and our lines had to project to the end of the hall. My Dutch vocal cords drove Mother Eleanor almost to despair; they blunted and blurred what was trying to come out of my mouth.

We had to dance a minuet, Ann Hathaway and I, a tricky manoeuvring which I never fully mastered. The concert, eventually judged a success, was a feat of endurance for the despairing nuns. 'How wonderfully boorish of you. Why not wear clogs and stomp about like a horse?' This sarcasm from one of the nuns cut so deep that she was shocked and changed her strategy to handing out compliments. I was only human, and it worked much better.

I sacrificed many precious weekend hours learning my part, and for weeks I walked around close to complete exhaustion. The nuns finally noticed and I was sent home early on occasion to get some rest. What exhausted me, and everyone else, was my shyness. Stage fright is a well-known sensation, but this ran deep, very deep, into a bottomless fear of exposing what I felt I was at the core: a rotten apple. I felt helplessly transparent. Phenomenal energy was needed to convince me that I could act well enough to get away with it. Poor nuns: how could they have guessed the white fear they were working with? 'All for Jesus through Mary' and 'Courage and Confidence' were the mottos they drew on to help them along with the extraordinary sacrifice of time and energy the production demanded.

The audience was appreciative throughout the performance, and thought it was funny to see my feet lose the plot in the middle of the intricate minuet. I gratefully warmed to their kindly attention, and managed to enjoy the performance. After the concert, as custom demanded, the whole choir of senior girls gathered to stand on tiered cloth-covered boxes, stools and steps to sing the school song and that glorious hymn to Mary, Gounod's 'Magnificat'. We sang like angels, our spirits soaring after our successful performance and with the beauty of the harmonies.

Afterwards a large young man with black hair in tight curls surrounding his chubby but serious face, and brown eyes, came up to me. 'Carla, this is Keith,' his sister introduced him to me. He had been in the audience. Touched by what he saw and heard, he had wanted to meet me, the star performer.

When he had me to himself, Keith's manner was shy but steadily determined. 'Can I call on you, Carla? We can go for a drive or something.' He didn't even blink when I told him straight off, 'Keith, it's no use us starting a relationship, because I'm going into a convent in three months' time.'

Completely undeterred, he arrived at our gate the very next weekend to take me for a ride on the back of his motorbike. What fantastic fun! He soon acquired a Holden with a bench seat in front, and we went for long drives, mostly saying nothing but our bodies burning with desire. I looked at him furtively and felt him aware of it, and wondered how long we were going to maintain this self-denial.

'Saint Maria Goretti, come to my aid!' I whispered to myself. Maria Goretti, a young Italian girl, had recently been proclaimed a saint after she was murdered for refusing to have sex. A huge picture of her filled a large section of the wall in front of the assembly hall, her eyes lifted dolefully to heaven for help and a bunch of lilies clutched to her chest. She had been proclaimed 'a saint for our times', a role model for all girls who were sinfully tempted — which occurred more in our times than ever before, it seemed.

Keith suffered from flat feet so we didn't go for walks much, and besides he had a tendency to be overweight and didn't like exercise. His affection for me grew and I loved him for his generosity in freely giving me his friendship and admiration. He asked me why I wanted to go into the convent. I forget what answer I gave him — it was the will of God, or something — but he never tried to dissuade me. For eight years he waited for me, only giving up when he was told that I had made my final vows.

IT WAS ASSUMED without question by all the nuns and the girls in my class that I would enter the convent, together with five others. That last year at school I was awarded the highest recognition for a school prefect: the Louise Grieve Prize, a statue of Our Lady.

Louise Grieve, we were told, had been an outstanding pupil of the school many years ago, and had instituted an annual prize for the girl with the best school spirit. I knew that wasn't me; I was cynical, both about school spirit and the prize for it, which smacked of bribery. I was the girl who took off my gloves on the way home from school, had once gone into the Greek Orthodox church, and regularly went to visit her Italian friends while in uniform. Apart from that, I was often late for school, did nothing at fundraising times and was never very flattering in my opinions of the nuns. However, the prize was as much a device for instilling the much-vaunted school spirit as a reward for it. My mother kept the statue. It fell once and broke, and she had it expertly mended at great expense only to discover later on that I didn't want it back. My sister, Mary, appreciated it as a symbol of the feminine and put it in her garden.

All the senior girls were expected to be members of the Sodality of the Children of Mary. We wore a shining silver medallion of Mary on a shining blue ribbon and fine white tulle enveloped our faces, giving us the illusion of being angels. The Sodality girls met in the chapel after school and were taught about modesty and all the virtues that the Virgin Mary stood for. We visited her blue-and-white statue in the grotto in the garden. Her hands were joined, her eyes looked up to heaven, and her feet were not quite on the ground.

On 8 December, the date for the feast of the Immaculate Conception of Our Lady, the Children of Mary busied themselves for hours, decorating her altar in the concert hall. I brought a bunch of late forget-me-nots, a little nothing in that sea of lilies, larkspur, delphiniums, gypsophila and roses, their exotic perfume even more heady in the humidity of the confined space. We cleaned the floor of the hall and were soaked in sweat by midday. At 2 pm the long procession began. 'Our Lady conceived without sin, pray for us who have recourse to thee,' was the special prayer that day for our souls that had been conceived in sin.

The long journey home on the trams was more crowded on feast days, because it was later in the day and working people were going home. At those times, it was impossible to read or even sit down; we had to make do with hanging on to a strap to try to keep our balance. On wet days, there were the steaming smells of offices, sawdust and oil, perfumes, talcs, warm clothes and wet mackintoshes. Hardly anybody said a word as we were tossed against each other with the tram's every stop and start. Some people managed to read a newspaper in those conditions, holding the paper close to their nose, tightly folded so as not to poke it in the eye of the next person, unwillingly pressed up against them.

It was on one of those crowded days that a boy managed to get his hands into my pants. I could feel his fingers but pretended I was dreaming, that he was not really there. Everyone else around me was also pretending — pretending that the others in the tram did not exist. I just went a notch further, going into a freeze. I was totally unable to stop him. My brain went into the automatic response of denial, just like long ago, when my father came to me in the night. I couldn't risk knowing fully, couldn't pull away; the best way to get by was to be as unconscious as possible.

I never looked at the boy who had jammed himself next to me, but I saw him as he left the tram, exuberant at the success of his subterfuge. Then the shame and the remorse hit me and made me turn scarlet. Walking the short distance home after alighting, I tried to erase it from my mind.

No medal of Our Lady on a blue ribbon was going to protect me from my inability to face my sexuality; neither would the brown cloth picture of Our Lady of Mount Carmel that we were obliged to wear under our clothes. I entered the convent for a multiplicity of reasons — one of them was the fact that I was totally unable to face life as an adult.

EVER SINCE I had come into contact with nuns, I had heard them talk about vocations, and dreaded the possibility that I might ever be cursed with one. Nuns seemed as cold as ice. In Holland they were cruel and self-centred; in Australia many seemed conceited and self-righteous. Most of them weren't real people, not natural, and the last thing I wanted was to become one of them. Even at the age of six, it used to give me awful shivers just to go near the convent walls. Those shivers had to do with a premonition, because I knew that in spite of all my dread I would be a nun one day, that it was an unavoidable fate.

At the age of seventeen, just in case my motivation to enter the convent had weakened after my friendship with Keith, the nuns provided powerful inelegant prods to engender fear. All the young women who were about to leave school were fed stories of girls who hadn't followed their religious vocation. Their lives, we were told, were full of misery because they had deprived themselves of the grace of God. It was like leaving a path that had been mapped out, the only route filled with God's grace. The results of refusal were unhappy marriages, stillborn babies, terrible illnesses and bad luck. Nevertheless, my stomach would turn into knots whenever I saw a mother with a baby. Babies were not to be for me, and I cried inside.

The tension in me was immense, because, in spite of the repulsion I felt, I knew there was no escape: I would *have* to go in. It was the will of God, I told myself. God would love me for my sacrifice. God would also bless my family, as the nuns had promised. I wasn't just searching for the Truth; I was searching to be loved, really loved. I was like the young man in the story, looking for a lost key. He was searching under a lamp-post late at night, when a stranger came by and asked him where he had lost the key. The young man pointed out into the darkness. 'Why are you looking for it here then, if you lost it there in the dark?' the stranger asked. 'Because,' the young man asserted, 'the *light* is *here*.'

I was compelled to do the best I could, and I would do anything rather than give up hope that the key would be found. And yet it was the perfect thing to do. The Divine somehow had it all sewn up, even as I seemed to exercise my shaky free will in such a paradoxical manner. To go in was to be my way out.

A month or so before I was due to enter the convent, my mother rushed into my bedroom. She had heard a loud sobbing and was horrified to discover me in a frenzy, tearing at my clothes and crying hysterically. I told her between sobs how terrible it was for me to go in. She listened to my despairing confusion: 'I don't want to go in, but I *do* want to!' She felt sorry for me and comforted me, but what else could she do? Besides having a vested interest in the honour that my entering would bestow on her family, she too was a firm believer in 'doing the will of God'.

With her expert skills, she quietly helped me to get ready. She made me the simple black dress, apron and short cape that was part of the postulant's uniform. I needed a net cap to stop my hair from blowing in the breeze or falling about, lisle stockings and the detested old black lace-up shoes I'd worn to school, with new soles glued on by Dad. Underwear as usual. Nightdresses were to be plain white. My mother and I made some from white flannelette and some from cotton sheets.

I did allow myself one statement before going in: I sewed large bright red buttons on every one of my white nighties.

PART TWO

ASKING FOR TROUBLE

FEBRUARY 1957, A hot day in Melbourne. A version of me I had never known before, accompanied by my proud and smiling parents, walked with straight shoulders past the cypress hedge that stretched all the way from my home to the convent. I arrived at the nunnery's back door to be received by a proudly smiling Reverend Mother. It was Cheshire Cat day; there were smiles such as I had never seen, the biggest from Reverend Mother Winifred, the Cheshire Cat herself, as I (strictly privately) called her.

I had become a postulant — literally 'one who asks'; in this case, one who asks to be admitted to become a nun. There were five other 'possies' with me, all girls straight out of school, like myself. I hadn't even done my matriculation year; neither had some of the others. In a few years my eager younger sister, Berta, would be accepted at the age of barely sixteen, ecstatic to get away from home and still have a roof over her head.

'*For fools rush in where angels fear to tread*' wrote Alexander Pope. If anyone had called me a fool in those days, I would have replied: 'Oh yes, I am; I'm a fool for Christ.' I was single-minded; a euphemism for blind.

I couldn't afford to examine my motives. Motives didn't seem to bother the nuns' consciences either. They couldn't afford to look too closely at their much-needed recruits, even if they'd had the psychological know-how to detect ulterior motives. It has taken thirty years of my own life, after all, to fully understand why I thought I had no choice but to go into a nunnery.

'*God beholds thee individually whoever thou art. He calls thee by name. He sees and understands thee as He has made thee . . .*' These words had somehow wafted their way to me, on a piece of paper I found floating in the street one day on my way home from school. They had touched me deeply, and I clung to the original scrap of paper as if it were a treasure map. I sure needed someone who knew me, as I didn't know myself, and nobody else seemed to either. I needed the promise of being 'beheld' by my God, who, it said, 'knew me by name'. I could not afford to turn my back on this. '*Thou canst not love thyself as He loves thee . . . He compasses thee round and bears thee in His arms.*' Such comforting words to one who doubted love.

I said goodbye to my parents, knowing that I would most likely see my father in the convent grounds every day, and, if not, he would make it his business to see *me* somehow. And my mother was only a minute's walk away. They had tears in their eyes. Had they known what was in store for me, they might have bawled or taken me away by force. But nothing like that happened. There was an unreal atmosphere of holy sacrifice and blind trust that day.

I was led into the inner sanctum, into which I had so often seen the nuns disappear; the domain where I imagined them to fade into vaporous non-human beings. I had been shocked at school when Mother Anthony took a handkerchief from the bottomless pocket of her skirts and vigorously blew her nose in front of her class. The shock came from the realisation of her humanness, and an aesthetically offensive one at that. It was an exotically strange feeling now, to be finally admitted behind the scenes. Understandably, I entered with the FCJs, the order which had taught me.

Out in the sunshine the next day, dressed in our black cotton frocks, aprons, short capes and white hairnets, each aspirant had her photograph taken — an innovative memento for the parents that year.

It would take stern self-discipline to stop me taking the opportunity to call in on my mother, as she was so near. Sometimes

I dreamt about it. One morning, I glided around the inside of the cypress hedge, past the nuns' washing lines and Sister Kevin's chookyard, and spied her hanging out the clothes in the backyard. I called out to her. She was surprised and looked so guilty that I had the distinct feeling that my furtiveness wasn't completely appreciated. Nevertheless, I discovered years later that my mother was frequently spotted slinking along the same cypress hedge by my brothers and sisters, to sneak a look when she thought the nuns wouldn't catch her.

My first letter home described the circumstances of my new life. 'I get up as if my bed is on fire,' I wrote, 'then we wash away all our laziness with cold water.'

For the first few months we rose at 6.15 am, in time for twenty minutes' meditation before seven o'clock Mass. A novice would run through the dorm, breaking the early-morning stillness by shouting 'Praise be to Jesus!' with as much piety and urgency as she could muster. She would not leave until she heard an 'Amen!' from behind every curtain. Getting up was the first joyful act of obedience. I literally bounded out of bed.

The dormitory for postulants and novices was originally designed to be a chapel, but it was never used for that, being situated high up on the third floor. The dorm, gowned with white curtains to made cubicles for twelve beds, felt more like a dreaming room for angels or fairies. Its large arched double oak doors looked like wings, and there were tall sash windows at the far end, set in a five-sided wall, giving the room a rounded look. The floors, as throughout the entire building, were polished wood. The metal wire-slung beds had very down-to-earth horsehair mattresses. At home, I had been used to kapok, dusty and lumpy but supremely comfortable compared with unyielding horsehair. It was something to get used to, and nobody complained.

In the morning, summer and winter, we washed in cold water. The water was collected in a pitcher the evening before, to be poured into a metal basin standing on a wooden locker in the morning. We would strip the bed and put the bedclothes on the single chair that fitted neatly in the small remaining space next to the bed, then sweep back the curtains as we left. The two people at the end of the dorm had more room than the others because of the rounded wall. I was one of the fortunates to be given an end cubicle, and slept beside an open window through which I could see the stars and the moon. 'The view from the window even beats the view from the top of the tree in our yard,' I wrote, to let my family know how wonderful it all was. 'FCJ stands for First Class Jailbirds,' wrote back my brother Willem.

Postulancy was, on the whole, a rather gentle introduction to the ways of the nuns. We shared the living quarters of the novices, who had been there for a whole year and wore the complete habit, but with a white bonnet and veil instead of the fully-fledged nuns' black. Except for the times we met in chapel, and for some readings, we postulants and novices were segregated from the nuns. It meant that, for the moment, we were shielded from the day-to-day routine of those who had taken permanent vows — or perhaps *they* were shielded from *us*! In spite of being an optimistic postulant, I was still in fear of the total blackness of the nuns' habit.

The only visible white on a nun was on the forehead: a half-moon-shaped strip of starched cotton which fitted between the brow and the hairline, known as a bandeau, inside a white, stiffly starched band around the face. In spite of the urgent advice of Pope Pius XII at the 1950 Congress for Religious in Rome that nuns should modify their clothing to suit modern life, no changes had been made. Ten years after entering the convent, I would have nightmares about this little bit of white on the forehead, the only part of me that had been symbolically left intact.

In this nightmare I dreamed that the nuns, who all lived precariously in a treetop house with dangerous holes in the floors, had asked me to skin a cat. The cat was black, but had a small white diamond patch on its forehead. I was handed the cat and a scalpel. The cat was limp, as if it had been knocked out, but was warm to the touch. Going totally against every instinct, and with complete horror, I proceeded to obey a command I did not allow myself to question. I proceeded to do 'the will of God'. Scalpels usually make me want to faint, but in my nightmare I managed to use one to skin the warm, sleeping cat. I skinned off all of its black fur, but hesitated when it came to removing the white diamond-like piece on its forehead. I couldn't do that! I *didn't* do it, and left the white piece intact.

I would wake up with pounding heart, but there was also a tiny flicker of triumph. The cat had fared badly (by my own hands), but it hadn't been *entirely* skinned.

THE BEGINNING OF postulancy was sweet: it was summertime; at first there weren't even schoolchildren around; and there were no harsh demands. We were given a lot of leeway to help us gradually get used to the rules of silence, and I had the comfort of the company of other souls who were just as new as I was.

The novitiate was a large square sunny room with a creaky floor, lined with large wooden desks. Each of us had her own desk in this friendly room, where we studied the rules of the convent, the scriptures, the life of our foundress, Madame de Bonnault d'Hoüet, and the lives of the saints. It was where we wrote our letters, and kept our missals and rule books.

A statue of the patron saint of novices stood on a pedestal decorated with fresh flowers. There was another Saint Stanislaus in our dorm sharing the honour with Saint Anthony, patron saint of all things lost, and therefore a favourite saint. Why did we feel that we were always losing things?

Every day we came together at recreation time, for a full hour after lunch and half an hour in the evening before prayers. Two large tables were placed together in the middle of the novitiate so we could all sit around them, postulants and novices together. Whenever the weather permitted we would go outside, walking leisurely to the friendly shade of a large tree, or watering two little oak trees we had planted in the horse paddock a short distance away. We adopted three pumpkin plants in the compost heap, but discovered one day that two had been pulled out by my father, the gardener. I complained about it in a letter to him, and received a reply explaining that only one could use the space. My father wasn't a sentimental man.

Our sense of fun was sharp in those days. Humour prevented the strange and unusual becoming macabre. All the same, the first time we joined the nuns in the common room for the daily reading session, and a nun knelt on the floor, accusing herself in a loud voice of some misdemeanour and asking her superior and us to forgive her and pray for her, I turned scarlet. I felt I was doing something indecent, just in witnessing this exposure. I stumbled into the chapel afterwards. Once there, I was in for another shock: nuns were kissing the chapel floor upon entering and leaving! Later, I saw nuns kissing the refectory floor — I never understood why — and, on especially penitential occasions, kissing venerable old nuns' shoes — most often those of the Reverend Mother Vicar, grabbed by grovelling hands from beneath her skirts.

A distinct feeling of having gone back to the Middle Ages overcame me. I was shocked to see a novice take her meals while kneeling on the floor, making her chair into a table. She was a little removed from the others and therefore from the possibility of serving herself. I came to understand that this happened quite frequently and was a sign of voluntary removal from the community for having broken a rule. To be fed by a compassionate volunteer meant that this humble apology had been accepted. Sometime during the meal, the superior would allow the sister to rejoin the community and take up her place at the table again. You could always count on being fed and forgiven, so the exercise was really a tame ritual.

Our first novice mistress had an act of cultured grandeur about her because of her very straight back, her age, her gaunt looks, her powers of observation, sense of humour, intelligence and fortitude. Mother Philomena was slowly dying of cancer, which gave her a chance to sort things out in her very astute mind. Once she had been feared as a strict disciplinarian in the school, but she showed us a rare compassion. She took us for slow walks around the convent grounds, made magnificent by the huge conifers, oaks and elms, and the dedicated work of my energetic and resourceful father. She knew the names of all the trees and taught them to us. Mother Philomena was full of stories of life in other convents in other countries and the women who had lived in them.

She loved our exuberance, although she made us keep the rules. Only one person was allowed to speak at a time. In her magnificently mild-mannered way she saw to it that everybody got a fair chance to contribute to our lively conversations.

We had many sunny days to spend outside at recreation time, and I was happy. To me, recreation felt so *civilised*; it was unaccustomed civilisation, the nearest thing to the genteel ways I had read about in E M Forster's *A Room With a View*, wistfully reminding me of my mother's lost heritage. Often, we'd take chairs with us and sit under a shady tree to do our embroidery or our mending. Poverty meant we had to mend our clothes. Doing it for the glory of God meant mending them to perfection; our darned stockings were worthy of a needlewoman's craft. Our embroideries too were works of devotion. They were sold to God knows where or given to God knows whom, and we learned the virtue of detachment by handing over the work of our hands and hearts without question. Later, much much later, I was astonished and angry to find out that my family had been paying their hard-earned money for the things I was embroidering.

Recreation was also a time for sharing tall stories, asking sly questions about the nuns, and much laughter. We laughed a lot — we were young, full of repressed mischief, and needed relief from the anxious business of adjusting to a new life. Laughter was the great tension-defuser, the thing that kept us sane and restored healthy blooms to our cheeks. My natural sense of humour found scope in those daily sessions when everybody listened to you when it was your turn. It was only in the third year of my novitiate, after my new novice mistress told me to be sure to cultivate my sense of humour or I might lose it, that I started to forget to laugh. She had triggered some warning about pride — it was like winning too many marbles.

Before this unfortunate reminder, I learned to tell jokes with flair, and wrote down the new ones to send home for the family to have a laugh. '*God looked over the walls of heaven at the souls in hell, who were writhing in terrible agony while the demons poured pitch over them and goaded them with red-hot pokers,*' began a joke of Scottish origin (perhaps it was one of Bertrand Russell's, who must have told it better than I did). '*His eyes searched out the souls among the flames and smoke. "Oh, God," the souls agonised, "we didn't a-ken it would be this bad." God looked them over and said: "Well, ye ken it noo, doon't ye?"*'

I always thought this was a very risque joke; in it there was such a firm belief in hell and the eternal wrath of God. We must have felt pretty smug and secure to laugh at these sorts of in-house jokes. Somewhere inside me a key turned, but I hardly noticed it. Laughter has a way of banishing the devil, if only temporarily.

Throughout my twelve and a half years of convent life, it was always the laughter and the togetherness that made any part of the experience seem worthwhile. The shared laughter created a camaraderie, a solidarity; the one thing that truly gave us a common identity. We even created a common noticeboard for jokes to be posted, anecdotes that everyone could read, not just the possies and novices. It was a friendly communication device between the two camps of the fledglings and the fully fledged. '*A housewife found a little live rabbit in her Westinghouse fridge one day. When she asked him what he was doing there, he said "Just westing." "Just resting?" she queried. "Yes, isn't this a westing-house?"*'

Sometimes I would catch sight of one of my little brothers. Once, my two-year-old brother Peter came wandering along with a teddy bear in his arms, looking for his daddy. I sent him on his way, not sure myself where Dad was, and he grinned and blew me kisses as he went. A few weeks later, during one of our outdoor recreation times, he sat nearby on the cement kerb, content just to be there. Every minute or so he'd say, 'Allo, Ca-la!' and smile. I was allowed to kiss him and send him home, pulling up his trousers because his belly was exposed. 'I can't find Mummy anywhere, Ca-la,' he said. Poor little boy.

The end of recreation time usually filled me with a feeling of great loss, even doom. Why couldn't we continue to dream, to recreate the world, for a few more hours? Why this forlorn obedience to a clock?

But 2 pm spelt sudden silence, like sudden death. The time was up; eyes down, hurry off to work duties.

There was plenty of work to do. We postulants and novices must have saved the convent from massive cleaning bills. We worked hard in the laundry, in the kitchen, in the chapel, in the linen room — sorting clothes, making new ones, doing large mending jobs with sewing machines, in the dormitories; in fact, everywhere in that enormous place.

During my time, there was not one hired hand; all the work was done by novices and nuns, who were rostered in their time off from teaching duties by the efficient Sister Kevin. I could not believe it when I was eventually told, many years after coming out, that my family was required to pay fees for me during the years of my novitiate, and for a full total of eight and a half years until my final vows. It had something to do with not having a dowry to bring with me when I entered; all I'd had was a portion of my parents' will to bequeath to the convent upon my death, and that wasn't considered good enough. I had no idea about this extortion.

'It's always the poor people who pay up, Mrs van Raay,' the sister who had been drafted into doing the dirty work of collecting the money told my mother. 'The rich ones can't be bothered; they never pay.'

It seemed that quite a few people hadn't brought a dowry, even those who could afford it. It was the wealthy who had the wisdom not to be intimidated by demands of payment while their daughters gave their lives to God and God's endless work.

My main job was to keep the corridors and parlours shiny and free of dust. I was shown how to strew discarded tea leaves at the head of the corridor and sweep them down methodically so the damp leaves gathered all the dust. I learned how to tame the large polishing machine that bolted away from inexperienced hands, and how to care for the carved mahogany tables, the Queen Anne chairs and every item in the opulent parlours, which made me think of the court of King Louis XIV (I wasn't used to antique vases, and some of these were three feet high).

It wasn't right to be seen cleaning when a visitor arrived, but sometimes it was unavoidable. I saw a fairly important-looking male visitor emerge from a parlour one day as I was mopping the corridor, and I ducked away into the Rev's bathroom, which had a recessed door facing into the corridor. This bathroom was a spacious, hallowed place, usually out of bounds to a hoi polloi cleaner like me. The visitor, however, had exactly the same room in mind, and wanted to bolt when he saw me. Dusting furiously, I said I'd just finished and, really, it didn't matter!

The refectory, where we had our meals, was a place of anxious feeling for me. We novices had our own refectory across the corridor from the nuns. Our mistress would usually preside and we would take our cues from her. Our foundress was French, but etiquette in her convents was definitely Victorian. It was nerve-racking. One day, she ate an apple with a knife and fork. I considered myself a total dunce at table manners and supposed that everyone else had been well brought up, except for me, a caretaker's daughter. But who learns to eat an orange with a spoon at home, or an apple with a knife and fork? So we must have all felt pretty much the same, stealing furtive glances at each other's manners.

We had become quite expert at not touching our apples with our fingers, when our novice mistress had the gall to announce dryly from the presiding end of the table: 'It isn't necessary to eat an apple with a knife and fork, you know.' She wiped her thin mouth with a large white napkin and left the room. I never did sort out the meaning of that particular lesson.

FOR CENTURIES, RELIGIOUS life had been an education in dehumanisation. Over and over again, the Church Fathers had defined religious life as a striving for perfection, synonymous with the renunciation of the world. 'The world' did not just mean material possessions; nuns were also to minimise contact with people. *Stern* is the word that comes to mind. Stern devotion. Efforts to break this austere attachment to rules and lifestyle made by Pope Pius XII and Pope John XXIII — who called Major Superiors from all the religious orders together in 1957, 1961 and again in 1965 — were met with a bland inability to imagine anything other than the way to perfection they thought they had already embraced.

Eventually, living by the rules and daily schedule became easier — it even became a crutch. To do the right thing, we had only to consult the routine or the rules; in cases of any doubt, there was the novice mistress to consult.

'Every little thing I do is always exactly what Our Lord wants of me at that moment, and that certainty is an ecstatic feeling,' I wrote in my first weekly letter to my family. The more rules we learned, the easier it seemed to 'do it right'. Until, of course, the burden of the sheer number of rules and the complexities of living them increased the chances of failure.

Everybody felt larger than life now, for we belonged to 'the community'. For a young woman struggling to have any identity at all, this was something to glory in. My ability to 'please God' seemed guaranteed. I had successfully transferred my need for approval from my parents to anyone in a position of authority within the convent hierarchy, the 'mouthpieces of God'. Such transference was openly encouraged; even the titles Reverend Mother, Reverend Mother Vicar and Reverend Mother General were a blatant claim on childish loyalties. These titles have now been abolished.

Our Reverend Mother was made much of. She had a lot of organising to do and was cosseted like a queen bee. The rank and file were also encouraged to love the regional Mother Vicar, whoever she might be at the time, and, most of all, the Reverend Mother General, affectionately known as 'Notre Mère'. She was the hardest to get to meet or know as she lived in Broadstairs, in England. We were taught to send letters of affection to this unknown, respected mother figure, assuring her of our constant prayers and our loyalty and love for her.

Reverend Mother Winifred had a mouthful of large teeth, but after the initial wide smiles at my reception she appeared to take a chilly dislike to me. She didn't have much time for postulants and novices in general, and luckily only made an appearance now and again to read the rules or give an impassioned pep talk called a dissertation. This she delivered with eyes down on her prepared written statement, while we youngsters sat in two rows at right angles to her, eyes staring at our folded hands in our lap.

Once in a while, though, we had to make a personal report to her. One by one we knelt beside her in the hallowed atmosphere of her private office, which reeked of rebukes, disciplinary measures, reiterated rules and regulations, regrettable decisions, humiliations, exhortations and admonitions — all of which I suffered myself, over time, in that room.

Reverend Mother sat in an armchair so that a kneeling postulant like me could look up at her large face. I think it was my particular brand of naivety that tended to upset her. She would twitch her large nose involuntarily and those bushy eyebrows would come down darkly as she answered my questions unsmilingly.

WHEN MOTHER PHILOMENA, our elegant novice mistress died, we were temporarily left motherless. She died of cancer without any of her 'children' there to witness her passing or to mourn by her bedside. As was the custom, Holy Masses were offered for her soul, six in a row on the first day, performed at double and even treble speed, making me wonder why we couldn't do it like that every morning and save heaps of time. After a week or so, we were appointed another mistress.

Mother Rosa was younger and much more emotionally expressive. She had kind eyes, and thought it her major duty to try and cheer us up, even if she didn't feel so bright herself sometimes. Mother Rosa had the unfortunate experience of having one of the older novices fall violently in love with her. I say 'violently' because Sister Miriam had very loud, disrespectful arguments with Mother Rosa, and even swore. Miriam was reluctantly sent home to her respectable parents after almost two and a half years of being in the novitiate. She left without saying goodbye to us.

Mother Rosa tried hard, very hard, to do her job, poor thing, but she cried too much at her own incompetence, and so we were given a third novice mistress, Mother Immaculata, a woman with large glasses that made her eyes sparkle deceptively and a prunish mouth set in a square jowl. Her beguiling upturned nose belied her nature. She was impish all right, and had a cultivated bright manner, but her nervous habit of constantly pushing her glasses back up her nose and the way she remained prudish even when smiling, should have made somebody think twice. There wasn't anything obviously wrong with her, except that she had no idea what she was doing. She had a blind faith in a God who spoke through her superiors. Her superiors had told her to be a novice mistress; it didn't matter that she knew nothing about the job, her faith told her that she would be miraculously guided. She was a holy innocent. She was also a child — every bit as I was. Trained in primary school teaching, she was used to dealing with other little children, and now she had a few bigger ones under her wing, that was all.

During this time, the mysterious and awe-inspiring Reverend Mother General came from England to visit her three houses in Australia. We didn't have enough time to knock up a concert to welcome her, so we simply had a religious reading for her in our common room, followed by a chat, during which she asked several questions in a crowd interview. A message got back to us later about her impressions: she wouldn't give sixpence for the lot of us! We bit our lips and giggled and snorted at the news. Surprisingly, the insult did not make us feel bad — it was so insulting as to be ridiculous. We simply couldn't believe that in such a short time she could have made an honest judgment about our worth or worthlessness.

Our giggles were accepted as a postulant's way to discharge pent-up tensions and they were tolerated for a time. The giggles would get hold of us in chapel, because we weren't used to prolonged silences, even though our meditations were initially for only twenty minutes.

After a month, the time was extended to half an hour, after two months, to three quarters of an hour. Our quick, youthful minds could not cope with the suppression of thought for so long. One of us might start to snigger silently and helplessly, then the rest would soon join in sympathy, shoulders shaking so violently that the vibrations could be felt through the wooden kneelers. All of a sudden, someone would explode into laughter. The shocking release of energy would calm us all down, as if our collective tension had found a way out through one of us.

On hot humid days we would simply go limp and suffer in perfect silence. The black cloth of our dresses stuck to the back of the bench if we dared to lean back instead of sitting bolt upright as was expected. One morning I had been leaning back for as long as five minutes when the Reverend Mother came up and asked me if I was sick, but I had merely wandered off into my thoughts and forgotten where I was.

The meditations were boring to the extreme. They were always read from the same book, in archaic language, on topics such as the Resurrection of Lazarus, the Last Judgment, Saint Patrick, the Devil and the Guardian Angel, the Glorified Body of Christ, the Eucharist, Silence, how the body would look and feel like after the Resurrection of the Dead ... etc. After a few years, it became easier in a perverse sort of way, because the meditations remained the same, repeated time after time after time!

At breakfast we always listened to excerpts from the *Imitation of Christ*, even after the shocking news that Thomas à Kempis, the esteemed author, would never be canonised. This was because he was found, after exhumation, to have died with his teeth sunk into one of his shoulders. He must have despaired of God after being buried alive and coming to in an airless coffin, and no saint would do that.

During the hushed bustle of serving and eating lunch, there were readings from the writings of the foundress, until such time as the superior would say the magic words, 'Praise be to Jesus!'. This was the signal for a few minutes of animated conversation, one person speaking at a time, while others behaved and kept in what must have been dying to come out. Only the lay sisters, who had not taken the same vows and usually sat the furthest away from the superior, broke the rule of one person at a time. Often they couldn't follow the in-house drift of the conversation, so chatted quietly among themselves, and were usually given an ineffectual rebuke by the superior. On feast days the reading could be counted on to be very short, creating delightful relief. At dinner, more readings and no talking at all, because after the washing-up came recreation time.

There was a strict routine to the evening supper reading, before chapel and dinner. Twice a week we were treated to the writings of Alphonsus Rodriquez. He had written several books in a series called *The Practice of Perfection and Christian Virtue*. The books had a transparent sincerity and we readily absorbed their peculiar reasonings and admirable solutions to living a Perfect Life. No other books could have shown us so adequately how miserable and worthless we were as human beings; how filthy, vile and rude our human bodies were, to be beaten into the habit of 'following the Spirit'.

On other days, the readings were from a shortlist lives of favourite saints, handed down from generation to generation. After the visit from the General, books by Abbot Marmion were thrust under our noses for some months, glorified by being the personal choice of the General, who admired the Abbot's scholarly phraseology. Ordinary brains like ours had difficulty understanding his ideas. Occasionally we had a fair thriller — such as the life of a humorous missionary in Africa, whose name I have forgotten but who at least made us smile. Then there were stories of male saints like Aloysius, who never looked at a woman, not even at the face of his mother; and the story of Father Petit, who would never touch an apple because of its connection with original sin set loose in the world by Eve. Father Petit asked for his pure heart to be cut out upon his death and preserved for Sister X, a friend of his. Nobody thought of ridiculing these stories; we took them as a patient takes a remedy: they tasted bad, but they were supposed to do you good.

The life of the foundress was on the reading list, of course. She had led an unusual, courageous and mysterious life, full of inexplicable coincidences towards the end, like being in two places at once, hearing voices and foretelling events which later came true. She was a pioneer of education for the girls of non-affluent parents, realising that education was the way to emancipation from the narrow roles women found themselves in during the early nineteenth century.

In 1820 she founded her first convent, followed quickly by four others, all in France, and before long more were established in England and Ireland. The first Australian convent was in Richmond, Melbourne, established in 1882, twenty-four years after the foundress's death. Were she alive in our time, the 1960s, when education was available to everyone, she would surely have packed up the schools and done something more useful. But this was inconceivable to the FCJs. The relevance of the teaching nuns was almost completely non-existent towards the end of the twentieth century, and vocations dwindled. It was all blamed on the godlessness of the times rather than on the lack of timely initiative.

SIX MONTHS OF postulancy sped by, filled with excitement, horror and humour, and soon we were ready for the next step: the awful thrill of shedding our simple black cotton frocks and net caps for the wildly professional-looking habit of the novices.

This took place in a formal ceremony meant to impress our families with the growing seriousness of their daughters' choice to live their lives for God, in God's house.

ASKING FOR MORE TROUBLE

THE SOFT SELL of postulancy ended on 8 September 1957, the day of the Immaculate Conception of the Virgin Mary. To mark the change there was a public ceremony in the chapel, formal and impressive, which our families and friends all attended. What they wouldn't see was the backstage crudeness when it came to hacking off our hair.

We six brides of Christ walked solemnly down the aisle, our hair still intact and covered with the same veil we had used as children at our first communion. Our hands were joined at the fingertips and held in front of our chests as we walked with bent heads. My pseudo-wedding gown had been sewn by my mother; it was made of thin white satin with a little dot in the fabric — needless to say, it had no plunging neckline or bare shoulders. I imagined I looked like Maria Goretti, or one of the saints from my holy pictures.

The chapel was crowded with the relatives of the six girls gliding over the red carpet towards the sanctuary. A few senior schoolgirls thought to be potential future 'entrants' were also allowed in. My parents and a sister were there, somewhere.

The chapel was filled with the scent of many flowers, predominantly white: white roses, white carnations, lilies, gladioli, gypsophila and lily of the valley. Strange to think of it now, but the scent of the flowers, which I can so clearly recall, was a reassurance to me then. Their fragrant presence carried the message that everything was all right. Everything *was* all right — not because I was assured of 'doing the right thing' to please God, which I wasn't, because God doesn't need to be pleased — but because I was doing what I felt I had to do then. In time, there would be different things to do. I had friends; I was being watched over.

We had rehearsed our lines for renouncing the world, asking for the habit we were going to wear, and declaring our willingness to be a bride of Christ, a Faithful Companion of Jesus.

The bishop asked each of us the ceremonial questions as we knelt before him.

'My child, what do you ask?'

'My Lord, I ask for the mercy of God and the grace of the holy habit of religion,' we replied.

'Do you ask it with your whole heart and with a free will?'

'Yes, my Lord.' Our words reached the many listening ears in the chapel.

'I espouse you to Jesus Christ, Son of the Eternal Father, in the Society of the Faithful Companions of Jesus. May God grant you perseverance, my child.'

And so, having wedded us to Jesus, the bishop placed the neatly folded nun's habit over our outstretched hands. When we had all received our new clothes, we rose and proceeded demurely back down the aisle, our heads bowed, heading for the door at the back of the chapel.

Once out of the chapel, we lost our sedate tempo and raced to the room we had dubbed the bridal chamber. Jesus had been given six more brides that day; this was a mystery I accepted as easily as the notions of the Holy Ghost and ejaculations. The cutting of the hair had to be done quickly, so that each bride could return with her head encased in a white bonnet and veil, the rest of her body enveloped in voluminous black, without making the whole congregation wait too long.

A strange feeling rolled over me as my novice mistress chopped at my hair, the symbol of my femininity. Femininity vanishes when you take your vows. A bride I could be, but not a woman.

What on earth was Mother Immaculata up to? Her nervous hands were even clumsier than usual as she struggled to cut through my thick healthy hair. This would take an age! Meanwhile, the fairy tale continued in the chapel. Organ music maintained the ambience of soft holiness, belying the agitation backstage. Someone with stronger hands and a larger pair of scissors took over from the struggling novice mistress. As my hair began to fall to the ground, something stirred in me, reminding me of the dream I'd had the night before.

I had been dreaming of Keith, soft sensuous Keith with his black curly hair and kind wise face. Without even knowing the words 'sexual intercourse', let alone what they might have meant, I had dreamed of him entering me. In the dream, he entered my body somehow and came into my heart. It was a physical presence so real and alive, and it felt so good, that I wanted things to be like that for ever. It was the consummation of a marriage, I thought vaguely, still dreaming, still in ecstasy.

When I woke in the dark, aware that some of the others in the dormitory might have listened in, I wondered if I could still become a nun. *But it was only a dream.*

Mother Mary Luke, who used to be my headmistress at primary school, smiled knowingly at me the next morning as I scanned the faces around me to spot who might have heard me in the night, panting secretly with nervousness. She must have heard it all before. But I was clear about my choice to devote myself solely to Jesus, to God the Father and to the Holy Spirit; the Trinity that was mysteriously all One, according to Christian belief, but which, alas, had no physical reality for me to relate to.

The hacking of my hair continued, accompanied by grunts and gasps. The dismal thought suddenly entered my head that I would never have a baby. I had this thought again during the years that followed, and each time I let in this grief, something seemed to dry up in my body.

The nuns were done, finally, and my spiky head was covered with a bonnet. We re-entered the chapel encased in our heavy black serge gowns and white caps, feeling so strange and looking so unearthly that some people burst into tears.

After the brave ceremony, my family was there to congratulate me. My father held me tight and kissed me on the mouth until my mother whispered urgently for him to stop. With his mouth still on mine, I opened my eyes and saw my mother's agitated face. She was looking around to see who might be noticing this tableau. In that strange unconscious moment of collusion with my father, I felt all the desperate collusions of the past paying off. My father was proud of me at last. I had finally succeeded! His daughter's achievement had excited him sexually. It wasn't appropriate, but I wasn't used to thinking things through. My desperate need for love and approval had kept me in sexual collusion with him since the tender age of three — though, as the young novice I was then, I had no idea of that.

When the hullabaloo of the party in the main parlour was finally over, everyone went home. The shiny tresses of my thick blonde hair — which looked a lot like Grace Kelly's after they had been kept for six months in a little net — were given to my mother. She placed my hair in a silk-lined box near an enlarged photograph of me and often put it on her lap and wept. When my younger sisters saw her weeping, they thought I had stolen her affection and that they were only second-best. I was both venerated and despised.

Little did anyone know about the welter of less-than-holy reasons in my subconscious mind pushing me to be a nun. My social, financial and emotional status in the world could hardly have been less promising. If I'd had any self-assurance at all, based on a sound knowledge of the world and a good self-image, I might have faced the future with confidence and excitement — but I felt bankrupt. By joining the nuns, I was doing what a politician does, who associates with famous and powerful people to further his or her career and reputation. To be a bride of Christ wasn't such a bad connection. To be a bride of Christ in the FCJ camp was an even

better prospect! But I was conscious only of sacrificing ora.
to take up a life of obedience, and was admired and congratu.
for this. I was like an innocent young soldier, ready to obey witho.
question.

I make this comparison because years later, one evening in 1992, a
TV documentary about a young soldier had me suddenly glued to
the screen. It was about Franz Lang, a German officer who could not
disobey an order from his superior. It told how Franz's absolute
allegiance to the Führer allowed him to coolly shoot his long-time
friend Klaus, who had joined the Communist Party. Klaus was in a
line with other captured Communists and recognised his erstwhile
buddy, Franz. He thought he could safely make a dash from the
group, since it was rearguarded by Franz. He died with Franz's bullet
in his head, disbelief etched on his face. Franz had acted without
question; he didn't think he had a choice.

A few days after my initiation, I met a little girl who was distressed
and lost on her first day at school. I knew the direction she had to go
in. I knelt down beside her to tell her, when I remembered the rule
of silence. I felt sad that I couldn't help her but I didn't speak. I just
got up and went on my way, believing I had done the grander thing
for having obeyed a rule. The urge to obey a command was stronger
than kindness, and much stronger than common sense. It was not
until 1967, well into the reforms instigated by Pope John XXIII, that
the spell broke for me.

I had vowed obedience as a Faithful Companion of Jesus, after the
style of Saint Ignatius of Loyola and the Jesuits, whose rules formed
the basis of our own. Our superiors carried the air of infallibility,
much like the Pope. I was unaware then of the strange and dark
history of the Catholic church, often led by Popes of dubious
character and downright worldly ambitions. Nor was I aware that the
Jesuits had been born in answer to Luther, the arch-critic who had
caused so much defection in the church because he had dared to
publicly point out institutionalised corruption. Added to my
ignorance was my emotional dependency and immaturity, which

...tion along nicely. Dependency was everywhere
...g sisters were addressed as 'child', and we naturally
...riors as 'mother'.

... Mary Carla, the name I had asked for. No male
... ny of my sisters had buried their femininity even
further by adopting a male saint's name.

Life as a novice was a quantum leap in strictness. Our new life had
begun in earnest. Letters to my parents, written in Dutch but always
translated so they could be censored, were now allowed only once a
month instead of once a week. Breaches of the rules, from ignorance
or carelessness, were dealt with more harshly. The reprimands were
more humiliating and the punishments more severe. Humility was
often taught by reducing novices to tears. Experienced nuns seemed
to be experts at shredding our impressionable souls to pieces.

'Get out of my sight!' was a common way of telling us we had
done something wrong. 'Go and clean the kitchen and make sure you
do something useful for a change.' 'What are we supposed to think of
you? Are you too dull to understand that a rule is a rule, even when
you don't feel like following it?'

The more rules we learned, the greater the chance of failure now.
We were made hypersensitive, reprimanded for looking around, for
using two sentences when one would have done, for being a few
moments late, for making a noise in chapel, for not doing chores
perfectly, for having a stain or lint on our voluminous black clothes
or unshined shoes, or for not addressing the superiors with enough
decorum.

I was given a whip made of five stiffly knotted lashes, to scourge
my legs and punish myself for certain breaches, such as for being late.
Whippings made my legs wobble at first, but in the winter it warmed
them up in a pleasant sort of way. I kept the same whip for the rest
of my years in religious life, and used it as part of my normal list of
punishments, especially to quieten sexual urges. The normal list also
included kneeling with arms outstretched until they and my knees
ached and ached.

PRAYING AT THE fourteen Stations of the Cross was a daily obligation. There we worshipped the suffering, dying and dead Jesus. Every one of the billions of crosses made around the world bearing the agonising body of Jesus, is testimony to this worship of suffering.

The weeks before Easter and Christmas were times for additional self-inflicted punishments. Penances were creatively dreamed up, shown to the superior for her blessing, then written up in a tiny pocket booklet called the Permission Book. We took to eating bread without butter, drinking tea without sugar or milk, adding salt instead, and doing without salt and pepper on food — as well as going without water.

General
Permissions.

1. For the use of Habit,
Rosary beads, Missal,
New Testament,
Imitation of Christ,
Holy pictures.
2. For the use of
notebooks and stationary.
3. For the use of
needlework requisites.
4. For the use of toilet

requisites.
5. To lend or borrow
small articles in
case of necessity.
6. To do a passing
act of charity.
7. To put in a stitch
when necessary, in the
Dormitory.
8. To speak when
charity, courtesy or
my work demands it.
9. To take a drink before
Meditation.

Other Permissions.
To use sewing
machine,
To use iron,
To use polisher for
Dormitory and Wing,
To use Reference books.
To enter Kitchen
for charges or late meals
To write in Linen Room
book for bundle and
mending materials needed
To write in Store room

~~book for supplies~~
~~needed in Children's~~
~~Refectory and Dormitory~~
~~charge~~
To use 2 cotton
vests weekly, or, in winter,
to change the cotton
under the woollen, weekly.
To take a drink
at either 2.30 or 5.30 p.m.
and last thing at night.
To use hand-cream
and cream for rheumatism.

Melbourne in the summer is notorious for an inverted air pattern that traps the heat so there is often no relief at night after an asphyxiatingly hot and humid day. My tight-fitting black woollen bonnet made me so hot I'd reel and almost faint. Perspiration stained the white starched linen around my face and continually prickled my scalp. Even just breathing was difficult under all those layers of black serge over a petticoat and lisle stockings. Imagine doing without water in such circumstances, by way of punishment. One predictable result was that my colon literally dried out (not that I knew then what or where my colon was). I did not connect the lack of water with the relentless constipation I suffered.

On one very hot day, we were given the relief of an extra shower. It was the summer of 1959, the hottest in fifty years, and we'd suffered 40°C and over for days on end. Normally we took only one bath or shower a week (dressed in a chemise so we wouldn't see our own bodies); otherwise we washed ourselves in a basin of cold water in the morning and hot water in the evening, so this extra shower was an extraordinary concession. The only pity of it was that we had to step back into our perspiration-soaked underclothes and black serge. It was in the middle of that summer that our habits were at last changed to creamy white for the season.

Sleep in the summer often happened just out of sheer exhaustion. We wore a nightdress and nightcap to bed. A basinful of water for our morning ablutions was on the locker by the bed, and a glass of water for brushing our teeth. I hallucinated about that glass of water, and woke up several times to find my arm travelling in its direction. But I had an iron will, so I succeeded in this penance of water-deprivation, time and time again.

For ten years I didn't have a normal bowel function because of dehydration, on top of nerves and anxiety. I hated toilets, for starters. Back in Holland, I had often kept in what wanted to come out, rather than go through the excruciating ordeal of the thunderbox toilet. At Genazzano, toilets were desolate places for other reasons. They were built six in a row on plain cement floors and had clackety wooden doors that shut with a big iron latch. The doors were painted grass green, appropriately enough because they were outside. The area was open to bitter winds, and the Melbourne winter rains splashed around our feet on our way there and back. It was also a peculiarly forlorn experience using the ancient pullchains. I avoided them, and paid the price.

I had been on occasional laxatives before I went into the convent, and now it had become a daily need. Sometimes the laxatives didn't work and then it was time for cascara, a herb that no bowel can withstand. It gave me tremendous stomach cramps, and then I had to run, while Sister Victoire, who had given me the potion, gently laughed at me.

Sister Victoire. In the face of all the medical crises that happened over the years, her smile and little chuckle often reassured me. It was worth getting sick just to get Sister Victoire's attention. Now and again I would do just that, running a temperature and a sore throat for a few days so I could get a special bed in the infirmary, a high-ceilinged ex-parlour, also used as a music room at other times. It had beautiful tall windows on one side, and was much more private and cosy than the dormitory. Sister Victoire would make a concoction of honey and lemon, infused with her constantly humorous and loving nature. It was always a shame to get better and move back to normal life.

THE PERIOD OF penance called Lent was coming to an end, the children had gone home for the Easter holidays and we were all very busy making the place look festive and extra clean. Sister Victoire was in charge of the flowers for the chapel, and she taught me how to make hydrangeas and gladioli last by crushing the stems and plunging them in hot water. My father grew chapel flowers in a special patch beside the nursery. There was never a shortage. Beautiful arrangements were the order of the day, and on special feast days the altar was smothered with exquisitely arranged vases.

On Good Friday I was cleaning in the corridors, shining the brass knobs on every door along the way, having already polished the floors to a beautiful shine with the electric polisher, when an arresting sound came from around the corner near the Vicar's office. I stopped in my tracks to listen and figure out what was happening.

Around the corner, supported by the big frame of the Reverend Mother, came the wizened old Vicar. She was perhaps eighty-five by then and very rickety on her feet. She was being very noisy, wailing aloud and lamenting the sorrow of the Virgin Mother at the foot of the cross, all the while fingering her rosary. As she shuffled closer, I could distinguish her words: 'Holy Mother of God, how she must have suffered! To see her son Jesus so cruelly treated! Holy Mother of God!' The old biddy had observed almost a lifetime's rule of silence, and now she was making a vocal spectacle of herself. It did not go down with me as genuine spiritual empathy with the Mother of God; instead I thought her histrionics smacked of the worst kind of attention-seeking in a feeble old age that had never transcended childhood. I stood silently by, mop upright, as the pair passed by into the chapel, where the commotion stopped.

Was this supposed to be a demonstration of great piety? I wondered. As a dutiful novice I should have total respect for my elders but I could not control my thoughts. The old bat was simply trying to impress us all with her so-called extraordinary sanctity. The display did not convince me. The Vicar was feeble, yes, but strong-minded enough to always interfere with any decision-making processes that she happened to overhear. Her position had become honorary when she was no longer able to act as regional superior; everyone sensed that she was likely to suffer a severe identity crisis if the role were fully taken from her.

Later that day, the Vicar insisted on kneeling on the refectory floor and eating her meal from the seat of her chair. Once more, she caused no end of commotion, with people struggling to find out what she needed. 'Salt? No. Pepper? Water? Butter? Too many potatoes, are there? More peas instead? Oh, your fork dropped, please let me get it for you ...' My disdain for the old nun was complete. Even her old pal, the Reverend Mother, stopped responding after an initial concern for her old knees on the cold bare floor, and remained silent with eyes cast down as the circus went on. I wasn't even ashamed of myself when I felt pleasure when she finally died and we were no longer treated to her endless platitudes.

I tried to be the very best novice I could be. I made the parlours look as if no one ever used them, and the floors of the corridors shone with my waxing, polishing and endless mopping. Nevertheless, I had a recurring nightmare in which I would *forget* to clean the corridors. The dust and scuffs accumulated, and everyone knew that Sister Mary Carla had fallen down on the job. How could it be possible to do something every day and then suddenly forget to do it? Because of an inner command from self-sabotage headquarters. The more I feared it, the greater the chance of it happening.

And so came the day when I discovered lots of dust in the corridor and realised, to my horror, that I hadn't done my job for days! Nobody had said anything. I swallowed hard. I had to cover this thing up! At the first available moment, I whipped out a couple of big mops and did an emergency swish-up. I could feel the heat of shame in my neck. My shoulders were rigid in super-tension, making me work as fast as possible.

In hindsight, this could all have been part of the dream. Sister Kevin, when I saw her years later, assured me that there was never any dust in the corridors when I was around. 'I can vouch for it,' she said; and if anyone could it was Sister Kevin, who was in charge of all cleaning work and very strict.

MOTHER PATRICIA CALLED me to her side. The date for my leaving the novitiate had grown near. 'It is time for a new postulant to take over your work in the parlours, Sister. Would you kindly show Sister Catherine how it is done?' 'Yes, Mother, of course.' My status as queen of the parlours was coming to an end.

Catherine was a sensitive girl, a musician, and as keen if not keener than me to 'do it right'. I recognised the trait in those big innocent eyes, in that long face with deep grooves already etched on either side of her mouth. Here was a vulnerable one, and she was going to get what she seemed to be asking for. I wasn't meaning to be cruel, but Catherine wore an open invitation on her face. Besides, who was she to muscle in on my domain? Petty politics came so easily in a hothouse of dimly lit egos. We vowed to be holier than the rest of mankind, and then we abused each other, ever so indirectly.

I showed Sister Catherine the routine and what to do if visitors should arrive in the middle of it. It wasn't a big deal, but I had written nothing down and she seemed to doubt her ability to remember the details. If she had been little less of a ready-made victim, Catherine would have written things down herself. But she didn't; she charged around my former comfort zone in floods of tears, the silly thing. Catherine came from a well-respected and wealthy family, which made her distress even more illogical to me. She wasn't likely to have ever been hit by her father, was she? It never occurred to me that for Catherine to behave in such a pathetic way, she might have suffered a different kind of abuse.

The novice mistress called me aside about my lack of cooperation. As required, I knelt down beside her chair and listened to her pursed mouth. 'Sister Mary Carla,' she said, looking up ever so kindly from her perennial piece of needlework, 'Sister Catherine is not coping well with her new task. She tells me you are not very clear in your instructions. Would you please be more helpful to her?'

So Catherine was in a tizz and I was responsible for her misery! I looked down and had trouble not to smile. It seemed ludicrous to me that Catherine's distress was so important, and I didn't have it in me to commiserate. 'Mother,' I said, 'I have shown her the work and told her all about it. There is nothing much to it.' Mother did not reply to that, as I had expected, and let me go.

Eventually Catherine's face wore its beatific smile once more. How I hated her tragic saintly demeanour! Her face pulled at heartstrings, begging not to be given any task except to play the piano, please. Now she had mastered dusting the parlours and shining the floors — a simple thing. I despised her for being a mollycoddled child who had never had to clean anything at all, and who had been overwhelmed by the challenge I found so easy. In the end, however, it was Catherine who stayed, and I who left. But she hardly ever got her hands dirty again, and is still teaching music.

When emergencies occurred that cut across the normal routine, we novices had to fill the sudden gaps. Just such a crisis happened one morning: none of the regular nuns was available to hold assembly for the girls in the primary school adjacent to Grange Hill. I was closest to hand at the time and was asked to hold the assembly in the open square until someone came to relieve me. I had no idea how to do this, except that it was necessary to keep everyone under control. I suppose we could have stood at ease in some way, but I found myself staring down at the girls with a grim determination caused by panic in case anybody moved and I would not be able to control them. As it turned out, nobody spoke a word, or did anything more than breathe uneasily. The replacement mistress eventually turned up, smiling away the tension and allowing me to disappear.

WE NUNS SHOWED extraordinary devotion to priests, especially the local bishop and archbishop. For centuries, religious women had thought of themselves as less than priests, and when canon law was revised in 1917 this attitude was strengthened even more. Apart from being thought of as less intelligent than priests, nuns were also assumed to be timid little creatures. Worst of all, though, they could be thought of as a threat to a priest's celibacy. So while nuns could venerate priests and fuss over them, they had to be careful to not overstep the mark in any way that could be misinterpreted.

Archbishop Mannix, who later became a cardinal and was very influential in the preservation of conservative Catholic thought, resided in Kew and was invited to visit Genazzano, the convent in his home suburb, on his ninety-fifth birthday. To the awful delight of the community, the revered old man accepted and naturally a welcome had to be devised. He was Irish, perhaps from County Londonderry, and his first name was Daniel, which wickedly inspired the Irish contingent among us to dare to sing ' Danny Boy' for him.

The deeply greying archbishop gave nothing away as he sat and listened to the lyrics of this sentimental love song, hackneyed, yet polished up like a new penny by the musical ability and fervour of our well-practised choir. We watched his impassive face. The song was meant to convey loyalty and appreciation; had we presumed too much familiarity? Daniel Mannix held his bishop's staff in his right hand, and when he used it to rise to thank us, our highly trained eyes detected the concession of a glimmer of a smile around his mouth. The relief that rippled through the ranks was almost audible.

ALL THIS WHILE, life in my family home continued only a hundred metres or so away. In the cottage behind the cypress hedge, my mother was pregnant for the twelfth time at the age of forty-four. It was an anxious time; Saint Gerard, the patron saint of expectant mothers (for some reason I have forgotten), was promised that the child would bear his name if all went well. It did, and my baby brother Gary, later known as Gazza, became the proverbial spoiled child of the family. When he grew up, he was absolutely resolved never to have children of his own.

I felt for my little brother when he was hanging on to Dad's hand one day, dragging tired little legs. Dad had just burned a rat in the incinerator. Gary's face was red with heat, his mind seemingly preoccupied with what had happened to the rat — a nasty creature to an adult, but to a child simply an animal.

After all the glamour of becoming a novice, the ceremony of making our first real commitment with the triple vows of poverty, chastity, and obedience, two years later, was a simple and humble affair. Once again, the words were pronounced before the local bishop in the chapel, but this time they were said with only my religious sisters as witnesses. My life as a novice had been a time for learning the ways of the order, a two-year assessment to determine whether I really wanted to live as a nun for the rest of my life. I was nearly twenty-one and had grown used to the lifestyle; anything else was simply unimaginable by now. I genuinely loved God and the togetherness of community.

And so, on a very ordinary wintry day, when the black serge was welcome cover for my skin, I traded my white bonnet and veil for black ones, received a large set of rosary beads to hang from my belt, and a cross of the dying Jesus. The Passion of Jesus wedded to the sacrifice of Carla. Two sufferings, the better to save the world.

ENGLAND

MADAME DE BONNAULT D'HOUET was a widow when she founded the Faithful Companions of Jesus, and her followers continued to wear her mode of dress after she died, as a tribute to her spiritual greatness and as a sign of their pledge to follow her example. It also gave them a recognisable identity in the world.

So in the 1960s we looked exactly the same as our French foundress did at the turn of the nineteenth century, complete with ruffled bonnet and long pointed shawl. For the sake of genuine antiquity we wore a white cotton camisole underneath instead of a bra, covered with a white cotton shawl that crossed our breasts twice, thick enough to hide our nipples. Our foundress had been a truly innovative woman, way ahead of her time. Her followers, on the other hand, had managed to freeze her example and dress into a way of life, as if it were an absolute.

Although we had professed our formal vows, we would not be considered fully fledged until after another two terms of probation, each lasting three years. Such was the rigour of making sure of a person before she took final vows and could no longer be expelled.

The powers that be (which never consulted us) decided that some professed novices would go to Latrobe University in Melbourne; and that six of us, a mixed bag of recently professed and older nuns, would be sent to the order's teacher-training college at Sedgley Park, just north of Manchester in England. Since I hadn't completed my last year at school, and so wasn't university material, I was to go to college.

We were to travel there by ship. Passport photos were needed and the photographer came to the convent. My passport was still Dutch, since I wasn't with my family when they became naturalised Australians in 1958, the year after I entered the convent.

As part of the preparations, I was sent to the doctor to have my ears tested. Mother Mary Luke, my erstwhile primary school principal with the wry smile and the bustling manners, and another nun accompanied me. I hadn't complained about my ears; others had complained about me for apparently not hearing things. I was often too wrapped up in thought, which can be a bad thing when someone sticks their head inside the room to make an impromptu announcement. My tendency to get things not entirely right or to understand instructions a little differently than intended had been observed several times, and had certainly been annoying to some.

The doctor was not simply to examine my ears — he could have done that during any of his visits to the convent — but was instructed to wash them out. He did so reluctantly because, in his opinion, my ears were not dirty, let alone so caked up that they obstructed sound. It was then that I caught the sly smiles of my two companions, and I understood: this was a charade, a highly embarrassing punishment intended to make me learn to listen up! I sighed with dismay. I was vulnerable to embarrassment, but they had demeaned themselves by stooping this low to strike their message home. Nothing was said on the way back on the trams.

We were to travel to England on the P&O ship, *Oriana*. Reverend Mother Winifred — the one with the Cheshire Cat smile who harboured a particular dislike of me and who was a stickler for the rules — was to be our chaperone. But not even she was going to stand in the way of the excitement the six of us felt about travelling across the wide, wide ocean. And I was to retrace much of the journey I had made as a child migrating to Australia, nine years earlier.

A jolly march played as the ship moved slowly away from the wharf at midday, and we huddled together to say a prayer for the safety of ourselves and our fellow travellers. This five-week trip was to be a first-class adventure, though we would have little, if anything, to do with the other travellers.

We had two large cabins to ourselves on D deck; I shared one with three others, sleeping on the top bunk. The floor was thickly carpeted, the porthole beautifully curtained with chenille, and the ship's soap was a welcome change from the plain yellow Velvet we were used to. The rule of silence was relaxed so we could talk to one another about what we saw, but not to the extent that we could communicate with passengers. We had a map so we could identify all the islands and places we passed.

There were four travelling priests on board, who said Mass together every morning and attracted a dozen or so passengers. We nuns prepared the altar and ironed the vestments for the priests provided by the ship. They had to be pinned onto the senior priest, who took central stage on the altar, as everything was size XL, which he was definitely not.

We had a dining room to ourselves, complete with our own waiter, a short young chap whose eyes boggled at the inane conversation of nuns. I think it blew his reverent Catholic ideas about religious women and their supposed composure and intelligence. He couldn't believe our blithe ability to order things without knowing what they were. We hardly ever consulted him about the meaning of words on the extensive menu, which presented us with unaccustomed choice.

'Gorgonzola; that's an interesting name. Shall we ask for some? Everyone agreed?'

Our waiter boy lifted his eyes to heaven and shifted from one foot to the other in a hopeless attempt to let us know that this was an unwise choice for the uninitiated, but he must have had instructions not to speak to us, let alone contradict us.

The gorgonzola arrived, and we examined the strange-looking cheese. 'Why does it have blue veins in it?' someone had the good sense to ask. Our young attendant's tongue was untied at last. 'The mould creatures,' he began enthusiastically, 'gradually creep through the cheese as they eat away at it. They multiply their numbers as they go and ... and ...' He hesitated, as if weighing up whether to inform us or not, and then seemed to decide it was his duty to tell us the truth in the politest language. 'They *defecate* as they go along as well. It gives the cheese its unique flavour,' he hastened to add. It was a good enough description to have the cheese sent back.

The voyage took us through a variety of weathers, conjuring up many memories for me. Colombo's steamy weather was followed by an almighty thunderstorm as we pushed out to sea. Great flashes of lightning lit up the dark clouds covering the whole sky, followed immediately by crashing claps of thunder. We watched as one particular flash turned into a fireball, which immediately came flying towards us. It fell in the water at close range, hissing and steaming as if angry for failing to hit the ship. 'A narrow miss!' said the awed passengers.

Night-time brought another electric storm that knocked out the ship's aerial. The explosive sound, followed by a strange sweeping wind, made us believe that the ship had caught fire. We just about wept for joy to find out it hadn't at all, and then slept so soundly that we almost missed breakfast.

Once again I came to the place where the young Egyptian of my teenage dreams had refuelled the migrant ship nine years ago. This time, as we briefly left our ocean liner to wander along the quayside, I noticed the poverty of the people. It struck me, however, that they were happy and quick to respond to kindness. Back on board we were surprised by a dark face peering into our cabin, and decided to close the porthole curtains.

We glided majestically through the Suez Canal. It was such a delight to see through adult eyes the utterly strange and amazing world that had unfolded before me when I was a child. Our convoy of eight ships rounded a bend, and looking back we could see all the others following the *Oriana*, stately and precisely placed as if they belonged to Nelson's fleet.

Then, out to sea, we hit the doldrums. The only doldrums I knew were those feelings of dull listlessness and indecisiveness, a kind of depression, but when there was talk of 'hitting the doldrums', I knew it must be a nautical term as well. After lunch I displayed a typical example of that naive ignorance that my superior so hated in me. We were all staring at the water, looking, I presumed, for the doldrums. After a while I confessed that I couldn't see them. 'Please, would somebody show them to me?'

Mother Winifred was affronted, probably thinking I was taking the mickey out of her. She couldn't imagine that I was sincerely ignorant. 'The doldrums is a belt of becalmed waters, where sailors of old were often stranded with no wind to push their sails,' one of the others explained. I shall always remember that piece of information!

Every day we went for a one-mile walk — seven times around the deck. Not once did I feel seasick.

It was Easter when we reached France, and very cold. The crane operators were in no festive mood, their faces frozen against our attempts to cheer them up with smiling sympathetic faces.

We reached Southampton at five-thirty on the morning of 27 March 1960, on a typically rainy day that blotted out all colours. The way through the harbour was littered with grey industrial buildings and dismal machinery. We were met at the quayside by a streetwise sister whose job it was to chaperone the 'provincials' through the bustle of city life to safety inside the convent walls in London. After our gear had gone through customs it was loaded onto a train. Our chaperone did the lugging that the porter refused to do — she had the physique of two porters, and there was a lot of heavy luggage. There was also more than a fifty per cent chance that some of it might get mislaid.

'Say a little prayer that our luggage is safe,' said our Reverend Mother, in a moment of inspired intuition. Only a moment later, our ears caught the name 'Sister Raay' coming from the luggage department. We were about to investigate, when an observant and sympathetic porter stuck his head through a nearby window and announced: 'Sister Raay, your luggage was found on the floor of the ship's cabin, but has now been put on the train.' Had I really left a case in the cabin? Thank God it had been found by this kindly porter, and was now safe. It must have been an answer to our timely prayers. The porter did not expect a tip, and quickly retracted his head.

The train was fairly packed. A woman kept up a very noisy stream of chatter just behind our backs. I tried the prayer trick again — I was on a little roll — and miraculously she said, 'I think I'll keep quiet now.' Mercifully she did.

Our intrepid Cockney sister hailed a taxi for the last part of our journey, and we passed some of the famous landmarks we'd heard about: Pall Mall, Westminster Cathedral, bridges over the Thames, the infamous Tower, the Guards changing at the Palace. We caught many glimpses, in spite of the eyes-down rule. Surely *not* to look would be more of a distraction to the spirit than to catch glimpses from a taxi? Tulips were ablaze everywhere, as if this were Holland.

We arrived. The very first thing everyone needed was to find a toilet. This London convent doubled as a large school for senior girls. With any luck, we could use the nearest toilets before the girls descended on them at break time. But we weren't lucky; four of us were caught in the loos.

This was a dilemma! We didn't know what to do at all. None of us spoke or made a sound; we all wanted to disappear into thin air. When that didn't happen after half a minute or so, we used our combined weight against the door of the toilet block to keep it closed. The girls on the other side pushed and shoved, and we pushed and shoved against them! They thought it was some kind of joke, not realising who was in there.

Eventually there was nothing for it: we'd have to face the music, come out, and not only confess to being human and needing to relieve our bladders, but to being ashamed of showing it. We emerged with eyes down, without saying a word. The girls gasped, 'Sorry, Sisters!' They had the enormous good grace to apologise instead of bursting into laughter. The apologies should have been ours! I often wonder what those girls surmised from our strange behaviour: perhaps that being human was shameful? That nuns shouldn't have to urinate and defecate?

After lunch, we travelled by bus to the Mother Convent at Broadstairs in Kent — Stella Maris, the home of our venerated Reverend Mother General. She was away at the time, but the place could not have been more impressive with its spring beauty and the sprawl of its several gardens and buildings. Tulips seemed to grow like weeds. Fruit trees stood in blossom, poplars showed their first green, and hundreds of daffodils lined the narrow paths through the gardens. One of the buildings was an old novitiate. We would have afternoon tea there, and sleep in a little round bedroom in The Knoll.

The Knoll's distinctive red-brick walls went four storeys high, narrowing to the top room, which had become a dorm for three. We were allowed to sleep in the next morning, and I awoke to the unusual pleasure of breakfast in bed, at eight-thirty! The kindness was overwhelming. I was even presented with a new block of soap by a sister who had spotted my tiny remnant from the sea voyage, but when I showed her my collection of similar remnants, squeezed into one bigger piece, she promptly withdrew her offer!

Our studies at Sedgley Park were not due to commence till June, so we spent our time at Stella Maris making ourselves useful in the garden, laundry and kitchen, and now and again studying Latin and French. During that time I felt attracted to young Sister Dehlia, still a novice, whose delightful English humour had a way of sparking my own wit. Walking outside in the fresh air of early morning, I showed her my hands, blue with the cold. 'I'm a blue-blood, plain to see,' I said, naughtily. She looked at my hands, looked at me, and caught something in my eyes that shocked her. Eyes down, she moved away, and for the rest of my stay there we never spoke again. I swiftly tried to bury the thought that I had tried to seduce her — into what? Into a conversation, when the rule of silence forbade it? Or maybe into a 'particular friendship', which was explicitly forbidden by one of the rules? I was so sorry to have upset her.

In early May, we travelled north-west to Manchester, to our new home. There, with summer approaching, we were able to relax for a few weeks, and get more acquainted with jolly England and the thirty or so nuns with whom we were to spend the next three years.

FORBIDDEN LOVE

 WHERE SEDGES ONCE grew in abundance, home to countless species of birds, now stands the manor and college of Sedgley Park. Most of the birds have gone, but here and there the sedges are trying to re-establish ownership of their land.

The original manor house was built by a Greek shipping magnate in the nineteenth century, and while not ostentatious on the outside was more lavish inside. In 1906 the Society of Faithful Companions of Jesus bought the place, eventually adding several tasteful extensions, including a chapel. They took care to match the architecture of the house, even extending the mosaic patterns of the hallway into the wide corridors of what was to be a college. The college entrance was given a rather humble set of steps leading up to oak doors, ensuring the adjacent manor remained without competition.

The Mother Superior claimed the manor's grand upper storey, while the gilded downstairs rooms flanking the hallway were turned into music and history rooms. The tall bay windows with their dark green velvet curtains and enormous pelmets were reflected in mirrors that sometimes spanned half a wall, illuminated by bracketed chandeliers on either side of their magnificent frames.

In 1960, when we Australians arrived, the FCJs had embarked on an innovative three-year teacher-training program. Affiliated with Manchester University, it was the first of its kind. Sedgley was a college for girls who hadn't made the grade to university, or didn't want to go there, and matriculation was not an entrance requirement. Sedgley's clever association with the university added some fudged glamour. Funded largely by the British government, it was administered by the FCJs who hired their own staff. The nuns thought nothing of tampering with the curriculum — they felt perfectly justified in banning the works of Oscar Wilde, as well as D H Lawrence's *Lady Chatterley's Lover*, from the reading list for English literature. Consequently English lit became suspect in my mind; a pity, for I loved to read.

I felt that it was important to choose wisely what to study, but I didn't know *how* to choose. Then, suddenly and urgently, all available nuns were pulled into an impromptu meeting in the main corridor, where we heard that our Reverend Mother General, Margaret Winchester wanted us to take geography. It was something to do with the importance of understanding the world. This solved a problem for me: my first choice just had to be geography.

I was surprised that not all of the nuns obliged. Now I understand what *they* saw immediately and I didn't: this message was a ruse. The geography tutor was a nun of doubtful qualities (old, odd and ugly) and a decent enrolment was needed to ensure that she remained on paid staff. Mother Gertrude was not only large, pasty-faced, bushy-browed and short of breath; worse was the impression that she was terribly conscious of her wealth of knowledge, which she imparted with an annoying degree of self-importance.

I was drawn to science, though I didn't have the necessary background for it (science for girls? I must have gone to the wrong school!). Unenrolled, I sat in on many lectures voluntarily, until news of this reached the ears of Mother Gertrude and she went through my superior to ban me from attending. I eventually received full marks for geography. It puffed up the chest of my oversized tutor, whose whiskery face shone with self-pride at the news.

I chose French because I loved the language and had a good ear for it. Now to choose the main subject! I wanted to major in art because I yearned to use my creativity. Someone should have warned me that Miss Nagel, a hardened middle-aged tutor, simply hated nuns.

'I'm considering taking art,' I told her innocently. 'Would you tell me something about the curriculum?'

She glowered at me. 'Most nuns don't make the grade, in my experience,' she said darkly. 'They don't have the imagination and . . .' She didn't say it, but I heard her all the same: *and they are boring to deal with.* 'Go and paint a shell,' she said. 'It'll give me an idea of your talent.'

I didn't have a high opinion of myself, but I thought that my delicate little effort wasn't bad when I showed it to her an hour or so later. Miss Nagel was surprised to see me again, but she was merciless. 'This won't do,' she blustered. 'If you want to be artistic, it'd be better for you to go for craft,' and she turned away from me.

Well, craft was creative too, but it was in no way a challenge for my mind. It was only at exhibition time, when students displayed their first and last works in order to gauge their improvement over the three years, that I realised what had happened. 'My painting of the shell was much better than any of these!' The words came out spontaneously, I was so aghast. Miss Nagel happened to be standing right beside me at the time. She said nothing and moved away.

I was either a slow learner or I had my head in the sand. How did other people see through these things, I wondered. Did they break the rule of silence and talk to each other? I guessed they were smart enough to do exactly that. They probably spoke to the girls too, who knew much more than we nuns because they got around in the outside world. I was too good, too naive and too preoccupied with an inner self that seemed to be in constant turmoil.

SEDGLEY PARK IS ingrained in my memory for two very different reasons; neither had anything to do with the curriculum. I was impressed by the magnificent rhododendrons, which grew to a glorious towering height along a great stretch of the building and its grounds' cool shady paths. In summer they took my breath away, and I saw them bloom three times over, long enough to start feeling that they were mine somehow.

The second reason was much more personal, and more deeply etched. I fell in love there, totally, uncontrollably, illicitly. I loved green-eyed Sister Alice, a rebellious Irish beauty with a bold sense of humour and an intelligence that outshone her loyalty to the order in the end. She was eleven years older than I and left in the early 1970s.

Sister Alice was a science mistress in an FCJ high school in nearby Manchester. At weekends, she and her teaching companions joined the Sedgley community because they were too few in number to form a nunnery in their own right.

I loved Alice's deep lilting Irish voice, her strong Roman nose, her dark eyebrows, her dry wit, her sociable gracious nature, and her natural ability for humorous sarcasm. She appealed to the very core of my romantic, passionate being. Above all I loved her sea-green eyes. They were brown most of the time, but when she became angry or emotional they would flash a marvellous green, and I was helpless in front of her. In ordinary circumstances I would have been able to speak to her as a friend, or laughed and joked with her. As it was, I internalised all my feelings because of our rule of silence, and because of one rule even more fearful than that: the rule regarding 'particular friendships'. These were to be *avoided*; they were '*the bane of religious life*'. So I felt obliged to fight against my delicious feelings of appreciation for this outlandish woman. The more I fought the feelings, the more they grew. '*What you resist, persists,*' is a psychological fact that escaped the careful wisdom of our foundress, who wrote the rule about particular friendships. And her matronly hierarchy of followers knew no better.

Sister Alice wasn't like the others by any comparison. To her, clomping comfortably along the polished corridors as if she were in a farmyard not a convent had nothing to do with not being a good nun. She got away with things because it was considered that her heart was in the right place, and because she was a brilliant and popular teacher. It was too difficult to contradict her Irish logic, anyway. I saw how her superiors would save face by quitting a discussion they weren't going to win. I heard her colleagues gasp, as if she had gone beyond every boundary. She wasn't afraid of punishment; it didn't seem to figure at all with her. To her, a good nun was one who was able to love a great deal. She did, and this was the main reason she was so popular with children. In the end, it was the reason she left: she became disillusioned by the rules that tried to contain her and were valued more than love itself.

I managed to hide my feelings well enough so as not to arouse her suspicions. All the same, I couldn't pass up an opportunity to be near her for some extra tutoring in French. There we sat, tightly squeezed together at a school desk designed for one. '*Ca va très bon, n'est-ce pas?*' She smiled her wide, gracious smile at me, and I melted. Alice was extremely good at French, and I wasn't bad, hoping mightily to impress her. Alice remained kind but neutral.

I wanted her to notice me, and so when she asked for volunteers to help cover science books at school, I quickly took this chance to be in her company. I stood in her classroom, motionless with strange passion as she showed me a special light bulb she had just acquired for a project. She caressed the bulb with such sensuous delight that my mouth hung open, my eyes slowly lifting to hers to read what was being expressed by her hands. She collected herself, vaguely aware that she had caused something in me that did not quite match her own pure enthusiasm for science.

A burden of guilt now grew in my soul because of my love for Alice. Eventually, it became a weight too heavy to bear. This was a breach of the rule that I would have to confess to my superior. I was granted a private audience and entered her study. If I had known that I was about to commit the equivalent of hari-kari, I might have reconsidered.

Mother Theresa, our superior, had not been chosen, I think, for her intellect. For that side of things she could rely on her offsiders. It may be unkind of me, but perhaps she was in her position because she was a good nun; she certainly was not a good teacher or a person with any great psychological wisdom. I knelt down beside her chair, obliquely facing her, as was expected of me. To my horror, I realised that I did not know this woman in whom I was to confide my deepest and closest secret, nor did she particularly know anything about me. All we had between us was the rule book.

My heart was full of the deepest dismay as I opened my mouth and spelt out my own doom. 'Mother,' I began, deciding that to be as direct as possible was the only way to break the news, 'I have fallen in love with one of the sisters.'

Silence. All my attention was on her, my superior, and the way her matronly body sweated. I could smell her perspiration, see her short, shallow breaths moving the black cloth of her habit rapidly up and down. Her face showed wild surprise, confusion, then, it seemed to me, her ardent but hopeless wish that she did not have to deal with this. Since she was speechless I answered her unspoken question. 'It is Sister Alice.'

Mother Theresa did not reply immediately. Her short breathing continued while she sat with eyes closed for a while, fumbling with her rosary. My heart, meanwhile, was suffocating. I felt I had done the right thing, and at the same time had make a huge mistake. I was being sincere, honest and good, but I was confessing to something very bad. So I could not win any points here whatsoever. Finally Mother Theresa regained her composure and lifted her head to me. Her look was severe. Her words were equally direct.

'Sister, you know that this is a serious breach of our rules. I must give you a penance. You will use your whip every time you are tempted to indulge in any thought of Sister Alice. Is this understood?'

'Yes, Reverend Mother. I am sorry, and I will do my best to follow our holy rules.'

It was late afternoon when I left her office. That evening, at dinner-time, I could not eat. That night, I could not sleep. It was in the dead of night, in the furthest toilet I could find, that I first used my whip to control my thoughts of Alice. When I returned to my dormitory bed, I cried, stifling my sobs and sniffles in the blankets. The tears did me some good and the relief gave me blessed sleep.

That following morning, straight after Mass, when the whole community was on its way to breakfast, Alice was informed by our superior of my damnable love for her. I was not supposed to notice, not supposed to see or hear. But I looked up just as Sister Alice was being beckoned to a door recess to be spoken to discreetly, then heard her stride away abruptly, shoes clomping in an uncontrolled distressed sort of way, and I knew then that she knew. No doubt Mother Theresa's intention was that this action would help us both. But I caught a glimpse of her agonised face as she watched Alice stride away. She might have doubted the wisdom of her decision then. It was a stupid action, even if well-meant, and one she never attempted to rectify.

Sister Alice was now implicated in my crime. Although she knew how to love, it was the overwhelming love *I* felt for *her* that she found difficult to cope with. I was convinced this wouldn't have been the case if we had just been given a chance to talk to each other. There was an unwholesome complicity in Mother Superior not telling me that she had told Alice, and in Alice not telling me that she knew, and in me not being able to say anything to her. It made the whole affair so sordid that my heart began to break.

Our French tuition ended abruptly, and I became conscious of Alice evading me. If we happened to be coming down a corridor in opposite directions — and the corridors at Sedgley were long ones — she would turn tail. In chapel she took care to find a pew on the other side. In the refectory she would take a seat where I couldn't look up and see her. She spoke less at recreation times, afraid of drawing my attention to her, and she always managed to position herself so that her back was towards me. The pain I felt was hardly bearable, not only because I was so deprived of the ordinary contact I'd enjoyed with her before, but for seeing her in such distress. She seemed to instinctively reject passionate admiration from someone of her own sex. Her normally free nature and broad mind drew the line there, and I felt the rejection personally, totally and sickeningly. I might as well have worn a bell around my neck, to warn her of my presence.

For her sake, to make it better for her, I was very, very good. I tried never to be near her, though I longed with all my soul to catch a glimpse of her. I wouldn't look at her when I had the chance and would weep when the chance was gone. Love became a sword that drove deeper and deeper into my heart. The image that was Alice became the image of all unrequited loves, tangled in one endless longing for reconciliation.

I was twenty-one and had never heard the word 'lesbian', nor even 'orgasm'. In all my years as a nun and a virgin, I never masturbated, because I didn't know about it. But in chapel I had terribly inconvenient spontaneous convulsions that went through my body whenever Sister Alice came close. Kneeling in prayer, I instantly knew when she came in and heard every step that brought her closer to me.

Here she comes; I can recognise her step, even if she tries to disguise it by walking lightly. She is still several yards away and I can smell her scent, a sort of wild heather or wet-from-the-rain smell.

Now what am I to do! Wild energy is pulsing and building up in my pelvis . . . Oh God, maybe if I cross my legs, I can control this. It's so hard to cross my legs while I'm kneeling! I wobble from knee to knee. The energy wants to escape . . . and now my hips start swaying . . . Oh God, I can't!

A force that was greater than my will exploded and ran up my spine. My head jerked up; it's a wonder I didn't yell out right across the chapel. My legs wobbled desperately in the aftermath of suppressed ecstasy. I bent my shoulders in shame. It had been impossible to hide what was happening. I was absolutely mortified by the thought that someone might have noticed, but how could they *not* have noticed? I froze to hear a gasp behind me and someone loudly muttering, 'Holy Mother of God; Jesus, Mary and Joseph!' with a noisy rattle of a rosary.

Nobody ever spoke to me about this behaviour, although it happened several times. If my throat had not been kept silent with the aid of desperate, brute willpower, I would, of course, have screamed and only God knows what would have followed.

Once a week, student nuns met in the traditional way with our immediate superior for exhortations and admonitions. We sat with our eyes down and our hands on our laps. We were told things like: 'Ignore girls who bring their boyfriends to the college.' Bringing menfolk onto the campus was against the rules, but the girls didn't care, and we frequently found couples kissing goodbye on the steps leading to the main entrance. Then one day our superior told us something that was meant to be a warning, but, as it happened, her action backfired.

'I want to remind you of the rules relating to your vow of chastity,' she began. 'You are to resist the temptation to visit each other in dormitory cubicles. Also, you are not to have private discussions.' (Wow! What an idea — to visit each other privately in the cubicles!)

No names were mentioned, but I knew that this wasn't just a warning, that it must actually be going on, otherwise our superior would not have been so nervous and the atmosphere would not have been so tense. In spite of the eyes-down rule, I glanced around. Who was the guilty party? Why had she not been spoken to privately? Why did I seem to be the only one not in the know? In hindsight, I wonder if this was an oblique message to *me*, in case I should contemplate doing such a thing. Or maybe I was *suspected* of doing it.

I never found out the truth, but in any case the admonition electrified my imagination. From then on, I dreamed of going into Sister Alice's cubicle, finding her asleep and looking at her as long as I liked, and then kissing her ever so gently on the mouth. I daydreamed in chapel, instead of meditating, about her coming to *my* cubicle, and of her getting into bed with me and holding me tight so I could feel her solid Irish body, smell the heather of her breath, feel her breasts close to mine — I could have fainted with the wicked pleasure of it.

Guilt set in after these self-indulgent daydreams. Sometimes I managed to keep it at bay for a little while, but sooner or later I would have to punish myself. I used the strongly plaited and knotted twine to beat my bare legs and thighs mercilessly. Sometimes it was very painful and made me tremble, especially when my legs were cold; at other times, there came a glow of warmth and wellbeing. The whippings aggravated the varicose veins I had developed as a teenager.

Over time Alice seemed to come to a more benign understanding of the whole thing. She may have begun to sense the utter and constant misery I was in, though I applied myself to my studies and took part in community affairs as normally as I could. One morning at meditation time she made a bold statement. She deliberately knelt beside me in chapel, as if to express her solidarity or her support for me — or maybe she even thought she could do with a bit of love, for heaven's sake, in that God-forsaken establishment. The trouble was that I didn't know *what* she was trying to convey and I pretended not to notice her. It didn't last for long; Reverend Mother spotted her and came over to tap her on the shoulder and whisper to her to move to the other side, which she did.

Late Friday afternoon was time for Benediction — the blessing of the faithful by the monstrance. Those who were in the choir went upstairs to sing. I loved the harmonies we made, the sweetness of it all. I enjoyed the melodiousness that came out of my own mouth, the mouth that had to stay dumb for most of the day. To sing was to express my deep soul and to feel energy running freely. It seemed to me that we sang like angels.

The clever organist was none other than our ungainly Sister Gertrude, the notorious teacher of geography. Her corpulent body swayed pompously as she pedalled the ancient organ, assisted by the skilled bellows operator, and turned out the beautiful music that she had the responsibility and good sense to pick out. Her fat fingers made magic as she flawlessly played anything from Palestrina to Paganini, Haydn to Mozart, Bruch to Albinoni to Verdi. Our ever-expanding repertoire included works by Weber, Scarlatti, Cesar Franck and Schubert, all apart from the thorough training in

Gregorian chant we received from the sober Benedictine monks, who sang in choir with us on rare occasions.

The nuns from the school often came home just in time for Benediction, and some of them joined us upstairs. And so it happened that Alice wafted in and knelt beside me once more. Up here in the choir space there was no Reverend Mother; she was downstairs with the congregation of older nuns and the students. Alice had the rain of the Manchester autumn on her clothes and she smelled delicious. I didn't dare look at her or smile at her. All I could do was drink in her magnificent presence, her free spirit, which I envied so much. *Oh God, this is just so delightful, and so extremely painful!* Tears began to roll down my cheeks, unhindered and uncontrollable, soaking the starched linen band under my chin. I didn't dare take out a hanky and give myself away. I kept singing. Love made my voice even sweeter and truer. I wanted her to hear it! I was singing my love to her through a *Te Deum* and *Ave Maria* that should have broken her heart. Afterwards, in the silence of contemplation before we went downstairs, I was one with my beloved beside me, holding us in an enormous brilliant light of love, if only she could have seen or felt it.

I have few strong memories of Sedgley Park other than those associated with Alice. Of course I remember the constant hubbub of going to lectures, the large high-ceilinged rooms, the ring of footsteps on the beautifully tiled floors of the main hall. There were the bus trips and walks to Manchester University to attend lectures on Freud, among other things. I learned from those lectures that tiny children are sexually awake, and that their need for skin contact, warmth and affection, as well as their sensual explorations, are forms of auto-erotic sexuality.

The lecturer was well aware of the presence of nuns in her audience and aimed to shock us out of our enclosed naivety, or ignorance, or both. We didn't have such fiercely opinionated and abrasive lecturers back at our college. What I remember best from those lectures is our walks back to the bus-stop, and then the convent, late in the evening. We walked in silence, keeping our heads down according to the rules. I couldn't help but notice the houses as we passed, their hedges and fences and gates, all evidence of ordinary human life and human relationships. I looked up from the bricks or pathways under our feet to catch a glimpse of the sky, often dark and swirly, and once my eyes caught a hawthorn tree silhouetted under a street light. I was awed by its beauty — its branches were bare and thorny, so lonely, so majestic, and so perfect in their symmetry. The tree was just there, oblivious to whether anyone noticed it, pouring out its beauty. The image burned into my heart, and I thought of it often, the way a soldier on a battlefield holds on to the picture of a sweetheart. It comforted me.

One Saturday morning Alice was entrusted with the duty of doing the rounds with an urgent message from our superior. I can't remember at all what it was, but I was so surprised by this sudden event that I was caught utterly off guard: there was Alice, right in front of me, looking into my eyes to make sure I had heard the message, head to one side in a questioning stance. I was supposed to answer her question, I think, but all I could do was whisper, 'Beautiful. You are so beautiful.' Like a fool, I was lost in her eyes, and would have stayed looking into them for ever, except that they winced and turned green with brown flecks. But she held my gaze as evenly as she could until she knew she would get no sane answer, then left me standing there as though I had just seen a vision. Obviously, I was incorrigible! Alice strode off, conscious of my stare, her heels clipping the parquetry floor, her wide hips swaying.

The summer holidays came; they were filled with diversions, including concerts. Nuns often holidayed at other convents, depending on the powers that be to send them there. Those who stayed behind had the pleasure of devising a concert for our visitors and for the older members of the community. It was a rare time of creativity and lots of fun. A few of our sketches were rehashed from previous years' performances elsewhere, but for me they were all new and I laughed long and hard at the silly things we came up with. Laughter was a painful thing, I remember. It hurt my belly and my face, which were used to too much seriousness and tears. I laughed at everything, helplessly. I doubled up for the slightest reason, grateful for the relief. I ended up with a heavy head from laughing.

Alice was especially playful at these times, although she seemed never to notice me. Only once did we come face to face again, in the theatre wings where a few of us were fooling around. She was caressing a silky piece of material, holding it against her face and trying it on for a headdress. The silk was a purplish colour but she called it by its proper name: magenta. It was exactly the same colour as a rhododendron bush I knew in the grounds. I was stunned by the picture before me: the magenta perfectly set off the darkness of her eyebrows and eyes. She had turned into a gypsy! She saw my stunned admiration and my weak attempt to smile appropriately. She threw the silk on the floor and turned her back. I felt mortified and close to tears. It was wrong, I told myself again, to be so obsessed with Alice. I gave myself a new punishment, which was to never again set eyes on the magenta rhododendron.

FOR THE NEXT two summers, I was sent elsewhere for the holidays, and enjoyed the magnificence of the English countryside. I walked with my companions along tall hedges full of different kinds of wildflowers, picking posies and filling baskets with blackberries. I sat under ancient trees on large stately lawns and read or sketched. My favourite subjects were trees — I sketched them with charcoal and pencil. *They were so beautiful! Their proud naked trunks, their bare muscular arms, the folds in their white flesh, their whispering leaves* . . . As in the chapel when Alice came near, my body convulsed with pleasurable ecstasy. I let it happen here, where nobody saw.

Being with a community of strange nuns during summer holidays was really no easy matter. The English niceties that came so easily to my companions as they talked with one another, even the décor of the rooms, had a frightening charm that made me thankful for the usual rule of silence. Since I knew no one there, I was left alone to silently absorb the expressions of a culture that was so different from the Dutch and Australian ways I had grown up in.

One tiny incident stands out from those summers with nuns whom I never got to know long enough to remember by name or face. I was sitting at a long dining table among a hubbub of excited women who were, for once, talking with unrestrained pleasure to friends. Being a stranger in a strange land, there was no 'Oh, hello! Great to see you again!' coming my way, but somebody there noticed my aloneness. She was an old and wizened nun but quick on her feet. I would never have noticed her; she was in the background, filling up cake plates and not participating in the talking. What she did was simply place one kind hand on my back, between my shoulders. It was such a warm touch, so extraordinarily good, that I never forgot it. It melted and relaxed me; a touch that spoke to my inner soul, reminding me that I was loved and that everything was all right. I always blushed very easily, and of course I blushed then at the suddenness and intensity of the feeling that washed through me like a blessing. I turned and caught her smile and then she was gone, an angel in the shape of an old wizened silent sister.

At college we were nuns first and foremost, and so we were excluded from the social activities organised for students, and didn't mix much at all with them or with the lay staff. All this changed dramatically when Sedgley Park became flooded after a downpour that went on for days. Panic built up as the water level began to rise over the gardens, lapping against the walls of the inner courtyards, then started coursing over the college floors.

Why was it impractical me who guessed what was going on — namely that the drains were blocked by summer debris? Water kept rising, and was soon at waist level outside, so I decided to do something. I was in a corridor with my English lecturer, Mrs Green, who was in her fifties — a strong character not given to sentimentality — and her younger friend, also a tutor. *These people are mature enough, surely, to realise that nuns are just people, with bodies like their own*, I thought, and took off my shawl and black bonnet and handed them to them. The plan was to climb through the window and duck under the water to grope for the drains. I couldn't afford to ruin the delicate stitching and ruching of my bonnet, and my shawl would have hampered my arm movements. I must have looked like something out of a comic strip with my hairless head inside a white undercap, and they were aghast. *Never mind*, I told myself, lifted up my skirts, clambered through the window and promptly submerged myself in search of drains. I found one, then two, in a relatively short time, removed the debris, climbed back in, dripping wet, to retrieve my dry bits of clothing. The water level dropped immediately, at least in that section of the college, so I had every reason to feel satisfied with myself. I put the dry bonnet and shawl over my wet clothes and walked, wet to the waist, past other nuns, staff and students as they were bailing out with buckets. I felt like a heroine, but nothing was ever said to my face about my ostensible heroism. *Well, the less said by anyone, the better!*

I probably generated some interesting conversation in the lecturers' common room. I was one of Mrs Green's favourites, since I displayed the kind of sharp, analytical mind in class that she admired. She found more and more difficult passages for me to read aloud, whole paragraphs written as one sentence, more convoluted than legal language. I had the feeling that she was running bets with other staff on how soon I would begin to lose the plot during a passage, but I enjoyed the rare delight to have my mind stretched. I was entered for a Special Mention, but let her down awfully in the exams, omitting a whole section that I thought was optional but wasn't, thus dragging down my total mark. The disapproval that followed naturally hurt me, but it sat more comfortably upon me than praise.

DYING AND DEATH happened at Sedgley, and a certain kind of madness.

We had a few elderly nuns in the community, perhaps to balance the large number of very young people. They were retired teachers and old lay sisters. Lay sisters were often women who had had a limited education and who served God and the community with supposedly intellectually undemanding work, such as cooking, running the laundry, cleaning and ironing.

Because the class system in England is so strong, and snobbery ingrained and unquestioned, there was no guarantee that such feelings of superiority wouldn't apply in a convent. The lay sisters often had a humiliating time of it; they just didn't have the credibility in daily life that the so-called educated mothers and sisters enjoyed.

One of the lay sisters, Sister Jeromy, complained about a pain in her chest for days and weeks. She was old— perhaps in her late seventies — and short of breath. She had rough hands, a short bent body, and a big wrinkly mouth in a coarse wrinkly face. She had been brought up somewhere in the muddy countryside of England, and had a pathetic way of insisting that she wasn't well. Lay sisters were usually the most silent and unnoticed of all. They were there to serve and never be seen if possible, let alone heard. So Sister Jeromy's pleas went largely ignored, dismissed with irritation. The infirmarian clearly had no remedy for her condition, and a doctor was never called.

After Mass, as we climbed up the broad staircase that led to the refectory, Sister Jeromy, who had been hogging the railing with her bent back, slumped to the stairs and stayed there, face down. Everybody filed past her, including Mother Superior, who no doubt resented such dramatic malingering. And that's how Sister Jeromy died, there on the steps. She lay in a casket on the landing for two days, so we could pray for her and show her our respect, which she never received while she was alive. I knelt beside her stern figure, which was relieved at last of the burden of constant hard work, humiliation and pain, and bent over to kiss her cold folded hands. A musty taste stuck to my lips that I shall never forget. I screwed up my face and ran away to spit it out, together with all sentimental feelings for dead nuns in caskets.

Shortly afterwards I witnessed the horrible demise of another community nun. She was in a room at the top of the stairs, beside the landing and not far from the refectory, so we passed her frequently. She was extremely restless when I visited her, breathing hard, rolling her eyes, unable to speak but apparently aware of her state and her surroundings. On the little table beside her was a bottle of glycerine and a dropper, to relieve her dry rasping throat. I took the dropper and moved it over to the dying nun's face. She saw it and opened her mouth like a starving fledgling bird. She couldn't get enough of the glycerine and kept opening her mouth for more.

One of the others there said, 'Don't give her too much, it's not good for her!' I respected her opinion, thinking she had medical knowledge that I didn't. The dying body on the bed did not seem to agree. Her eyes grew wilder, her mouth gaped wide open and her breathing became even more laboured.

I could sense her utmost fear, and realised with cold surprise that whatever she had learned from her religious life meant nothing to her in the very real face of death. Any thought of eternal reward for her life of sacrifice appeared to be wiped from her mind; any feeling or conviction of being loved by God, gone. In her hour of dire need, her beliefs seemed to crumble and count for nothing, her sacrifices had been egotistical nonsense that had not schooled her in true surrender. She was abandoned — or so it seemed to me. Her tens of thousands of pleas to the Mother of God in every Hail Mary, to pray for her in the hour of her death, seemed to have gone unheeded.

We had no skills for the process that is death, no ability to help this woman, one of our sisters. We could only mutter platitudes and exclamations of horror — 'God, how awful!', 'Jesus, Mary, Joseph, come to her aid!' — and the banal recitations from the daily prayer book.

The poor woman took days to die, in terrible agony. I don't know how people die in common hospitals, but I can't imagine anything worse than such a slow death in absolute terror, suffered in full consciousness but without the ability to ask for relief, with the only wisdom offered being a mixture of sympathy and platitudes. We nuns, who witnessed this for days, could have stopped to question what was wrong with our lives if they had to end this way — but no, we were living in basic ignorance and denial. Truth filters very slowly through to consciousness that believes it's got everything right already.

THE SEASONS OF autumn and winter taught me something about surrender. I often sat near the large bay window of the library on the first floor, up among the branches of the linden trees. In autumn the trees' branches relinquished all their leaves, and in winter they bore a couple of inches of snow. My heart went out to the trees, especially the one closest to me. It seemed so patient, so long-suffering. The thought brought tears to my eyes. I wrote a poem, in which I asked the tree what it had done for it to be condemned to stay frozen and carry the burden of snow instead of leaves. Sentimentality comes easily to people who keep their sorrows to themselves. I told the tree that one day the birds would come to sing among its leaves again, and it would feel the warmth of the sun on its branches.

The season of my sorrow would last much longer than this winter. It would take many years for me to wake up to an inner sunshine that no one could ever take away.

I GAINED MY teacher's diploma after three years at Sedgley Park. The day for goodbyes came. *I shall see Alice at last, and speak to her, and for once it won't be wrong of me!* I hoped it would be an especially good time, an excuse for a loving hug, but it wasn't like that. I stood in front of her shaking like a leaf, trying to hide it while extending a hand, being as casual as possible.

'Goodbye, I'm leaving now,' I said, and was unable to say any more. How I detested my awkwardness! Why did I have to be this stultified, tongue-tied Dutch clod of a person, the opposite of Irish sociability?

Alice took my hand politely. There was no sign on her face of any special recognition. She was distressed at losing another friend, Sister Imelda, a Canadian, who, like herself, was blessed with the gift of the gab. Standing before Alice, I felt I could read her mind, her feelings, and a realisation swept over me like a betrayal. Alice had felt nothing more for me than occasional pity. She had not shunned me just because my love for her was against the rules, but because she simply didn't appreciate me. She wasn't beyond strong attachment herself, for someone more inclined to her own ways. It was a bitter moment of clarity, draining away any hope I had ever entertained of being loved by her in return.

How was it possible that great love did not produce love in return?

I ran outside to say goodbye to the magenta rhododendron bush, hoping against hope that it would have some flowers on it in June, but of course it didn't.

My years at Sedgley, then, had been the years of my absorption with Alice. When I finally stepped in front of a classroom in 1965, I might as well have come straight off the street, so useless had my training been to my preoccupied mind.

SILENT MADNESS

 STELLA MARIS, 'Star of the Sea', the mother house near Broadstairs. I was sent back there for a refresher course as a Faithful Companion of Jesus, an intensive year or more of relearning obedience and practising silence.

I was not alone. All of us six Australians who had arrived in England three years ago travelled south together. We left sooty Manchester to emerge onto the glorious green fields of England, and then to London, where we were met once more by our streetwise nun-guide and stayed overnight.

Off again at the crack of dawn to avoid the crowds. I had time to admire the magnificent old ceilings of Victoria Station filling with steam; enjoy the thunderous clatter of incoming trains, the dignified whistle of others announcing their way out. I revelled in the beauty of the old-world wrought-iron gates and seats, the detail of the paintwork on the trains and, after we were ushered into our sequestered first-class carriage, the luxurious comfort of the leather-padded seats.

We left the train after many hours and boarded a bus. The double-decker wended its way through small villages built well before the time of motor cars, lurching through their narrow streets and allowing the passengers close-up views of quaint crocheted curtains in the upstairs windows.

From Broadstairs town we were chauffeured to North Foreland, a patch of coastline that was mostly owned by the order. At last we had arrived.

It was as if I was seeing the place for the very first time. I had forgotten how long it took to walk from one end of the property to the other, and that a public road ran right through the middle of the complex of gardens and buildings.

'We welcome our Australian sisters to Stella Maris! Have you travelled well?' The choreographed welcome came from the ancient nun who had greeted us at the door three years earlier. She was the Vicar, the second-in-command, a bit like royalty, and she knew how to quickly make us feel at ease. The old dame had been a grand duchess once, and had been allowed to keep her graces.

The Vicar's house was a former mansion which retained the feel of English country homeliness. We were shown our sleeping quarters: large rooms made into upstairs dormitories. The building was close to the convent's exclusive little primary school, and from our dorm window we had the exquisite pleasure of hearing the Kentish children reciting their prayers at assembly. Their accents were so pure and song-like that it brought tears to my eyes.

Our duchess-Vicar ordered high tea for us, after which we were shown through the orchards and gardens to the main residence. Although we would sleep at the vicarage, we were to study, work and eat in the main house.

It was the height of summer and espaliered pear, apple and peach trees were in fruit along the south walls of the vegetable garden. Roses of all colours climbed up every available wall, ramblers and large-flowered cultivars. Wallflowers graced the sunny bay windows along the front of the main house, their perfume luscious in the late afternoon. Ivy crept up the red-brick walls, trying to enter the open upstairs windows, reaching right over the chimneys.

We were shown around the creaking complex: the study rooms, the linen room, the kitchen, the bright convening room and, in a separate building, the laundry. An enclosed wooden passage joined the two main houses. There were odd little rooms and useless spaces, and the toilets were in a row of five. These were new: the pine cladding still gave off a refreshing scent. We weren't shown the parlours at the front of the house, nor the sleeping quarters of the resident nuns, or the General's quarters. The General lived in a secluded part of the complex (she was expected to arrive back from a journey the following week).

I so wanted this to be a good place. It was beautiful: such precision in the garden, contrasting with the crumbling grandeur of the old mansions. It all promised the possibility of homeliness, of comfort, even of friendliness. All this turned out to be true at times, and yet the place was dominated entirely by the influence of one stern woman: Margaret Winchester, the Reverend Mother General. She was treated with extraordinary reverence, not only because of her position but because of her force of character — something I was to experience first-hand.

She was very tall, with a wide broad face and staring eyes made larger by the many circles of sagging wrinkles around them. She reminded me strongly of an orang-utan. I smiled at her when she met us upon her return to the convent, thinking that she was deliberately trying to create a funny impression, but was soon stared down by her steady eyes. Neither feminine nor masculine, she had a power bestowed by enigma. While she was imposing, she walked with a humble gait on feet that always ached with gout, head bowed, watching her step. Her hands flailed beside her swaying body to keep balance as she walked, typically orang-utan-like; something we would never dare do ourselves, no matter how unbalanced we might feel, because it would look too ostentatious, or out-of-control.

The General had a very poor constitution by the time I knew her. She burped constantly and her devoted personal attendant took infinite pains to find recipes and cook her meals that might suit her stomach. The General took her job extremely seriously. In time I would find out that this woman, to whom I had sent loving letters during my postulancy and novitiate, believed that her main mission in life was to make sure nobody had a swollen head, that we all remained humble.

To be humble meant being slavishly submissive, never speaking up, and never complaining or arguing. We were also to be obedient without question, and our obedience was measured by the degree of self-abnegation or mental, emotional or physical suffering we could endure in the execution of orders. We were frequently given contradictory orders to confound and confuse us, and publicly humiliated whenever we failed to carry out these orders based on impossible expectations.

The General got away with it because her subjects willingly bestowed a sort of infallibility upon her as the mouthpiece of God — although it takes English stoicism (which I did not share) fortified with heavy doses of religious fervour (which I did share) to ascribe a special holiness to the whimsical madness of an ageing, eccentric woman — and because Stella Maris was a testing place anyway. It was a place where the wayward were pulled into line, and the as-yet unshaped — or perhaps crookedly-shaped, like us college graduates, influenced by lay studies — were moulded in the true spirit of the order. She also got away with it because of her mad sincerity and her innovative flair. Her innovations were cruel, but their shock value drew respect. Lastly, and incredibly, she had a sense of humour, and sometimes a kindness in her eyes that belied her madness. She may once have been an especially gifted woman, but she had become a victim of her own institution and her own convictions. The General was often with us in chapel, and gave us talks at least once a week, yet she remained a terrifying mystery because she hardly ever conversed with us on an individual level.

The nun in charge of tertiary novices was Mother Mary John; she was about sixty-five years old, rotund and serious but with a little smile close to her brown eyes. Her olive skin gave her an Italian or Spanish look and tiny, dark whiskers grew above her lips. She was a tower of stability and kindness, but steadfastly refused to become a mother figure of the consoling kind, which might have been her natural tendency. She was stern whenever she thought it necessary, not habitually like the General. She sat at the head of the long narrow L-shaped table at which novices and lay sisters sat in the refectory. There was hardly enough room for so many of us.

Conversation, when it was allowed, was supposed to go around the corner of the L shape, to people who couldn't actually see each other. This peculiar arrangement encouraged witty asides that were tolerated by Mother Mary John if they did not too obviously reach her ear. She appreciated laughter, and that was our saving grace. It was like balm to our young adult souls to be allowed this indulgence in high spirits at table and at recreation time. Her large body would shake when she laughed; her eyes would close up and her lips would soften and she would lift up a serviette to hide her mouth. I loved the way she could not control her mirth; she was obviously enjoying our company. She had a way of sending us into stitches too, with unexpected moments of dry wit, but mostly she was quiet, keeping aware of the group dynamics, checking that each of her charges was there and seemed to be all right.

It was Mother Mary John's job to bring to our notice directives from the General, to coordinate household tasks, to hold monthly interviews with each of us to check on our progress or otherwise, and to correct us when necessary and impose punishments. She also presided over some of our afternoon recreation sessions. I had the distinct impression that although she was thorough in carrying out the punishing chore, it went against the grain for her. Somehow that made receiving punishment from her more palatable — and more hurtful. The question arose: 'Why punish if it feels wrong?' and the answer had to be, 'God's ways (meaning the General's rules and ways) are mysterious, and we are here not to question but to make a sacrifice of our obedience.' Mother Mary John had compassion, but her sense of devotion took absolute precedence.

Since space at Stella Maris was terribly cramped, we Australians often did our morning meditation in the Vicar's chapel to reduce crowding in the main chapel. It was a small stone building, set apart in a garden, with tiny archaic windows at just above head height. The wicker prie-dieux were only two deep on each side of the aisle, and there were about eight rows of them. The windows were usually open, winter and summer, and the sweetest fresh air would drift in. At six o'clock in the morning even the dew had a smell, and many a meditation of mine was but a pure appreciation of the roses and wallflowers and the song of the birds. The air was like a pure angel, cool to the brain, bringing on a kind of euphoria.

I would let my poetic nature have its head and joy filled my heart. I would remember some line from Gerard Manley Hopkins, like '*The world is charged with the grandeur of God . . .*' or something else I'd read. This little stone chapel was a precious jewel, as still as stillness itself, exuding a rare atmosphere that the darker and larger chapel at Stella Maris did not, even with its wonderfully carved and polished wooden sanctuary rails and pulpit, beautifully architraved ceiling, wooden pews and parquetry floors. There, the smells were all traditional — of wood and the remains of incense. The Reverend Mother General knelt at the back — a vantage point for her watchful eye.

STELLA MARIS EMPLOYED a professional groundsman who knew how to grow vegetables and flowers all year round. He would often get disgruntled when he received contradictory orders from week to week and ended up doing a lot of work for nothing. Early that autumn he gave up and left. This was something quite unexpected from a mere servant! The nuns forgot that he had not made a vow of obedience. 'He loves his garden, and he has a great respect for his work. He'll come back,' I heard them say, but they were wrong. The weeds accumulated in the vegetable patch and still he didn't come back. That's when we were asked to fulfil one of the General's unforgettable crazy orders — about ten of us were told to pull up nettles with our bare hands. We were not to stop until the last nettle was gone.

If you have ever been stung by an English nettle, whose barb lodges in the skin, you will know that the pain can stay for quite some time.

Getting stung feels like a tiny — or not so tiny — electric shock, depending on your sensitivity. We hesitated, but only to make sure what was expected of us.

I grabbed a nettle with both hands and was, of course, shocked by the sudden stings, but decided that the best policy was to proceed with a will. The nettles grew high and thick over a couple of large patches, as if especially cultivated. Soon the stings reddened our arms as well as our hands. We worked for about two hours, until the last weed came down. Then we tried to wash the pain out of our hands — and couldn't. Water was a cool blessing on the raging heat, but the raw stinging would not go away. I couldn't sleep that night from the burning and throbbing sensations, and found that nobody else could either.

'Why did we pull out all those nettles without gloves on?' The question came from a small Irish nun and was spoken gently at recreation time.

All of us were interested in a reply and we listened expectantly. Mother Mary John heard the question, but because there was no rational answer she gave none at all and looked steadfastly down at her needlework.

WE OFTEN HAD to listen to words about the value of suffering. The thought of getting closer to Jesus through pain held an immense attraction for our collective ego. Life at Stella Maris was intense; suffering seemed to be on the menu daily.

In the main chapel, I always had the feeling that it was better to stay quite still, to avoid attracting attention. It was bad enough that, being so tall with a straight back I was sometimes mistaken for Mother Clare, the General's personal assistant. She had a ramrod back and very square shoulders. We were both slim and nearly six feet in our shoes. The resemblance ended there, except when I did a deliberate and very naughty impersonation of the way she walked, holding my shoulders very straight.

Mother Clare had a classic face; she was a dark, stern beauty, with eyes that sparkled behind her large glasses, giving an inkling of her brilliant mind. She had a great intellect and had been a marvellous disciplinarian and organiser in her day. I imagine that she was sadly missed by her school. Mother Clare's phenomenal ability was now shackled to working out how to make the General more comfortable throughout her many discomforts.

In the chapel it could be very disturbing to feel eyes trained on you most of the time. If I sat down when I was expected to be kneeling, I could expect an enquiry as to why. It wouldn't do to explain that you were menstruating rather heavily and felt a bit weak in the tummy. The General walked up and down the aisles to see who was awake and who was not, and to gauge what the quality of our meditation might be. She preferred that we used no book to prompt our meditation other than the one read out in chapel, though written reminders were not forbidden altogether. When I used my missal one morning to prod my brain, she kept walking agitatedly past me. I was usually at the end of the pew, beside the aisle, so I wouldn't obstruct the others' view of the altar. The swish-swish of her habit went back and forth, and I kept my eyes down. She rattled her rosary beads with flailing arms, to see if that would make me notice her. I pretended not to, daring her to rip the book out of my hand. She didn't, but it must have been a close thing.

Later that day, we were called together in the convening room for a talk by the General. Seats were arranged in rows in a room barely large enough for us all to breathe together, and a table and chair were set up in front. As usual, I was at the end of the row, this time on the far side away from the door, beside the large expanse of latticed window.

The General began by challenging some individuals about their practice of the rules and their religious life. Sister Bridget, a brilliant history teacher, was well known for her innovative chart-making and her students were achieving particularly good results. This Irish nun in her mid-thirties was the coordinator of studies in her school and obviously frantic that she had been forced to leave her department and classes suddenly unattended. I saw her distress as her charts were ripped up at the General's command and she was ordered not to return to the school at all. Sister Bridget was beside herself with confusion, unable to make head or tail of this.

The General's attention suddenly turned to me. 'Sister Mary Carla,' came the voice, interrupted by little burps of indigestion, 'what do you think about when you meditate?'

My reply was immediate, panic-driven. 'Nothing,' I replied, turning scarlet at the attention I was getting and the silliness of my answer. I had given it instinctively, the kind of classic denial used in TV soapies, though I had never seen one.

The General seized on the error. 'I thought as much,' she retorted, producing a giggle in the audience.

I kept my head down, determined not to say another word. I was so overwhelmed by the sudden attack that my mind went numb anyway and I couldn't have responded even if I'd wanted to. It wasn't any fun for the General to keep on talking to a moron, so I was left alone and a dissertation on meditation followed.

After that, I became acutely aware of the questionable nature of the trances I spontaneously fell into. For example, I might be reading a book and a passage would so inspire me that I would become oblivious to my surroundings. This could last for some time, and it might take a bell to wake me up.

One summer afternoon I walked to the end of a pathway that finished at a fence with a wheatfield on the other side. Being tall I could look over the fence easily. I was in rapture at the soft winds rippling the wheat and the sight of red poppies and blue cornflowers that I used to know as a child in Holland. On this day, a lark was singing. The little creature seemed to be tireless. Whenever it dropped back into the wheatstalks for a breather, it wasn't long before it was up in the sky again, singing as if its lungs would give up at any moment, chirping to . . . what? Its creator? An invisible mate? I chose to imagine that it sang to praise God, and my heart joined in with the music.

Long after the song was over, and the sun started to set in the sky, I remembered where I was. I had been standing in that one spot all the time, totally transfixed. This peculiar behaviour didn't go unnoticed by the others. When the General had asked that question, there were several nuns who had looked at me curiously and were keen to hear the answer themselves. Well, they got none. And no amount of humiliation would make me stop using these escape mechanisms. Even when I was very little, I had learned how to escape into the painted woods on the ornately gilded picture in our sitting room. My father and I used to walk in the real woods portrayed there, so it was easy to imagine being on the track that led through the forest, smelling the fallen leaves as they were crushed underfoot, noticing the spiders hanging in their diamond webs, spotting the toadstools and being on the watch for fairies and gnomes.

A SPECIAL ASSIGNMENT came my way. The General gave me the instructions herself; this was most unusual. Sister Angela and I listened together and I was fascinated by this opportunity for a close-up look at the 'orang-utan'. The resemblance was so striking that it filled my mind and the softly spoken instructions got lost in my reverie and an endless series of interruptive little burps. I didn't think it wise to ask the General to repeat herself; besides, I believe now that she deliberately swallowed most of her words so we couldn't possibly understand her. Her powerful presence was the only thing that stayed with me from that meeting.

I hoped that Sister Angela had listened and understood better than I had. All I had gathered was that I was in charge of picking tomatoes for distribution to all the houses, and Sister Angela was to help me. There were up to five locations to think of, including the children's boarding school. Did the General tell us how many people were in each house, so that we could distribute the tomatoes in the proper ratio? I couldn't remember anything more than her mumbling something about 'Here' and 'There'.

Picking the ripe tomatoes with the effervescent Sister Angela (I had known her since postulant days) was pure pleasure. The smell of tomato leaves brushing against our clothes was intoxicating. Plucking a ripe tomato from its bush, with the stalk still in its centre (I did remember this part of the instructions!), and filling my hand with its healthy red roundness, felt like a little miracle each time. The hothouses held the luxury of mystique and sunny, warm light.

Our canvas bags laden with loot, our difficulties began. 'Sister Angela,' I said, 'how many people do you think are staying at Stella Maris just now? Do you know how many live at the vicarage and how many elsewhere?' Alas, she knew no better than I, so we made rough guesses and went around surprising the occupants with our gifts. Certainly, nobody knocked back any of our tomatoes!

Talking was not authorised, and I felt so guilty about breaking this rule with Sister Angela that my head was bent low when we crossed the public road. A car was cruising slowly by — probably full of sightseers lucky enough to come across a couple of local 'penguins' — and we were both so self-conscious and kept our heads so bent down, that we crossed the road at widely different angles instead of side by side. The sight probably caused merriment in the car, but our silliness made me grit my teeth.

We had been carrying out our tomato routine for about two weeks when we found out we weren't doing a good job. The news came via an open talk by the General to the gathered communities in the convention room. The crowded gathering was treated to a sarcastic description of our stupidity, ending with, 'There was no rhyme nor reason in what they did. The allocation of tomatoes showed a complete lack of common sense.'

Had the whole thing been a set-up to make us look bad? I had no idea. Sister Angela didn't seem to mind very much; she was a bouncy person, always smiling, with a wonderfully good heart and happy to have no brains, the kind who barges in where angels fear to tread. I, however, was feeling slightly desperate because I dimly realised that, in this humble institution, the only way to get a responsible job —

a tangible sign of esteem — now or in the future, was by impressing your superiors.

Sister Angela and I were relieved of our tomato-picking duties.

IT WAS THE time of Vatican II and ecumenical rapprochement, which meant that Christian churches began to respect each other's sincerity and essential sameness.

Pope John XXIII had bravely called a Vatican Council during his short reign, in January 1959, three months after coming to office. It was an extremely difficult thing to accomplish; the Council didn't open until October 1962 and even then the bulk of Pope John's work was not completed until after his death.

The story of how he dealt with the machinations of the scheming, self-important Curia makes fascinating reading. The spirit of Pope John somehow managed to get past conservative thinking. The result was the now famous movement called the *Aggiornomento*; loosely translated it means 'bringing things up to date'.

So now we were to study the research into the Bible that had been done by the Church of England (Catholics had not been so keen on the Holy Book after Henry VIII ran off with it). Mother Clare was in charge of Biblical studies and she dealt decisively with our scandalised reactions.

'Of course Jesus may have had brothers!'

'Clearly it is true that he could not have been born on 25 December, because at that time of the year it is too cold for sheep in the vicinity of Bethlehem to be outside. The Wise Men from the East were probably just symbols, like their gifts of gold, frankincense and myrrh.'

We were treated to some really eye-popping possibilities.

'Jesus may have been the illegitimate son of a Roman soldier, and that was why Joseph agonised so much about whether to get his promised wife stoned or not. That might have explained why Jesus grew up secretly with the Essenes and studied for the priesthood, which he later betrayed when he let their secrets of health and other forbidden knowledge out into the open.'

Such first-class scandalous hypothesising! This was the kind of open bravery that the Catholic church largely withdrew from when Pope John's great spirit left the earth, and his too-frank successor died after only thirty-three days in office. After this, the politicians in the Curia succeeded in installing their puppets once again.

It was curious that some FCJs were so open, at that particular time, and yet progress within the order slowed down and came to a halt. In Ireland in particular, FCJs loved the status quo and stuck to what had seemed good enough to them since time immemorial.

When we weren't studying or praying, we were doing chores, and there were plenty of them. I daresay we earned our keep, working inside the house and in the gardens. We also did exquisite embroidery at recreation time. I dressed a series of dolls, and even embroidered their petticoats. I never knew what happened to them, or any of the tablecloths and doilies and napkins that we made with so much skill.

Suddenly, I landed myself a very different kind of job. Mother Mary John stopped me in the corridor. 'Sister Carla, the sister who usually prepares the parlour for the priest's breakfast and serves it after Mass is ill. Would you like to do this service while she is absent?'

I was asked not ordered, I noticed, and said I was pleased to step into the breach. I was surprised too, because I didn't think of myself as having such fine sensibilities as parlour manners. Well, there was no time like the present, so I took on the job with courage and a little bit of confidence.

The job required two women: one sister to prepare the food tray in the kitchen and the other to do the serving. There was one nerve-consoling factor: everything was the same from day to day — the same food, cutlery, crockery and napkins, trays, and the same procedure of 'this goes first and that comes next'. The only thing that ever changed were the flowers in a little vase. The best part of my job was definitely picking a little flower here and there from the lush garden for the breakfast table.

I was the server, and all was fine, except I wasn't prepared for the possibility that the priest might talk to me. The priest that week was a human sort of guy who must have been curious to get to know the new sister. He threw out the occasional small talk, which was naughty of him as he must have been aware of the tertiary novices' rule of silence. I answered politely and briefly and so survived a week. The sick nun I was replacing either never asked for her job back or never got better, so I continued into a second week. I was really getting into the swing of things. The priests weren't always the same, but they were normally reserved, polite and unengaging.

I was to become undone, however. One Irish priest started asking me questions about what I was going to do that day, and why was I in England. It was all very disconcerting — somehow too human, too friendly — but I didn't think of asking for guidance from my superiors. Then one morning I couldn't resist telling him the old joke about the Rolls Can'ardly. He had told me a little joke and I thought it was appropriate for me to tell him one in return.

'My father owns a Rolls Can'ardly,' I said, with wicked pleasure in the humour I was encouraging. 'It rolls easily down the hill but can 'ardly get up!'

The laughter which followed must have reached through the walls. The General had been having her breakfast in another parlour not far away and, inevitably, Mother Mary John called me to her side that very morning. I knelt down as was the custom and listened to her reprimand. Cracking jokes was not part of my job, I was told, and was a serious breach of silence. I was to be relieved of my parlour job at once.

Well, I wasn't too upset — that morning of laughter would be a hard act to follow, anyway. The trouble was that the job was now the sole responsibility of my partner, and she was having great difficulty doing it all smoothly and properly by herself. I would see her rushing through the refectory with the tray of cutlery and crockery, then the tray of food, and not getting to her own breakfast till everything was cold.

This went on for days, until Mother Mary John took me aside and hinted that I should apologise and ask to get the job back. What? The notion was so preposterous that I flatly rejected it. 'No, thank you, I will never go back to that job again.' If I wasn't good enough then, I wasn't good enough now, and the fact that the other sister was struggling had nothing to do with me. If this was some strange test, I was willing to fail it wholeheartedly!

AUTUMN TURNED TO winter, the time of great winds and storms. They swept the foreland mercilessly. We had to walk from the vicarage to the main residences and back every morning and evening; the objective was to arrive without losing anyone over the cliff. Umbrellas being useless in the gale, we left them behind and held each other's gloved hands in a row of six or so, proving that there was strength in numbers! Together we would pull each other through the wind, cloaks plastered against our bodies, plodding along in gumboots. How we enjoyed those wild and windy days! Yes, we got wet, but our cloaks were made of good serge and the plastic bonnets over our heads saved us from the worst of the rain. There's nothing like a refreshing physical challenge to rehumanise spiritual people. Among the genteel, mollycoddled older members of the community, the Australians acquired something of a heroic status for the way they tackled nature. Well, it was something. Crossing the grounds at least four times each day between the main house and the vicarage had a cooling and refreshing effect on us; it probably contributed greatly to our relative sanity. The eyes-down rule kept me in contact with the things that grew in the ground and around our feet as we walked. Nature was my ally, as it had always been.

Christmas drew close, and so did the snow-laden skies and the cosiness of a heated recreation room. During the six weeks of Advent we chose to do extra penance, easily achieved if you suffered from the cold. However, we all did compulsory penance when the breakfast tea was served not hot, not warm, but cold. Here was a *ready-made* penance, we were told. Worse was to come: the General decided at lunch that *no tea at all* might be an even more suitable penance for the duration of Advent.

I could sense a few hackles rising around me, especially from the resident lay sister in charge of the laundry, who year after year had been thwarted in her bid to get warm water to rinse the washing. She had been at Stella Maris for some years and the mystique of the place had apparently rubbed off a bit. She had a loud voice too. 'We'll all get sick!' she shouted.

And she was right — people started to display all kinds of withdrawal symptoms. Hot tea was reinstated after a week, much to everyone's relief. We were all thoroughly addicted to it. How ordinary we were, in spite of our grandiose ideas of leading lives of detachment.

On Christmas Day we waited expectantly for festivities to begin. The long ceremonies in the chapel were over and we were all congenially crammed into the recreation room, eyeing the many little bowls of sweets on the table, waiting for the General to appear so we could wish her a Happy Christmas and get stuck into the chocolates, humbugs and boiled lollies.

The General had a real fear that we took too many things for granted. Mother Clare swept into the room like a broom on fire and swiped all the bowls off the table. The sweets gone, the General came in and planted her large frame squarely in a chair at the head of the table, one hand on her knee, a forearm draped over the table, like the King of the Castle.

'Jesus,' she said (pause), 'was born in a cold stable (pause) and we (pause) are His Companions. Indulgence in sweets is not a proper way to celebrate Christmas!' Her manner was impeccably choreo-graphed and impressive. Eyeing all of us around the room, she added, 'There are many starving people in the world. Let us think of them today.'

It was this sort of superior-sounding wisdom, this bold way of stating her truth, that for many years had earned her a special respect. It takes nerve to come out with persuasions like hers, and a certain flair to impose them on others. She spoke softly and intently, with many pauses, conspiratorial half-smiles and knowing eyes. She made you believe that if you did not understand what she was saying, you were stupid. Small, intimate groups like ours were her little playground.

WINTER WAS ALSO a time for colds and flu. For a while I helped out when others fell victim to influenza, then succumbed to something mysterious myself. I developed such a raging fever that someone was assigned to watch over me and administer medicine at certain times. She was a young nun, who was rather obviously anxious about something other than her present job. I had my eyes closed, but I could sense her restlessness. Finally, she spoke up.

'Listen,' she said earnestly, 'can you take those tablets yourself?' and mentioned a time. In my delirium, it seemed perfectly fine for me to believe that I was capable of taking the tablets as instructed, and I said yes. After a while, alas, I had no idea what I had and hadn't taken. Had I swallowed the tablets or only imagined it? What time did she say they were to be taken? I decided to take the tablets I could see on the saucer close to me. My guardian came back, seemingly only moments later, and was aghast. Why hadn't I looked at the clock properly, she wanted to know. She ran away again, very agitated, but I promptly fell asleep.

I woke during what I thought was the middle of the night, needing to go to the toilet. It was pitch dark. I couldn't make out a thing, but knew where the toilets were, so groped my way out of the dormitory into the passageway and into a toilet. I switched on the light, I thought, but there was no light. I went into the next toilet and tried the light there, again with no luck. There was a power failure, I presumed, or else all the globes had blown. I managed to use a toilet, made it back to bed and fell asleep again. When I woke up and opened my eyes, I still couldn't see. My world was pitch black but I knew it was daytime from the noise of people around the place. Whatever those tablets were, they had sent me blind.

Someone came to question me about the taking of the tablets, reprimanded me for being stupid, and left me alone. I had no idea if

I would stay blind or not, and was curiously resigned to whatever might happen. For days I woke up in darkness, checking for sounds to see if it was day or night.

Then, one morning at dawn, my eyes saw the world again, softly. I was on the mend. I asked for little jobs I could do in bed as I improved, like peeling potatoes or apples, or shelling peas. The amazing hothouses in the garden produced vegetables all year round.

The sister who had made the mistake came to apologise, as was her duty, and that was that. All in all I enjoyed my illness as a respite from the daily round of tensions.

I BECAME BADLY constipated again, like I had been back in Australia when I was a novice. Laxatives didn't work this time, so I was given a big cup of the sweetest tea ever and was made to lie down on the infirmary table, on my side, buttocks exposed.

The infirmarian looked at me as if she wondered if I knew where all this was going to end, but her rule of silence apparently prevented her from explaining anything to me. She put on some gloves, swirled a hand in a pot of Vaseline, and approached the end of my intestines as if she was holding a gun. I watched her face during all this: she kept it turned away from the work at hand, watching me in her turn, but her expression gave nothing away.

When the strategy started to work, I finally caught signs of relief and disgust before I was told to slide down onto a commode. I decided then that it might be a good idea to leave penitential salt out of my tea in future, and take a lot of sugar instead.

Later in the year, my periods stopped. I was unconcerned, having experienced a similar hiatus as a postulant in the convent at Genazzano. Kneeling alongside Reverend Mother Winifred's armchair, looking up into her large face, I had shyly come out with an issue that was bothering me. 'Reverend Mother,' I began shyly, 'I haven't had my period for four months.' Her body had rocked in her chair, then she had replied with all the surety of bluff, 'It means absolutely nothing, Sister Carla.' But for the nuns at Stella Maris, it was another matter entirely!

Mother Mary John responded to the report from the linen mistress that I hadn't ordered sanitary pads for five months by calling me to her office. There, she and the linen mistress quizzed me about my activities. 'Where have you been, Sister?'

Been? I had been nowhere special. My interrogators watched me closely. The tension was electric.

Mother Mary John finally became more specific. 'Did you go to the village at all, Sister?'

'No, I haven't gone to the village. Not at all. Why?'

She seemed relieved and handed me over to the infirmarian, who judged that I was suffering from a shortage of iron and gave me some tablets. In a short time, my periods returned and 'all was well'. It was years and years before I understood the reason for their anxiety: *they were wondering if I was pregnant!* This was a preposterous idea, but I smiled at the implication — I guessed that if it had been suspected of me, it must have happened before.

SPRING CAME. I wanted to shout my delight at seeing the snowdrops come up; then the jonquils and daffodils that waved to me *en masse* as I passed, and the hyacinths, tulips and bluebells. The crisp air made their perfumes sharp and delicious. I longed to talk to someone about the beauty I saw, as if it would otherwise be lost. It couldn't be done, of course, except at recreation time. I felt very foolish then, speaking hours afterwards of feelings that were so private and poetic. I wasn't ashamed to cry as I walked among the flowers. For once, I desperately wished for a special friend to share life with, someone with whom I could share my deepest soul. Jesus was too far away; I wanted someone real that I could talk to. My truest relationship was with something I could feel at my core, but as for Jesus — I couldn't put a face to him. A physical description of him was nowhere to be found, and the sentimental holy pictures showed an effeminate, meek man, not the kind of Jesus I could believe in. The Gospels never once describe Jesus as laughing, smiling or hugging those close to him.

I had been at Stella Maris for about nine months when a flu epidemic, accompanied by severe diarrhoea, swept the Foreland. Quite a few sisters fell foul of the germs, but I hung out for a bit longer. The usual procedure for communicating with the infirmarian was through a written message, deposited in a box. It worked well if the infirmarian bothered to empty the box regularly, or if there were no emergencies.

When the stomach cramps finally hit me, I stuck a note describing my symptoms in the box. Then I waited for the response. I knew this was silly, and even perverse — the sooner I got attended to the better — but I wanted to show up this system and the rule of silence that prevented me being able to say anything directly and out loud. Finally, I was becoming angry.

I spent most of the day near or in the toilets. It was Easter, and the place was crowded with visitors; there was an awful lot of to-ing and fro-ing for the Easter ceremonies in the chapel. I didn't attend prayers and didn't turn up for lunch, but wasn't missed.

The toilets at Stella Maris held a particular fascination for me, because of the pictures I saw in the pine-clad doors and walls — the kind you can also see in clouds. There was a snarling wolf, a dragon, a nymph, faces, trees, a whole landscape in the whorls of knotted wood. I whiled away the time by admiring the animals and the fairies in the pine slats, then decided to draw what I saw, so took my sketchbook with me to the toilets. An amazing thing happened then: the animals and fairies disappeared! It was the strangest experience to see them one moment, then have them disappear the very instant I wanted to draw them, even though I only took my eyes off them momentarily. It was as if they were playing hide and seek. I felt stupid and baffled; I may have been delirious by that stage.

The cramps got worse and I paced up and down the deserted passageways and empty rooms for hours, while everybody else was in chapel. All of a sudden an anxious and angry infirmarian appeared. The note had finally reached her after two whole days and she couldn't believe that I hadn't simply said something to her. We went into a nearby room, where she grilled me about the symptoms, then asked me to wait. Back she came with Mother Clare, eyes large with consternation, and the upshot was that I was sent away immediately to isolation in the The Knoll.

The Knoll served as a guesthouse every so often, but most of the time it was empty. It was the furthest building from the main house, a red-brick structure with four floors and a winding staircase. It looked like one of those tall, skinny buildings you see in ghost stories; each floor dwindled in size, so that the little room at the top held only three beds. I was to sleep in that top room, which was more like an attic and had no curtains. There was no light — the globe had blown a long time ago and nobody had bothered to replace it. At night it was hardly dark, though. The North Foreland lighthouse swept its invasive beam right through the room at regular intervals.

I was the only soul in this lonely place. The doors on the bottom floor were always kept locked. A novice left a tray of food at the back door for me three times a day and sometimes some clean underwear. The infirmarian came once to ask me for a stool sample, then ordered samples to be collected by a silent nun every few days. I was never told of the results, but written messages arrived intermittently under the teacup on the food tray, such as: 'Clean all the stairs today, Sister'; then, perhaps the next day: 'Do nothing today'; or 'Keep to your bed today'; and once a note from Mother Mary John asking me if I needed any books. At least it indicated that she knew where I was and hadn't forgotten me. I had the life of the foundress with me, a biography of Saint Theresa of Avila and the rule book. I had no idea what other book to ask for when given a choice. It never occurred to me to ask for a novel. In the end, I asked for a book on the lives of the saints.

My mind had shut down more than ever. I had no means of knowing when my isolation would end and I adjusted myself to the possibility of a long haul. I kept on cleaning the rooms and the stairs, collected my food from the back door, usually ate it cold, read, and meditated a lot on what I read. I really wanted to understand the rules and the importance of the life of Madame de Bonnault d'Hoüet. At night, I would undress between sweeps of the lighthouse and begin my solitary night's sleep.

The weeks passed as if in a dream. The diarrhoea had long since disappeared, but I felt terribly weak. I was so hungry! I could have eaten at least three times the amount of food left for me at the door.

I felt that the only person who had any shred of belief in my sincerity was me. It was a painful feeling, but I coped by submitting to everything that happened as the Will of God. I didn't rave, I never complained, never even checked the door to see if I could get out or run away. I was unquestionably, and frighteningly, obedient. I may even have dared the General to kill me, or at least do her worst. It would have made no difference to my equanimity.

The day came when I was told to return to the community. I was a wraith who had to leave her homeland of shadows, her ghostly house, to go back to the land of the living. The world had changed. Everything was too bright! And everything moved so fast! Mother Mary John explained to me that I had been suspected of a transmittable disease but that the danger had passed now. I could tell from the calendar that I had been in isolation for six weeks.

My body had become frightfully thin; my wrists were transparent; there was nothing but skin on the bones. I longed for FAT! At breakfast the next morning, which must have been a Sunday because there was bacon, I sent my plate back for more and whispered for 'the juice, please'. The message didn't get through, but I could have licked the tray clean, I was so hungry for grease.

Recreation time arrived. It was such music to my ears to hear voices! I joined in whenever I could, quipping, laughing, and was surprised to hear Mother Mary John, who was presiding, ask me to speak up more. She was actually providing a space for me to do some talking! The gesture touched me deeply.

I was now even more conditioned to endurance, and to doing any silly thing for the sake of obedience. I rather expected the bizarre to be normal. I heard silly orders even when they were not so, and regularly misunderstood directives. I walked in big rubber boots every time I went outside that wet spring, and took myself around the front of the house when the express directive was to not do that. I had lost my sense of judgment and was blithely unperturbed about it.

I was finally summoned by Mother Mary John for a talk. We sat in the cushioned alcove of the recreation room. She looked at me over her glasses and I could see from her brown eyes that she wasn't angry, but slightly perturbed.

'I have to give a report soon on all the tertiary novices,' she began. 'What shall I say to Reverend Mother General about you? That you are stupid?'

She wasn't being unkind, I could feel it. She was merely chiding me, inviting me to save myself. I could feel laughter growing inside me, helplessly. It came from the understanding that here was someone who cared for me; she was a reminder that I was loved by God and everything was all right. A wave of relaxation swept through me which made me reckless.

'Yes! All right! Do!' I laughed, then smothered my laugh and said, 'Oh no! Please don't tell her that!', but couldn't stop myself from laughing. 'Oh dear!' I said, in fits now, 'I might be going mad!'

Then I told her what was absolutely true at the time: 'I don't care what the General thinks of me!', and laughed some more. My superior looked at me quizzically, compassionately, even humorously for a little while, then the twinkle in her eyes died and she turned away. No doubt she knew that this sort of attitude wouldn't get me far. I was both sane and insane at the same time. I could feel fresh, irrepressible humour bubbling up in me like a freedom, and recklessness like a death warrant.

I had no idea that the die had already been cast. It was made to look as though I wasn't professionally fit enough to return to Australia and be put to work there, but the fact was that because I held a Dutch passport, I was a foreigner as far as Australia was concerned. After having been away for more than four years I would have to seek re-entry as a migrant. Since I wasn't aware of these issues — no one told me — this gave the General the opportunity to do her ghastly ego-destroying number on me.

I was called in to see her. Her great eyes watched me with contempt as I knelt nervously in front of her. I noticed with fascination that they were grey and watery, and amused at my expense. If I didn't know better, I might have read compassion there; but those eyes were so deceptive that they fooled everyone, even the people closest to her.

'You will not be going back to Australia.' The words came like a prison sentence. 'We can't palm you off the way you are,' and she brushed the palm of one wrinkly hand with the other as she spoke. 'You will go to Brussels instead, where you will be trained by Mother Josephine.'

I bit my lip and fought back the tears. The other Australians were due to sail home in a month. I would miss them, and miss the fun of the informality on board ship. Besides, Mother Josephine's name brought desolation to my heart; she was an Irish woman full of energetic ambition, clever and determined.

When the ivy on the walls started to change colour, my Australian companions left Broadstairs for their homeland. The lucky five had just been through an English summer and were going home to an Australian one. They would begin teaching in the new term. Goodbyes were swift and subdued. Neither they nor I could fathom the exact reasons why I was being left behind, nor for how long. It wasn't for any of us to ask any questions.

WINTER OF BAD DREAMS

A FORLORN FERRY took us from Dover to Calais; then my new Reverend Mother and I boarded a grey, dirty train to take us to Brussels. We travelled in silence all the way, which seemed oddly rude because Mother Josephine was the epitome of refinement. Maybe she was just very deep in thought.

Mother Josephine was heading back to a pretty serious job. Her convent in Brussels was a huge responsibility; it would need every bit of her phenomenal wit, courage and tenacity to keep it on an even keel.

The Reverend Mother was not an ordinary woman. She was about forty when I knew her, a well-made Irish woman with a very pale but beautiful roundish face. In many people pallor would not be attractive, but it somehow suited Mother Josephine very well, bestowing a kind of ethereal beauty to her regular features and giving her a deceptive air of delicacy. Her most distinguishing feature was her full, pink, mobile mouth. Such kissable lips! I was sure that her sacrifice of celibacy was a much bigger one than mine; after all, she could have been a phenomenal social hit! When she opened that mouth of hers, you were likely to be carried away by the magic of her Irish lilt, which stirred vague dreams of Celtic witches, elves and fairies. Glasses worn over her expressive eyes made them seem even bigger and, to the simpler minds of some of the people she dealt with, intriguingly innocent.

Mother Josephine was definitely not naive, nor delicate. She could have been successful as a politician, had women been active in politics in the 1960s. In Margaret Thatcher's time, she would easily have topped that lady's intelligence, strategic flair and verbal dexterity, as well as floored the chamber with the sheer beauty of her feminine Irish charm. Mother Josephine put these skills to use within her own domain of influence, for the sake of the convent's survival.

Being a natural psychologist, she learned to use people without entirely losing compassion for them.

Belgian women, like the Dutch women I used to know, love to gossip, and many reputations were made or broken in the parlours of the wealthy. It was important for Reverend Mother Josephine to be well-spoken of. The convent's bank account, on the other hand, owed much of its success or failure to the menfolk.

Montjoie was a convent of huge proportions. It took up an enormous frontage along Avenue Montjoie, while two adjoining properties, Longchamps and Le Chateau, faced onto another road. It took bottomless funds to maintain this ancient, three-storeyed structure. The heating of the enormous complex in winter was granted by the benevolence of one of Brussels' rich and famous. The oil bill must have been fabulously high, as the interior was kept at a constant twenty degrees on all three floors throughout winter. The convent school took in about nine hundred boarders and many day pupils as well. Everything in the boarders' quarters was super-sized: the dormitories, the dining room, the classrooms, corridors, even the chapel. The ceilings were so high that the windows were set above head height, to be in proportion.

The chapel on the second floor was a Gothic gem. It held about a thousand people, very nearly losing the intimacy of a chapel. Wooden beams arched from end to end, focusing attention on an impressive raised and marbled sanctuary. There were wooden carvings throughout and the communion rails were of carved wood and marble. The chapel statues were magnificent; the Virgin Mary had the sweetest, pale marble face I have ever come across. She resembled

Mother Josephine somehow. It was a most beautiful chapel, but it echoed to the sound of footsteps. I so missed the intimate immediacy of the tiny stone chapel at Broadstairs.

I was introduced to everyone during talking time in the refectory, and was placed next to the lay sisters in accordance with my lowly status. After all, I had not done any teaching work at all and had no 'image' as yet. I didn't want one, for that matter, but that attitude was a mistake: people who were able to prove themselves as image-makers were useful and highly respected within the system of things. I felt completely inadequate when it came to image games. All I could do was hope to convince everyone of my good intentions and prove my as yet untested abilities as a teacher.

The long refectory tables were arranged in a U-shape, with one at the head and two down each side. This way we were all in sight of each other and it was easy for the servers to do their jobs. The room itself was ancient, dark and creaky-floored, as all of them were. Each morning the reading from the *Imitation of Christ* was read out by a volunteer, who offered on the spur of the moment — a surprising arrangement in such a militarised institution. I was keen to practise my French and show it off, so I became a frequent volunteer. I loved the musical sound of the French language. It was a rare joy, as a foreigner, to listen to others speak it in this bilingual city, even if rules usually prevented me from joining in.

MONTJOIE CONVENT WAS embarking on a daring new venture: to provide education for the young children of rich American businessmen. American families did not want to expose their children to the deep and sometimes violent Belgian prejudice aimed against them (*Americans are upstart foreigners who think they know better than we do, and they're robbing us of our business opportunities*). By sending their children to a specially established school the Americans deepened the social rift, and Mother Josephine had to field the annoyance of her Belgian benefactors. She did this with her usual grace and diplomacy.

St John's, as it was called, catered for all the primary school grades, but from its inception was short of space. I was given the task of teaching crafts to each class. There was nowhere to store the craft materials and the children's work, except in places already occupied by things like books, so they very often ended up on the floor.

Mother Josephine's ambition was reflected in her demands that the children do well; especially in craft. After all, hand-made objects were something concrete. A five year old's coordination isn't as advanced as that of a nine year old, but why not push them to expand their limits? The children became fodder for the convent's image machine, and I was there to be tested anyway, so it didn't matter how impossible the task.

I ended up doing quite a bit of the work myself, in countless attempts to correct the little children's inevitable mistakes. All the same, I recognised that American children had an undauntedness about them that was different to Australian, English or Belgian children. They had a self-confidence that was astonishing and refreshing. They were open, talkative and sociable, and obviously not used to coming into class in silence, as we were all taught to do. I secretly hoped that they would never be asked to conform to such arbitrary rules.

Needless to say, I had nothing to do with policy-making. I wasn't even placed in charge of a class. Sister Stephen, the slim, quick-witted, young Irish principal had obviously received a briefing that hadn't put me in the best light. She had an unconscious way of curling her thin lips in disdain, pointing her chin in the air and disregarding everything I said. The impossibility of keeping the craft materials and children's work tidy gave her endless opportunities to reprimand me. As a last resort, I put the stuff in boxes and placed them at the front of the classroom, officially the teacher's space, where they wouldn't be walked on.

I was proud of the children's efforts at needlework, and so were most of their parents. I was even proud of myself for helping them to learn so well, until I saw that a few who had not managed so well had lost some of the confidence in themselves that this sort of work was supposed to instil.

It's too petty to describe how everything I tried seemed to be sabotaged. Sister Stephen's harping criticisms felt like continual harassment. I was there to be tested, but how was I supposed to get it right? I gave up and decided to submit to whatever was happening. Let my superiors judge me the way they wanted to, and let the future be what it would be.

To my surprise, I was asked to teach English. My training had included mandatory English teaching, so the assignment was fair enough. I couldn't find a syllabus of any kind, so I made up some lessons in a hurry. I enjoyed the challenge, but it came to an end rather quickly during a surprise inspection visit from Mother Josephine. On the blackboard I had written the parts of the verb 'to eat'. The past tense was down as 'ate': 'She ate an apple this morning'.

I was bluntly told in front of the class that I was wrong. 'Ate' should have been spelled 'eat' in proper English, Mother Josephine asserted. I argued politely with her, but she wouldn't budge.

'Sister, you have probably missed something during your schooling, since English wasn't your native language. Please correct it.'

She watched while I replaced 'ate' with 'eat'. At that moment, I sold out another fragment of my integrity to obedience, and more of my self-respect along with it. To this day, I don't know whether Mother Josephine was being pedantic — since 'eat' is an archaic form of the past participle — or whether it was a test to see if I would cave in or hold my ground. In any case, I was relieved of the teaching of English.

The General's conviction that I wasn't good enough for Australia was the reason given to me for my presence at Montjoie, as if at a finishing school. So my mind was geared up to expect harsh treatment. Had I been in a different frame of mind, I might have had a totally different experience. I most likely would not have put up with harassment and silly pettiness as a matter of course. If only Mother Josephine and I had been able to speak as one human being to another, even just the once, who knows how different my Montjoie experience might have been.

MY WATCH BROKE down. That doesn't sound like a big deal, except for the fact that there weren't any clocks around the place, except for the one in the chapel on the second floor. 'Your watch can't be mended, Sister, and we don't have watches lying around for people who break them.' My superior spoke in a hurry and she was gone. The rule of silence prohibited me from asking others the time — at least, I *allowed* it to stop me from asking. An interesting few months followed, where I guessed the time, often got it wrong, and suffered the consequences with apparent equanimity. What had happened to my state of mind? Why didn't I find an alarm clock to carry around with me, for instance? I was in a kind of hypnotic trance, responding to an unspoken edict: you are here to be tested, but are already pre-judged and won't be able to get anything right.

Mother Josephine sent me out of her sight one day. I had waylaid her as she left the refectory, desperate for an opportunity to talk to her. I had been at Montjoie for more than a month and had not had a single tête-a-tête with my superior or with anyone else. It was as if I didn't matter at all. She told me to go for a walk outside, by way of getting rid of me. It was a bitterly cold winter's day with an overcast sky. I put on my gloves (they had developed holes all of a sudden, as if gobbled by invisible moths) and went out to the playground where I walked and walked. I hadn't asked how long I was to walk, and I wasn't going to stop until I received an order to come in again. But how could I expect Mother Josephine, responsible for a thousand people, to remember me, walking outside in the cold? Stubbornly, I wouldn't entertain the option of going inside to ask her if it was enough. No, I walked on doggedly for five solid hours, until dusk, and would probably have walked on into the night or until I dropped, waiting for my superior to finally admit she was unreasonable.

'Sister!' I was pulled up by the urgent voice of a young nun, running towards me. 'Mother Josephine says for you to come in now.' She came closer to look at my frozen face. 'I saw you from a window,' she explained, 'and I asked Mother Josephine what you were doing, walking for so long in the cold and now the dark.' Mother Josephine had apparently been taken off guard for a moment, but 'You can go and fetch her in,' was all she said.

Snow started to fall as we headed back inside together. With blue-cold lips I thanked the nun for her kindness. She asked one of the lay sisters to make me a hot cup of tea and then she disappeared. I was given some leftovers from the dinner table with my hot tea.

The next day I had a temperature, not surprising after my long exposure to sub-zero temperatures. It was a secret relief, because I thought I'd get a break from teaching. I was sent to the infirmarian for a check-up and for medicine if necessary. To my surprise, she told me that I didn't have a temperature at all! I sat there feeling stunned, my cheeks and forehead burning, my lips cracked and dry. Was the thermometer faulty, I ventured to ask, but was brusquely rebuffed. Had she been told to ignore me? Was that part of my punishment?

I stood outside the infirmary room, not knowing what to do next. The infirmarian was rumbling about inside, so I plucked up the courage to ask for another temperature check. She agreed reluctantly, but came up with the same conclusion: it wasn't abnormal. I began to wonder if my regular body temperature was lower than other people's, so that a rise in temperature might make it seem normal. I received no sympathy and no medicine, and sat around feeling hot and befuddled, with an overwhelming desire to get under blankets and sleep. I quickly succumbed to a heavy cold and was told to stay away from others; so I did get a few days' respite from teaching, but without the comfort of being in bed.

Then came a new challenge. One of the nuns said to me, 'Old Sister Norbert needs a new bonnet. She can no longer do the fine stitching herself and nobody else has time to do it for her. Would you do it?'

I could have refused; I was being asked, not ordered. The only reason I could have for refusing was that I had never done that sort of thing before. But why not try? I accepted, probably hoping that acceptance without demur would help improve my reputation.

The trouble was that I had to do it after school hours. Being winter, the natural light faded early. I sat working by the window until the interior lights were switched on and black on black became impossible to distinguish. It took months, but I succeeded in finishing the bonnet, and the old sister was grateful to have it at last. That very evening, I saw it being taken apart. It obviously hadn't met the standard. I glanced at the old sister, who blushed sheepishly and kindly tried to smile at me. No one ever spoke a direct word to me about the ill-fated bonnet, and no one showed me how it should have been done.

MY PARENTS HAD embarked on a trip from Australia to Holland, and decided to call in on me in Belgium. It was wonderful: I was overcome with indescribable emotion to see them again, and they were so happy to see me. 'How are you, Carla?' asked my mother, watching me closely. I hesitated. What I wanted to do was break down and tell her how miserable I was, but my face managed a dead calm. I was totally constrained by my loyalty to the order: never disclose anything unpleasant to an outsider.

Mother Josephine was as hospitable towards my parents as if they were a king and queen. Graciousness oozed out of her. There was no shortage of cakes for tea, and they were given a guided tour, culminating in the chapel. They weren't shown the nuns' quarters, however, or the place where their daughter slept. If they had, my father would have approved of the horsehair mattress! All the while, I was dying to come clean with them and tell them about my life. A huge desire welled up in me to ask them to take me away, please! The terrible longing I'd had as a six year old for my parents to hug me and make me feel wanted came over me again. Nothing happened when I was six, and nothing happened then. Inevitably, the time for goodbyes came and then they were gone.

I WOKE UP on Christmas morning in my attic dormitory and looked out of the tiny window set in the sloping roof to see snow lying over the rooftops and the street below, like a silent cloak in the pre-dawn light. It was a magical morning. I broke the ice on my basin of water and washed myself.

On Christmas afternoon, the young ones in the community had a great time shovelling and sweeping snow from the wide flagstoned footpath in front of the convent. Large shovels and stiff brooms helped us pile the broken snow into the street gutter. About a dozen of us worked for more than three hours.

A few days later, there was fresh snow. It melted a bit, then froze over, and we were sent down to scrape it off with salt and spades. An elderly couple passed by, watching us. If only I hadn't looked up to catch the eyes of the elderly man; as if cursed by looking at me, he slipped, falling heavily on the ice. His wife helped him to his feet again as he moaned with surprise and pain. None of us spoke or went to his rescue: the rule of silence set us apart, kept us from being human.

The boarders had gone home for the Christmas season, so the whole community went into a three-day retreat, as was usual in the holidays. A Jesuit priest was hired to lead the retreat, and gave inspirational talks in the chapel twice a day. Here was an opportunity to improve my French; I hadn't been able to listen to so much of it ever before! Lord knows what it was like for the unfortunate priest, who was required to speak enthusiastically to a group of women who sat there like statues and, out of prudery, never even looked at him. I sometimes glanced at him, and realised he must have been instructed not to catch any nun's eye. Instead, he enthusiastically addressed the statues and the wall at the back of the chapel!

For the rest of the retreat time, free from the daily grind of teaching, I escaped into blissful trances. When I was without any pressure to perform, a sun would burst forth in my heart, filling it with joy. My body would relax into delicious feelings with the slightest prod: the sight of a single flower somewhere, the sound of a bird.

I started to write a letter to my family during this Christmas break; the only letter I managed to send during my entire six-month stay at Montjoie. It took me more than two months to finish it, because, incredibly, I was given only one sheet of paper each time I put in a request, and it took several days before each (written) request was granted. The stationery was kept by a nun who had grown grumpy and graceless from the loss of female hormones. She seemed to think it her duty to frustrate my requests for paper, an envelope and a stamp, turning the process into a silent, tortuous saga.

My mother noted that the four-page letter was dated 26 December, but didn't get to her until March. It was this, as well as what I had written, that made her anxious about my welfare. I admire my mother for her perspicacity, for the letter was cheerful enough in the way it was written. Alarm bells went off, however, when she read the remarks I made about the recent retreat. *'You know, you can be miserable and sorrowful, and as poor and isolated as a church mouse, and still be happy, so long as you are not God-forsaken.'*

My mother started asking questions about why I hadn't come back to Australia with the others. She directed her questions to the superior at Genazzano, insisting that she write away to England. After a while, she put her foot down and demanded answers, feeling that something was really wrong. It was my mother who got me out of Brussels; but not before another two more months had gone by.

DURING THAT TIME, a pupil asked for English lessons, as she was going to live in England shortly. I was asked whether I'd be interested in coaching her and I agreed with pleasure. When asked by her parents what I would charge — as if I had any clue at all about Belgian currency or the going rate per hour for tuition — I simply said 'Not much!' and that was all they got out of me over the next weeks.

The girl was about sixteen and we got on famously. She taught me a good deal of French, so I felt well rewarded. We had our lessons in a tiny music room that smelled of its teak walls. It had the usual creaking floor, with a low window, below waist level, which overlooked the playground. The tuition progressed well and did wonders for my self-esteem, because here was someone who expressed only gratitude! It was fun. When it was time for her to leave and I still hadn't stipulated my fee, her father gave a rather large sum to the convent. The nun in charge of accounts made a public announcement about the generous gift at the lunch table, acknowledging my contribution. In one fell swoop, I had redeemed myself in that place and it felt very good. I never found out how much money I earned for them.

Something in me changed after that little incident. My relations with the general community continued as before — everyone was very busy with their work, and diluted to invisibility for most of the day in the vastness of that establishment — but I began talking to the lay sisters, to maintain the feeling of being a human which I had recently gained.

In contrast to the teaching nuns, the lay sisters were a much more cohesive bunch. They worked together in the laundry, the kitchen and the scullery. I joined them after meals when I could, helping to dry the dishes. I enjoyed their company and also sensed a certain independence and assertiveness among them. They were simple, kind, uncomplaining and dedicated women, with only one exception.

This woman had a big mouth, always speaking up when lay sisters should not be seen or heard. The most that was expected of them was to contribute a funny anecdote now and then; for the rest of the time, their assumed lesser intelligence demanded their subservient silence. The lay sisters accepted their lower-class status, except for Sister Bigmouth, Soeur Patrice. Soeur Patrice had a way of stating the truth, to the frequent embarrassment of Mother Josephine and her offsiders. She didn't mind arguing with them either, and often refused to obey a command to stop. I found her funny, daring, courageous, stupid and enlightening. She definitely served to diffuse some of the unquestioned reverence for the superior that reigned in the chateau, and brought things down to earth a bit.

One day, Soeur Patrice announced that she thought the girls were not being given the right kind of food. Mother Josephine was trying to save by scrimping on food bills. There was a revolt, not long after, in the senior girls' refectory: they declared it was dog food and refused to eat it. It was a highly embarrassing incident. This was a crisis Mother Josephine had to field with all of her skill. The storm was weathered, as all storms were, but it could have easily been prevented if the wisdom and honesty of one angry lay sister had counted for anything.

I began to absorb the camaraderie among the lay sisters; it was the secret to their perseverance in that convent sweatshop. They all came from a peasant Flemish background and were used to hard work. They probably knew that life out there would not be any better, most likely worse. Here at least they had some security, and would be looked after in later life if they needed care. In those days, not having a husband might have been a good thing: the astute could opt for a life in a convent. I got to know these women well and they were far from naive.

One of them, Soeur Helene, was totally self-effacing. She was delicate with a thin, angelic face and a smile in her slightly crossed but calm eyes. I never heard her speak; she was either very loyal to the rule of silence or perhaps she had a speech impediment. She didn't seem to need to speak. This little sister was a balm to my soul; there was a consistent feeling of peace and kindness about her. She would look at me occasionally with those quiet eyes and any soreness in my heart would disappear.

I began to talk to the sisters as I worked with them. It was against the rules, but the little bunch of washer-uppers had agreed that talking was necessary for their sanity. They spoke about what they thought was happening on the floors above them (they worked in the basement), and since they were never told about the things that weren't supposed to concern them, like happenings in the schools, they made it their business to find out for themselves. There was always a fair amount of gossip and laughter. I joined in with guffaws which made them warn me to be more quiet!

I had found an underclass in them that I identified with. They seemed to understand that even though I was a visitor and a teacher, I was not in the hierarchy's good books, and young and vulnerable. They trusted me, and gave me to understand that they were behind me.

Soeur Helene showed me something strange and wonderful one day. She motioned for me to follow her and opened a cleaning cupboard. There I espied a statue of the Black Madonna, hidden in a corner. Just looking at it made my hair stand on end. There was a curious energy about it; her features were strong, not pretty or sweet, and her colour was black, with a shiny finish, giving the impression of sweat on her face and on the infant in her arms.

Why was the statue hidden in that cupboard and not standing in some venerated place like a great many other statues, such as The Little Infant of Prague, Saint Philomena, Saint Anthony, Saint Joseph, and Our Lady of This, That and The Other? And why did the little sister show it to me in such a surreptitious way? She watched my face intently all the time, and I felt that the statue was somehow not kosher, or had unappreciated influences. Now, I wonder if the objections were racist. A *black* Madonna! I had heard of one in Russia, where a secret Catholic movement was challenging the official Communism, but Russians were not like the rest of the world — they were feared as subversive. The Spanish also venerated a black Santa Maria at Montserrat, but at the time I didn't know about her; nor, most likely, did anyone else in the superstitious and judgmental Belgium of the 1960s.

I loved the statue so much that I thought of stealing her. The sight of her stuck away in a dark cleaning cupboard as though she were evil, simply because she was different, brought tears to my eyes. I must have identified with her plight and, symbolically, wanted to rescue myself by carrying her off. Sadly, I didn't think I had the right and left the statue there. Over the years, I have often wondered what became of her.

I BEGAN TO experience nightmares. The old attic where I slept was not only creaky, dusty, draughty and cold, but had dark, unfathomable corners. At night it was easy to imagine that some stranger was prowling around. Maybe a man would get in through the unlined tiled roof of the attic. There were so many Belgians disgruntled with the convent's involvement with the Americans in Brussels that Mother Josephine took me seriously when, one night, I knocked on her door in a nervous state, convinced that I had heard the footsteps of a man.

She called the porter nun and they searched up and down the attic with powerful torches. There was no one there, except perhaps the many ghosts of centuries gone by that worried me on other nights. They were plentiful, bringing with them shades of ghastly memories of times I felt I had surely known.

One day I was creaking along the corridors when Mother Josephine stopped me and stood in front of me. She was the shorter and so looked up at me. Her face had an expression that I couldn't read, and what she said was a complete shock to me.

'Sister Carla, I am sorry —' she began.

'It's all right,' I interrupted quickly, wanting to spare her the trouble of whatever she was about to say.

Mother Josephine seemed to push aside some annoyance. She started again: 'I am sorry —'

Again I interrupted her, feeling strangely panicky. She gave up and walked on. I was stunned. Had she intended this to be a confession? Was she trying to make up for something? I never found out. I let her off the hook, which didn't do me, or her, any good, but there it was.

SUDDENLY, THANKS TO my mother's insistence that I be sent back to Australia or she would personally go to fetch me, I was told to leave. An agitated Mother Josephine came to me with the news that I would travel to Broadstairs the next morning. There was no time to arrange anyone to replace me, I was to leave as soon as possible; those were the orders from the General. There was an unusual urgency in Mother Josephine's manner and she looked sickly pale. I was stunned, confused and pleased, but there was no time to get emotional, or say goodbye, or any of those things. My passport was in order now and in Mother Josephine's hands. My suitcase was retrieved from the storeroom and I quickly packed.

We were up at four in the dark of morning. I stuffed some cold cereal and an unripe banana into my unwilling stomach, pulled on my gloves with the pathetic holes, and Mother Josephine and I were on our way to the port in a taxi.

Once more I was on a ferry, this time going from Ostend to Dover, with some farmers for company. They were sympathetically inclined towards the uncomfortable-looking nun passengers.

'*C'est très dur*,' said one of them after a while. He had been studying our faces, which were white and drawn. I was fighting seasickness, something I had never before experienced on an ocean liner, but the green banana in my stomach would not go down.

In the end, nature got the better of me. No time to explain, no time to ask where the toilets were — those things we always pretended we never needed in public. I blindly made it to the passageway, blundered into the lavatories and threw up. I gagged again at the awful mess in the washbowl. It didn't wash away all that well. I came back quietly to my place beside Mother Josephine, who was preoccupied with her own thoughts. Murmurs of sympathy came from the farmers, whom I didn't dare look in the face.

We were sitting there, lurching gently, when Mother Josephine handed me something to read. It was a small booklet called *How to Improve Your Willpower*. It contained a good deal of pop psychology about the benefits of a strong will, which I took literally at the time, especially as it was given me by my superior. I assumed that she had chosen it especially to help me. I was so grateful, and even felt that Mother Josephine was sharing a secret with me — one of her personal strategies, perhaps. The implication that I had a weak will didn't matter!

I kept that tiny booklet for several years. With each exercise — like shredding ten sheets of paper slowly into a hundred pieces —

I conjured up the feeling of a strong will. I thought it was exactly what I needed: more control over my feelings. Mother Josephine's iron will became my model; a desperate hope for control that would eventually collapse. But during those years it helped me to be stoic, to remain unmoved by whatever the gods or God might send to try me. That is how *I* wanted things to be. The gods or God had other things in mind.

BACK AT THE London convent, I met the nun with whom I would share the journey back to Australia. Sister Marian had just finished a few months of retraining at Stella Maris. She was an introvert who seemed always to be aware of her surroundings. She liked keeping her mouth shut even when the rules allowed her to speak; for example, when travelling at sea.

Our voyage back to Melbourne was uneventful. Taciturn Sister Marian steeped herself in a book most of the time, but there was one memorable break in her silence when we left the boat during a stopover at Calcutta, to find the Jesuit monastery to go to confession.

My first glimpse of the Indian people moved me deeply. From our ship, I watched a small group of children dancing outdoors with their teacher. The grace and ease of their movements had me enthralled. When we alighted, we were met by a woman whose handshake I shall always remember because of its feminine fluidity. In it, she carried the grace of the Ganges, the soft winds of her country, everything that flows naturally. She smiled warmly but shyly, and I lowered my curious eyes that seemed to embarrass her.

Sister Marian and I began the long walk to the monastery. She seemed to have a map in her head and walked resolutely, as if she did this every day of her life. She obviously had been given accurate instructions on where to go, how to get there and how to behave in these unfamiliar surroundings. All I needed to do was copy her. There was no communication between us as we walked.

We ignored the groups of children who crowded around us, asking for money. They didn't see us as holy people — how could they? Our dress and our skin showed that we were foreigners. I noticed bodies in the gutters of Calcutta, immobile, either drunk, asleep or dead. I saw flies on the meat as it hung in stalls open to the street. I saw many faces crowding the pavement, cameos of lives, snapshots in my mind.

We made it to the oasis of the monastery and were cordially received by the Father in charge. Sister Marian untied her tongue and did all the talking, which was just as well as I seemed to have forgotten how to carry on a normal conversation.

We were ushered into a cool parlour and treated to the finest cup of tea I've ever tasted. Whether it was the heat, or the fact this was the purest Ceylon tea, or that it had been prepared with so much care by the young priest who served it, I couldn't tell. Perhaps it was a unique combination of these things. What was certain was the magic of the young priest, for he enchanted me with his touch as he shook my hand. Electricity flowed between us, forming an instant bond, and I smiled happily at his young face, which beamed back at me. He was truly delighted that I liked the tea so much.

We were shown to the confessionals in the quiet haven that was their chapel: cool, with the scent of sweet incense in the air. The confession itself was a gruelling and humiliating experience. Having met the senior priest personally, I now had to tell him how awful I was. Feeling a terrible cringing inside my chest, I told him how I'd had sexual fantasies. I quickly added that I had also had rebellious thoughts — they were less sordid than sexual feelings ... It was all so pathetic. Why did a beautiful afternoon have to be spoiled with this sort of soul-baring? After all, it was a one-way contract: the confessor told neither of us what went on in *his* secret mind! Never, ever, would a priest officially confide his sins to a woman.

We shook hands again, the young priest and I, to say goodbye. His masculine hand clasped mine with warmth and firmness. Three years later he turned up at my convent in Australia to see me. I wasn't there at the time, and wasn't told about his visit until months later, when no one could remember his name nor where he came from. It was one of those strange incidents that made me wonder: were we meant to meet? But if so, then why didn't we? What difference might it have made if we had met again?

Why do human beings wonder about these things?

WELCOME HOME, SISTER

 MY FACE HAD become pale from the longest winter ever, but my mother knew I would be all right again now that I was back in Australia — even if it was at the beginning of yet another winter. Her face glowed triumphantly when she and my father came to see me. My father grinned with pleasure. I would not stay long at Genazzano, however. I was needed in a country school and no time was wasted in getting me there. It was the middle of 1965.

Sister Marian and I were taken by car to sleepy Benalla, a country town in Victoria with one Catholic church and two adjacent schools, both taken care of by the FCJs.

That day — the first in my new community of eleven teaching nuns and one lay sister — was a chance for a new life, a productive life at last, a life with no history, or so I thought. Only two people — Sister Anna, who had entered a year after me, and Sister Madeleine, a year older than me, and both of whom I could trust — had known me before. Sister Marian had been my companion on board ship, but I discounted that short time. The Reverend Mother had never seen me before in her life.

There were such things as personal reports, of course, with the power to establish a view of someone as yet unknown and unproven in a new community, and such a report naturally had preceded me.

In my keen expectation of a new start in convent life, I had forgotten that this would be the case.

At the first evening gathering around the common-room table, which concluded with some practical announcements, Reverend Mother Clare ended with, 'We need someone to take on the job of waking us at 5.30 am. Is there a volunteer?' I saw an opportunity for proving myself willing and useful. 'Yes; *I* will,' I said quickly, and wondered why my offer was not taken up immediately. Reverend Mother Clare smiled ruefully, but not at me, and then said to all the listening ears, 'All right, Sister Mary Carla will be given the bell. We can expect anything to happen now.'

My heart stopped. Why had she said this? A soft murmur of giggles went through the gathering. They had understood the joke, which was obviously based on information shared before I had even arrived. A young person's reputation was of no importance to the Reverend. She wasn't intentionally cruel, just pressured from being in charge when she wasn't well suited to the task. My heart sank, but I knew that I would do this job perfectly.

THE CONVENT WAS on a small acreage, a couple of hundred kilometres north of Melbourne, and inland. The winters were chilblain frosty. 'Our Lady of the Angels' was carved in stone relief on an archway over the front porch. In front of the building was a garden large enough for a car to turn full circle; at the back was the playground for the schoolchildren and the convent's vegetable garden and chicken yard. The small size of the community fostered friendly interaction; the beauty of the rooms and their brightness induced a feeling of homeliness and relaxation. It was such a change from the comfortless spaces the nuns had to put up with at Genazzano.

The thirty or so boarders were farmers' daughters whose homes were too far away for daily travel. There were also a few boys, but they were day pupils. All the dorms were upstairs, accessible by two sets of stairs: one at the back of the building, used by the boarders and young or able nuns, and a beautifully polished and curved wooden staircase close to the chapel door, used only by the superior and the senior nuns, to spare their legs. Apart from Anna, Madeleine, Marian and myself, the household was middle-aged or older.

Sister Marian was the infirmarian, but a number of nuns were trained to look after the sick in order to minimise contact with male doctors. Sister Madeleine was a small, sweet nun, with rotund, pale cheeks, beseeching eyes, a shy little smile and a soft voice. She was given to hiding in a corner. She and Sister Anna — who was more robust than Madeleine in every way, bright, fairly tall, talented in English and sewing — became my friends. We shared a freshness of mind because of our youthfulness, and would later team up against the forces that mistrusted youth.

The oldest nun in our community, Sister Imelda, was a wispy woman with rumpled hands who worked magic on the piano and organ. She was the unassuming elder of two music mistresses. She could hardly see, had wrinkles all over her kindly blind face, a large, spongy nose and a very wide smile. When Sister Imelda spoke, which wasn't often, it was music that came out of her mouth: she had the proverbial melodious voice. One of the things she never wanted was to be in charge of anything. Whenever she was asked to take on authority, such as in the temporary absence of the Reverend, she would always smilingly shake her head, never even uttering the word 'no'.

As I was the newest arrival, it immediately became my job to keep the corridors and the common room spotless and shiny. I'd had plenty of experience in this sort of thing! And because I had gained craft skills at college, I was given the delightful task of dreaming up themes for festive days and making the decorations. The convent became a hive for one feast day: bees galore festooned the refectory, attached by strings to the rafters, and everyone had to choose a card with a message beginning with B, such as 'Be happy' or 'Before it is too late'. Next came a wondrous butterfly theme; and on another day, an ocean made the refectory swim with magic fish. The immediate effect of this kind of happy occupation was that I was no longer constipated; after more than ten years, my intestines were suddenly perfectly functional again. I felt a precious sense of usefulness.

I WAS ECSTATIC to be assigned the job of teaching art and craft to several classes of children of different ages. It was so good to have direct human contact and feel useful. I noticed, however, that I was not made a class mistress, and was never trusted with the responsibility for the wellbeing of any particular class. Even in times of dire need, or if anyone was sick, I was never even temporarily placed in charge of a class. Was it an order from above? Whatever it was, I tried not to think about it. It might have been more helpful had I been encouraged to grow in confidence, but self-affirming psychology wasn't a strong feature of religious life. Unavoidably, as a result of this unspoken and unbending mistrust, I was never fully integrated into the community, in spite of my best efforts and in spite of the otherwise happy environment.

I soon discovered that my training at Sedgley College had not prepared me for secondary-school dynamics, nor given me any organisational skills. We had been taught content (what to teach), and the principles of learning (how children learned). Thank goodness I had gained some practical experience in the schools of Manchester, watching veteran teachers at work and having a crack at teaching myself.

That was two years ago. Now I had to learn as I went and I enjoyed the challenge. After all, maintaining discipline among Catholic girls was a cinch. These girls were so passive! In art classes I had trouble stirring up any kind of passion in them to get them to express themselves in paint and colour. I brought a tape recorder to class and played evocative music, but they just looked at me helplessly and could only produce shadows of the ideas I put before them. They were practical farmers' girls with an 'I-hope-this-will-do' attitude to creativity. The older the children, the lower their ability to be experimental. I went for bold colour instead, and at the end of the year we managed to put on a bright exhibition.

My other responsibility was needlework and I had a rich store of experience in this field. I loved creating with stitches and fabric. The farmers' daughters, unfortunately, took badly to fancy needlework — broderie anglaise, shadow work and such — which was done only for show. They would have been better off learning how to put together overalls and aprons. The standard I elicited from them was questioned by a visiting inspector. I don't know what pieces he criticised since I wasn't there when he examined their work. He left without giving me any ideas on how to improve the situation. Maybe he was the apron and overalls type too.

In time, I became almost like one of the family. A precious camaraderie flourished among the members of our small community in spite of the rule of silence. We cleaned the chapel as a team, well organised by the nun in charge. On a sunny day, we would all lift the pews together and take them out onto the front lawn. The old wood was cleaned and polished, the floor dewaxed and waxed anew, the stained-glass windows washed, and all the silver and copperware for the altar polished. To keep our arms free, we tied up our shawls and aprons. I became acutely aware of my inadvertently revealed figure at those times and those of my sisters. A travelling salesman happened to call in during one of our cleaning sprees, catching a number of us outside in working mode. He caused a fast retreat and was left standing alone among our undusted pews.

I settled into the feeling of belonging to a group of people whose lives, like mine, were dedicated to God, and who were mostly kind and humorous. My perception of how convent life might be was realised at last, in this little place in the country. For many years after leaving, it was this intensified and idealised feeling of community that I searched for in my dreams. I had a recurring dream in which the nuns I looked for were standing in the vegetable patch. As I approached they looked up and said to each other, 'Here she comes again; I wonder how long she'll stay this time?' I would wonder, then, how many times I had indeed been back, and why I had left again and again. I would fall on my knees and tell them how much I loved God and wanted to serve him, and they always allowed me to try again. I wore a strange mixture of habit and secular clothes in those dreams, and once I was there, I would wonder why I had returned. When I got really close to the nuns, a dark cold chilly energy, like an angry wind, would hit me and I knew it couldn't last.

Our lay sister at Benalla was a tiny woman with a harelip, whose eyes shone mischievously through round metal-rimmed glasses. Sister Antoinette was no longer young when I knew her, but in spite of her size and middle age she was undaunted by any task. She was the cook-in-charge and prepared meals for all the nuns and boarders with panache. She was Irish and missed her homeland sorely, having been sent to Australia when she was only twenty. As the sole lay sister, she was doubly lonely. She wasn't included in any of the discussions about the main business of the convent — the running of the boarding school or the parish primary school. She was just a workhorse.

Sister Antoinette and I became good friends. I enjoyed helping her out in the kitchen. One week she and I made ginger beer. The recipe was deceptively simple, and for eight days or so we added sugar and ground ginger to the 'plant'. Finally, it was time to put the liquid into the bottles we had scrounged from all around. So far, so good.

While we were having breakfast a few weeks later, an explosion rocked our silent thoughts. It came from the kitchen cellar, and one glance at Sister Antoinette told me what was going on. I caught her looking helplessly at Reverend Mother, with a twinkle in her eyes in spite of the tragedy going on below us.

The first explosion was followed by another a few moments later, and soon there was a veritable barrage. Breakfast continued in silence as if nothing were happening. All we could do was wait until it was certain that the last bottle had exploded and then deal with the mess. Sister Antoinette did not have to ask for help for this job — everybody pitched in to remove the shards and slivers of glass embedded in our vegetables and cheeses, as well as in the walls. It was a mammoth task. Ginger beer-making was never attempted again, not least because it proved to be alcoholic instead of a pleasant-tasting ginger-lemonade.

I would have done anything for Sister Antoinette because she was humble and ordinary, friendly and non-judgmental. She also had a reliable sense of humour. She often helped me to laugh at myself, God bless her kind soul. In the end, she was forced to watch me grow distressed beyond redemption, looking on in her quiet way. But she was always there for me, she always prayed for me, and her prayers were genuine; her heart never judged.

We both loved the garden and the chicken run. The vegetable patch could never keep up with the demands of nearly forty-five people, but the chooks laid all the eggs we wanted and more. Many an hour was spent spreading Vaseline over the shells to preserve them for future cakes and other recipes when the chooks went off the lay. I asked Sister Antoinette to show me how to make patty cakes — I still have her recipe in my scrapbook of favourite things.

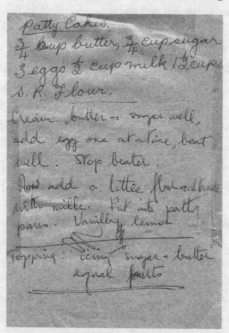

'Sister,' I said one day when I had some time on my hands, 'I'll clean the kitchen windows for you.'

'Don't you worry about that, now,' came Sister Antoinette's swift reply. 'The windows are dirty because they are much too high up and nobody can reach them.'

It was true; the windows reached nearly to the ceiling, which was very high up indeed. They hadn't been washed for years, the top parts perhaps never, and this meant the kitchen never felt as sparkling clean as a good kitchen should.

Antoinette knew it wasn't possible to stop me from carrying out a good deed once I got hold of the idea, but she tried to warn me. 'Take care, now, Carla.' She eyed the wooden ladder I'd dragged inside. 'Those steps get slippery when they get water on them. So don't get them wet. And make sure now that you don't touch the sides of that hot urn.'

I climbed up with a bucket of water in one hand and a cloth in the other. I looked down — Sister Antoinette was praying for me, I could tell! Just below to my left was the large electric urn, full of water and close to boiling.

I was near the top of the ladder when my lace-up shoe with its shiny leather sole slipped. The bucket left my hand and dropped violently, and I came down just as swiftly, the sleeve of my habit catching the boiler's frame. The boiler let go of me — as if by a miracle — but my body landed sideways on the edge of the large stainless steel washbasin below.

The commotion attracted the attention of the infirmarian. My upper right leg was severely bruised; the flesh visibly impacted by the fall. 'Get yourself into a bath and soak in it,' prescribed Sister Marian, in her casual manner.

Well, it was better than nothing, given her attitude of 'no malingering in *this* convent!' An application of arnica, even some Epsom salts in the bath water, might have done some good, but alas, convent infirmarians were no herbalists. Herbal wisdom, once the province of monasteries and convents, had been neglected due to the new reverence given to science. My thigh retained a deep dented mass of damaged scar tissue. For a few days I had a limp, then forced myself to ignore it, the same as I tried to ignore the rest of my body.

Something else clamoured for attention, however; a disagreeable disfigurement on my hands: *warts*. My hands were once so beautiful that Sister Marian had taken photographs of them, and my novice mistress used to sit and gaze at them. I wasn't supposed to know this, but I did, the way people do who, for their own survival, have to guess all the time what others around them are thinking. Secretly I lapped up the adulation, but then, of course, came the guilt after the pride, and the inevitable self-punishment. So I grew warts, a large one on my left thumb and several spread over my fingers. Not exactly the thing for a teacher of needlework and craft, whose hands were always on show. The warts might prove risky in handling food as well, so it was decided that they had to come off — at the hospital.

Benalla Hospital had never had a nun within its walls before. They did the best they knew, putting me under a general anaesthetic. Perhaps the anaesthetist thought it took a lot to knock out a nun, because he gave me such a large dose that I didn't wake up for a very long time and then just long enough to vomit all over the floor. A woman patient sharing my room looked on helplessly as she watched me struggle not to vomit, and fail. By the time assistance arrived I had slumped back into unconsciousness.

'Sister Mary Carla will not be going home until tomorrow,' my enquiring superior was told.

I was feted as the Sleeping Beauty on my return, and my swathed hands were kept away from work for a few days. At recreation time I was teased. 'Sister, you didn't keep your rule of silence while you were under!'

'What? What did I say?' Nobody would tell me, and I blushed to imagine what on earth could be so unrepeatable. Ah well, *que sera, sera*; what else could I do except shrug off the uncomfortable thought and join in with the laughter.

RAISING MONEY WAS a constant affair for the convent and the school, and each year a fête was organised for that purpose. They were busy events, not especially memorable, except for the time when I took charge of a stall. Numbers matching numbered prizes were scribbled on pieces of paper and, together with a few blanks, were placed in a cotton-string bag. For twenty cents, people could try their luck. The most coveted prize was a good bottle of sherry. I soon noticed that it was the bottle that drew the gamblers, so didn't want to lose it too soon. I looked up the ticket with the bottle's number and pocketed it. Somebody else took over from me while I wandered about, looking at the sights and taking advantage of the relaxed rule of silence to talk to parents and children.

When I looked around again I caught the quizzical and half-alarmed eye of my offsider; there were only three prizes left, with the bottle still sitting ever more lonely on the top shelf and a determined punter going crazy trying to win it! Swiftly I seized the bag and returned the ticket in less time than it takes to look around — too fast for anyone to suspect that they had been swindled. Luckily for me the bottle finally went to the right person, who was uncomplaining in spite of having paid for so many tickets. Why didn't she suspect something? Was it that unthinkable that nuns might cheat? Probably. I was an undiscovered rogue nun, but I was praised for the great success of the stall and that was all that mattered.

WHEN I WAS a girl at Vaucluse College, I had been taught by Sister Anthony that kissing made you pregnant. That wasn't such bad information in itself, being a half-truth, except that nothing was ever added to that initial, shattering revelation. Sister Anthony had either been ignorant herself, or unwilling to divulge any more. Now I too was participating in the cult of disguised ignorance.

I was nearly thirty-one when I found out where babies came from — and fifty-four before I discovered why *kissing makes you pregnant* had produced that vivid image of semen travelling down my throat when I was seventeen. My knowledge of things sexual took a giant leap when the convent finally obeyed a directive from the bishop to provide pupils with proper sex education, following reforms instigated by Pope John XXIII.

The person to teach it was Father Gregory, our senior parish priest, after heavy persuasion by the nuns. In the summer of 1967, the nervously sweating man visited the convent to explain conception to a hallful of students. As a teacher, I was allowed to sit in.

Father Gregory presented a slide of the statue of David by Michelangelo. The projection was a shadowy image that made it difficult to work out what and where the testicles were that the priest was talking about. Inside the body, were they? And what was the scrotum? One thing was for sure: the penis was on the outside and we were told it had to go inside a woman's most private parts, called the vagina, to cause conception.

Well, that was one piece of information that just couldn't be true! The idea was so hugely gross that my mind couldn't register it. It reeled at the thought of a woman taking off her knickers, exposing herself to a man who had *his* pants off too, and him sticking his — *penis*? What an *ugly* word! — anyway, the thing that he peed out of into the woman! Outrageous! Abominable! No wonder Jesus opted to be born of a virgin, who never had to suffer such debasing goings-on!

My burning mind clung desperately to what I'd learned when I was seventeen: *kissing* makes you pregnant! Maybe the priest was wrong. Look at how he was sweating! Something wasn't right, for sure. Mercifully, a question box was circulated and questions could be anonymous.

'Is there any other way a baby could be conceived?'

My question was read out by the priest in the half-light. My heart stopped. It sounded such an ignorant question, and of course it was. The answer came like the sentence of a judge in court — final, irrevocable, no longer deniable.

'No, this is the only known way, except in the case of the Immaculate Conception.'

I'd been duped! Rage against Sister Anthony's sex education boiled in me, but most of all I was overcome by shattering humiliation and shame. Shame at my ignorance; shame at my parents; shame at *all* parents who were now 'exposed'. I felt shame at the thought of adults copulating all over the world to produce all those children; shame at the beauty of romance destroyed. All these thoughts rioted through my mind, threatening to fuse my brain. Audrey Hepburn, Bing Crosby, Grace Kelly — *how could you do it*? How could anyone look so innocent and do such things?

The mother of one of the girls stood up. Here was a woman who had 'done it'. As I looked at her, the question in my mind was not 'Had it corrupted her?'(I took that for granted), but 'How was that corruption visible?'

She was about forty, had permed hair, and held herself quite steady on her feet. She wasn't pretty, and she wasn't scared to speak. She seemed unaffected by the electricity in the air. 'You didn't say,' she addressed the priest, 'that the sexual act is very pleasurable.'

Silence. She continued. 'It isn't just a functional act. It can be highly enjoyable, and you never mentioned that.'

My mind went into a further state of shock at this woman's words. I felt that she had openly betrayed her fellow adults by this statement. She had let out a secret, an adult secret, to a hallful of adolescents. It was like publicly proclaiming to children that Santa Claus wasn't real; it set the seal on the destruction of innocence.

Father Gregory fumbled with the papers in his hand. No sound came from him, just a nod of approval, or of admission. He didn't say, 'Is that so?', which he should have, since he was a priest and shouldn't know about such things. But someone might have told him, or he might have read about it ... My brain-on-fire was trying to save him. It was significant, of course, that he hadn't mentioned the pleasurable side of sex. That was a message in itself, which sank into all the minds in that packed and steamy little hall, for each to interpret for herself.

This woman had touched on the main reason why sex was

reprehensible: it was obviously *perversely pleasurable*. Obviously perverse? Oh yes, otherwise it would have been mentionable in the first place.

Naturally, Jesus was not conceived like other people; he was born of a virgin, untouched by a human penis. The inferences are clear: conception is sullied by sexual intercourse, and normal human birth is therefore inferior.

Human beings hadn't yet figured out how to give birth without having sex. As it is difficult to populate the earth without sex (and so make the Catholic Church grow) sexual activities somehow had to be condoned. So the Catholic Church had made up a sacrament called Holy Matrimony, or marriage, a concession to human frailty. Sex was to be strictly for the purpose of procreation. And a church which had put so much energy into sanctifying pain could hardly sanctify the pleasures of sexual intercourse ...

The lecture was over. Unable to risk meeting the glances of any of the girls or my sister nuns, I left the hall and slipped into the chapel. There I knelt bolt upright, stiff with embarrassment at my own extreme ignorance, cheeks ablaze. I stared at the tabernacle with a huge question mark on my face, but no enlightenment came forth from the silent space on the altar. God appeared to be totally indifferent to my dilemma: how to absorb the shame?

'Yes, well, I ... er, made people this way, yes, but well ... er ... at least my Son was born of a Virgin! That's the best I could do. You were born in original sin. At least I sent my Son to save you from your sinfulness. I created temptation, but Adam and Eve should have been strong enough to resist it. Too bad; it's done now. And didn't you throw away that booklet your mother gave you when you were seventeen? There were libraries in your world — why didn't you ever get out a book on sex?'

Yes, it was true: I seemed to have deliberately not wanted to know anything. *Why?*

Time ticked by, but I didn't notice. At last, there was an urgent whisper from Sister Madeleine at the door. 'Sister Mary Carla, it's time for reading!' It was six o'clock. School had been out since four. I flew to the common room and took my place among my sisters, who mercifully had their heads bowed to listen to the text being read by our superior. I didn't hear a word she said. For the hundredth time, I tried to put away the image of a penis entering a vagina.

I had many torrid dreams in the months to come, followed by repetitive weekly confessions to the priest. Who knows what words escaped my dreaming mouth in the dead of night? It was not for nothing that I was never chosen to be a dormitory mistress, one who slept in the same room as the boarders. But what had been stirred up that afternoon started to melt a kind of ice within me, awakening feelings that I grew to not entirely dislike.

Within a few weeks, the tone of my confession had changed. 'Father, I don't think these feelings are sinful. I think they're natural.'

The priest sighed. He wasn't game to venture an opinion. 'I think you should discuss this with your bishop,' was his careful reply.

NOT SO FAST, SISTER

OUR GENERAL WAS suddenly deposed in 1965 amidst turbulent events in England which were kept as quiet as possible elsewhere. In Australia we were simply told that she had resigned for health reasons. For months the FCJs was without a General, then, in the following year, an Irish woman with a sparkling social talent and a brilliant gift for organising, Mother Raphael, took over the post. It was now up to her to get things moving; it would be like trying to turn a dinosaur into a gazelle. Margaret Winchester had been made General in 1948, and had stayed on for nineteen years.

When the General died in 1967, her death provoked such little ceremony that I can't remember exactly when it happened. What I do remember is the shocking announcement Mother Clare made about her, on a day when we heard more than one thing that would change our lives for ever.

Reverend Mother Clare was nervous — we could tell by the colour of her cheeks. They usually had an attractive bloom, which ruddied when she got excited or stressed. On that day, her face was blotchy and held an ambiguous smile while she fidgeted with the papers in her hands. Her back and neck were stiff as she moved; another sign of stress.

We were asked to put away our needlework, the better to listen to a special announcement. Everybody knew then that something serious was afoot and the room came to perfect silence. We sat with our eyes down, holding the tension.

'The announcement I am to give you is a formal public notice, worded in legal language,' Mother Clare began. Then, before she uttered the news, she took on her sternest tone: 'You are *never* to comment upon what you are about to hear, as a mark of loyalty to our late Mother General, whom we have all revered.'

We could hardly believe what we were hearing, or what came out of her mouth next.

'Margaret Ellen Winchester,' read Mother Clare, 'formerly known as Superior General of the Order of the Faithful Companions of Jesus from 1948 to 1965, has been declared to have been of unsound mind during the last three years of her life. In view of her insanity, it is not possible to attribute to her any form of malicious wrongdoing.'

We drew in a collective deep breath. Had we heard right? *Insane!* Our General, mentally ill to the degree of insanity, *therefore not held responsible for her actions*? I smiled into my lap, ruefully gratified at hearing these words spoken in public in our private domain. Would this have to formally appear in the newspapers? But my mind was working overtime. The events pertaining to the reign and deposition of Madame Winchester were to be kept secret in archives in the Bishop of London's residence. I suspect that Mother Clare made a mistake in reading that announcement to her community. As far as I can make out, it was not repeated in any other convent. And the order was never sued.

Claiming insanity to avoid litigation was one thing, but to deny that injustices had been committed was quite another. The statement was an admission of guilt, but, because of her madness, the General was deemed innocent and irreproachable! There was no hint of apology, reparation or offer of counselling for the poor nuns who had suffered at her crazy hands. This news produced a welter of emotions in me — triumph, anger, betrayal, and sneering disdain.

The second announcement came as a clap of thunder.

Mother Clare held in her hand fateful discussion papers from the bishop of the district, which he had received from his superiors in

Melbourne, who in turn had received them from Rome. They were belated papers based on the Decree on the Adaptation and Renewal of Religious Life (*Perfectae Caritatis*), proclaimed in 1965.

There had recently been a summit in Broadstairs. The FCJ order, which had been so courageous at the beginning of renewal, had by then largely given up in the face of resistance from its ordinary nuns. After all, nuns in FCJ convents around the world had been taught to keep silence, not to talk. After lengthy deliberations, the Chapter of Superiors from around the world came to a decision: namely, to be as conservative as possible about Vatican II's suggestions pertaining to nuns; which, in practice, meant doing almost nothing. The Church had assumed its nuns had the maturity to instigate and implement sensible changes to make them more relevant in the world, as well as more human, but that wasn't the case.

In faraway Australia, we hadn't even been aware of mooted changes. The local Catholic hierarchy, responsible for disseminating news, had been far from enthusiastic and had kept us in the dark. But now the superiors were obliged to tell their communities that changes had to be made and that in each convent *the whole community* was to suggest how *it* would introduce those changes.

'We have been asked to do some serious thinking and debating,' said Mother Clare, in a barely controlled tone. 'In a spirit of renewal, we will be asking ourselves what is the purpose of our religious life. We will also re-evaluate all three of our vows, especially the vow of obedience.' She allowed the words to sink in. 'Everyone will participate. Everyone will have an equal voice.'

This was a monumental change! But there was more to come. Mother Clare seemed bent on destroying the last vestige of normality that day.

She went on: 'As a religious order, we FCJs have resisted changes brought in by Vatican II in the past. This is to end. Changes will now not only be considered but *implemented*, or we will be disbanded or amalgamated with another order.'

Disbanded! Amalgamated with another order! The twelve nuns around the table shuddered and swayed. Most of them, including several in the hierarchy, had been convinced that the whispered changes were concessions to human weakness and it was up to them to preserve their true religious ideals and customs. For them, ignorance of the world was considered wisdom. The only news of the wider world that filtered through to us was if the schoolchildren happened to mention something, or it was universally important enough to be announced formally in the common room. I remember well the day John F Kennedy was assassinated; I was still at Stella Maris and the announcement was made to anyone who happened to be in the common room at the time. The custom of waiting for the reading was dispensed with so that we could immediately pray for the dead President's soul. Of course, Kennedy was a Catholic.

Only a month before Mother Clare's shocking announcements, Sister Patricia, the domineering middle-aged nun in charge of the primary school, told us about a child who had brought a meat sandwich to school on a Friday. 'I told him it was a mortal sin to eat meat on Fridays,' she said — no longer true, according to Vatican II — 'and he began to tremble, speechless with fear, because he had already taken a bite.' She thought this was terribly funny.

One of the biggest sacrifices we had made in the past was to avoid making judgments, or even hold opinions — the major side-effect of childlike obedience. I had taken to this with the instinct of a martyr. Whatever was good enough for the Jesuits was good enough for us, we'd been told. I forgot to notice that the Jesuits were encouraged to think very sharply indeed, as well as to obey.

'Do not judge' caused me to ignore the fact that many of the older nuns did not always keep to the rules they imposed on the younger ones. They huddled in door recesses, animatedly breaking the rule of silence when they thought no one was watching. They cultivated those 'particular friendships' called the bane of religious life in our rule book. In spite of the agony I had gone through trying to be faithful to this rule, I still didn't judge them. They read magazines and

books that we had no access to. They drank tea when ⌐
and helped themselves to things in the kitchen, ignoring the ⌐
there, whose job it was to not judge anything.

When the rule of silence was finally relaxed to a degree, and I felt free to push it a degree or two further, Sister Antoinette and I would often laugh together about these things.

Sister Antoinette was a consolation to my spirits, every bit as effective as the Rawleigh's ointment she gave to the beggars who came to the back door complaining of piles. She was disturbed when told she could no longer assist beggars: 'We're a teaching order, not a charitable institution, Sister. And these beggars could be dangerous to the boarders and students!'

Sister Antoinette was nobody's fool. She realised that the presence of beggars at the back door threatened to tarnish the convent's precious image. But the beggars were well known to her, they had been coming for many years, some after long journeys around the country. In return for food, clothing and remedies, they would shake out heavy mats she couldn't manage by herself and do chores like cleaning the chimneys. She continued to help them surreptitiously, telling them to hurry off afterwards.

'BLIND OBEDIENCE', WHERE a sister took no responsibility for her own actions in her efforts to do the will of God by simply following commands, was no longer acceptable to the spirit of reform. 'I'm only doing my job' could no longer be considered an excuse for stupid or immoral behaviour. For submissive nuns like me, this was a challenge to progress from childhood into adolescence, a painful growing-up. For others, the transition would not be possible. They would be children or nothing. Their struggle was a pitiful one, but could be absorbed by a convent that had housed them for so long. It was the 'adolescents' — noisy, vocal and rebellious — who proved to be the headaches.

And so began the time of great inroads into conservative thinking and the status quo. As I read the notes we were given to study, on

e paper — one colour for each vow — an ugly
been severely duped came over me. But who had
p responsibility for thinking for herself? Only me,
ief and alacrity!

AFTER THAT MEMORABLE day of introduction to the changes, the
newspaper was placed daily on the common-room table and a TV
was installed in the little room next door. At the same time, we were
told that even though we were now obliged to have such things in
the house, it was better not to touch either.

Of course I read the newspaper, in full view of the others, their
silent disapproval sweeping over me as they passed. I was more aware
of their reaction than of the words I was reading, and when the news
did penetrate I had to pretend not to be deeply shocked by the things
that were happening to other people all over the world.

And I watched TV. At first I chose fairly innocuous programs, such
as religious services performed by other denominations on Sundays.
They seemed harmless enough. In spite of the much-vaunted post-
Vatican ecumenicism (of Christians of all denominations coming
together), I overheard nuns judging the program to be subversive to
our Catholic faith. The next week, thanks to the moderating
influence of one of the older nuns, who pointed out that it was a
good thing to try to understand our Protestant brothers and sisters
and discover what we had in common — and also, perhaps, to prevent
the total isolation of their adventurous sister — this Sunday program
was watched by several of the nuns over several weeks. I felt
vindicated to a degree.

Movies were different. Even Anna drew the line there. I could
count on her to talk to me, to help me shorten the hems of my skirts,
even redesign the whole habit, but she wouldn't watch midnight
horror movies with me. So I watched them by myself. My very first
TV movie was a psycho-thriller about a murder which had been
vibrationally recorded in the stone walls of a cellar. As the stones were

activated, the murderous events played themselves out again, fatefully, inexorably.

The lights all went off at 10 pm but I stayed in the little room, mesmerised by the story. At way past midnight it was time for me to find my bed. I entered the dark hallway and couldn't see a thing. The floor creaked under my stealthy feet, agonisingly loud. There was no way I was going up the outside stairs at this hour of night. I headed for the main stairs, finding my way by groping along the wall. The stairs also creaked, but if anyone heard, they didn't come to see who was causing the noise. I reached the landing and was now sure of my way to the dorm. There was so much adrenaline in my veins from the excitement of the movie and the fearsome trip to bed that I couldn't sleep for hours. The adventure was worth it, I told myself. The next day I had a heavy head from lack of sleep, but felt a silly kind of superiority. Nobody asked me if I had enjoyed the movie, so I was alone in my supposed victory. It would have been a greater victory if I'd watched something useful, like current affairs programs and local and world news!

THE SKIRTS OF our habits were so full that walking in them without the material twisting around our cotton-stockinged legs was a skill, one that was mastered better by some than others. I had perfected it to such a degree that it seemed I had wheels under my skirts instead of legs.

One morning after prayers in the chapel I passed the vestibule where our superior was saying goodbye to the priest who had just said Mass for us. I looked neither to the left nor right but noticed that their conversation stopped abruptly as I passed by. Then the astonished priest's remark filled the vestibule: 'Is *that* human?'

Shocking words. I couldn't just take them as a compliment for my skill in the art of gliding.

Sometimes I would slow down, when the line of a poem I had heard as a schoolgirl came to mind: '*the incomparable pomp of ease*'.

I would take a breath, let the phrase sink in and recapture a sense of being at ease. Then I would practise walking more leisurely, letting my hips move me a little, feeling like a queen.

The new regulation stated that if at least two nuns agreed upon a design, the new habit could be worn by its innovators. Anna and I took time off together to sew new-look habits. She was better at sewing than I was; she knew how to make things fit. So I followed her directions and was very grateful for her cooperation, since she was risking the judgment of some of the nuns who saw what we were doing as a conspiracy. A conspiracy aimed against *them*.

Anna thought that it would be wise to sketch out a design and then get others' opinions. She drew a slimmer-looking skirt, the hem neither short nor long but hovering undecidedly midway, topped by an untailored jacket which just touched the skirt at the waist. Instead of the bonnet we chose a veil over a stiff white band. This was already regulation wear but no one had adopted it as yet.

There was absolutely no interest in our new design and no suggestions for improvements were forthcoming, so we went ahead and made them for ourselves in the off-white, summer outfit material.

I wore my new habit for the first time to my youngest sister's wedding. By then, I had grown my hair just long enough to show a ragged fringe. It felt strange, after all those years of having my head shaved every week, to let my hair grow again. Would it still be blonde? To encourage my scalp into action I secretly sunned it on the tiny balcony at the end of our dormitory, one storey up and facing the convent's driveway. I had to crouch low so as not to be seen by anyone (the balcony was in sight of the road and rather low) and choose a time when no one was in the dorm. Hot, prickly sweat soon made me retreat from the sun's glare, only slightly dulling the wickedly sensual feeling of fresh air on my scalp.

I felt extremely vulnerable at my sister's wedding without my armour of voluminous folds of cloth.

Anna and I also wore our new design to a funeral in the chapel. It was attended by several Jesuit priests, who were there to show their solidarity with the FCJs, forged from a long association. For many decades they had enjoyed a mutual admiration society. It didn't do any good trying to hide us near the back; it was there that we were most easily spotted by those in the very back pew and others who had standing room only.

'Where do they come from?' was the ungracious question whispered to our superior by a Jesuit. I glanced furtively at the questioner and caught the response of our chagrined superior.

'Those are the new habits,' she whispered, turning away from us as she spoke, indicating her helplessness at having to witness and accept such absurdities, and hoping that the priest with the querulous voice would understand that it wasn't *her* idea.

The new habit went no further than Anna and me. Nobody attempted to emulate our bravery, called brazenness by some. A 'proper' design for a new habit was carefully researched by two nuns at Genazzano and they eventually came up with a model that represented a more gradual change; one which was superseded every two years or so, as courage and acceptance of smartness grew. I was long gone by then.

THE DISCUSSIONS ABOUT renewal were lively. I felt like a visionary; my imagination was fired: I could easily see how we could move into the future without unnecessary shackles. But I was also an idealist, approaching topics and ideas without considering others' feelings, without acknowledging or respecting that my sisters were not all like me and needed much more time to change.

Their resistance to my forwardness was both outspoken and subtle. As talking became easier, so did politicking — people bunching up into groups. Isolating someone is easy in a community: all you do is stop talking to her. You can make it hard when she wants to talk to you, by being in a hurry. You can make plans that she won't know about by announcing them when she isn't there, and so on. Gradually, I was being ostracised.

I complained to my sisters at a meeting that they weren't accepting me. The superior headed off the psychological equivalent of a lynch party. The storm of angry comments only confirmed my belief.

I received letters from various superiors who had known me in the past. 'Be patient and kind, Sister,' was the tone of every one of them. But my heart hardened. I replied in plain language: 'No one wants to listen to me; and all you want is to sweet-talk me into being a "good girl", to be quiet and stop being a nuisance.' It did not go down very well at all. This was not the FCJ spirit I had been brought up in.

I lived with a bunch of people who were emotionally more stable than I was, but not necessarily more mature. They were able to sacrifice themselves for the common good, weathering the storms while they resented those who rocked their boat.

A NEW CONCESSION allowed nuns to choose their own priest as confessor and mentor, which meant they were no longer reliant on the likes of the local parish priest for confession and guidance and also less dependent on their Mother Superior.

Father Doherty, who had led our seven-day retreat that year, became my mentor. I liked him because of his admiration for Teilhard de Chardin, the ex-communicated heretic with a scientific and lyrical passion for God. Father Doherty was stationed in Melbourne, so our communication was by correspondence. I poured out my frustrations to him and he replied with soothing letters, offering understanding and dispassionate good advice.

'I trust that you will not forget,' he wrote, 'that it was the patience of men like Congar, de Lubac and Karl Rahner that eventually made possible the great work of Vatican II.' Well, that made me feel so humble and insignificant! I was no great brain compared to these famous characters; he was gently pointing out that I was just a nun (not terribly well informed) and shouldn't take on too much responsibility for changing anything. 'Do try to be patient, Sister. Try to see the others' points of view. The way ahead is a gradual one, which means we all have to move together, in mutual respect and charity.'

I did try. But I was on fire, and didn't understand the hesitation of my sisters. 'Father,' I replied, 'my sisters are deliberately obstructing change, and they are doing it to obstruct *me*!' He did not reply to that. What can you say to a young nun who is developing the first signs of paranoia?

I was not the only headache in the order. If I wanted to go too fast, some did not want to move at all. The suffering of some of the older, very faithful sisters was intense. These nuns inwardly endured the crumbling of the whole premise of their holiness. The changes 'proved' that the foundation of the rules had been shaky all along — like the church's doctrine of limbo, for instance. They had given themselves up to what they thought was righteousness and were now faced with having been wrong. Had they been living a life of foolishness instead of ultimate perfection?

The minds of a few turned to jelly at this destruction of their inner security; they became senile. One such nun spent all her remaining days in the top storey of her convent, among the linen. She was always carrying parcels of linen from one place to put them somewhere else. With her very fine face, large staring eyes and tight mouth, she became the living ghost of the convent.

THE NEW REGULATIONS allowed nuns to spend time away from the convent, to visit their families. In the past we had been told over and over that to be a nun was to 'leave your father and your mother and brothers and sisters and come, follow me' — words attributed to Jesus. Now we were allowed to return to our relatives and even spend several days with them.

Our families were delighted and a little embarrassed, not least of all my parents. The daughter once so far removed had suddenly come among them again!

We went to the movies together, my mother, my sister Liesbet and me. We saw *Far From the Madding Crowd* and *The Sound of Music*.

We nuns were still heavily obliged not to divulge any 'religious community matters' out of loyalty to the order and the community we belonged to. I was completely loyal and never uttered a word of complaint or blame to my family. I reinforced their picture of me as a happy nun, the same picture they knew from the regular letters I sent them. For their part, they didn't share any of their own worries, thinking it their duty to entertain me.

NEW THINKING SOON inspired more new thought. It occurred to me to ask to learn to play the piano. I had always been attracted to the piano but there wasn't one at home, and when the Billingses from across the road had offered to let me use theirs, I was thought by the music mistress at Vaucluse to be too old to start learning at sixteen.

So here I was at the age of twenty-eight, feeling the urge to train my long fingers for the piano. I knelt by my superior's chair and put my request to her. She busied herself with some papers while she considered it. She didn't seem particularly inclined to refuse, but she couldn't feel any enthusiasm for the idea. Then she came up with a suggestion. 'I shall ask Sister Cecilia to give you an audition,' she said, 'to gauge your ability.'

I was happy with her answer and confident, because I knew one thing for certain: I had rhythm and pitch in my blood; I could sing both alto and soprano. The day came, and Sister Cecilia, who had won a prize at some time in her life for brushing her teeth correctly, demonstrated a few musical phrases for me to imitate, then a few more, and a few more. She said nothing, but her verdict came about a week later, when I asked my superior.

'I'm afraid you don't have any talent for music at all,' came the cool reply. 'Sister Cecilia is very sorry, but in her opinion that is so. I can't afford to give lessons to someone who has no aptitude, Sister.'

My heart didn't want to accept this. It was one thing to be refused, but quite another to be told I had no musical talent whatsoever. This wasn't true, but there was nothing I could do about it. The insidious snake of anger injected some of its venom inside me; another drop into the poisonous pit.

Soon after, something else occurred to me: this time I wanted to learn to drive. Since the introduction of the reforms the convent had acquired a car, and nuns could now visit the doctor and dentist, instead of them having to drag their gear along to the convent. The car was also used for shopping and for outings. At first, however, no one knew how to drive! When necessary, we had always been chauffeured by a lay teacher or a friend of the convent. It was considered a favour to the community to learn to drive and so be of service. I offered with a great deal of enthusiasm and was surprised by the total lack of appreciation for my offer. An immediate flat refusal came, with no thanks, not even a lift of the head this time.

If the hierarchy had no control over the way I discussed our vows and religious life, they certainly had the power to frustrate my desires to grow into a more useful and expanded human being, or to ask for anything out of the ordinary. My heart thumped in desperate frustration, but what right had I to assume that I would be allowed to drive? I so much wanted to spread my wings, but others might be better at it.

A week or so later I noticed Sister Madeleine with a sling around her arm. 'I caught my arm in the steering,' she said honestly. I smiled wryly. It wouldn't have happened to me, I said to myself. The hot feeling of having been denied was still with me, but it was funny to see my superior's choice walking about with a broken arm. Yet I knew that if all the nuns in the convent broke an arm, I would still not be chosen.

If I was not to play the piano, I could still choose to play records at recreation time, under the new regulations. I stood up so everyone could hear what I had to say. 'Does anyone want to come with me to the concert hall to listen to music and to dance?'

There was a silence so that all might consider my suggestion, but no one wanted to come with me. I didn't really expect anyone to. Waltzes, minuets and ballet music — I danced to all of it, magnificently and totally alone, with the music resounding so loudly that it must have reached the ears of my sisters in the common room. I thought that maybe if they heard the music they would feel like dancing, but it never happened, and from week to week my dance became more lonesome and poignant. Self-pity beckoned seductively; the lid of Pandora's box of hidden emotions was slowly opening.

THE NEXT TIME I went for my weekly private session with Reverend Mother, I asked her if she would be a mother to me for a little while. What did I have in mind, she asked, her tone cool as her cheeks took on a deeper colour and her eyes glinted in her attempt not to look at me too closely.

'I want you to hold me,' I said, 'like a mother.' And she did, God bless her kindness, while I cried helpless tears.

My sobs spoke to Mother Clare's heart, and she held me patiently against her bosom, so I could smell the special soap she used and feel her softness. Neither she nor I had any idea what these tears were about, but they seemed endless, coming from a pit of sorrow she hoped I would soon see the bottom of. Instead, my need grew bigger. Sometimes I wouldn't be able to function at all unless I was first held like a child, kneeling beside her on the floor, wetting her habit shawl and taking up her valuable time.

The schoolchildren were exposed to the fact that their nun teacher was human: she came to class with red eyes and nose. They might have talked about it among themselves, but took no further notice. I was more a function and utility to them than a person, and what they couldn't understand they easily dismissed. Nuns were supposed to suffer.

The changes hadn't done away with penances; they were still very much in vogue. This was an area of convent life I did not challenge. Instead, I adopted a new penance that was particularly painful for me, which was to stand up in the classroom when my legs were tired, until I could hardly stand up any more. My legs had varicose veins, and they hurt.

Even more painful, and unplanned, were the premenstrual cramps that had begun to attack me, sometimes in the middle of a lesson. The blood would leave my head, I would turn pale as death and become unsteady on my feet. I stumbled out of class one day, asking a girl to run and tell the headmistress. I didn't know that it was premenstrual tension; I just thought I had a bellyache. The infirmarian wisely gave me a hot water bottle to hold against my stomach as I lay curled up on the bed.

During that year a host of emerging energies — forbidden and dangerous — leapt up within me. I used all my desperate willpower to suppress them in order to stay functional, but the volcanoes inside clamoured to erupt. I became more and more confused, and would have happily buried myself in my superior's bosom to cry myself to death.

One of the older nuns accosted me and said she was worried about Mother Clare. 'You are taking up too much of her time,' she said, 'and your behaviour worries her. I beg you to be more considerate.'

Sister Antoinette managed to cheer me up. She would lift her eyes to me and whisper words of comfort from her hare-lipped mouth. As a virtual outsider to the process of renewal — she was a lay sister and therefore hardly counted — she had plenty of time to reflect, and was able to assess better than most what was going on.

'Don't take any notice of them,' she'd say with her lovely little rabbit smile. 'They can't hurt you if you don't take any notice of them.' Such simple, wise words. That is exactly what *she* was doing: letting every new thing wash over her. Sister Antoinette knew that it was important to love God and keep your mouth shut, but secretly she admired me for my vocal stance. She agreed with my views, but wisely knew her limits.

MOTHER WINIFRED WAS now a well-recognised resident of Broadstairs and was sent on an official visit to the convent of Our

Lady of the Angels. We prepared a musical concert for her. Along with all the others, I sang my heart's devotion to God, to the Society and to her. I earnestly wanted her to know, from my singing, that my intentions were good; that I had 'the right spirit' after all. But, alas, Mother Winifred seemed not to notice me. Her eyes went everywhere as she smiled with that full set of good teeth in her broad, ruddy face, but they never met mine. I felt I was shouting into a vacuum.

The purpose of her visit was to gauge our progress and report back to Broadstairs. She saw each of us, one by one. When it came to my turn, as soon as I knelt by her side I was warned not to be critical of authority. 'Sister Carla, it is my duty to remind you of the spirit of our society, and to beg you to honour it.'

Her bushy eyebrows frowned as first she pleaded with me, then commanded me, to toe the line. She would have preferred it if I never opened my mouth again on any subject, instead waiting mutely for improvements to develop in their own time.

I knew it wasn't any use opening my heart to her and asking for her understanding, never mind her support. She wasn't unkind, but she obviously had a preconceived agenda on that visit to Benalla. She did not make any effort to befriend me or to make me understand that she appreciated anything about me whatsoever. There might have been overarching changes, but nothing had happened to change her attitude towards me; nor did she show any sign of respect for those who, like me, wanted to throw their energies into suggesting and making improvements.

Upon her departure, she did not say an individual goodbye and left me with a deep pain in my heart.

I WAS CALLED to Mother Clare's side once more. 'Sister,' she said, 'you are no longer to write to your sister at Genazzano. I have it from her superior that you are influencing her the wrong way. This is an order, and I expect you to obey.'

This was very painful, because my letters to my sister were a sort of catharsis. I tried to obey, but I needed *someone* to listen to me. So that no one would see me, I wrote to her on toilet paper, while sitting on the toilet. I stole an envelope and stamp from my superior's desk and watched what happened to letters left in the vestibule for collection. I got to know the regular time and surreptitiously added my letter in among the others just before collection time. Genazzano was a big convent. My sister received my letters and no one noticed that they were from Benalla.

THE BOARDERS WERE allowed out more often as a result of renewal. One day the senior girls attended a concert in a nearby civic hall. A group of German women singers, backed by the Victorian Arts Council, were making their way around the country to present their songs, accompanied by the piano. We nuns accompanied the boarders.

I was not prepared for the power of this music. The women let go a stream of passionate songs: songs of praise for the beloved, songs of unrequited love, and songs of devotion. The pure, fresh energy of the music went straight and unexpectedly to my heart, and cut it, so that my breath was taken away and deep, deep tears started to flow again. I couldn't stop them and didn't really want to.

In spite of a couple of huge cotton hankies retrieved from one of my bottomless habit pockets, grief soaked the starched linen under my chin and made its way right under my collar. No one spoke as we moved out of the aisles of wooden chairs and onto the late-afternoon street. Everyone was moved in her own way and nobody said a thing to me; not then, nor afterwards.

It must have been an unusual sight, though, for a nun to be so affected by songs of human love. What could set off such a reaction but a feeling of missing out, of desperately wanting to experience love; a yearning for a trusted, warm, humorous embrace of affection and devotion, of mutual appreciation? I had never been able to imagine such a thing before, not even when reading Jane Austen or the Brontë sisters' novels. But this music had flowed from a composer in love, and I felt the force of it for the first time.

Was it this pure love of a man for a woman, a woman for a man, that I had sacrificed to God? Such a sacrifice sounded like lunacy. *What* exactly had I given up for God, and *why*? In the normal course of life I had only experienced the kind of love that is easy to do without. Anything beyond that, I had told myself, was all imagination. But how could I now be sure that a life lived for God, in a convent, really *was* the ultimate life of love?

THE DIE IS CAST

THERE CAME A last-straw event — though I didn't recognise it at the time — which set me on a path of no return.

I was called to the head of the large polished table in the common room, where the superior sometimes sat to read her mail and make herself available for requests, permissions and reports. It was almost time for the six o'clock reading, when we would all assemble around the table to listen and do our needlework. I had entered the room with the idea of starting my needlework early, when Reverend Mother Clare summoned me. I went over to kneel beside her.

'I am taking your art class away from you, Sister Mary Carla,' she said evenly. 'I've heard that you discussed religion with the students after your class yesterday. I want to ensure that the students are taught *art* when they are supposed to be learning art, and *not* religion.'

She kept busy with the mail as she spoke, her tone somewhere between angry and righteous, and avoided looking me in the face until she had finished.

Rage welled up in me. Yes, it was true: three students had asked me questions after school, sparked off by a discussion about a classical painting of Adam and Eve. I had been reading some of the works of Teilhard de Chardin, and had presented his ideas in class as an alternative interpretation of the official version of creation. The girls had heard of Teilhard de Chardin, the excommunicated poet–priest and thinker, and were keen to explore more open ideas. They had an emergent feminist streak and had also wanted to know my opinion about wearing hats in church. I had no trouble telling them that I thought it was probably a custom introduced by Paul of Tarsus, who, I had read, looked down on women. We had talked amicably for half an hour or so. Either I had been overheard or one of the girls had betrayed me. The new rules allowed me to speak freely, but apparently not about religion! The hot flush of anger I felt gave me immediate courage.

'OK,' I said breathlessly. 'If you want to make sure that the pupils learn what they're supposed to learn, you'd better get someone else to teach them. I'm quitting!'

I just had time to take in her complete surprise and the stunned reaction of the nuns who had filed into the room, before leaving to go upstairs to my cubicle bed. And there I stayed.

I came down for meals, making sure Sister Antoinette understood that I would be there, so heading off any chance of my sisters pretending they didn't know and arranging no place for me at table. I came down for meditation and Mass the next morning, had breakfast and went back to my room, determined to stay on strike unless the decision to remove me from my art class was reversed.

I knew my sudden departure from the workforce would be sorely felt because I had a full timetable and my sisters would have trouble covering for me or finding a replacement. My anger sustained me into the third day, when they sent Sister Madeleine — the little shy one, a friend to me because she couldn't be my enemy — up to my room to negotiate. I was begged to come down and help because everyone was overworked; no word about reinstating my class. I sent her down with my commiserations and the message that I would resume work as soon as my class was given back to me.

Several times Sister Madeleine came up to reason and plead with me and, in the end, I gave in. Unprincipled as I was then, I thought I'd better do the right thing as my sisters had suffered enough. I let myself down badly for the sake of their doubtful approval, since I did not get my class back. 'Never mind,' I told myself, 'I've got more free time now,' and devoted it to redesigning my habit. But my heart had been insulted and compromised in a way that was not going to heal.

Soon letters from previous superiors in Australia, England and Brussels, and even from the local bishop, began to arrive on my desk. People had been active during my strike.

'I am most disappointed to hear that of late you have been missing some of your classes with the children, and that you are not always in the places where duty lies,' began the letter from my erstwhile geography lecturer at Sedgley Park, Sister Gertrude, who was once so proud of my getting perfect marks in the finals. 'Sister, this is most unprofessional of you and it is letting Sedgley down badly! Sister, what has come over you that you seem to find it so difficult to act like everyone else? Do you think that if you find life such a strain, you ought to see a psychiatrist?' And, 'You must think of your community, Sister. It is most distressing for them to have to live with you if you are not going to live our life properly.'

The worthy Gertrude ended by asking whether it might not be best to ask to leave. *Leave!* That was a red rag to a bull, as was everything else she and everyone else said. They were taking sides against me while steeped in ignorance of the real situation. I was unmoved by their attempts to intimidate me.

Instead of being apologetic, I wanted to be vindicated, somehow. I sent a statement to my mentor; it read something like a police report, detailing my conversation, word for word, with the three students. I wasn't just angry; I was outraged. I wanted to show how authority was being misused to blacken the name of innocent people like me. I suggested the creation of a tribunal to deal with injustices. My argument read quite well, and could have worked, except that this was a *convent*, for God's sake, not a political establishment, a war zone, or a gathering of war criminals being tried for their crimes against humanity. Alas, humility and meekness, the traditional cure for a sore heart, had become foreign, useless concepts to me.

The worst letter, three pages long, came from someone in my community I had thought was on my side: Sister Albion — a short, nervous nun with an attractive smile, striking face and very dark eyebrows. Sister Albion had been practising her public speaking techniques on us: giving talks, moving motions and answering imaginary questions, all to gain confidence and skills in the Westminster system. Was she getting ready to enter politics? Not quite, but she did become my next Reverend Mother, after which her natural shyness disappeared for good, replaced by an unbending personality, ready to break wills and hearts.

She sent her letter while she was on holiday, where she was secretly being prepared for her new role. The tone of the letter was kindly, pleading with me to participate more and not be so much on my own. It was sane advice, but I was unable to hear it because none of my grievances were acknowledged.

'Make people conscious that you care about them,' she wrote, avoiding the main topic of my recent rebellion. 'We can never judge anyone,' she continued, referring to my complaints about the way I was treated, 'and if we develop the habit of always suspecting others, thinking that they underrate us or thinking they are always against us, then we shall have no peace of soul. Besides, it is not Christ-like.'

She was right, of course. She was telling me I was being paranoid, and I was. The proof was my continued and increasing distress at all the 'evidence' I saw around me that I was misunderstood, mistreated and underrated.

'When you hold on to your own opinion, pride is at the root of it,' she urged. 'Forget yourself, put all your energy into helping others and you will find that you will have no worries, no heartaches, for most often our biggest heartache is ourself. Oh dear, how I preach!' she admitted. There was no doubt that she meant well, but she didn't realise that it was impossible to appeal to my good side while so much lay unaddressed. Her letter was an invitation to sweep everything under the carpet and go back to being a good nun, for Christ's sake. How did she think this would work?

THAT CHRISTMAS I hung the decorations up as usual, getting happily lost for a while in the creative fun of the job. It was also my task to store them all away a few weeks later, in boxes kept in the attic. Mother Albion, who had taken up her position as superior in early January, came to see how I was getting on. She inspected the boxes, then, to my astonishment and grief, blithely turned them all upside down and started packing them away again herself, insisting that I watch. I was soon in tears, but she took no notice. She seemed to have plenty of time, chatting to people who came to her for one thing or another as she worked, before finally she asked me to take the boxes away. Her newly-invested superior power had instantly wiped out her former hesitant manner.

Mother Albion's power grew over several years, as she was moved from house to house to fulfil a term here, there and everywhere, carrying out her role of stern management. It was due to this that the declining Society eventually regained the wealth it had once enjoyed in the days when many women took up the vocation. Mother Albion came into power at a time when new entrant numbers were in serious decline, necessitating the employment of more and more lay teachers. She understood the importance of hiring only the best teachers — at least for the all-important Genazzano convent — in order to attract the best students (that is, the best payers) and, in turn, secure the future wellbeing of the FCJ order in Australia. For a while, this strategy worked. However, eventually the lay teachers were not content to work under nuns less qualified and so lay headmistresses and a board took over much of the schools' management.

My father wholeheartedly hated Mother Albion, convinced that she was responsible for the sufferings inflicted upon him by the board at Genazzano.

The members of the board did not appreciate the forty years my father had dedicated to building up a dazzling display of beauty in the convent gardens, nor the expense of keeping them up. And they didn't think twice about knocking down his garage and workshed when they needed the space for an Olympic-sized swimming pool.

My father was a simple man. When he saw trees that he had planted thirty years ago knocked down because they were in the way of a straight path, he blamed Mother Albion, who was by then the Mother Vicar. She probably no longer had the power of veto over the board, but my father could never understand that. His jaws worked, his eyes popped in rage, his hands and arms, muscled and veined from the supreme effort he had put into his work, felt the lameness of terrible impotence.

ON AN ORDINARY but chilly morning, I woke up and couldn't move. It was like being stuck in a bad horror movie. The sister doing the 'Praise be to Jesus!' wake-up call should have waited for my 'Amen!' before taking off, but as I was usually one of the first to jump out of bed she didn't bother to listen for my familiar confirmation. The others in the cubicles next to mine (the curtains had been replaced by thin walls) went about their usual routine in bustling silence. I tried to call out, but the small sound that came out of my dry mouth was muffled by the noise of shoes on floors and the thump of bedding being piled on chairs. With a big effort I reached to knock on the wall next to my bed, but still there was no response.

After breakfast an annoyed infirmarian entered my cubicle. She had been called by Sister Madeleine, who had missed seeing me around and had poked her head in to find me when she came back upstairs. Sister Marian's face made it clear that she suspected me of pretending to be ill, but as she couldn't make me get up, the doctor was called in. He prescribed anti-spasmodic tablets to persuade my muscles to give up their catatonic state. My body had literally seized up, somehow matching my feelings of being in a strait-jacket.

After a few days I was well enough to resume duties, for which everyone was grateful. The boarders greeted me with, 'Glad you're better, Sister,' and smiled when they saw me back in the refectory where I served them dinner. That little human touch did a lot to relax the clench in my back.

ORDERS FROM THE bishop made sure there was more human diversion in our lives. One of the best innovations that trickled down from Vatican II was the extra fun in our holidays: they were full of talk and laughter, guitar-playing, tennis, group dances — we danced in circles like the fairies might have done in Ireland — and *swimming*. The society had purchased a forty-acre section of the Peninsula Golf Course at Frankston, a beach suburb not far from Melbourne, for a new school. Its guesthouse was easily transformed into a convent and I spent a vacation there in 1967. We went to the beach early in the morning, dressed in black cossies that were meant to be inconspicuous but were anything but, accentuating give-away white skin everywhere.

My sister and I were never housed at the same convent in the five years that she was a probationary nun. Her buddy at Genazzano was Sister Anna; they shared an iconoclastic attitude, although Sister Anna's was more intellectual and guarded, and therefore more diplomatic and acceptable. Anna also showed a sweet humour about all the things she ridiculed or derided. My sister, however, transformed her ideas into action, and immediate action at that. Eventually, in spite of the shortage of vocations, she was considered 'bad blood' because of me and wasn't allowed to stay on.

However, in the autumn of 1968 she was at Genazzano, and I wanted to be near someone who could understand me and make me laugh. The Easter holidays were coming up. I fronted up to Mother Albion, without much hope, to ask if I could be with my sister for their duration. This unprecedented request was refused, as expected, so I decided to take matters into my own hands.

On the day before Good Friday I packed a small bag with toiletries and a few underclothes and headed for the highway, which passed close by the front gates. No one saw me leave because they were all at prayers; ostensibly, I had left the chapel to go to the toilet. I wrote a little note and left it on my superior's breakfast plate, both hoping and not hoping that it would give her indigestion. 'I've gone to visit my sister at Genazzano,' she read later with unbelieving eyes. 'I'm travelling with friends, so don't worry. Sister Mary Carla.'

The 'friends' I was referring to were whoever might pick me up to travel south. I simply trusted in God to send me friendly people to take care of me.

It was a drizzly day and I headed for the protection of a leafy tree. I looked along the bitumen highway, the only arterial road going south, and my heart thumped when I saw a shiny black car coming towards me. As if I had done this all my life, I raised the thumb of my right hand as it came nearer. My white habit made me the most visible target in the world, even under a shady tree on a grey day.

The car slowed down and stopped close by, off the road. There were three men in it; from where I was standing I guessed the driver to be Italian — an instant plus for me, bringing back memories of the warm-hearted Italian friends of my teens. Relying on the instinct that would protect me in so many situations in the future, I knew I would be safe with these men. The back door swung open to let me in — an invitation to share the seat with an open-mouthed Australian farmer, a heavy man with a big stomach and spreading legs.

We were well on our way when they asked, 'Where are you going, Sister?' 'To Melbourne,' I replied. 'Is that all right?' 'That's all right with us,' said the driver decidedly, heading off questions from the others for the time being.

They were heading for Melbourne, but not necessarily for Kew, where Genazzano was located. It never occurred to me that their destination might be elsewhere in Melbourne's vast metropolis. I was deeply grateful, and thanked them very much for their kindness, showing a cool that I hoped was convincing.

The men said they were Catholics, to make me feel better. They must have had a strong inkling that this tall, white-faced sister travelling with them was in a bad way. Surely, the convent would have put her on a bus, at least — and certainly she should not be travelling alone.

The driver spoke up again. 'Where in Melbourne are you going, Sister?' I explained it was to the convent on top of the hill in Kew, and one of them remembered the row of cypress trees along Cotham Road. 'To see my sister,' I added, as if it were a perfectly reasonable explanation.

A road map was taken out and, once they were sure of the way, silence fell. They were polite enough not to talk about worldly things, because I wouldn't be able to join in. They sat lost in their thoughts, casting an occasional glance at the nun in the back seat, who had half collapsed against the back door, her little brown suitcase beside her like a barrier separating her from the big man next to her. Other than the odd banal comment, no one spoke, as if we were all spontaneously on retreat.

It was a fairly long journey — about 180 kilometres — but we didn't stop along the way. The man behind the wheel lost absolutely no time in his effort to deliver me as soon as God was willing. The country road entered the humming business of the suburbs. The driver knew exactly where he was going. As soon as I recognised a familiar tramline I offered to catch it, but they wouldn't hear of it. When the ornate convent gates on Cotham Road came into view, I offered to walk down the driveway, lined with magnificent flowerbeds planted by my father, but again they didn't want to risk losing their passenger, especially now, so close to target. The black car sailed down the winding driveway, around the oval with its stately trees and stopped at the porch with its oak front door. They waited while I rang the echoing bell. When the heavy door swung open, they shouted farewell and drove off — these men who had turned out to be truly my friends.

The portress was shocked to see me, and called the Reverend Mother, who had been warned but hadn't expected to see me so soon. In her little study — which I recalled from postulant and novice days — I explained my reason for coming and asked if I could stay for a few days. How I had got there was already obvious. The superior appeared genuinely nonplussed about the whole affair but decided to let me have my way, and did so with kindness. She called my sister and asked her to make tea and look after me.

My sister was delighted to see me. We sat on the kitchen bench as she got the story — and all my other stories — out of me, saying, 'Oh man!' and, 'Oh geez!' I could count on her to be on my side! She made tea, raided the biscuit tins and found some cake in the fridge, all of which I gobbled up with gusto, even though we were in a serious period of penance before Easter. It was mid-morning and I hadn't had breakfast yet.

On Easter Friday, I took on once more my old familiar task of sweeping the corridor. I strewed tea leaves across the width of the lino floors so they would absorb the dust as I systematically swept them up. Memories of miles of corridors crowded into my head, along with memories of terrifying nightmares of having forgotten to mop the floors and seeing dust collected in swirls of soft downy fluff.

After Easter, I returned to Benalla by car with four Genazzano nuns who were to spend some holidays there. My time with my sister made me feel infinitely better, for having had a sympathetic ear for a change.

Back home, nothing was said to me. The only person to hear my story was Sister Antoinette, who enjoyed my adventure, but held her breath for me. This, she knew, could not go on. Meanwhile, the little circle around Mother Albion advised her to send me to a psychiatrist for an assessment.

There was a retired, much respected, psychiatrist by the name of Dr Brown, who had close connections to Genazzano. He lived in Melbourne, within walking distance of the convent. An appointment was made and I travelled south again, accompanied by the same four silent nuns who had come up with me.

I was ushered into the venerable old man's study, accompanied by the grim and accusatory Vicar of Genazzano. She was tight-mouthed, but her usually dull brown eyes were alert. Also present was someone not well known to me, who had arrived at Genazzano while I was overseas. She was a so-called neutral second person, but really they were there to get the opinion they wanted to hear.

Dr Brown was a gentle man who had the greatest respect for the reality of suffering, having observed it in his many patients. White-haired, soft-footed and slightly stooping, he nevertheless carried himself with rare grace. 'Sister Mary Carla,' he said, 'tell me what is troubling you.' He sat down and gave me the impression that he would listen with the utmost attention.

'My reputation was torn apart even before I came to Benalla,' I began, glancing at my companions. What would they know of any of this? They weren't even members of my community! Dr Brown asked me to clarify, and I answered honestly and without hesitation, in the presence of my two witnesses. I told him about the injustices I had endured; how I had felt deliberately picked on for years. Finally I was able to speak out passionately and truthfully to someone with some authority whose job it was to listen.

Several times my companions tried to interrupt with outraged denial, but they were silenced. Finally he asked me, 'What do you want, Sister? What do you think would be a solution to your problems?'

I knew the answer to his question the moment he asked it. 'I would like to be sent to another convent, away from Mother Albion, preferably to be with my sister at Genazzano.' It immediately occurred to me that the latter would never be granted, so I added, 'I would like to make a new start with people who don't know me.'

Dr Brown then spoke with my two companions, to give them his opinion.

I had no idea that he had been asked to give the verdict that I wasn't fit to be a nun and should be expelled. It was extremely difficult to force someone to leave once she had made her final vows; in fact it was impossible, unless someone with the right credentials was prepared to declare me psychologically unfit. But he did nothing of the sort.

In my presence, he told the two nuns that I showed symptoms of paranoia. When they spoke up and gave him what they thought was the real version of events (though neither lived in my convent), he explained that this was proof that my interpretations of reality were paranoid. At the same time he noted that I was passionately devoted to religious life, and intelligent with a high sense of integrity and idealism. He wrote a note there and then — which he showed me before he gave it to the Mother Vicar — recommending that I be sent to the new small community at Frankston, where nobody knew me and I could be given the fresh start I looked for.

It was sound, workable advice — and surely that's what my companions had come for? But their sour faces showed their disappointment. It came as no surprise to me, once back at Benalla, to be told the decision of the hierarchy: nothing was going to be done. I was to stay where I was.

The eyes from abroad continued to watch me, and more letters landed on my desk. They had been advised of my latest exploit — hitch-hiking to Melbourne of all things! — and were co-opted to lecture me. Nobody understood the distress that had prompted my action; they saw my behaviour as an outrage, a slight on authority.

The most direct letter came from Mother Winifred. She didn't mince her words:

'Notre Mère is distressed that you are the cause of so much unhappiness in the community and wishes me to say to you that this must not continue. Sister, you are not satisfied with the way of Renewal settled by the Chapter and you are critical of authority. It is important that you look into yourself; and as you are not happy in the Society, it is possible that your Apostolate is elsewhere. Your way of acting and your want of respect for authority are quite contrary to our Spirit. Sister, if you are unhappy and dissatisfied there is something radically wrong in your religious life and it is time for you to seriously examine if you are in the right place. God bless you, Sister. Affectionately yours in JC, M Winifred.'

The letter, dated 25 March 1969, was well-considered, polite and diplomatic, and it really made me think. My loyalty to the Society was still intact — so much so that I had never opened my mouth to anyone on the outside, not even my parents — but it was true that I no longer embodied the Spirit of the Society, which relied entirely on joyful obedience and a respectful and intimate association with superiors.

AT THE END of April, a whole year after I thumbed that lift to Melbourne, my constant prayers were answered — and probably those of the community, too. My mantra in those days, months and years had been a desperate *Lord, that I may see*! for I had felt for a long time that I was as blind as I had been that time in Broadstairs, when I had taken the pills at the wrong time.

I was in the chapel as usual at six in the morning, settling into the silence of meditation, when suddenly I saw a vision of the whole community, as from above. It showed my sisters hard at work, hard at prayer, and the unity among them contrasted starkly with my isolation. I felt keenly their normal state of happiness — once mine also — and their distress at the constant disturbance I was causing. I understood clearly that the more I fought for renewal, the more shut off I would become. There was no way back. I could no longer just toe the line and be peaceful. An urge grew in me to move on, to venture out into the unknown. It was more important than trying to fit in or being unquestioningly content. I also saw that no one would be going with me.

This was not a dark vision; it was infused with wonderful light, filling me with excitement. I knew in that very instant that I should leave; that my heart and spirit longed for it. It wasn't just a question of no longer fitting in as a nun, although I did not know that then. I needed to heal wounds which had their origin in my childhood, and the convent was not the place for these wounds to heal. Thanks to *Aggiornomento*, it was merely the place where they had re-opened.

I left the chapel, found paper, envelope and a stamp, and wrote straightaway to the Bishop, informing him of my intention. I placed the letter on the little escritoire, the collection point for the morning post. It was gone before breakfast. Only after breakfast did

I inform my Reverend Mother. I was surprised at her annoyance that I hadn't consulted her; I thought she would be relieved! She was after a little while, and the news soon spread around the community.

Only Sister Antoinette and Sisters Imelda, Madeleine and Anna came up to me to wish me well. The others must have felt betrayed as well as relieved: all their hard work in accommodating my neurosis, all that time I had taken from the superiors as they tried to counsel me — all for nothing. And they would have to share among themselves the teaching responsibilities and many chores that I was abandoning in the middle of the teaching year.

The Bishop sent his reply to Mother Albion, suggesting the next step, which was to write to the Holy See for dispensation. I was also to write formally to the Reverend Mother General, which I did. Father Doherty was told of the news and came to see me to give me advice on the wording of the letter to the Vatican.

'Dispensations are not always granted, Sister,' he said, 'but if you could find a way to state your *unsuitability* for sisterhood, you would have a good chance.' I noticed his emphasis and at this late stage was politically astute enough to realise that he was trying to head off the kind of report that might incorporate my views about my order's failure to comply with the dictums of renewal, which might have caused unnecessary trouble for the FCJs.

So I tried to make it sound as if the reasons for my leaving were all my own doing. 'I have never before been conscious of my motives for entering the convent,' I wrote. 'I have discovered that they were not purely to serve God, but were based on insecurity and a mistaken idea of what it meant to do God's will. At the time of my entering, I had no clear idea of why I wanted to be a nun.'

I wrote a few more sentences like that, but it didn't feel quite right. I couldn't stop myself from adding: 'Holy Father, as a result of my desire to bring about renewal, tensions within my community have become unbearable. I cannot stay and be happy. I cannot stay and expect my community to be happy.'

The letter was approved and sent off, sealing my fate in the eyes of all concerned. After the briefest of goodbyes, I was removed from the scene, away from the turmoil that my continued presence would have caused among my sisters, and sent to the convent of my secondary school days, Vaucluse.

I enjoyed my stay there. Here was a new community, though many of the faces and names were familiar to me from my time as a student. Vaucluse had a distinct and intimate identity of its own. The convent even had ornate toilets, like some I had seen in England, with peonies and roses painted on the bowls.

'I would like to welcome Sister Mary Carla among us as our guest for a few weeks,' was the brief formal announcement at breakfast by the tall, wizened Reverend Mother. She wore a wise and weary look, and dabbed at her mouth with a hanky before she spoke. 'Sister Mary Carla is on holidays and therefore not obliged to hold to the schedule.'

There was a murmur of welcome. If anyone was curious as to why I was 'on holidays' in the middle of a working season, nobody asked. Only a few suspected the real reason for my stay, which was to await the reply from the Holy See.

No one knew exactly how long this would take, and it never occurred to me — rebellious as I was — to leave without official permission. In spite of all my posturing against authority, I was deeply obedient and wanted to do the will of God.

And so I whiled away the time at perfect leisure. Sometimes I helped with the washing up, but I was given no regular chore that I would have to suddenly drop when I left. I was given the use of an empty room and filled it with a table and a chair, a borrowed sewing machine, a record player and all the paraphernalia for making clowns. I sat on the floor mostly, making the clowns from many colourful scraps of material, playing Spanish music that my sister Liesbet had sent me a short time ago.

La Paloma filled the room and my heart. I was happy, much happier than I would be in a few weeks' time, out there in the cold of Melbourne's winter, feeling like an orphan. I made the clowns for the

Vaucluse community to sell at their next fête, and kept one as a gift for my mother. It was dressed in a golden jacket with ruffles at its wrists. My mother treasured the clown and kept it in her parlour, where it appeared to chat cheerfully to invisible company. It was offered to me after she died, but I declined, and now my sister Liesbet owns one of the world's strangest clowns. It has Spanish blood in it, I told her, and that's why she likes it.

THERE WAS THE problem of what I would wear to face the world. This was only the second time that a sister had left the order. The first was four years ago, in 1965. Due to the prevailing rule of silence, it hadn't been a talked-about event. The sister had once been the headmistress of Genazzano, and decided to leave after a lot of controversy about her handling of the pupils. My leaving, on the other hand, would cause a lot of talk — and would spark a veritable exodus. Before the end of the year, six more would leave.

My mother was asked to take me shopping, using $200 authorised by the Vicar at Genazzano for my new wardrobe.

It wasn't easy for my mother because she didn't drive, but she wasn't ready to give her husband the news that his daughter was coming home again. She feared the scenes that would ensue as my father asked questions she had no answers to as yet, and his agitation as he protested the loss of the halo he envisaged around my head. She hired a taxi at her own expense. I was overjoyed to see her, and to see that she was pleased to see me; more pleased than puzzled or distressed at my imminent departure from religious life. It was May and very cold. I needed a coat, which cost $45. There was enough money for a hat, gloves, shoes and underwear, and one dress.

My family lived in Kew, so that's where we went shopping — not the cheapest place, but I wasn't to know that! My mother must have thought that a department store or an op shop was no place for a nun to be taking off her habit and veil to try on clothes. So instead of shocking the hoi polloi, we gave boutique proprietors nervous attacks by exposing the flesh and short hair underneath my hallowed black, pretending that we did this every day of our lives.

The dress I chose was a heavenly blue with a white collar and belt. Unconsciously, I had chosen the colours of the Children of Mary that I wore as a girl. The material was a thick, rather stiff polyester and the hem reached just below the knee.

The Vicar at Genazzano asked to see our purchases, with the receipts. The sour woman berated us, making no distinction between my mother and me, for spending so much money on one item, the coat. She made it clear that there was to be no more financial assistance for clothes, or anything else. 'Please say thank you, Carla, and get out of my sight, because you have destroyed my belief that this could never happen. Goodbye, Mrs van Raay, goodbye.'

THE LETTER FROM the Vatican said, 'Go, Carla, go!' It arrived six weeks after mine was posted and was written in Latin, which to this day I haven't bothered to decipher. I was sent upstairs to my room to take off the habit. I left everything behind except a few toiletry items and prayer books.

The ritual of taking off the habit moved me unexpectedly. For the last time, I laid down the veil, noticing that my hair had grown to a boyish length. I packed my prayer book and, on the spur of the moment, the sturdy, faithful whip that was showing signs of wear. I had no intention of using it, but nobody else would want it!

When I came down the broad winding staircase usually reserved for convent royalty, dressed in my civvies and carrying my little brown suitcase, all the Vaucluse nuns were lined up to say goodbye. It was a scene to remember: those faces turned up to me, hoping to be seen for the angels that they were. I was touched by their wish to see me off with their hearts open, even if I wasn't a member of their convent. Each one took my hand warmly and said something encouraging to me as I passed. Only Sister Anthony, my maths mistress of years ago, couldn't help herself. 'May God forgive you!' she blurted. 'See what comes of disobedience!'

Others murmured their disapproval of her outburst. 'Take no notice, Carla.'

The feelings that enveloped me took me completely by surprise. I wasn't used to being the centre of such friendly attention. The kindness of their farewell that day was a blessing I sorely needed. It prevented the sorrow of rejection from taking up all the space in my heart.

PART THREE

FREE!

 FREE AT LAST! I relaxed in the back of my father's old Chevy, feeling like singing something silly, if only my father and mother hadn't been so serious about it all. I was on my way back to my parents' cottage, my old home. It was 1 June 1969, and my mother's bittersweet fifty-sixth birthday.

My poor parents. My mother, who had shown such optimism when we went shopping together, seemed to have come down to earth under the barrage of my father's loudly spoken incredulity. I remembered one of my father's extremely rare letters, composed in a fit of pride. '*We feel secure and happy when we remember that our eldest daughter is praying for us,*' he had written. To him, my prayers had been more powerful than his own. I had been a sort of insurance policy with God; now cashed in way too early and with serious losses. But their sweet bubble had to burst some time, and that time was now. They were coming to terms with the fact that the daughter they had worshipped had feet of clay. I saw the pain in their eyes, a deep sense of having been betrayed.

My father, who no doubt smarted from having been kept in the dark about my imminent defection, was also surly. 'Will you explain what happened,' he began with his characteristic forthrightness and impatience the moment we walked inside the familiar cottage. 'What's wrong with you that you couldn't stay put where you were? What wasn't good enough for you there?'

That was my cue. For the very first time I had the strange, wonderful and cleansing experience of telling them the truth of the last few years, what I had been aching to say. 'I was so miserable and unfulfilled that I was willing to die.'

They looked at me open-mouthed and with wide eyes.

'What sort of talk is this?' said my father, knuckles on hips. 'You didn't tell us that when we visited you, or when you came over for your holidays. You've been lying to us!'

His face was a mixture of derisive accusation and genuine puzzlement. He looked as if he didn't know whether to laugh at me or whether he was stopping himself from crying. I looked at my mother. Her expression was hard to read. She was barely breathing, intent on trying to understand me. Their pain finally hit me and it broke my heart. I sobbed terrible tears, bent in half with the sorrow I was causing, and we all finally sat down.

What my father had said was true. It was galling, the way I had never confided in them. I had to try to explain, even if it didn't make sense. 'Dad, you never heard a word of complaint from me, because I had to be loyal to the order.' My voice faltered; where, then, had been my loyalty to *them*? Or to the truth? 'It was one of the rules we had to keep.'

Loyalty was the first and foremost tribal rule of the sisterhood. It was an unwritten rule, but, ironically, one that I had been well schooled in from childhood: never betray the family by talking to others about what really goes on. Do not air the dirty linen to people who do not belong to the tribe. My convent community had become my most immediate tribe, at the expense of my blood family.

I told them how I had wanted to bring in changes, and how my sisters had resented me for going ahead by myself. How extremely frustrating it all had been for me. It was like opening a sluice gate, freeing water carefully dammed for years. Tight muscles in my face that had worked so hard to keep my mouth silent could now soften and let go. Fresh, clean energy filled my body as I confided and confessed.

They listened with total attention. My father swore and uttered loud 'Tch! Tch!' sounds interspersed with incredulous guffaws. My mother's breathing was rapid now and shallow and she made occasional guttural sounds of acknowledgement, her hands held tightly to her chest in a ball. She finally spoke up.

'I knew something was wrong when we didn't get a letter from you for a long time, and then all you wrote about was how beautiful your surroundings were in that English place.'

I saw her pitiful look; a mother's helpless love and sorrow. And now what did she have? A beloved daughter whose tales were destroying her images of convent life and threatened to turn her own religious beliefs upside-down.

Her intuition had been correct, especially when she had visited me in Brussels. I had lied to her there, when she asked her questions. It had seemed the best thing to do at the time. Now, I could explain to her hurt face the allegiance to the convent that had been demanded of me, and she seemed to understand. I drove the knife deeper as I went on to explain the vow of poverty and how I had been required to give away all the things they sent me as presents.

My mother reminded me of one especially valuable gift — an irreplaceable set of Reader's Digest records of classical music, sent to me during my third year at Benalla. 'What happened to that, Carla?'

'The trouble was that sometimes we were allowed to keep gifts, and at other times not. We never knew in advance,' I said. I had been too miserable to warn my parents. 'Sorry, Mum.'

My poor mother suppressed a sob. Those records had been bought from her own personal savings and were no longer available.

The immediate upshot of my confession was that both my parents became so disillusioned about nuns and the religion they represented that they stopped going to church for a time. My father was the first to relent. He had nothing better in his life, and told himself that even if the nuns were bad, God might not be.

But my mother never fully regained her trust in religion. She couldn't drive herself to church, and her occasional excuse of being unable to come with her husband because she had to mind the kids at home became more frequent. She no longer confessed her sins either; her cynicism reaching new heights when she learned about the exploits of the local parish priest, a mean-minded little man, who stroked the thigh of her friend when she went to him for advice.

There was something, however, that my mother had been hiding from *me*; something I wouldn't find out about for many years to come. For the eight and a half years before I made my final vows, my parents and my sister Liesbet had been sending money to cover a list of 'expenses' that the nuns regularly presented for payment. For all that time, while I worked hard as a cleaner and a drudge in the convent, and produced many exquisite pieces of embroidery, they had been duped into subsidising my lifestyle. My sister took it in her stride, but my brothers were less forgiving — and it showed in their attitude towards me when I first came out.

SO I WAS OUT, with one dress to my name. I wore the unlikely madonna number to meet my brothers and sisters and their curious husbands and wives. I was a showpiece. Everybody watched how I sat — rather like Grace Kelly on a dais, legs together and slanting, ankles crossed, hands folded on my lap, neck straight. I offered no juicy titbits about the convent, which they might have enjoyed. I let my mother do all the talking and was no more interesting than a doll in a box. Mercifully, people were sensitive enough to guess a little of the culture shock I was experiencing. Even though I was unimaginably agitated, I hoped I showed no trace of it.

No doubt the nuns had banked on the likelihood that my mother would use her skills to make me dresses and blouses and skirts. She did, but she sewed them the way *she* liked them. I hadn't a clue about what was fashionable. With my vows still so fresh in my mind, modesty and poverty were my only guides. I was offered a fur coat by my loving sister Liesbet — not real fur, but real enough to be super-warm — and I thought it looked very posh. But my vow of poverty prevented me accepting it. The glow I felt in indulging my self-righteous virtue almost made up for the lack of warmth during that freezing Melbourne winter. My poor sister gasped in disbelief when I refused her offer.

My blue madonna dress also gave me my first experience of being the object of a male sexual fantasy. On a sunny winter's day, during my very first shopping trip without the veil in nearby Camberwell, my psychic sex sense picked up a mumbled conversation between two sixteen year olds lounging against a shop wall on the opposite street corner. 'Look at that one!' I saw the lanky guy saying to the shorter fellow, keeping his hands in his pockets and nodding in my direction. 'Now *that'd* be an easy one to get into,' meaning my dress. 'No buttons at the back. Just a big zipper all the way down the front!' And he made a tell-tale unzipping gesture.

I smiled, tingling with pleasure at this first experience of being eyed up! It was a warm, human sensation, which helped me feel more at home on the planet.

During those early weeks, I still entertained the delusion that I might want to return to the convent after six months, so I kept up the morning and evening prayers. As I was no longer hampered by the droning group of somnambulant nuns in the convent, I found myself fairly racing through the words.

It took less than a week for me to realise the utter idiocy of the practice. It had become the most literal form of lip service. Somehow, these prayers worked through the devotion of the whole group; one individual wasn't enough — and certainly not *this* individual. Maybe I had never been pious enough, or maybe everyone left it up to her companions to fill those dry, repetitious prayers with energy and meaning. Maybe lots of small weak lights, of which I had been one, added up to a single bright light. Anyway, my tiny little bulb began to falter when I opened the book of prayers, then died, never to spark into life again.

I still went to Mass quite often. This freedom of choice was like a delicious, cool current running through my spine: I no longer *had* to go! I had barely missed a single Mass since I was old enough to go to church. Now nobody would say a word if I didn't go! In lucid moments, I realised with shock how conditioned I had become, and how childish was my pleasure in choosing.

In my parents' house, I slept once more in the double bed that I had shared with my sister more than twelve years ago. I was reminded that my parents' bedroom was next door when I heard my mother squeal 'No!' during the night. But my father still refused to take no for an answer. Soft objects hit the wallpapered wooden wall, slippers and pillows, then heavier things, like an ashtray. My mother's suppressed squeals turned into suppressed screams.

I was bold one night and called out, 'Stop it, you two! I can't sleep for all the noise!', thinking that I was protecting my mother. But my father was not about to 'cop flack' from his daughter — not even if she had been a nun and thought she had some sort of moral authority. He appeared suddenly in the doorway of my room, dressed in an assortment of nightclothes and gaping dressing-gown, looking like something out of Dickens. He was uncompromising: if I didn't keep quiet, he would let me have it. That was my cue to leave.

A FORTNIGHT AFTER I left the convent, I also left my parents' house. I rented a room in a large manor house converted into flats with money borrowed from my sister. No one guessed how completely unnerving it was for me to take this step into the anonymous secular world, but nothing could stop me from plunging headlong into it. I started teaching French at Templestowe High, one of Melbourne's most notorious and overcrowded high schools, the day after I moved into the flat.

My life as a 'normal' person had begun, whatever that means. I still don't feel normal, in the regular sense of the word, but at that tender stage of my life, at the age of thirty-one, I didn't even know exactly what a post office was for.

The principal of the school asked me into his office. 'If you need to know anything, or need help, all you have to do is ask, Carla.' He was a genuinely kind man. I *did* need help. My head was often spinning, making me tighten my neck muscles. I experienced frequent momentary blank-outs from the pressure of having to adjust to so many things at once.

I didn't know how modern adults behaved socially. I watched the people around me to give me some ideas and listened to their banter. Even ordinary language had changed. 'Nerds' now existed; at first I thought a nerd was a dimwit! It would have been good if I could have trusted my principal, but I was humiliated by the fact that he knew about my immediate past. Shades of my supposed new start at Benalla! I sorely needed a mentor, but instead I swallowed Valium before going to school.

For six weeks I lived in a semi-conscious state, until I threw the Valium in a bin and adapted with incredible tenacity to the ways of a secular high school. It was my impeccable French and my love of the subject that earned me the respect of the students and enabled me to struggle on.

They called me The Frog that first winter, because of the snugly fitting green knitted suit I bought with my first pay. It was an appropriate compliment for a French teacher. Within a month, I was given a new name: The Flying Nun. Somehow all the children knew by then that I had been a nun. Maybe it was the way I moved — fast, and seeming to glide rather than touch the ground. Sally Field flew across the TV screen as 'The Flying Nun' and I flew across the schoolyard and through the corridors like her real-life counterpart, without the wimple.

Some members of staff queried my position in a high school because I hadn't graduated. Well, I hadn't even matriculated! They talked about it among themselves loud enough so I could hear, but never said anything to my face. I gathered that they thought Sedgley College's affiliation with Manchester University was just a smart trick. I reacted by sitting for the very next Matriculation exam, and then becoming a member of the teachers' union. This was an accreditation in itself. My salary could have been affected if they had refused me. I found that my principal was on my side, and I had the explicit support of one of the staff, Ron.

Ron was a guy with a moustache and a naughty smile who loved to make me blush, which was very easy. He shared a broom cupboard converted into a staffroom with me and four others. He never forgot to ask how I was every morning. He was my main lifeline: married, and therefore no threat as a possible boyfriend, with a nice sense of humour. Ron came into the little staffroom one day with a ditty he'd found for me. My recent history had never been mentioned to my face, not by him or by anyone else. But any doubt of whether he was aware of it was dispersed with Ron's verse, which went like this:

There once was a monk in Siberia,
Who found life getting dreary and drearier.
He met a young nun,
They had lots of fun,
And he made her a mother superior!

To his satisfaction, I blushed deeply.

The teachers in my broom-closet staffroom had warned me to watch out for the 'sleazebags' — doctors employed by the education department to examine new teachers and give them their medical clearance.

The surgery was large, old-fashioned and well-equipped, and the doctor was a fit-looking man of about forty, frocked in white. The new priesthood, I thought, in white instead of black. Having been forewarned I was cool in my demeanour, an attitude I'd had excellent training in. All the same, I was naive and new to the procedures of a normal medical practitioner. It was highly probable that this doctor knew about my background.

'Please take off your clothes and lie down on the examination table. There is a chair for your clothes over there,' he said with the greatest nonchalance. *This is what I ask all my patients to do*, was the inference. I hesitated. All of my clothes? Should I ask more exactly what he meant? He saw my hesitation and repeated his request in a more commanding tone so I could be sure. 'Please take off your clothes and lie down on the examination table, Miss van Raay.'

There was no screen, but he turned his back while I placed my clothes on a large, comfy chair, then walked over to the white table near the wall, stark naked, to lie down on my back. He didn't bother to cover me up and started the routine of placing his stethoscope here, thumping his fingers there, and so on. I sat up for him to examine my knee reflexes, and was asked to lie down again, this time on my tummy, while he stroked the entire length of my back and buttocks with a feather, explaining that this was also to test my reflexes.

The feather trailed along my very white, virginal skin. I felt I couldn't object; my brain went into a scramble and refused to reason clearly. For one thing, I was unfamiliar with medical practice, as well as overawed by his authority. He made a fine mother superior substitute. However, I was careful not to be seen to react; I didn't want to satisfy this man's curiosity.

Finally he sighed and told me I could get dressed again. He did not take his eyes off me as I walked over to my clothes and started to put on my bloomers. Before I had quite got them on, he lunged over and put his right hand on the crease of my groin. 'To test the lymph glands,' he said. I stopped mid-movement to allow him to carry out his last-minute mission, coughing obediently when asked and remaining completely cool even while feeling that this was distinctly off.

It didn't occur to me that I could have slapped his face, or reported him. Sexual harassment was not an indictable offence in the early seventies. I wonder if he would have given me the required certificate if I had not cooperated. As it was, I could sense his excitement — and his frustration. A naked ex-nun in his rooms who didn't smile at him. She hadn't even become hysterical, which would at least have been interesting. I dressed as he watched, feeling his rude curiosity. But I gave him nothing. That was my only revenge.

I taught French to several streams of classes, to children with various levels of interest in the subject. When the inspector came around, I was pleased to hear him tell the children they were lucky to have a French teacher with such an excellent accent. It was then that I appreciated my six-month experience in a French-speaking convent in Brussels! I also played the mouth organ — something my father had taught me — as an aid to teaching French songs.

I only had minor problems at Templestowe High. '*I am sorry I corsed you so much trubble,*' wrote Melinda — one of several students who had a limited ability in English, never mind French, but had been forced to try to learn a foreign language in her second year of high school. She gave me a little bouquet of flowers.

I BEGAN TO have money in the bank. After I'd had my front teeth capped to hide the blackened legacy of my father breaking them when I was ten, my thoughts turned to buying a car. I was being driven to work every day by a kind woman who went out of her way to help me. To own a car, I would need to get a licence, and to get a licence I had to get out into the Melbourne traffic. It was then that I wished I'd kept the Valium to cope with fear bordering on terror. It might not have been such a big deal if my father hadn't bet with me that I would fail. It wasn't just spite; he reminded me that none of our family had so far succeeded on their first attempt, so the likelihood of me doing so was tiny.

When the big day came I was more nervous than when I'd had to win the races around the block as a child. My examiner noticed and tried to put me at ease. He sat in the front seat and my instructor relaxed in the back, as we launched into peak-hour traffic on a Friday afternoon in St Kilda. I had to manoeuvre us through a five-point intersection. I had been taught well, but forgot to turn off an indicator light, causing some confusion among my fellow travellers on the road. I thought that was it, that I'd blown my chances, so it was a huge surprise and relief to learn that I'd passed. I was so delighted that I drove all around on my way back, trying to get lost.

When I went to collect on my bet, my father was unable to be gracious; he hated parting with his money. He looked incredulous, then envious; that sinister desire to dominate his children, even if it meant their failure, was still there. He didn't want me to achieve what he himself had been unable to.

BACK IN THE parish of my childhood — Our Lady of Good Counsel — Sister Bartholomew continued the drama she had started in 1950, when the van Raay family first went to school there. Now it was 1970 and she had my sister Liesbet's children in her class.

Beatrice, the oldest girl, came home with welts on her hands, arms and legs from the big iron-edged ruler. Beatrice was a spirited girl but with good manners, so Liesbet went to school to investigate.

'Beatrice is *insolent*,' Sister Bartholomew explained in her defence. 'She doesn't *say* anything, but I can see it in her eyes: *they're just like Carla's!*'

Liesbet was not about to accept this line of reasoning. 'Frustrated old bitch!' she yelled. 'You're just jealous because Carla's out, leading a normal life!' She locked the office door and, with the instinct of a furious mother, punched Sister Bartholomew on the shoulder. Sister Bartholomew was made of good country stock and a regular tennis player, and her muscles leapt instantly into gear, trying to return the punch. She was at a disadvantage with her veil swirling around the tiny room, and she lost it to the firm grip of my sister, who gave it one decisive yank. It was enough for Liesbet to see Sister Bartholomew's utter consternation and to hear her yell: 'Get off me! I'm a nun!' The incongruous remark changed my sister's anger into mirth and great satisfaction.

Sister Bartholomew desisted from using her ruler on the girl who reminded her of Carla, the van Raay who had disgraced the order by leaving it and caused so many headaches in the process. She still had the temerity to warn my sister that she would stop her children from going to school at Genazzano, but the threat was an empty one.

'Whatever made you think your girls would not be welcome here?' said the superior when Liesbet enquired, and both Beatrice and her sister were duly enrolled at Genazzano, Melbourne's most prestigious convent.

WHEN I FOUND out about my family's financial subsidisation of my previous lifestyle I decided to confront my mother about it.

I couldn't believe my ears when I heard the facts from my mother, who broke the silence at last. She had been the main contributor — (How did she manage to do it? She refused to say.) — and my brothers Adrian, Markus and Willem, as well as my sister Liesbet, had all chipped in. I was livid.

My poor mother, she hadn't wanted any trouble with the nuns. The family was dependent on the sisters for their livelihood, for the very house they lived in. For nearly twenty years, harmony with the nuns had been essential: my father was their gardener and caretaker, and my mother worked for them as a casual seamstress.

For a while, I considered suing the order. My leaving had inspired a string of others to leave as well — six more by the end of 1969 — and I thought of joining forces with all the other women whose parents had been treated like mine. We could create some publicity and get compensation for ourselves. We should never have been put out on the street with nothing after so many years of hard work, which had been supplemented for years by funds from our own families! Yes, we had been trained as teachers, thank goodness. But I had taught at Brussels and for four years at Benalla without wages; I should at least have been given enough to make a new start in the world of houses, furniture, cars and clothes. But I did not pursue it because of my parents' precarious position. Besides, what did I really know of my legal rights? All in all, it seemed best to let sleeping dogs — or cats — lie.

The 'cats' are very grey now, if not exactly lean and hungry, and both my father and mother have died. Their home has been returned to the nuns. The time for litigation has long gone.

LIFE IN MY flat threatened to become lonely. I was only just coping with reality. But then I met Cheryl, a stylish, extroverted girl with a good heart, and we decided to share. She loved dancing and once again I found myself on the dance floors of the Melbourne suburbs. Had they always been full of people who couldn't look their partner in the face as they executed the barn dance? The guys would pass me on as if they were dancing with a bag of wheat with legs. Never mind; the music and the exercise did me a great deal of good.

The question of my getting married was now on everyone's mind, including mine. 'I think I know of a good match for you,' my mother said, trying to sound casual. 'He's Dutch and his name is Bart. His mother will ask him to take you out on a picnic in the country.' His mother did ask, he agreed, she packed a basket and off we went in his car.

Bart was a tall fellow in his forties who had never left home and had never been kissed. He worked hard as a window cleaner from dawn to dusk and was probably too tired for a social life. He had amassed quite a fortune from having nothing much to spend his income on. My mother made a big point of this fact.

He had just been to see the doctor, he confided to me as we sat on a grassy slope in a park somewhere. The doctor had recommended a book, *The ABC of Sex*, which he had bought and read. There was nothing more he needed to say to me: I didn't need a holy innocent like myself; I needed an understanding man, or at least someone who knew what he was doing. I wasn't tempted in the least by his wealth and I found his awkwardness terribly boring; in short, I had no compassion or understanding for this timid little boy in a grown man's body.

The expectant faces of our mothers fell immediately upon our return. They sighed: my mother for me, his mother for her dejected son. What were they to do?

But did my mother really want me to get hitched? Months later, when I was staying with my family again for a short while, and invited a dancing partner home for a chat — and nothing more than a chat — my mother was stupefied by moral indignation when she found us tip-toeing through the kitchen on our way out.

'Carla! That's prostitution!' she almost wept in her broken English, her trembling hand held to her mouth. She crumpled over with grief and horror and disappeared into the bathroom. She didn't mean it, of course. She knew about her husband's occasional waywardness with prostitutes; perhaps she was preoccupied with thoughts of them and didn't have the right words to express her disapproval of my late-night visitor.

When my mother's friend Eileen came to visit, they brought up the subject of marriage once again. 'What about enrolling her in an introduction agency?' Eileen suggested.

'A what?' I said. All was explained to me, and I relented and went for an interview in the city.

The tiny office had a counter at chest height as soon as you entered the door. The secretary sat at her desk in the canyon below the counter, and there was an interview room to her left, from which the boss emerged. He was in his fifties, slim and darkly dressed. He looked me up and down quizzically, as if he wasn't quite sure I was human. They had no qualms about taking my money, but it was months before I rang them and asked what they had done to find me a partner.

'It has been difficult to find someone for you because you are so tall,' said the boss. Even so, within a week I was given the phone number of someone of impeccable character, they said, who was divorced — was that a problem?

It wasn't. I met Leon at the agency and he whisked me away in his Mercedes to a restaurant. It was a brilliantly seductive introduction for me. I love elegance and style and he had the money to buy it.

He appeared to be a gentleman: not in a hurry to get me into bed, not suggestive, not rude. The one odd thing was that he didn't seem able to keep his attention in the present for long. I laughed about it one evening over dinner. He was startled to hear me mention it, and most apologetic, but the habit continued.

Leon, the sophisticate, was probably bored out of his brain by me. Maybe it was his curiosity about this singular woman with good looks and the mind of a child that made him take me out regularly. He even took me on tours of display homes, to discuss my taste in houses! I didn't know until later that he was in real estate and was combining research with the pleasure of my company.

Only once did he ask me to choose a movie. 'Let's go and see *The Robe*!' I enthused, and he looked incredulous. 'I saw it as a teenager and it'd be great fun to see it again,' I explained, all the while feeling that I was like somebody from the last century for this guy. All the same, I didn't care that Leon suppressed his yawns while Richard Burton (Marcellus) was once more converted as he put on the seamless robe worn by Jesus on the cross. I enjoyed the nostalgia of going back a full fourteen years.

Finally, the day came when Leon took me to his house; a rather fabulous pad for a bachelor. 'Well,' I remarked innocently, 'this place looks as if it has the delicate touch of a woman's hands. Lovely lace curtains, velvety carpet. Beautiful vases and flowers.' His wife, he explained, had left him. And left him with the house.

It was in the bedroom that he made his first move. I believe to this day that Leon had no great sexual interest in me. I wasn't mature enough for him and he probably had a string of mistresses. Nevertheless, he wanted to see the body of this girl-woman who had been a nun and was still a virgin. How tight would her fanny be? Would her hymen still be intact? Was that even possible these days?

The sun streamed into the bedroom window from the private, enclosed garden and made the room pleasantly warm and bright. I allowed him to undress me gently. He laid me down on the bed, on top of the covers, and began to stroke me ever so lightly. I felt myself drifting off, less and less aware of what was happening ... trusting him. He kept all his clothes on; all he did was loosen his tie.

He asked me to spread my legs. 'Is that all right?' I nodded yes, and he peered between my legs to see what he could discover among the blonde hairs, parting them slightly. He was the first boyfriend ever to lay eyes on my fanny, and the only one whose sole interest was in looking, not touching or having sex.

When Leon's curiosity was satisfied, he said, 'Enough for today?' and I nodded again, trusting his lead completely. This experienced man knew how to treat an inexperienced lady!

And yes, my hymen *was* intact. The doctor confirmed it when he came to my bedside a week or so later, when I thought I had caught the 'clap' from using a public toilet. 'You silly girl,' he said. 'How could you have venereal disease when you haven't even had sex?'

Back at the flat, Cheryl told me my mother had phoned. She had sounded anxious and wanted me to go over there. I did so promptly, and found her embarrassed and agitated.

'That man you've been going out with,' she stammered. It was obviously difficult for her to come out with it, but she decided to be direct. 'Eileen found out that Leon is married ... and he's a bad man. He's always taking out women from that introduction agency. It's just a place where he can pick up women!' There! She had blurted it out and was biting her lips now, looking so sorry for me and so angry at the man who had misled me.

She felt she had been instrumental in my deception. She knew I had come to like this man and had started weaving dreams of how my life might be with him in the house of my choice. But even she could not have guessed how hard this news would hit me. The sense of betrayal was so overwhelming that I became ill from emotional distress and couldn't go on teaching. I was submerged by a grief that could not be explained solely by Leon's actions; all the betrayals of my life seemed to be rolled up in this one.

Cheryl was kind to me; like an angel. After six weeks of misery, she suggested I went dancing with her again. 'You need to get out,' she said.

'I don't want to meet another man for the rest of my life,' I whined, but eventually I agreed and we went.

It was good to be dancing again to a live band playing the old familiar ballroom tunes. The room was full of migrant lads that evening, many of them from Britain. One of them had such an honest face that even someone as bitter as me could not put him down. He had no sense of rhythm and couldn't dance properly; he kept treading on my feet. But he smelled nice, of Scottish tweeds and fresh heather. His boyish face with its fair skin and a few freckles was topped with red wavy hair. He said his name was James. He had a lilting voice and was slim and athletic. He begged me to have the last dance with him. That seemed safe enough, so I agreed, and he kept standing on my toes, apologising. When the dance was over and I was about to disappear, he asked if he could see me again.

I stood there, literally swaying between yes and no. Yes, this was a truly honourable man. No, this was a *man* — and one who couldn't dance! My life was in the balance. But do we really have a choice, I wonder? He didn't have a car, so I drove him home, with great merriment from both of us — this is what the girls do in Australia, didn't he know?

I accepted his telephone number, but for weeks I deliberately didn't see James. I just wasn't all that attracted to him. Nevertheless he was the man I eventually married, much against the advice of all his British friends. They pointed out that I was seven years older than him, with no experience of life and unable to make a proper choice. They were right, but he was truly in love. I wasn't. I appreciated him, but in love I was not.

My mother gave me her advice. 'There is no such thing as real romantic love,' she confided to me — this was her brand of ultimate wisdom distilled from her own life experience. 'Romance only happens in the movies!'

James was kind and he always wanted to be in my company, but he didn't spoil me with romantic gifts — perhaps because he was a Scot, or perhaps because he was an original romantic, not a copy-cat. Since he didn't have a car, it was I who picked him up on our nights out. How unromantic is that? But I loved the purity about him and his sweetness. Romance was for the movies and didn't exist in real life. I was more than willing to believe my mother, having observed the quality of several other people's relationships.

James wasn't the one to take my virginity and break my hymen. That unique honour was bestowed on a man from Manchester, whom I met before James officially became my boyfriend. Brian and I got talking at this new-fangled thing called a supermarket, while waiting in line. He epitomised all the men I had read about in English novels: wild (meaning a bit unkempt), dark-haired and dark-eyed — and therefore mysterious — and humorous in that friendly, straightforward way I had noticed about Manchester people during my teacher training there.

Brian did not quite live up to my image, however. He was considerate enough as we both lay on his bed and the moment of losing my virginity came nearer. I felt strangely detached, as if I wasn't fully in my physical body, as if part of me was removed into unconsciousness. I had no control over this sensation. Brian was on top of me, supporting himself with his elbows, making determined efforts to enter me. His hard penis hit against my even harder hymen. He groaned, with pain, I presumed. Was it an ordeal for him to try to have sex with me? Brian didn't try to reassure me with kind or endearing words. His face was grim, determined, focused, and he wasn't looking at me. I just lay there, waiting for the next development, when he gave a tremendous shove and broke my seal. My virginity had been taken with a blunt instrument and the shock and pain of the tearing made me take a sudden deep breath and burst into tears. I sobbed because of the physical pain, and because of the sudden desperate feelings this act had evoked. I felt alone, abandoned.

Brian became irate at my crying, thinking it was a criticism of his lovemaking. 'What's the matter, woman?' he asked gruffly. I had trouble telling him. It was an anti-climax, yes, and a painful event for me physically, but why this welter of *emotional* hurts?

Words came to me while he dressed, and as blood trickled from between my legs onto the bedsheet. 'I only wish that it was a husband who had taken me.'

The words were meant to help him understand, but I think they made matters worse. I wished it had been *love* and not just *lust* that had broken my seal. If this was so, why had I chosen Brian? Why, indeed! When I tried to see him again, he had changed address.

Life continued, now as a non-virgin. In spite of Leon's deception and my unromantic experience with Brian, I looked at *all* men in a sexual way. My antenna was honed to receive sexual energy coming my way, always on the alert. It was this that James's friends could sense and tried to warn him about.

James and I decided to share a cheap bedsit for a while, to test how we would be living together. His sexuality was simple, uncomplicated, clean and sweet. It was all I wanted then. I loved his decency, his honesty and his tender, generous heart. That James had no money yet was something in his favour — it hadn't had a chance to corrupt him, so my thinking went. He found a job as an electrical draughtsman and walked to work rather than have me drive him. James was fit and walked with a healthy, brisk gait, radiating a steady, endearing brightness of spirit. I watched him from the window of our flat as he walked away, thinking how much I loved him and wanting to crank up those loving feelings. He did so deserve to be loved! Would marriage gradually make me fonder of this man's body? I thought of his freckled face, red hair and fair skin, also his slenderness, narrow shoulders and boyish chest. He wasn't quite a match for my own body; would that matter? The question was not quite formulated in my mind. We were to be married.

Some of the nuns came to our wedding, including Sister Bartholomew. Their presence was totally unexpected — they wanted to surprise me. I wished several times that they hadn't done me the honour, as it turned out to be a memorable event for all the wrong reasons.

ABOUT SIX MONTHS earlier, I had stopped thinking of myself as a Catholic. I had gone to confession for the last time, told the priest of my repeatedly wicked thoughts and gone to do my penance contritely and obediently, as usual. The Stations of the Cross were depicted in relief, the figures painted in lurid colours and half falling out of their frames. Vivid red paint oozed from the abused body of Jesus. As I looked at them I experienced one of those rare moments when the comical irrepressibly transforms the tragic. I started to laugh, but bitterly. I laughed at the ridiculousness of it all — at the endless rehearsal of this piteous and brutal story, and at the Church which continually ropes people into guilt. I felt such disdain that for a crazy moment I toyed with the idea of doing a handstand on the altar. I decided it wasn't worth the effort. I ran out of that church into the light of day, gulping the sunshine. After that, I shunned churches of all kinds for a very long time.

Which is why our wedding, on 19 December 1970, was held in a backyard in North Balwyn, near Kew, at the home of a woman called Joan who had befriended me. Joan was drunk on the day and useless, so I did all the running around myself, including preparing the food for the guests. Getting dressed was a last-minute operation. I had chosen to wear lemon yellow, in deliberate contrast to the white I had worn as a bride of Jesus. I thought of this as my second wedding. Instead of a veil, I wore a diaphanous broad-brimmed hat that would have gone down well at the Ascot races.

The priest was true to his word: meaning that he stayed only for the ten minutes he had promised, just long enough to whizz us through the ceremony. He had not been pleased to discover, when he asked for our addresses, that they were one and the same! We saw his surprise and displeasure, but it was too late. This wedding ceremony was sham Catholic in every way. James was a non-believer, who was willing to learn the basics to get married. And I only agreed to a Catholic wedding to please my parents, so they could tell the nuns all about it.

Berta was in charge of the music. Her job was to conjure up Handel's Fanfare and March from a record player as the bride came down the few steps separating the patio from the garden to meet the assembled guests. The magnificence of the occasion was ruined by the scratching sounds emanating from the speakers as I appeared at the top of the steps and Berta fumbled with the equipment. The music was abbreviated by silence as I reached the bottom step a few seconds later, then the candles on the makeshift altar wavered in the wind and went out. To make matters worse, my make-up was badly applied. I'd had to wait ages for the bathroom to be free, so one eyebrow ended up darker than the other and my lipstick didn't quite cover all of my mouth.

This was my wedding to James. One photograph shows a group of desultory nuns trying to smile their approval. If anybody had a good time, it was in spite of the mishaps and most likely thanks to the joie de vivre of my youngest sister, Teresa, who cleverly used her characteristic wit and flair to turn a semi-disaster into an amicable occasion after all.

I MARRIED JAMES because he loved me, and because I thought he was the opposite of my father in important ways. He was a sweet-tempered soul, gentle to the core, honourable, faithful, kind, generous and humorous; in short, a treasure of a man. But poor James: he had married a ticking time bomb. There were dark forces in me, unconscious demons that I hadn't yet faced, and they would not let me settle down like a normal married woman, with a normal family life.

For a while, everything seemed all right. We decided to leave Melbourne's cloudy skies and unpredictable weather to look up the sun in Perth, Western Australia. It was sad to leave my family; but on the other hand, I wanted some distance from them while I developed in my own non-Catholic and non-orthodox style. I didn't want to risk offending them all the time, or have to explain myself. We drove across the Nullarbor in the Falcon station wagon we had bought together, taking a leisurely week to do it. It turned out to be our only honeymoon.

Newly registered with the Education Department in Perth, I was persuaded by the eager head of a convent primary school to take on a fifth-grade class. She recruited me personally by visiting me at home, believing that an ex-nun would better for the children at her school than a lay teacher.

I negotiated my conditions. Would I be free to implement the curriculum in my own way, and not be bound by any timetable constrictions other than playtime and lunch bells? She agreed.

All was well — the children and I enjoyed ourselves. We did not have to interrupt a project when a bell rang; I did not apply any of the usual rules. I had read Neil Summerhill's books on education, and asked the children to suggest suitable punishments and rewards for certain behaviour. The headmistress and the parents approved, but it was pointed out to me that next year these fifth-graders, who had tasted such freedom with me, would be taught by the strictest nun in the school. Wouldn't they rebel? Wouldn't strictness be needed in double doses then? I sighed. Yes, it was probably inevitable, but it was not a strong enough reason to deter me.

My freedom in the classroom continued unchallenged as agreed, but the way I dressed didn't. I alighted from my car in a red pantsuit one day to find the Reverend Mother of the convent, the headmistress's superior, standing in front of me. She was outraged and stiffly ordered me to go home and change. I laughed; this was a challenge to my liking! 'What is it about my suit that isn't decent, Reverend Mother?' She chose not to answer me and walked away.

At lunchtime, I badgered her for a reason. She eventually blurted it out. 'If I allow you to wear a pantsuit, all the staff will ask for one, including the nuns!'

Had renewal gone so far as to allow nuns pantsuits if they wanted them? Intriguing thought! The whole situation seemed so ludicrous that I wrote a letter to the newspaper, which stirred up a lot of public interest and prompted a call from a television station. During the ensuing turmoil I was given a fortnight's notice, by way of a note delivered to me in the playground by a child from the third grade. The Reverend Mother recognised her mistake when she realised that I was going to air her cowardly way of firing me on television. She also received a number of phone calls from parents who were ready to remove their children from the school if she dismissed me. She pleaded with me humbly and so I agreed to end the conflict. I would not do the TV appearance, plus I would wear dresses, and not sexy pants, if heaters were installed in my classroom.

A FEW WEEKS before the Christmas of 1971, when I was six months pregnant, my destiny changed drastically. It happened due to my inexperience of life and people, which made me a sitting duck for the unscrupulous.

A Dutch woman had roped me into a networking company — the soon-to-be-notorious Golden Products. She was like a mother to me, taking an interest in my affairs and treating me to cooking creations. I never suspected her, not even when she knocked me and James out of bed in the middle of the night to sign a contract 'because it has to be in by morning, sorry I didn't notice before now'. James grumbled, but did not want to deny me. We were soon in possession of a tonne of water-adulterated soap products, which we eventually gave to a monastery because we couldn't sell them.

James didn't know how to husband a woman. In spite of his good qualities, he had not fully come into his own manliness. His horror of the macho made him too pliable and agreeable; he didn't have a strong will and relied on my lead. This was a big mistake.

James and I lost all of our savings to Golden Products. It was this that made him decide to head for the north of Western Australia, to work as an electrical engineer for good money. I was to be a temporary housekeeper in Perth until the baby was due. We left our belongings with a friend.

Suddenly I was without a husband and without a private space to call home. During the day, I kept house for a farmer and tried to cook Australian meals for him and his son. It was hopeless and the farmer had nothing but complaints about me. I cried as I walked around on the farm, feeling utterly alone and abandoned. As my baby's due date got nearer, an irrepressible desire grew in me: I wanted to be with my mother for the birth of my child.

I quickly hatched a plan. Two co-drivers appeared in answer to my advertisement for a non-stop journey to Melbourne, and we left immediately in my Ford station wagon. One was an experienced male driver, the other a young American girl not really used to driving on the left side of the road, but she would do. One person was to talk to the driver to keep him or her alert, while the third slept in the back of my station wagon. That third person was most often me, at the insistence of the male driver, who wanted me to stay in one piece until after our arrival. We made it in a blur of forty-five hours, stopping only for toilets, food and petrol.

My parents were welcoming, although completely at a loss to understand my irregular actions. No information was forthcoming from them to prepare me for birthing; they didn't appreciate that it was all new to me, and that being thirty-three years old would make a first birth more arduous. The pains soon took over. My father took me to the Box Hill hospital, where they strapped up my legs, then cut me to let the baby through. On the morning of 27 March 1972 my beautiful baby daughter was born. They whisked her away and I found myself alone in the operating theatre, where an uncontrollable urge to vomit overtook me. By the time someone arrived to clean up the mess, I had passed out. Once more — as when the warts were removed at Benalla — the after-effects of the anaesthetic would have their way with me.

I first saw my little girl at four that afternoon, when I finally woke up. I was full of remorse that she had been such a long time without her mother: I imagined life-long scarring from emotional deprivation, and trembled with guilt and anxiety as I offered her her first drink at the breast. What a pleasant and relaxing sensation to have my baby suck from my nipples! I felt we were bonding.

Still thoroughly washed out, I went back to my parents' place two days later, while the stitches were still healing.

JAMES FLEW TO Melbourne to be with me and little Caroline. He arrived three days after the birth and felt terrible about it. When I was well enough, we said goodbye again, piled all our belongings into and on top of our station wagon and once more crossed the great continent, to a town far to the north of Perth, where a good income awaited us.

James worked as an electrical engineer. I was employed in the company canteen, a lone woman in a sea of men with hungry looks, while the kind wife of the personnel manager looked after baby Caroline. I took away the dirty dishes and cleaned the tables, all the while catching with super-sensitive ears the opinions about me flying about the room. Three tables away, a group of men were discussing the size of my breasts, wondering if they were real. Because I was breast-feeding, my breasts were larger than they had ever been, but they were still on the small side compared with the posters I imagined to be in their rooms. Their interest was not in the size, but whether my breasts were real or not. It bothered me. Without looking at them, I moved so that they bounced.

'Geez!' one of them exclaimed in a subdued tone — he didn't want me to know they were talking about me. 'She bounced them just as we were talking about them!' 'They're real, all right!' said another, but there were no favourable comments about their size. Ah, well.

In the kitchen was Kev the chef — a small, round, congenial man — and his offsider, Ross. Kev was Irish and had a very welcome sense of humour. His jokes brought out the best in me. I genuinely liked him and could feel his private glow of satisfaction at being such a hit with me; but that's where I believed it ended — until one day when Kev had to go to hospital for an operation on a cyst.

The next day when I turned up for work, I was confronted by Kev's stocky wife, Janice, menacing me with a large scullery broom. 'You keep out of my husband's way!' she shouted, waving the broom at me hysterically.

I was nonplussed, but Ross filled me in. Kev had talked under the anaesthetic and said all sorts of things about me in his unconscious state, proving to his dismayed wife that he was in love with the 'tall willowy blonde'.

When Kev came back, things weren't the same. He avoided eye contact with me, and made a point of blaming me when a chicken went missing from the freezer. It was thoroughly miserable and I planned to quit by the end of the week.

But Ross wasn't done with me yet. He believed Janice's story that I'd been dallying with her husband and he wanted a piece of the action for himself. Ross's wife was expecting a baby and she wasn't available for sex. I was appalled when he approached me and said he wanted to meet me at my home. I refused outright, not only because I was married to James and had no intention of being unfaithful to him, but because I felt not the slightest attraction towards Ross.

He came to my house anyway and would not take no for an answer. He was in my living room, all on fire, raving mad. Why hadn't I locked the door? I knew I had to be quick on my feet, think of something to prevent him touching me, but my mind had gone numb, my limbs refused to show me what to do. I backed away as he came for me — uselessly, since we soon hit the wall. He had me in his grasp and started desperately groping. Spotting the bedroom, he steered me into it, pushing me backwards. My legs shook with apprehension and loathing, but at the same time it registered in my reeling brain that he would do worse things if I resisted.

He smacked me onto the bed and dragged my panties down. 'Take those off!' he thundered. He was all fired up now, his hair falling over his red contorted face. I did as I was told, and he entered me with a sickening thud. It was over in a moment: he gave some more desperate shoves then went limp. His animal lust had been satisfied.

Trembling, I cleaned myself up. I didn't realise I had been raped. I was still shaking when James came home, but I said nothing, not wanting to upset him and not wanting Ross to get into trouble for his temporary insanity. Ross had begged me not to talk, of course, after he had zipped up and regained a shaky sanity. Wasn't Ross like my father, except that *he* had forcibly demanded silence?

Unconsciously, I was repeating the old pattern, adhering to that childhood response of acquiescence and silence. Ross was fortunate to have chosen as his victim a woman who was true to her word. I resigned from the canteen and spent more time with my little daughter, Caroline.

THE MOST INNOCENT event can bring about huge change. My parents announced their intention to come to the west to visit their two daughters for Christmas and New Year. They would stay with Berta, who now lived in Perth.

I decided to head south in the car and leave ten-month-old Caroline with a couple who had become our friends. My advertisement for a co-driver was answered by Aaron, who worked some distance away at the iron mine in Pannawonica and was going home to Perth for a break with his friends from university who were all on the loose for the summer holidays. Aaron got himself over to my town. The deal was that on the way back from Perth I would drop him off at Pannawonica and then make my way back home alone.

He was nineteen, tall and slim, with loose blond wavy hair to his shoulders. Our hands touched as I explained the workings of the Ford's gears to him. The spontaneous charge was so electric that it caught us both by surprise, and we couldn't help showing it.

If I had been a mature woman, I would have closed off that circuit which connected me sexually to Aaron. But I wasn't mature. I hadn't enjoyed anything like a normal teenage life, and had minimal experience of boyfriends. That in itself made things difficult, but there was more: I felt a powerful urge to explore my sexuality, to unravel its mystery. I thought of James and my love for him, but James's friends were about to be proved right: I didn't have it in me to deny this fantastic new stream of adolescent energy. Although I spent some time with my parents in Perth — notably New Year's Eve, when I fell asleep from sheer boredom well before midnight — my attention was with Aaron.

He was a student of architecture on a six-month break from university to earn some money up north. Most of my encounters with him were at his parents' house, while they were away on holidays. We saw movies together. *A Clockwork Orange* was everyone's must-see and made me incredibly wild with sexual energy and the satisfying feeling that I was, finally, a woman of the times. It was a strange thought, since I was thirty-four after all. We swam in the pool with lots of his friends, partied to his music — new and wonderful experiences for me, full of the beat of life — and spent many hours in embraces so natural and sweet and young that I forgot my other life.

The time finally came to return and Aaron and I packed everything into the car. I said goodbye to my parents, whom I had neglected, hoping that my sister had made up for my absences.

Neither Aaron nor I were wide awake at the start of our journey; the night before had been one last party, and the last night we would be together. We stopped once along the way to fall into each other's arms under the shelter of a bridge — which didn't add to our alertness. We did notice, however, as the car swung off the main road onto the dirt track leading to Pannawonica, that the rainy season had begun. What that meant, Aaron explained, was that we couldn't risk stopping again — we would have to travel non-stop to the very end to avoid getting bogged. Getting bogged was unthinkable; being stuck out in this bush might mean death. Few people were mad enough to travel long distances by car in the wet season, and if we broke down we would be isolated with scarcely any supplies.

Hour after hour, Aaron drove on in the faithful Falcon, a silver machine with a powerful engine. Suddenly the car went off the road onto the shoulder, then into the adjoining paddock, jumping wildly over rocks and uneven ground, jolting Aaron awake. He had fallen asleep at the wheel!

It was my turn. To change seats, we climbed over each other, grabbing at the steering wheel, keeping the accelerator down and the engine going. We agreed to keep each other awake, but it was no good. I fell asleep too after a while, and it was sheer luck that there was no ditch at the side of the road to halt our madness, no kangaroos, no sheep and no insurmountable rocks. The ground beneath our wheels was mostly mud, sometimes gritty sand. Temporary firmness would suddenly give way to more slipping and sliding. It was safest to ride on the tufts of grass in the middle of the track, to keep at least two wheels from sliding.

Our indescribable exhaustion overshadowed the feeling of relief when we finally reached our destination. At Pannawonica, the officer in charge of the camp came out of his office as we drew up. Suddenly it was time to say goodbye. Aaron left quickly, so quickly that the pain of it only registered in a very tired part of me.

The officer saw the fatigued state I was in, sat me down in his office, and left to get me some dinner. When he returned, he found me sitting bolt upright on his hard wooden chair, so fast asleep that he thought I was dead! I woke up and ate some food, but the car — poor abused horse — was too overstrained to start up again a few hours later. I wasn't sorry; I was glad to rest overnight. I flew home early in the morning, in a Cessna with the postman.

JAMES DESERVED BETTER than this, but he had chosen me for his wife. It was hard to watch him suffer because I no longer wanted to be with him, so instead I turned my attention away. I didn't intend to hurt him, but how else could he interpret my behaviour? I didn't clearly know myself what was driving me to break up what we had together; all I knew was there was a restlessly growing urge in me to leave.

James found it impossible to discuss the details of our separation. I had my own money and would use it to rent a house in Perth. As we no longer owned a car, we both flew to Perth. From there James boarded a plane for Sydney, wanting space and time to get over the bitter wounds of our parting. His letters to my sister Liesbet, whose sympathy he could rely on, carried his grief and, briefly, his anger.

I still carry a great regret for his hurt, for he was a thoroughly good man.

Our marriage was over. Aaron — the catalyst for my newly awakened sexual drive — was also gone, but I was now open to a new sort of passionate connection. I looked in the mirror and saw that I was beautiful. My long blonde hair fell gracefully around a face with smooth fair skin and clear grey-blue eyes. My body was lithe and graceful and I had long shapely legs. I was in my prime at thirty-four and I felt invincible.

'This is how I am going to be for ever,' I told myself. It would take years — decades, in fact — for me to come to my senses. I had no idea then of course, how I would feel at the age of fifty-five, having been cavalier with the vitality of my own body and the emotions of others. 'Your biography becomes your biology,' says Caroline Myss in her book, *The Anatomy of the Spirit*. I think she is right, although the statement is a little on the grim side.

I installed myself and my daughter Caroline in a house with generous proportions in Floreat Park. Barely two weeks later, I advertised for a new husband in the personal columns, stating that to be eligible the pretender had to beat me at chess. I wasn't all that good at chess, but it had been too easy to beat James.

Several would-be suitors turned up, and one even returned three times, but I beat them all. None of them had the presence of mind to kick the chessboard aside and just take me out, for goodness sake! Shortly after, I told my tale to a taxi driver, who quietly stopped at a convenient coffee shop, took out his chess set from the boot and beat me convincingly. It took me down a peg or two, and redeemed my faith in men. No, I didn't marry him. I never even saw him again!

In spite of my confidence in my good looks and my adventurous spirit, my self-esteem was really still in tatters. Deep inside was an unacknowledged hurt, abused and frightened child.

BUY ME

 IT WAS EARLY spring, 1973. I never thought of asking James to support Caroline and myself, and as for social security — it was some time before I even learned of its existence. When I did, my heart filled with appreciation for such a generous welfare system. I used it when I needed to, but I didn't believe a person could live decently off social security. I started looking for work in the local papers. The option of teaching felt totally uninspiring, and so when I saw an advert for unskilled workers to make plastic rainwear in a clothing factory in Balcatta I went to check it out. I wanted to see what life would be like doing something useful with my hands. My mother was a seamstress; was there something of her in me that could help me earn my living here?

The manageress looked askance at me, but ushered me into the large shed that was the factory. The air was saturated with the smell of plastic and the oil that the women used to stop the slippery material escaping their needles. A steady drone filled the air from the rows and rows of sewing machines, all tended by women with bent backs — mostly Italians and Greeks, I thought. I suspected I was in a sweatshop.

'How much an hour?' I asked. The manageress had to answer this one, but how could she coolly say '$2.50 an hour' when the average rate of pay was about $8.00? 'Before tax?' I said in surprise. 'Yes, before tax.' The manageress studied my face. Was she wondering if I would report her factory to the unions for the exploitation of women who didn't have enough English to know their rights?

These women are prostituting their skills and energy for a pittance, I thought to myself. *Prostitution!* Once the word entered my head, the next thought appeared:

I would do better, I told myself. I would prostitute my body for good money and have fun, as well.

As long as I enjoyed myself, my young, inexperienced and only seemingly sane brain rambled on, I wouldn't be prostituting myself nearly as much as those poor women in the sweatshop. Or anyone else, for that matter, who worked just for money — as I might have done, by going back to teaching when my heart wasn't in it.

My first step was to find a woman to share my house. Her name was Kelly, and although she hesitated when I told her of my imminent plans, she agreed to be my babysitter. Caroline now had a little playmate: Kelly's son, Jimmy. Sharing was not new to me, having lived so much in community, and it was much less lonely, having Kelly and another child around.

I knew no one in the sex industry and, typically, asked no one for guidance. I began exploring the possibilities for this different, daring career by perusing the personals in the daily newspaper. *Escorts required to accompany gentlemen; phone Stella's for interview* caught my eye.

'Stella's Escort Agency. How can I help you?' A husky voice, almost male but soothing, answered the phone.

'I saw your advertisement for escorts,' I told her, my heart beating hard inside my chest. 'Er . . . I'm phoning because I want work.'

Stella, if that was who it was, talked to me in an upbeat way to make me feel very welcome to come and see her. No questions about what I looked like, if I had any experience or how old I was — luckily. My voice was young and musical and always belied my real age. And in terms of maturity I was thirty-four going on eighteen. That short conversation proved to be the only interview.

I WENT UP the flight of steps of the older-style Leederville house. On that first day on the game, I wasn't exactly dressed for the job in a smart but unobtrusive dress that might have done for the office.

I entered the hall and my footsteps resounded on the wooden floor, incongruously bringing to mind images of convents. The vestibule had been transformed into a tiny office with a desk and a chair against the back wall. Two more chairs against the other wall completed the furniture.

I spoke briefly with the woman at the desk; the scorched smoker's voice from the day before gave her away as Stella. She greeted me, quickly looked me over, then pointed me to the waiting room next door. Good; I wasn't especially unsuitable then.

I entered the girls' lounge room with the same feeling of doom as when I jumped into the lime pool at Box Hill during that last summer before entering the convent, falling fast and inevitably into the dark still water far below. My bathers had slipped off my shoulders, I remembered, from the sheer pressure of water rushing at my body.

The lounge room was in semi-darkness and permanently dusty. An old dark-red carpet patterned with pink roses lay over another, even older carpet and nondescript pictures of still lifes and horses were displayed on discoloured walls which had long stopped caring what was hanging there. The musty smell reminded me of my paternal grandparents' home. The curtains at the windows were drawn and the only light came from a dim shaded lamp in the ceiling. There were a number of armchairs crammed into the room; they were good for waiting in, and wait we did.

A turmoil of feelings swirled around inside me. The place was seedy and uninspiring, and I *hated* working without feeling enthused. I felt like a fish out of water, but uppermost in my mind was a burning desire to get an education in this business. There was no conversation while we waited. Some girls read a magazine in the dim light. Some chewed gum. Most sat wrapped in thought. If anyone was nervous, no one showed it. If anyone guessed that I was new, it didn't mean a thing. Silence reigned. In that room we were in competition with one another.

The girls smoked on the back porch, and even in the kitchen, but never in the lounge room. This rule wasn't to protect our health — it wasn't an issue in the early 1970s — but to keep the smell out of our hair and clothes. Stella had her minimal standards.

A stir of stale air heralded the entrance of the first client. My heart did a flip. Would I even be noticed? I wasn't, and it gave me a chance to watch instead. A lightning-fast appraisal of what the guy might be worth decided the play: whether the girls would compete for him with smiles or pouts, by unfolding black-stockinged legs, showing a hint of lace panties under a short skirt, or a suggestive turn of half-naked breasts. One girl rose from her chair, in readiness for his nod. His glance swept over me, but he seemed to recognise the one who stood and off they went without a word.

My silent co-workers were a mixed bunch who were generally more glamorous and explicitly sexy than I was. They did their best to show off their breasts, real or false — either way a definite asset in this business — and wore the reddest nail polish to match the invitation of their shiny lips.

I wasn't overtly sexy enough to fit the stereotype. I traded on standing out by being unusual, which is probably why I didn't make a fortune out of it. I had nice breasts, but they were on the smaller side. I hated nail polish and garish colours. I didn't know how to pout, seduce with my eyelashes or affect a sexy walk. My allure rested on understatement; I could create excitement from what could be hinted rather than displayed. Of course there was my elegant slimness, my Dutch blonde hair and what a friend once described as my 'deliciously long legs', in spite of some varicose veins. My best feature was perhaps the shape of my bottom: I knew it was 'cute' from the reactions so far received from admirers. My knees were slightly knobbly from the many hours of kneeling in the chapel, but not too bad. Another string to my bow was lively wit and conversation in a situation where I was the centre of attention. Yet another was my innocent friendliness, since I hadn't had time to grow cynical, mistrustful or hard, took no drugs apart from the contraceptive pill and had none of the ulterior motives that drove many of the girls.

I watched and waited but no other clients arrived that afternoon. However, Stella now knew she could depend on me to turn up. 'I'll put a new advertisement in tomorrow's paper just for you,' she promised. That was her way of saying she wanted me to be on her team.

The next day I came dressed in a white lace top with a pink velvet short skirt over white lace pantyhose. In spite of my height, I wore high heels. Shoes have always been a problem for me: I'm size eleven, which restricts my choice. I had to settle for a pair of shiny black ones I'd stashed in the back of the wardrobe. The colour didn't match, but they were pretty and I was surprised at my pleasure in seeing my own feet: eleven measures of sexiness on tall, slim, shapely legs. I found some flashy fake gold and pearl drop earrings and a matching necklace, and put on brighter pink lipstick. I looked myself up and down in the mirror: it wasn't really me, but it would do.

When Stella came into the room on behalf of the client who had asked for the new girl from the advertisement — 'Long legs, blonde Monica, very good to talk to' — I stood up in my high heels, feeling so tall that I was almost dizzy with fear that he would be overwhelmed by my height. But he didn't seem to care; he was just in it for the novelty. He paid at the desk and we left for his motel.

Acting as nonchalantly as I could, I made it gracefully down the steps to Tony's clean and newish car, and he took me straight to a motel that let rooms by the hour, with its own car park — very handy, I thought.

Tony was straightforward and businesslike. He showed me in, locked the door, instantly proceeded to take off his clothes, got himself on the bed and was ready for action. Even so, he whispered, 'Not too fast,' as I cat-crawled to him on the bed, having undressed more leisurely and deliberately while my heart was pounding and my mind worked overtime. What was expected from me? I had no real idea. I decided to gauge the situation moment by moment by trying to enter his world: what was *he* feeling, thinking?

I touched his naked body and felt it thrill. I was gifted with a special touch and wasn't even aware of it. Feeling welcomed and wanted, my hands were ready to become bolder, when he took over from me, stroked my body boldly up and down and entered me as he rolled me onto the bed. His body was impetuous and he came very quickly. Was this it? No; Tony stopped me from moving off the bed. 'Please stay a while,' he begged. Why not, I said to myself and relaxed beside him.

Tony lit a cigarette with slightly unsteady hands, lounged against the pillows and surveyed the body he'd hired with a bit more attention than he'd given it at first. He watched me as I turned to conjure music from the motel radio. From the corner of my eye, I noticed his penis begin to regain some of its life. His cigarette almost finished, he slid down from the pillows onto the bed and I turned to him again and put a friendly arm around his waist. He took my hand, indicating wordlessly that he wanted to be stroked, so I stroked his thighs, his belly, lightly touching his testicles and the length of his now fully revived penis, murmuring that he had a nice body. Tony threw the end of his cigarette into the bin by the bed, turned around and surprised me by powerfully lifting me up to position me over his penis.

This time, it was even more satisfying for him. For me, in spite of a raw shocked feeling of newness, the whole thing was enjoyable. Tony was decent and paid me extra. I took a shower and left him smoking another cigarette. It had all been so thankfully easy.

And so I was introduced into the game. 'Escorts' the advertisements in the papers said. At first I thought I would be a sort of geisha, providing company for men without sex being involved. 'Ah, yes,' the girls said when I asked them, 'that happens now and again, but don't ask us, we're not interested.' As it happened, shortly after I joined Stella's a young man rang wanting someone to escort him to a wedding. Being the new one, I was offered the job and, to Stella's relief, I took it.

I had two reasons for taking on this particular assignment. Firstly, I had never been a guest at a real church wedding before, and secondly, I had to pretend I was his girlfriend: the professional complicity delighted me. Everything went well in spite of my client's extreme nervousness, especially when he introduced me to his family and then suddenly realised he would have to do without me once his two hours were up. He paid me on the spot for another two hours, nervously extracting the money from the internal pocket of his jacket where he had it at the ready. For some reason, it was extremely important to him to give the impression that he was hitched. The deception was carried off with panache well into the reception, and my partner thanked me with true gratitude when I left. Stella let me keep his fee, as there was no profit to be made this time. She had to keep up the facade of an escort agency or risk being busted by the police, who knew what was going on anyway.

Sometimes we girls went out as pairs, posing as lesbians, which provided us with an opportunity to talk. One woman was angry with a former partner and wanted to teach all men a lesson by making them pay for sex. She also hated men because she had been sexually abused when she was an adolescent. Others just wanted quick money, for drugs or whatever else was obsessing them. These girls had no trouble showing their clients who was in charge and how much they wanted. A man had to watch his wallet with them.

Most of the women I met were not hard types. One girl I paired with was dropped off and picked up at Stella's by her boyfriend. She was a university student in a hurry to get on with life. 'I'll only stay until we've got our deposit for a house together,' she smiled, looking absolutely like the girl next door in a glamorous mood. We pretended to be lesbians with gusto, kissing, moaning, licking — sometimes catching each other's eye in amusement when we thought the drunken lot who'd hired us wouldn't notice. They laughed a lot, these men from the construction industry, who had stayed on after work for fun and drinks in the belly of the new hotel they were building, at the invitation of the boss. I didn't care if they were laughing at us, or because they were embarrassed, or just out of their brains. It didn't matter when both of us girls were also having fun and getting paid. What they did with their excited libidos after we left, I have no idea. They probably called for the non-lesbian types. Oh, well.

In those days, most men took a complete health risk with hookers: they seldom thought to use a condom, and neither did I. Stella had only casually mentioned using condoms for protection from venereal disease. She knew, of course, that men preferred sex without them, and if her girls didn't use them so much the better for her business.

What on earth was I up to, exposing myself like that? It wasn't that I didn't think of the risk. I had two strategies. The first was my instinct, which told me when I could trust somebody, even a voice over the phone, and improved with time and experience. Secondly, I went to see a doctor every week for a check-up with a blood sample.

Doctor Dayton was a nearby GP with a soft spot for the girls, taking extra good care of them. He was also an expert in venereal diseases.

'How much do you charge for your services?' he asked me one day, surveying my naked body on his table. 'Not enough, not enough,' he responded emphatically when I told him. I wish that I could have heard him then, because he was speaking the truth. But I was always far from perfect in my own eyes. I thought of my smallish breasts: they didn't fit the bill, did they? How could I charge more?

One day I received a phone call from Dr Dayton, asking me to hurry to his clinic for a penicillin shot. Usually when one of his girls came into the waiting room, she received immediate attention. It was all part of his gentlemanly attitude towards us. This visit was the only time this didn't happen for me. I arrived at the clinic to see an internationally famous rock star sitting nervously in the waiting room with his chauffeur bodyguard. When they were shown in before me, I knew the reason for his visit. Dr Dayton must have been a very good specialist GP to be known in the circles of the rich and famous! I chuckled to myself, until I remembered that the reason I'd been summoned was because I'd been diagnosed with the first stages of gonorrhea.

I am terrified of injections, just watching them on TV can make me feel faint, but I give Dr Dayton full credit for gliding the needle in so gently, and uttering soothing words all the while as if I were his own dear daughter, that I hardly felt it enter my buttock. He was a treasure.

WHAT WAS REALLY dirty about working for others in the prostitution business was the so-called containment policy, which meant that some madams were allowed to operate brothels and escort agencies in defiance of the law prohibiting organised prostitution, and others were not. How did those madams please the police to stay in business? That was, indeed, the question. Another evil permeating the industry was the undermining of the competition, and, where possible, the elimination of it. People could — and did — get murdered for mysterious reasons.

What bothered me particularly about my new career was that I never seemed to get to be myself. I was this make-believe person, an inauthentic imitation of a hooker; I was playing a game and nobody said, *who are you, really?* Prostitution is, after all, called 'the game'. Nevertheless, it shocked me that nobody seemed to *want* me to be anything different! After about a month at dingy Stella's, doing daytime hours, I set out to find another, hopefully more classy employer.

I discovered Marinette, who touted a French connection. She ran a different sort of business: men never seemed to come to her place at all. After speaking with the client on the phone, she and I would wait under a street lamp for him to show up and the transaction was made there and then, on the street. Her clandestine yet careful attitude made me feel safe with her. She was a sort of crusty mother figure to me, talking to me frankly about the art of sexual love, which my own mother never had the courage to do. I admired that about Marinette, and learned quite a bit of useful information.

'The missionary position is for Catholic missionaries,' she joked in her pleasantly distorted French accent. 'Avoid it. It is terr...ibly boring.' She spoke as if she knew the Kamasutra off by heart. I was lithe, but not a yogi, and quite happy to keep experimentation within the limits of my clients' expectations. After all, they were no yogis either.

Marinette must have been a beauty in the past; her signature was her shiny black hair, which she wore in an elegant bun. I liked and trusted her, until she let me down by sending me to a client well-known to her, who had the kind of penis that King David might have envied. My fanny, tight from its long-lasting virginity, had trouble accommodating him and it hurt. She had the grace to blush when I complained, but I left her soon after for a male pimp called Rick, who had once been mentioned to me by one of Stella's girls. It was mere curiosity that drove me to work for a man instead of for a woman.

Rick was middle-aged, of medium height and a rather thin fellow who had already been in jail a couple of times for living off the earnings of prostitutes. He had a certain hold over women because he came across as a real Aussie battler who had a soft heart for them. In other words, he was a sort of dinky-di father substitute.

Rick lived in the house he operated from — a ramshackle, wooden place with lino on the kitchen floor and three ducks flying in formation on the living-room wall. I had the impression it had once been his mother's house and he hadn't bothered to change anything, including the faded cotton curtains. Rick's girls hung out in his house, making tea and toast for themselves whenever they wanted to, even cleaning the place for him, until they were sent out on a rendezvous.

Only three weeks into this new liaison, I arrived at the house to find Rick in a drunken state, feeling very sorry for himself because he had just found his cornflakes box — which ingeniously doubled as a cash box — was empty. It had probably been raided by one of his girls, who had discovered the stash when she was looking around for something to eat. I was surprised to see I was the only girl there. Rick sat down in an armchair and imperiously called me over to have sex with him. 'Sit on top of me,' he grumbled, undoing his fly and taking his organ in his hands. A few strokes and the horny thing was standing bolt upright. I obliged him with extreme reluctance, and only because I feared that refusal would mean a nasty reprisal. He relieved himself ungraciously into me. 'There,' he announced with a sneer, 'you'll have cystitis now for the rest of your life.' Rick's penis burned with the infection as angrily as he burned with indignation at being robbed, and he had deliberately tried to pass on his disease to me in revenge.

Not realising that cystitis is not a transmittable disease, I ran for Dr Dayton, who calmly advised me to wait and see what would eventuate. Nothing did, but for the next two weeks I didn't dare have sex in case I transmitted the disease. I used the time to plan the next stage of my career. I wanted to work on my own, convinced that it would be infinitely better than anything I had experienced to date. I heard on the grapevine that Rick had gone behind bars again for pimping. The girls must have known that something was up that day and had left before the police showed up.

I still had a lot more to learn about the real rules of the game, and probably missed out on some of the better opportunities out there, but after three months I was ready to work for myself. I so longed to be free to set my own standards and working hours. This wasn't the done thing, but I had been lucky enough to be working for a pimp who had gone down, so I was unlikely to be penalised for being an upstart. Competition was serious business; even a girl working on her own was considered a threat, as I found out some time later.

KELLY AND I discussed my working from home. Our house in Floreat Park was well-suited: it had its own separate entrance at the back to a bedroom, and the bathroom could be reached without entering the main living quarters. I offered to let Kelly and her son stay on rent-free, and she agreed. She continued to look after little Caroline while I worked. Caroline and Jimmy got on well together and I made good friends with Kelly.

Kelly was taking a risk, living with me, as she could have been considered an accessory. It was perfectly legal for a girl to work on her own, but to have help in the house amounted to running a brothel — or so I was told by a client who sent me into a spin when he identified himself as a cop. 'It's all right,' he said in a fatherly way, 'I won't do you in. But be careful.' Kelly was even more nervous after that, but then she was the worrying type anyway.

I placed a small advertisement in the *West Australian*, among much more prestigious escort notices, and waited nervously. I was a woman on her own — would anyone notice me? The phone gave me a fright every time it rang. When would it be my first potential client?

One day I answered the phone to the give-away beep-beep of a long-distance call. It was a gent who said he was ringing from Sydney. 'Hello, Carla. I liked your advertisement! My name is Michael.' (I knew I didn't have to believe that.) I listened to his voice, and knew he was doing the same. A phone interview to determine whether we would meet up or not! I felt the thrill of this game: the excitement of the unorthodox and the potentially dangerous.

'Do you like chocolates? And roses?'

I laughed. It was just the thing to ask a woman who might feel a little awkward at being wooed for a sexual interlude with a stranger! Michael was due to arrive in Perth in three days' time, and was scheduling some recreational activities among his business appointments.

'I have two rows of standard roses at home,' he explained when we met face to face and he handed me his gift. (Swiss chocolates, dark: my favourites.) 'Red and white.'

Roses were obviously his passion and he was genuinely delighted to talk to me about them. Michael's suit showed a superior taste and he gave the appearance of being in charge of any situation, but underneath he was eager to please. I made the first move as we continued to talk, undoing his expensive tie. He smiled. Yes, we were well suited for this sort of encounter. I felt the pleasure of initial success, of a dare paying off. If this was wicked, it was a glittering wickedness, conjuring up the sensuousness of the 1920s. It was completely satisfying, a mixture of luscious leisure and eager excitement. When we had finished, Michael put money on the mantelpiece for me. It was more than I had asked for.

'Do you get many clients from interstate?' he wanted to know before he left. 'You are my first client,' I confided. 'That makes me very special indeed!' he flattered, then gave me his advice as a businessman. 'Be very choosy,' he said. 'Businessmen like me want to feel safe with a person who doesn't have too many different clients.'

I understood what he meant, and now I knew what to aim for. Michael wanted a mistress, not a hooker. There are some distinct differences. He wanted to get to know me, to make me like him and want to take care of him. He also did not want to be seen entering a known establishment — a mistress provided better discretion. Sex without condoms is always unsafe, but with me the risk was very much reduced because of my high standards of hygiene. From then on I specified 'businessmen only' in my advertisement, and gave preference to clients from interstate. These men became my regulars and a mutual trust developed.

Being a mistress in my own home suited me superbly. I could be generous with my time and friendship and I enjoyed having sex with men who knew and respected me, and with whom I did not have to pretend.

My house was usually filled with flowers from satisfied customers, one of whom was a florist, a wrinkly, good-humoured man. He often left bunches of flowers at my back door early in the morning. I would smell their fragrance upon waking — such a nice way to begin the day!

I felt myself wholly a *woman*, in love with sex, enjoying men's compliments and attentions — and they did me the honour of paying me well. Payment, to me, was a form of appreciation, of approval; it gave me a sense of self-worth. But I didn't really know what to do with the money. I bought peacock-blue silk furniture that reminded me of the 1920s, but it was in danger of being ruined by the two toddlers. It didn't enter my head to invest my money in real estate, which would have been a smart move. For financial astuteness, I deserved a zero. The truth was, I felt embarrassed by money — a leftover of the vow of poverty that I had lived for twelve years and renounced only three years ago. I had no difficulty breaking the vows of chastity and obedience, but poverty hung on, with its values of detachment and doing without.

I was still prepared to do some work away from home. One evening I answered a call to one of Perth's swankiest hotels to attend a party of guys celebrating a business deal. This sounded like a challenge, but I soon realised the guys weren't 'regulars'. They were just ordinary blokes out for a wild and naughty night. They had got my phone number on a recommendation from a client, so I felt safe to oblige them.

They were looking rather dishevelled, though still wearing their suits and ties, when I arrived at their large hotel room. It was fitted with lounge furniture, a double and a single bed, and had access to a smaller room. Music blared from the hotel radio and the air was already rank with the smell of alcohol and sweat. I was greeted with various gestures of welcome — especially from Barrie, who had originated the idea — and was offered a drink. I asked for cider. They had none, but it was soon delivered and the merriment began in earnest.

I was wearing a little red skirt and a billowing white silk blouse. I lounged on the double bed while my shiny red shoes were removed by helpful, eager hands. I gulped the sweet cider. I never normally needed alcohol or any other stimulant to get me going, but having to play up to six men I needed a little bit of help! The music inspired me to dance on the bed, and in moments I was joined by at least three others, all shouting gleefully and slopping their drinks on the covers. The guys began to clap in unison and I got the message: I was to do a striptease before leading them off to their ultimate ruin!

The mattress was really too soft for dancing, so I stood on the long dressing table in front of its large mirror and began to take off my blouse. I was untrained in the art and not sure what to do next, but their appreciation of every move I made was so tremendous that I soon forgot to feel embarrassed, even by the varicose veins revealed when I removed my pantyhose. My legs and body sported a light tan — I had taken to putting my pale European skin under artificial sun lamps to give it a healthy glow. I sang as I gyrated, trying to avoid falling off the dressing table and into their arms or onto the floor, and they whooped as each item of clothing was flung through the air and landed, whenever possible, on someone's head.

Alcohol had been flowing so freely that nothing was going to stop anyone doing anything he wanted now. I had exposed all, including my tantalising blonde patch of pubic hair — which was quite enough, I thought, when suddenly I was caught up by one man and turned first on my back, then upside down. He held me on the bed while he called out to a mate. To the brutish delight of all present, my fanny was doused in beer while he and his mate held my legs apart. The beer ran into my mouth and hair, and I wriggled in mock distress — 'Let me go, you Neanderthals!' — and, after much laughter on all our parts, they released me. Once upright again, I told them it was time for the real fun to begin, in the small room next door.

There was no margin for finesse as they traipsed in one by one and tried to get it up — an onerous task for the more intoxicated. In the end they were all satisfied, and not nearly so rambunctious when I left after a shower. The room was a veritable shambles: the bedclothes and mattress were soaked beyond saving; booze stained the carpeted floor. I was paid generously and returned home for a well-earned rest, wondering if they would think the night worth it when they received the hotel bill for the damage.

Sometimes things didn't go quite so well. Like the night I answered a call to a hotel from a captain whose merchant ship had docked in Fremantle. The room I entered was tasteful enough, and so was the dinner, nicely served on a trolley. The captain was dressed in his uniform — no doubt to impress me — and it did the trick.

He was a lightly moustached fellow of about forty-five, spreading a little around the waist from indulgent dining, but looking smart. He took off his jacket and we stood at the window, admiring the view across the harbour. We were a good match in height: he was at least two inches taller than me, even in my high heels. I put my arms around him, my back to the window, and then I made a fatal mistake. Unthinkingly, intending to create intimacy, I stuck my hands in the back pockets of his trousers and patted his buttocks playfully, rocking him gently from side to side. I gave him my best smile, intended to indicate the good time in store for him, and pushed my body closer to his, so he could pat my buttocks too. But suddenly he pushed me away from him, a changed man. 'You were going to steal my wallet, weren't you?' he bristled, his face alight with fury.

I was completely taken aback and could only shake my head in disbelief at his reaction. Was the man so blind that he couldn't recognise me as an honest woman? What *had* he seen in me? Nothing but a scheming piece of flesh? Did he think I was play-acting? I had been enjoying myself up to this point — I could never just 'act', because acting meant hiding that you were *not* enjoying yourself. I picked up my jacket and bag and left, feeling close to tears.

DURING THAT FIRST year of self-employment, one of my strangest experiences had nothing to do with work at all. It was the seduction of a famous pianist, with whom I locked eyes in the foyer of a Perth hotel. I was there on business, but he wasn't to know that. Between clever flourishes on the hotel piano, he gave me his card.

'It will be more fun if I come over to your place,' Philippe said on the phone. He was carrying three bottles of chartreuse when I opened the door to him. After scanning me deliberately, he declared me to be beautiful before committing himself by stepping through the door. I had no piano for him to shine on and his manner was more brusque than in the hotel, but I told myself that fame may make a person arrogant as well as intriguing.

He plied me with the pleasant liqueur, but I am one of those people whose brain cells die by the millions when they encounter alcohol. I am even more sensitive to the preservatives in wine, which have a toxic effect on my liver and often a drastic effect on my looks. It was approaching midnight when I felt my energy changing. My musical maestro was lying on top of me, joking about something. As the clock struck twelve, I felt a tiredness flood over me.

Philippe stopped speaking mid-sentence. I watched his horrified eyes, as he elbowed himself off me, shouting with sudden abhorrence, 'You've become ugly! U–u–gly!!'

His mouth convulsed with repulsion. His reaction was so unexpected that I felt very calm, even amused, in spite of the insult. I was exhausted, and after so much alcohol I couldn't possibly hide it. I felt like Cinderella in the coach that turned into a pumpkin on the stroke of midnight. The thought made me laugh, but Philippe was deadly serious. He got into his clothes, ran for the fridge to retrieve the rest of the chartreuse, and left without saying goodbye.

No manners from *this* French beau! Midnight might have turned him into a rat, but the whole thing was so funny, and the evening had been so exhausting, that I was glad to reach for the light switch and go to sleep without even bothering to brush my teeth.

MY THEATRICAL SIDE came out to play. I took to wearing a shiny top hat with anything that seemed to go with it — knee-high boots, sometimes a dinner jacket, lace gloves — and I smoked small port cigars, although I was never a smoker before and I didn't know how to inhale. I wore this marvellous gear at home for some of my guests, and to parties with my friends.

I posed as a lesbian at my friend Victor's party. Victor was my masseur at the clinic I frequented; he was from South Africa, an easy talker, young and muscular, exuding sexual charm as if he was the originator of it. On that cold evening, I greeted young women as they entered the door, offering to warm their hands or fetch them a hot cocktail, leading them to the fireplace, making complimentary remarks about their make-up or their hair, and asking them to sit on my knee. It was funny to watch their surprise — at first pleasant, if a little overwhelmed — then see it change to suspicion, and eventually, without exception, to wordless rejection.

I expected the shake-off. I would have been embarrassed if anyone had taken me seriously! In mock disappointment I joined a group of gay guys, imitating their stance and manners and enjoying their wit. However, I had to admit to myself how nice it was to feel female hands; something women don't often experience. I realised that there was a real lesbian inside of me, who could come out to express herself, if she chose to.

The occasion presented itself one lovely magical day.

'Julie is my girlfriend,' said Andy, when he rang and asked me to join them in their hotel room. Andy was one of my less attractive customers; a lecherous streak in him made me hesitate. On this afternoon, he wanted to see what a threesome would do for him.

As it happened, Julie and I gave him a first-class demonstration of how two women can enjoy each other. We clicked immediately, and seemed to understand without saying that although the plan was to please Andy, we were going to ignore him altogether. I felt such pleasure and pure abandon at throwing myself into Julie's arms, and feeling hers around me in a welcoming feminine embrace.

We rolled on the bed, indulging our every whim to touch, nudge, caress, lick, suck and delight every part of our bodies. Julie's hair was long and fragrant and her pubic area was clean and oh! so new and delightful. We both knew instinctively where we liked to be touched. The sensation of her naked body against mine told me what it might be like for a man to feel soft breasts against his chest. It was wondrous to suck her nipples and know exactly how she was affected by what I did. She found mine: they were large and prominent from having breastfed my baby for a year, and ecstatic to be caressed by her gentle mouth.

We were shameless in our desire for one another and didn't let Andy in until we were both satisfied and had gently rolled down into a soft blissfulness. Andy couldn't have asked for a better performance, but of course he was peeved. I vaguely remembered hearing his calls for attention, but we couldn't have cared less. He had his revenge later when I asked to see Julie again and he refused to let me have her phone number. I suspect that she wasn't his girlfriend at all, but another pro like me. I gave Andy the flick after that, and I hope Julie did too.

After that wonderful experience, I hung out at a gay pub in Perth for a while, the Red Lion, and watched the dynamics between the lesbian clientele. Would I meet another woman like Julie? I saw women who had rejected men dressing like men and imitating their behaviour. I also witnessed jealousy and outrageous cattiness. I was turned off and decided that was enough to know that I was bisexual, but definitely leaning towards heterosexuality. I would not go looking for lesbian sex. In honour of Julie and everything I had experienced with her, I would keep one perfect memory.

NEAR THE END of this first year of my new career, my lovely blonde pubic hair became home for a despicable brood of insects. I'd vaguely heard of crabs, but hadn't considered them a real possibility in my world. It got prickly down there, but not exactly inside my fanny, so I didn't think it was anything serious. I ignored the itch, scratching absentmindedly now and then.

A client who'd hired a waterbed at a hotel by the Swan River surprised me with, 'What you got down there, sweetie? You sure didn't get them from me!'

He pointed and I had to look close to discover the rude creepy-crawlies in my hair, sucking red blood from my body. I was so shocked that I jumped out of bed screaming and ran towards the door stark naked, as if I could run away from them. George said good-humouredly, 'It's not so bad, you know, Carla. Calm down!'

I stopped screaming. Nobody out there appeared to have heard a thing, or if they had, had taken no notice whatsoever. I had screamed blue murder and no one had come running. That was sobering in itself. 'Get yourself some DDT cream,' was George's sensible advice, and I did that very same day.

When I confided in one of my gay friends, he took pity on me and did the kindest thing ever: he carefully shaved off every bit of pubic hair around my infected vulva to remove the vermin, eggs and all. Now I had the French look, he told me, but the initial eroticism soon wore off with the regrowth of short scratchy hair. No way was I going to keep up the shaving routine — my hair being blonde, I didn't even use a shaver on my legs! I kept the DDT cream for years, just in case, but never had to use it again.

ON THE FERRIS WHEEL OF LIFE

 JAMES RETURNED TO Perth to live. He had regained his usual placidity and often came around after work to play with Caroline, and sometimes stayed for dinner. It was good to be friends with him. We didn't speak about the past, or about my new lifestyle. James was without criticism. He seemed to have come to terms completely with our separation, so he scared me one evening by predicting that eventually I would come back to him, just like the woman in the movie *Ryan's Daughter*. He was so sweet and undemanding that my heart started to soften towards him. Should I go back to him?

It was during one of those evening visits that Fate made a dramatic entrance: James brought with him his best mate from work, Hal.

I was sitting at one end of the oval dining table, doing some sewing, when I looked up and was stunned by a sudden sense of inexplicable familiarity. I saw a Japanese kamikaze pilot in the shape of the tall Caucasian man standing at the other end of the table, being introduced to me. What gave him away was not his leather jacket, but the way he lounged with one arm on the edge of a chair and the other on his hip. I recognised this stance, however silly that may sound, and his easy grin was also familiar. From that moment, I couldn't get Hal out of my head — even while I was thinking about going back to James. He was like a puzzle, a magnet.

Some part of me wanted to be ordinary, and a full-time mother. Life with James would certainly give me that. I had been on the game for a year; perhaps it would be best to leave while I was still enjoying it. In a move designed to end my licentious lifestyle for ever, I sold all my furniture in one weekend, pulled out the phone and disappeared without notice to any of my clients — a lack of courtesy I have always regretted, but it seemed necessary at the time. In a single day I reverted from a prostitute with a busy clientele to a dutiful housewife. Caroline and I said a sad goodbye to Kelly and Jimmy, but Caroline was overjoyed to have her daddy so close by. That is what pleased me most of all, to see her so happy.

James must have thought that he had finally conquered his wayward wife, but alas, poor man, it wasn't so. It was strange between us after that year of separation. After my year's experience with other men, I needed someone stronger than me, in every sense. I respected James for his strength of purpose in getting me to come back to him, but my reasons were based on wanting to be a good woman and a good mother, not because I loved him deeply.

HAL WAS A tall, rather well-set, soft-bodied man, quiet but humorous, who delighted his friends with a unique gentle quirkiness. His large round head was covered with a thin layer of blond hair parted on one side, and he had a careful intelligence. His was a sensitive soul, open to deeper things. He had once been drawn into Scientology, only to end up feeling badly used and disillusioned.

Hal drove his car as if flying a plane. Going for a drive with him was like taking a ride in Luna Park — he used such precise, hair-splitting judgment in his manoeuvres that he often caused terrible consternation among other drivers. He lived alone with his mother, having emigrated from Estonia to Perth in the same year that my family had settled in Melbourne. When we met, he was still a virgin.

Hal made no advances towards me — out of respect for his friend, James — and so it seemed *I* seduced *him*. It was I who went to visit him, and found we could discuss deep things like metaphysics. I was in awe of Hal's intellect; I loved his keen book radar (sci-fi and metaphysics) and his penchant for gentle, soothing music. What did he see in me? An ardour that was too flattering for a shy virgin to resist?

In hindsight, I think we fell in love because there were dynamics from previous lifetimes to be worked out, issues to be resolved. Several experiences over the years had opened my eyes to the possibility of reincarnation and how it can sometimes give insight into why people's lives become intertwined.

Within weeks I had fallen helplessly in love with Hal. I confessed this to James as we lay in bed one morning. 'I have to leave you. I need to be with Hal.' James, with characteristic leniency, did not berate me. He couldn't look at me, though, and I saw him swallow hard.

James's heart was broken once again. But for the sake of Caroline, the four of us lived together as a household for two years. Both James and Hal were soft-hearted, generous types and we always managed to remain amicable with one another. I discovered later, however, that Hal found it very difficult to cope and was close to leaving until I made the decision to be his sole partner.

JAMES, HAL, CAROLINE and I were joined by baby Victoria in 1975, born to Hal and me when Caroline was three. On the morning of her birth, I woke early to get ready. I collected my clothes and cosmetics, then woke Hal. This time I wanted to do everything right for my baby. I had arranged that Hal would be present at the birth and that my baby would stay with me beside my bed.

They were both promises the matron had no intention of keeping, but my loud protests made her change her mind. All the same, she made sure Victoria was taken away while I slept — why, I am not sure, since she was the only baby born that week in Warwick Hospital.

I was anxious and angry, but helpless. 'Did she cry in the night?' I asked each morning. 'No,' they told me, again and again. Were they lying? I couldn't tell. Meanwhile, my milk was in oversupply, hurting my breasts. One of the nurses was a kind sort. She told me to massage my breasts and came over to demonstrate how to do it. It was such a relief to feel her kind hands taking away the pressing pain. We were both shocked by the matron's stern, shrieking voice: 'Sister, get back to your work and leave her alone!' The confused nurse scurried away.

I left that hospital as soon as I could. Back home, I knew the bliss of motherhood once more. I was good with tiny babies; I would not be so patient and attentive when they became older and more demanding.

In 1976, James, Hal and I founded a rural community in Queensland, which still exists today as a community farm. James built a cabin house there for Caroline and himself, and Hal, Victoria and I lived in a pole house proudly built by Hal.

Our dream of a utopian farming co-operative soured and we left the rural community feeling broken-hearted. Hal, Victoria and I moved to Brisbane, where we shared a house with a family who had a little girl of Victoria's age. James, on the other hand, had been offered work in Melbourne. Caroline was asked who she preferred to live with — her father or me — and she chose to be with James. It was a pivotal moment, but even though she was so young, I had the distinct feeling that Caroline knew what she truly wanted when she chose to move south with her father. And it was the best thing, we all agreed, since the two girls did not get on together at all. So Caroline had to do without her mother throughout her growing years. It is hard to think of how much she must have missed me. I even missed out on seeing her for her birthday when she turned six. Now that I'm a grandmother, it is almost inconceivable that I could bear to be parted from such a sweet, vulnerable and beautiful girl.

HAL AND I HAD moved to a rented house in Ashfield, Brisbane, when he decided to take a break to visit his mother in Perth, his only relative, and also spend some time with an old friend there. I folded myself into his big chest as we said a fond goodbye. Hal was such a good match for my height; people who saw us together always said there was something about us that looked just right. Hal's eyes gazed deeply into mine. I wouldn't see him for two whole weeks. Then, to my great surprise, he foraged in his trouser pocket and gave me a condom.

I looked at him with wide eyes: what did this mean? I had never been unfaithful to Hal. 'Do you expect me to go rampant just because you're going away for a while?' I was incredulous.

Hal chuckled, his wide shoulders lightly shaking. 'Just in case,' was his cryptic reply.

Was this a test of some kind? At the time, that thought didn't enter my mind. I took this gift to mean that he did not want me to be lonely while he was gone. We were both liberal in our thinking; for instance, we had joined the Sunshine Nudist Club and regularly enjoyed weekends away with them, taking Victoria along. The activities were full of innocent fun for adults and children alike.

Nevertheless, I didn't expect to end up, one week later, in bed with a guy I hardly knew! I hadn't gone looking for him; he was a predator, a friend of a girlfriend, who was interested only in charming, conquering and leaving. He was very suave, so different from any man I had experienced before. I wrote to Hal about the encounter in glowing terms, thanking him for the condom. It had served its purpose after all!

Hal was deeply hurt. He wrote his black disappointment in a terse letter. I was confused, but in hindsight I can see I should not have been surprised. I determined to be more careful with Hal's feelings, and to stay out of the way of other men.

I had not reckoned, however, with Bill, also a nudist, who wanted me to acknowledge that there was a special bond between us. And there was. Bill loved my particular brand of elegance, and I admired a certain loyal gallantry in his character. There were many subtle aspects to our attraction. I delighted in it, but didn't see why this specialness couldn't remain non-physical. Bill was older and taller than me, intelligent and married — *happily* married.

During one of Bill's visits to me we had a lively discussion about politics, his favourite topic. I was showing him out when he took charge of the situation. He pinned me against the wall of the hallway and looked me in the eyes as his hands went up my skirt and pulled down my panties. It was his clear intent, together with his lack of aggression or lack of lust of the selfish kind, that held me. His soft grey eyes were tender, his face was like an angel's and his curly hair, lit up by the light, looked like a halo. He entered me while we were both standing. I was overcome with sudden bliss and clung to him. How could I be so ready for him, and he know it so exactly? It proved that true love is just what it is, beyond all morals.

It sounds strange, but this one act bonded me to Bill for the rest of my life, in spite of my commitment at that time to Hal and Bill's lifelong commitment to his wife. Bill hid nothing from his wife, that person dearest to him in all the world, and I stayed friends with both of them. Bill and I have kept up a regular correspondence for the last twenty-three years. To me he is a chivalrous knight. To him, I am his dear Valentine. We shall always remember that single act of love.

HAL WAS WORKING as an electrical draughtsman and I was teaching again, when life took another turn, as if orchestrated from afar. A massage course I took in Brisbane in the winter of 1979 resulted in an invitation to work as a masseuse for a new suburban clinic.

I spent six months there, receiving pleased feedback from clients who said I had a special gift, a touch that made them feel immediately better. Some of the guys responded by getting sexually excited — there was something in me that called it forth in spite of myself — and I would playfully slap them on the buttocks to mock their erections. I had to become more and more serious to control the situation.

In the end, though, I relented. I tried to keep it secret from the proprietress, but the noises of ecstasy must have penetrated the walls. Nothing was said, but she upped the rental fee on my room. It was then that it occurred to me to save both rent and further embarrassment by striking out on my own.

I was a good masseuse, well-trained, skilled and conscious now of my special gift of touch. Soon I became Queen of The Massage Parlour — my own business located in a convenient granny flat in the backyard. Hal did not object, since I did not sexually involve myself with my male clients. Besides, whatever he may have been feeling, Hal valued his liberal thinking above all.

At the end of 1979, Hal, Victoria and I moved back to Perth to be close to Hal's mother. James and Caroline returned soon after and we temporarily shared the same house again. Caroline was almost seven and attended the local primary school. She seemed a healthy and lively child, full of excitement about being close to her mum again. However, she and Victoria still could not be together for long without fighting. In later years, both confided to me that she thought of the other as the specially loved one and was jealous.

I continued with my massage business, setting up in a room at home. I gave relief massage to clients that wanted it, but did not agree to sexual intercourse or to being touched up. I insisted that performing relief massage with these sorts of boundaries would not affect our relationship, and Hal did not complain. All the same, around this time I underwent tubal ligation surgery, freeing me from the need for contraceptives. My mind had not turned consciously to promiscuity, but is it possible to make plans that we keep secret even from ourselves?

IF ONLY I HAD never parted from Hal.

After our lovemaking, when I rested in the feel of him, breathing easily, wholly satisfied, he was exactly what I wanted him to be. I loved his ambience, the soothing, gentle aura around him.

Our friends would bring any broken electronic gear to our place to see if Hal could fix it. He would put his hand on the thing and, most of the time, that's all it needed. Hal had a special love of angelic music and taped all of Jaroslav Kovaricek's Dreamtime programs, which were played in the dead of night on ABC FM. Apart from all that, Hal was the most considerate and accomplished lover — my perfect sexual partner.

So why on earth did I leave him? What do we know of the script in our deep subconscious that we feel obliged to follow, this blueprint hidden in our psyche? Forces beyond my reckoning or control were continually asserting themselves, guiding events unerringly. Some may call it the will of God unfolding, but it might just as well be called the unstoppable human urge to grow, to enter chaos in order to find a greater perfection there.

Or it could be seen as even simpler than that. No man is without his faults. And a woman can't stay with a man if she isn't willing to accommodate them. Hal had traits that sent me up the proverbial wall.

He was a pacifist, meaning, among other things, that he would not tolerate boundaries being set around our daughter. Powerfully intellectual, he could floor me with his immutable reasonings, sending me into a frenzy of impotent outrage at what I called his dishonesty.

'Victoria's pocket money is my gift to her,' he would argue, 'and it isn't to be used as leverage to make her behave better. You know how I hate teaching children even to say please and thank you. It should come naturally or else we are raising children with false manners.'

And so Victoria felt free to be rude, free to not contribute to any chores around the house. In my view, her generous pocket money was probably construed as a reward for bad behaviour, coming plentifully and faithfully no matter what she did or did not do.

Hal never lost his cool when I lost mine. He would laugh softly, enjoying the power he had over me. He saw in my eyes the contempt I felt for his dishonesty, and still mocked me. Nothing is more sure to undermine a relationship than contempt.

I left him in a fit of total pique one day, settled in a house nearby and brought Victoria — at school now — to live with me. After a few months I relented and went back. Then I would leave again, or send him away. For twelve years this went on, the breaks getting longer and longer, our daughter staying sometimes with me, at other times with him, until he put an end to it.

'I have never actually loved you,' he said by way of closure, a week before he did what he had always said he never would do: get married — and to a woman twenty-one years younger than me.

GOD'S CALLGIRL

 ON MY OWN again, I was free to indulge my clients — and myself — without restrictions. But I wanted to find an inspiration for my work, to lift the level of my game. I started to look around for a good source of motivation. If a person has to *create* a positive motive, mightn't she be covering up lesser ones? If she has to manufacture justifications to reinforce her desires, mustn't she feel doubtful about them in the first place? I didn't want to think that deeply. I just wanted to pinpoint what it was that I wanted to express, to give it words, an image, an ideal.

I found my inspiration unexpectedly at an exhibition of ancient Chinese vases in Perth. I was completely mesmerised by the pictures painted on their roundness of Chinese nuns, fully dressed, but clearly in coitus, offering their eager vulvas to well-hung men who looked like travelling merchants.

A story instantly welled up in my brain, explaining everything. These merchants were far away from home for long stretches at a time as they travelled on foot or with pack animals around the countryside, so my tale began. In ancient China, men who needed female *chi* to balance their energy were not forbidden by society to visit nuns. (I didn't know whether their wives might forbid them visiting any other women.) Yes, I decided, that's what it was about for the men: balancing out their energy in a much more wholesome way than masturbating, which did not include an exchange of female energy. It was a simple, natural wisdom; unlike the Western world's attitude towards sex, sullied by centuries of repressive religion.

The nuns, so my heady story continued, needed the men for their own purposes. They used the sexual act as an ecstatic meditation on God, and at the same time provided themselves with a living.

There were rules to the game. It was vital for the nun and her client to share the right emotional approach in order to excite the desired psychic and spiritual energies. Through his respectful attitude, the merchant could participate in and benefit from the nun's state of spiritual ecstasy, I told myself, getting more and more excited, fervent even, as I grew more certain of the purpose of my own work.

I saw some younger men in the paintings. Students, I imagined. So students, being single, could also avail themselves of the nuns' service. These Chinese students were not country bumpkins without manners, and they became even more refined through their sexual encounters with the nuns. The purpose of the sex was not self-indulgence, but to achieve equanimity of the spirit. Whew! The movie in my head sent me reeling, my blood was up — there would be no stopping me now.

The fantasy suited me — and that was the whole point, although I suppose there could have been some truth in it. Were there ever nuns in China? Buddhist ones, perhaps? No matter; from now on, I would visualise myself as someone who served her customers out of a pure desire to balance their energy by offering them her precious feminine juices. They would leave feeling peaceful, blessed and cleansed — God's Callgirl would bring out the best in them! And in return, my customers would do me good as well.

I never told any of my clients about my vision. It did none of them any harm, and my new attitude paid off in one very important sense. For a long time — until I forgot my vision and became lost in the mire of reality — I was able to feel good about what I did.

Creative juices flowed easily from my heart and body. Grace seemed to pour out of my hands and nectar out of my fanny. I enjoyed touching and giving pleasure — and being touched in return by so many different hands, tongues, bodies. I got to know the lovemaking habits of many men and admired how they could take command in a gentle directive way when I invited them to. When they were stuck in an unimaginative routine, I would help them to vary it. There was no position out of the question: on the edge of the massage table, on the floor, on a chair, against the wall. Or in the shower. I loved to wash down some of my clients and share the sensuousness of slippery soap between our bodies. The missionary position was my least favoured: it didn't give the right fit for the best sensations. After a soothing and sensual massage, I preferred to climb onto the table and right on top of my client, who was more than ready by then.

I didn't find my work tiring, as long as I was on the receiving end of a penis. To have my cervix massaged by a *lingam* just the right size was bliss, giving me more than I gave. Even so, I did not have sex with all of my clients; only those who had gained my trust and to whom I was sexually attracted. Most clients received a quality massage with relief for their excited organ at the end.

I was so pleased when clients wanted to try their hand at massaging me. I was getting paid for being pleasured! Some had been to classes, others just wanted to stroke my flesh and gratify my sensual delight in being touched. I knew it was an opportunity to look my naked body up and down, to let their hands wander gradually from my feet to my thighs to the ultimate intimate place. Provided my clients were gentle — that was the key point — and let up as soon as I requested, I was happy.

The feminine in me came out as never before. Without domestic disagreements to deal with, I was able to be radiant with my men, beautiful and tender, nurturing and naughty. I met mostly businessmen, some famous, mostly not: two doctors, a dentist, a TV newsreader, two architects, taxi drivers, removalists, footballers, sportsmen, musicians — and, sometimes, a person out of work with whom I'd strike a special deal. They were German, Dutch, French, Chinese and Thai as well as Australian.

I was often awed by the transformations I saw happening in front of my eyes. Men who entered with downcast eyes and tired feet left looking soft and bright. Many of my clients were men who didn't see themselves as lover material: those suffering from a deformity, chronic illness or mental illness; some who were very short, scrawny or clumsy; and many who just had poor self-esteem. I gave them my very best and they rewarded me with their friendship.

More than one of my clients had a problem with premature ejaculation. I wasn't able to help them, no matter how I tried. I felt sorry for them since they were able to experience so little of the truly sensual. I tried to relax their stiff, often petrified bodies, but a mere touch would electrify them and any stroke near a buttock would be enough to make them come. Even so, they kept coming back; often with little gifts, as if in apology.

I had more luck with men who were supposedly impotent. Often married, they easily managed an erection and orgasm in the presence of an anonymous person who took the time to caress them with music, soft lights and unhurried touch, and who never said there was something wrong with them.

Skill plus caring read my advertisement in the Saturday papers, though I didn't have to advertise all that often. For one thing, I didn't want to be too busy. Money, handy as it was, was seldom my first objective. If it had been, I should really have run a special kind of brothel, but that idea came when it was finally much too late.

Only one or two close and long-standing friends knew they were having sex with an ex-nun. I never capitalised on the financial advantage my past might have given me, because my new hybrid identity was too personal and sacred to me. My hands were gifted with an electric but soothing touch, a gift of the Divine that made my work so much easier, and it was enough to know that my clients seemed to feel particularly good. They often showed their appreciation with gifts of flowers, chocolates and sometimes music.

Mel, who came to see me regularly after he knocked off on a Friday afternoon, called my gift 'the laying on of hands'. I looked into his wicked eyes, topped with untidy red hair, and guessed from his words that he had been a priest once, or had studied for the priesthood. Now a shoe repairer and a married man, he seemed to be short-changed by life somehow. Something in the depths of his eyes was always crying, even when he laughed.

One Friday, while he was undressing and getting ready to lie on the massage table, I confided that I had once been a nun. His eyes lit up hugely when I said this and he gave me the biggest, most cordial hug.

Mel enjoyed the leisurely laying on of hands as if it was a cleansing ritual, something that made his world whole again. His tiredness seemed to dissipate with every touch, until his skin was no longer sallow and a brightness came back to him. To me it looked like a halo of light around his smiling head.

MY CLIENTS WERE often professional men with failed marriages who didn't want the ructions of a divorce. They had adjusted to loveless home lives, looking to success and prestige in their work for the bulk of their satisfaction, and getting their sexual release and pleasure from anonymous women like me. Other clients' marriages had simply collapsed — these were men with broken hearts and bank accounts, who would not easily expose themselves to the risk of losing more of their property by marrying again. It was cheaper and easier to pay a prostitute, who would never grow old and never nag him — what a bonus.

Some of my clients were simply addicted to sex. They often had a wife or girlfriend, but it was never enough. Luke was one of these men. A Catholic, he felt immensely guilty for his indulgence in illicit sex, but was hopelessly unable to get sex out of his mind. I have never met a more confused man.

Luke said he loved his young wife and hated to betray her, but sex with her was a routine performance without passion. He loved her so he couldn't fuck her. For him to have unbridled sex with his beautiful wife would be to deflower something precious; the idea was repugnant to him, and impossible. Luke had swallowed hook, line and sinker the idea that sex was evil, and marriage hadn't succeeded in sanctifying it for him — he was still thinking of his mother and the Virgin Mary when he turned to his innocent wife. So he needed a whore to fuck, to take the pressure off his woolly brain.

The more he blamed himself, the worse it got. Luke confided in a priest, which he felt did him good, until the priest confessed that he himself was fornicating with a married woman.

Luke came to see me as often as he could — several times a week — so he was usually short of money. I took pity on him and drastically reduced my fee; his interludes with me were so maniacal, so short. The only thing that seemed to give him any kind of brief peace was another round of copulation in the arms of a woman he saw as the opposite of his virtuous wife. His frenzy was like a fervent prayer for freedom from whatever possessed him. I think he was grateful that I was a whore who didn't scorn him.

I tried to make a deal with him. 'I'll give you a leisurely massage that you can enjoy and a relief massage, so you won't feel guilty and you'll get value for your money.' He'd agree and then fight with me to have sex; he almost raped me once. I knew he needed help, but didn't know what to suggest until I found out about a therapist who worked exclusively with men. I gave Matthew the information, hoping he would act on it, but when I last saw him he was receiving phone counselling from a Catholic centre in Adelaide. I'd say that the devil doesn't easily give up on his own.

When Matthew — a successful, talkative and brash lawyer — first came to me there was nothing wrong with him. Except that he spent so much time complaining about his wife and family — there was plenty wrong with *them*! But his disease, whatever it was — muscular dystrophy, perhaps, with progressive Alzheimer's — caught up with him rather rapidly. The last time I pinned his nappy back on, he had barely enough money in his pockets for a taxi fare home. 'I don't know where it all goes to,' he simpered from between his thinning lips. I had my guesses, as I knew he visited regular prostitutes. Matthew had been married twice, both times against his own better judgment he said. One very hot day he took me to his house, where I swam in his pool while he watched from the shady pergola. 'A mermaid,' he called me, but wanted me to stand on two firm legs while he held me close. Matthew needed his hugs most of all.

Among my friends was a threesome of schizophrenics. They lived a few suburbs away and travelled together to save petrol. Mullet, the biggest of them all and probably the eldest, did all the arranging and talking. One by one, they came in for half an hour, paid me their pensioner's rate, and waited for the others to drive home again. I loved these men. They were sweet, simple and undemanding, just grateful for whatever they received. Their bodies were not as muscled as other men's, nor as self-conscious; they were more like big babies.

They usually came once a fortnight, but after a time I suddenly realised I hadn't seen them for a while. I rang Mullet (he had left me his mum's phone number, 'just in case'). When he came to the phone, he started to lecture me in a high voice: 'How could you do those bad things to blokes like us?' Mullet explained that he now belonged to Jesus, and that I was one of the worst people on the planet, corrupting men and doing the devil's work. I felt hurt, but understood.

A few months later, Mullet phoned to make an appointment, just for himself this time. He pretended that things were the way they used to be, before he'd developed a conscience informed by religion. 'What happened, Mullet?' I asked. 'I'm a bad person, remember? You told me so. What do you want to see me for?'

'I changed my mind,' he said, sheepishly, and was relieved when I said, 'OK, see you tomorrow.'

He started to enjoy himself with me once more, although I never saw his two friends again. I admired Mullet for taking a stand when his two mates were still embroiled in their guilt.

I suppose every hooker has her passionate lover. Mine was a very fit young dentist with no scruples about his enormous sex drive. From the moment I opened the front door to this whirlwind, the clothes started flying. I have seen the cliché many times in the movies, but Neville was no actor. In his own way, he too was addicted and possessed — the difference between him and Luke was that he did not have religion to torture his conscience. Ardour personified, Neville kissed me non-stop as he progressed us to the bedroom, undoing our clothes, dropping them along the way. It was nothing for him to come six times in an hour. I had to stop him when my fanny dried up from exhaustion, and push him towards the bathroom. He would leave with arms outstretched for more, his tie off, shirt still open.

Neville was one of the few people I ever kissed. I was incredibly cagey about kissing. It was a disappointment to many of my clients, but it was something I couldn't explain. Kissing engages the mouth, the part of me that had been hurt when something was forced into it — perhaps that's what it was. For me, kissing just had to be a genuine expression of *my* passion. Affection or friendship wasn't enough; to give my lips meant that something more than an exchange of money for sex was going on — it had to be a partnership of equals. Equal lust, if not love. If my lips could not be sincere, then I might as well give up on integrity altogether. My clients just had to accept that when the extra ingredient was missing, no amount of decency they showed me was going to persuade me to give them more than a friendly peck.

I WENT TO A great deal of trouble to make my room pleasant, warm and clean and my massage table was superbly comfortable. I used quality oils, pink towels and I put poetry into my work with a background of classical music. Soft, pink light from a small lamp created intimacy and other-worldliness. It also did wonders for my skin, which takes to pink colours. Often I added a candle and a few flowers in a little vase. Once I repainted one room in French pink and bought matching curtains. When I didn't like the feel of nylon under my bare feet, I had the room recarpeted in New Zealand wool. The owner of the house was aghast. Luckily I had stored the awful grey nylon stuff in a shed and threw it back on the floor before I vacated his property.

I had always had a soft spot for musicians, but to meet Pietro was to be taken by storm. Pietro, as his name suggests, was Italian; he was also exotic, eccentric, spoilt and, sadly, rather cynical. He was short, but carried himself well, as if dressed in silks of the eighteenth century. He was talented and tantalisingly good-looking, but, in spite of that, poor and unappreciated. His cynical response to the lack of recognition verged on the self-destructive.

With Pietro on my massage table, I allowed my imagination to gallop. As far as I was concerned, I was dealing with a man straight out of history. That huge mop of curly hair — a lion's mane — (although Pietro was a fiery, self-opiniated Aries, not a Leo), those bold eyes, that sensuous mouth (wide but not too wide), the perfect teeth and that easy smile — it all added up to an imagined reincarnation of my beloved Mozart.

Trembling, I tried to calm my feelings; I was literally out of breath. My cheeks were turning an unusual shade of red and it wasn't just from the exercise I was getting that late February afternoon. Anxious not to appear a nervous, shy, over-excited middle-aged woman, I grasped for my professional attitude. I concentrated on doing a good job on Pietro's back and legs as he lay prone on my table, sinking into its softness. Meanwhile, the mystical nature of the moment continued. . .

I had recently seen the movie *Amadeus*, twice. I'd loved the reckless, mischievous side of Mozart's character, and identified with his love of beauty, his mismanagement of money, and his fear of his father, even after his father was dead. The cinema had made the man and his music larger than life, and I had adored his tragic-comic brilliance.

Amadeus — I mean, Pietro — turned over. He opened one curious eye to see who was playing his body the way he played the piano. I smiled, hoping it seemed as if my feelings were under control, and he closed his eyes again. I watched him. He appeared deep in thought for a moment, then asked, 'Do you know why people come to see you?'

'I've got some ideas,' I replied. 'Can you tell me what your reasons are?'

Pietro's answer was slow and languid and he kept his eyes shut. 'To be touched,' he drawled, and in three words he had told me of the agony his body contained, as well as his present pleasure. There was a pause, then he added with a soft sigh, 'To relieve some of life's horror.'

Did he mean the horror of his personal life? Pietro was married — I had noticed the wedding ring amongst others on his exquisite fingers. I imagined a stormy love: he, too possessive of the woman he loved; she, jealous if he looked sideways at another woman...

Pietro interrupted my musings. 'You don't know,' he said, but didn't want to tell me more. He clamped his hands over his ears dramatically. It was a gesture so like Mozart's — at least, as I imagined the composer had been — that it took my breath away. Perhaps he was hearing the doleful Piano Concerto No 27 creeping up on him.

'Either you don't like my music,' I ventured (the soft bamboo music coming from my tape recorder), 'or you don't want to hear your thoughts.'

He replied that he liked the music; so what were the horror stories that he couldn't switch off in his mind? I sensed in him the self-pity that comes with an addiction to exaggerated wrongs and bitter grumbling. Pietro had paid me in advance, mumbling that he couldn't really afford this massage. Perhaps he could give music lessons to my daughter in exchange for the massage, I suggested. 'I don't charge as much as you do,' he'd quipped, and didn't take up the offer.

After he'd gone, I wondered where I'd got the mad idea that this man was a present-day Wolfgang Amadeus Mozart. The phone rang; it was someone I had met at a recent workshop, who wanted to have a coffee with me. It was merely a coincidence, of course, that his name was Wolfgang!

I HAD MY regulars with whom I could be completely comfortable. Like Daniel, whom I privately called Dan the Great because he was a giant of sorts. On his first visit, he left a big impression on one side of my new massage table — a semi-circular gap the size of his larger-than-human bottom! It happened while he was dressing after his shower. Unfortunately, he chose to sit on the short edge of the collapsible table to get his socks on. The table gave way instantly and Great Dan's bottom followed hard, resulting in what I later called The Great Impression.

It was a testimony to the craftsman who made the table that it hadn't given way when Dan had initially launched himself onto it at the start of the massage. I stood with my mouth open, taking shallow breaths in suppressed fear, as I made a hopeful calculation of Dan's weight vis-à-vis my table's load-bearing capacity. Getting off might be more of a problem, I thought, but Dan was a truly resourceful man. He figured out a coordinated way of rolling and turning that changed the daunting operation of removing a tonne of human flesh from the horizontal to the vertical into child's play.

Dan rested on my table like a cherub, rolls of fat covering its surface to the very edges. He used gentle direction to get maximum benefit and pleasure from his time with me. Because he was obese and his voice had been made soft by congesting fat, I imagined he probably received a lot of sympathy and condescension — all totally unnecessary and unwanted by Dan, who was an ingenious and deliberate man, very well adjusted to his size — at least then, in his youth.

He wasn't like any other client I'd ever met; no one compared with him when it came to plain sensuality. Dan, I concluded, had grown a huge skin so he could enjoy it more. He was ecstatic when I stroked him gently on his neck, his ears, his scalp — I might as well name every part of his body. His immense enjoyment was magnetic: it drew me into its peculiar spell, like entering a different dimension, where solid objects become fluid. My sensitivity went up a notch or three to match his. I had entered the world of Dan the Great.

The hour waltzed by with energising intensity. I felt his every thrill at my touch — on the rolls of fat hanging from his arms, his oversized but delicate fingers, the roundness of his calves and thighs, the mountainous layers of his back, his abdomen, his huge chest, and of course his penis. Compared to the rest of his body, his penis hadn't put on much weight at all; it had kept a dignified distance from the rest of Dan's developments. I don't know what Dan thought about this. The only time he saw his penis was in the mirror. However he felt about it, his obesity made intercourse impossible. Orgasm, of course, was still readily available, especially with the help of a friend like me. Dan's delight could not be described. I felt it through my fingertips, through the ripples that travelled like miniature tidal waves through his flesh when he came.

So this sensitive giant came down to earth with a violent thud after his shower, when he perched on the edge of my massage table. But Dan was a man not easily flustered. He had firmly adjusted to being different, had been through all that self-recrimination crap. He apologised, and I apologised for the let-down, and he was content to sit on the chair after that.

With men like Dan, who could abandon themselves to the exquisiteness of total sensation in every part of their body, I could find myself weeping strange tears of excessive sensuality. To be with such men was like lying in a field of pleasure, vibrating with overwhelming music, at the point of orgasm again and again — when all I might be doing was stroking a leg.

EVERY WHORE NEEDS a good removalist as a client. I had a strong and generous one, Brett, who amazed me with his stories about his happy home life: his nice wife, his baby girl. I never asked him why he needed me; I think he chose to come to me the way another person might choose a different menu, to keep life interesting. Brett was an intelligent but uncomplicated, practical man. The constant lugging of furniture was hard on his body and the strong therapeutic massage he asked for helped to keep him in good shape. He wouldn't dream of leaving it at that, though. Never. His relief massage was the icing on the cake — or was it the other way around? Would he have come to me if I wasn't in the business of offering relief? I couldn't tell.

When Albert arrived on the scene, a truck driver with the face of a child, I didn't know how to handle him. He answered my advertisement, *Skill plus caring*, and said he needed caring, but would I please spank him? I was so innocent about this form of sexual arousal that it appalled me, but then I remembered the pleasure I once used to get from whipping myself around the legs. Whipping was what Albert wanted, hard on his buttocks with his trouser belt. He told me it was good for his circulation and looked at me so full of hope that I reluctantly obliged him.

He lay face down on my table and I brought the leather belt down on his sizeable buttocks, which were pimply and unusually rough-skinned. His body quivered with pain and satisfaction. He thanked me and asked for more, please, and harder.

I had strong arms and soon red welts appeared on his trembling flesh. 'Harder!' he called again. There was no doubt that he was getting something out of this. Then he asked me to call him a bad boy as I struck him. 'Bad boy! You're a very bad boy, and I need to whip you!' I repeated as I tired myself out. Finally he began to whimper and I stopped. There had been no satisfaction in any of this for me, except to gratify my curiosity. What was this all about? And where was it leading?

Albert climbed off the massage table with the demeanour of a child who had been beaten for being naughty. Now he walked over to Mummy, to have her forgive him and hold him on her lap and soothe him. 'There, there,' I said, as he sat his large bottom gingerly on my knees, 'you're a good boy now and Mummy loves you.' Only then was he able to receive a massage, having his sore bottom soothed with soft creams and gentle strokes.

I saw Albert a few times, but each visit his demands for more severe punishment grew — he wanted me to hit him harder and harder. In the end, I couldn't do it any more. I hated playing a game in a loop that was going nowhere. Albert was devastated. I felt for the child in him who had grown used to this so that he now could not imagine anything better, but I was clear that this was not my way of treating people.

IT WAS DURING this honeymoon period of my career that I finally learned to masturbate. After all the resistance I'd carried, I found it surprisingly easy. 'How come a sexually free woman can't masturbate?' Hal used to say, chiding and challenging me. I had always thought of masturbation as something you did only if you were desperate and lonely. It's not natural, I thought, and so I made myself dependent on a lover if I wanted to orgasm.

One Saturday evening, when I was home alone but tuned into the excitement of all those people out on the town, instead of feeling that I wanted to be there with them, I dressed up in lacy panties, scanty bra and silk dressing-gown, lit a few candles, grabbed a long mirror and put it on the floor. I took my very special rose-perfumed oil and knelt in front of the mirror with my knees apart, my gown open. As when performing for my men, I liked gradual excitement, gradually exposing my breasts and my delicate parts, my nipples and the soft lips of my vagina. My hand removed only part of my gown, part of my bra, as if an invisible lover were slowly undressing me. I found myself taking the part of a man, exciting the woman in me. I became wild with the beauty and the passion of my own body.

I made up a character called Father Kennedy and fantasised that he had a darkroom where he loved to fuck Sister Mary Carla on his developing table.

Father Kennedy watched me walk towards him. It was recess time at the primary school where I taught seven year olds. The wind caught my veil, waved it above my head as if in welcome.

I had pinned my black shawl behind my back, in work mode. I was aware that my clothing, plastered to my body by the wind, would reveal my shapely legs and hips, and my nipples, standing out at the tips of my small, firm breasts.

As I advanced, he remembered that the pockets of my habit were literally bottomless — I had cut out the fabric — and that his hands could reach through them, down and down. . .

He waited for me near the door to the room where he developed his photos — where he would take me. Wishing to seem casual, he moved towards me only as I drew near, then wheeled to saunter beside me.

He was in his cassock, buttons all the way from chin to hem. His dress was designed to obliterate the shape of his body, but the wind made a mockery of all pretences. And so he put the wind into his back, hiding himself from any curious gaze.

Unobtrusively, his right hand found its way into one of my large pockets and he saw my eyes grow large and luminous as his fingers found what they wanted.

Now he must take me inside, or reveal to all the world that his penis was pushing at his cassock.

In the ruddy light of his studio, he gently laid me on the table in the middle of the room and lifted up my skirt to lick my eagerly opening vagina.

It was easy for him to lift up his cassock and insert his gleaming penis. He undid the buttons of my bodice to expose my heaving breasts. My nipples yearned for the touch of his fingers, the lick of his tongue, the gentle suck of his mouth. My breasts cupped in his hands, he bent over me and kissed me full on the mouth, stopping my scream as I came, lifting my body towards him.

A bell rang to announce the end of recess. I buttoned up, unpinned my shawl and modestly draped it around myself. A kiss goodbye and I left the dark room to rejoin my charges.

Father Kennedy bent languidly over his developing tray. His pictures of the parish church were coming along well. . .

My orgasm was prolonged, sweet and satisfying.

The glow of achievement stayed with me in my dreams that night. I dreamt of being a novice nun once more, who went to the forest every week with some of her sisters to meet the young men studying for the priesthood in the monastery next door. Everyone was involved in one massive explosion of sexual energy.

I woke from this orgasmic dream in the middle of the night feeling exhilarated, and laughed aloud at my choice of symbols for sexual excitement. I knew real priests usually to be the most unimaginative and uninteresting males you could possibly meet. The sublimation of their sexuality seemed to leave them dried-out, or else holy in a way that made me want to puke.

Nuns were not much better off. Too often, their God-given female juiciness dried up into pale wrinkles. The sculptor Bernini saw it differently, judging by his statue of the saintly Sister Teresa in the Vatican, but how many nuns looked like that these days? Nuns like Teresa of Avila and Hildegard of Bingen have been dead a long time.

TO MY UTTER surprise, my anus became spontaneously orgasmic. It happened when I was having a normal evacuation. Sitting there, I became aware of the pleasure of feeling a large stool roll easily down from my bowel into that last section before it left my body. Tears came involuntarily into my eyes and streamed down my face as this most ordinary of functions became the apex of pleasurable sensations. I sighed with ineffable pleasure as the last stool plopped into the water. My body was letting me know that all was well with the bowel that had once been so constricted and dried-up.

I understood, then, why my men liked being stroked around their anus so much, even the most conservative, and some even liked a tiny poke in there (clean holes only), and how homosexual men would find anal intercourse entirely satisfactory. Not that anyone had ever enjoyed anal pleasures with me. When I was with one of my pimps, one guy tried, but it hurt so much and I cried so miserably that he gave up, lucky for me. Only once did one of my own clients make a pass at my anus, when we were doing it doggy fashion. 'Wrong hole, mate,' was all I needed to say.

GOD'S CALLGIRL WAS happy. With my clients I had what few achieve in a marriage: a life where my innermost essence found expression. I was the giving goddess who took nectar from her God in the shape of many men.

I felt pleasure in being with most of my clients and a true heart connection with some. I appreciated my customers — at least, what I got to know of them during the short periods we spent together in such out-of-the-ordinary circumstances. They certainly seemed appreciative of *me*, which was even more important. Not many words were spoken, but there was respect, appreciation, friendliness and humour. 'I like your special touch, Carla,', 'I feel at home with you,' and 'You give me a decent massage as well as making me feel great,' were some of the words that satisfied my constant question: *Am I on the right track?*

These men gave me their money but none of them ever took me out to dinner or wanted to be seen with me in public, and I went to bed alone all those nights I was separated from Hal. It was enough to be loved by several men in secret, to be pleasured to orgasm every day, or twice a day — some of my men dared to say that *they* should be paid instead.

My independent nature learned to appreciate having the house to myself at night. Victoria often chose to stay with her father; it was easier for both of us this way. I was forty-four but looked at least ten years younger. I never felt the need to dissociate from my work by taking drugs, or by smoking or drinking. I was radiantly healthy and could be forgiven for thinking I had it all, for ever.

THE VASE CRACKS

 PHIL LAY ON MY massage table, a burly man, thickset and about fifty-five years old. He had his eyes closed and was breathing rather noisily. Phil was one of my regulars and I had poured all my care into his back, his neck and his legs. He now turned over and I got busy with the front of his legs, his chest and the most important part of his anatomy — his penis.

I knew bodies. Phil's had been in an agony of longing this last half hour. I could tell by the unconscious slightly upward thrust of his pelvis, propelled not just by my touch but by his myriad of unused sperm — hormones unsatisfied by constantly deferred lovemaking. Phil came to me because I could relieve him of this stress while giving him the most intense pleasure he'd ever experienced — a heightened sexual climax. Years of practice had taught me where the tender spots were, where to be firmer; when to be slow, when to be fast. I knew how to build up a wave of energy slowly and let it drop, then pick it up again, and again.

Phil came closer to climaxing: I expected a feeling of the greatest wellbeing begin to surge through him. Phil's longing — and my hands — made him come. It was a great orgasm. Surely better than when he last had sex with his wife, which, Phil had confided, was several months ago. He should have been happy, but I heard a sound I'd not expected: with one hand over his eyes, Phil was suppressing a heart-rending sob. His naked, vulnerable body shook helplessly as he lay beneath my wondering eyes, penis flaccid now and every ounce of spare fat shivering around his frame.

I didn't know what to do so I reached for a towel to cover up his exposed distress. I laid one hand gently on his forehead, and when he opened his eyes I saw an inexpressible sadness. What I read in a single glance was that he was infinitely more lonely now, after his indulgence, than before. That his spilling of sexual energy had proven to him how empty life was without love, without real intimacy.

I helped Phil sit up. Silently he wrapped the towel around his waist and made his way to the shower.

Something of Phil's feelings found a corresponding reverberation in me, and I did nothing to stop it. Whatever Phil had been looking for, and had received, from me was not the answer for him. The greatest pleasure in the world seemed to have produced the greatest emptiness. I felt disturbed. A small crack had appeared in the pristine Chinese vase that was my icon.

Still, I told myself, not all of my clients were like Phil, coming to me with unrealistic expectations. But surely, said another voice, many of my clients were substituting sensual massage for a real relationship. If that was so, then what they had with me was a false relationship.

A *false* relationship! Was it true that the men who came to me equated sex with love, even with nurturing? If so, the more skilled I became at providing sexual services, the stronger I reinforced their illusion! I wanted to be a real person in a real relationship while I did my work. In my lucid moments, I knew that my fantasy of the Chinese nun wasn't real. Oh, it was all so confusing!

A terrible thought — too terrible to look at for long — hissed into my unwilling ears: *You might be making your clients' alienation worse. You might be intensifying their inability to have real intimacy and underpinning their lack of self-confidence* . . . Like Eve, I heard the snake in the garden, but unlike Eve I wasn't able to distinguish where the voice came from. I knew, however, that the choice between good and evil beckoned. If only I could distinguish between the two.

After Phil left that afternoon, life would never be exactly the same again. More than anything, I now wanted to be real. To learn to be real, so my reasoning went, I needed to define more exactly what was good and what was bad. Having thrown out my Christian God at the end of 1969, I had failed to replace him with any other sort of God. I felt now that I was missing something in the depth of me, a longing that wasn't being fulfilled by my work. There must be some kind of wisdom out there that surpassed what the Catholic Church had to offer; I just hadn't come across it yet. I wanted an *ultimate* truth, something that could command my entire devotion.

Not that I had neglected the search entirely. With Hal, I had become interested in metaphysics and had begun to study Madame Blavatsky's huge tomes of esoteric knowledge from the Theosophical Society. Now I accepted an invitation from June — a woman I had met in a bookshop — to go and live in the country with her for a while. I was profoundly grateful for a break from life in the emotional fast lane. The rent would be low for the makeshift cottage a little distance from the main house (where she lived), which functioned as a country post office, sandwich shop and a petrol station. I expected to be there for about six months, and had my furniture stored.

I also used my time there to recover from having some varicose veins removed. I had put up with the pain and disfigurement in my legs for long enough, and looked up a specialist with a good reputation. He made me stand on a chair, hitch up my dress and turn around slowly while he scrutinised the possibilities. 'Hmm, worth doing,' he concluded, but warned me that it wouldn't be easy. 'The pain will be bad for at least two months while your blood vessels adjust to new pathways.'

'I'll be delighted to massage away the pain in your legs,' June said in her sweet, light voice; she was a healer and a generous woman.

Victoria and I enjoyed our new surroundings. Victoria found a friend in June's daughter and loved learning to ride the neighbour's horses. We both enjoyed living with the sound of chickens, turkeys, geese and guinea fowl. As soon as my legs allowed it, I rode a bicycle around the magnificent summer-dry countryside, breathing in the smell of hay and of trees giving up their eucalyptus oil to the heat.

As soon as I was well enough, I helped June in the sandwich shop and around the yard. I enjoyed having a girlfriend, and June enjoyed my company, especially since she had become estranged from her husband, Sam. A quiet, practical and rather handsome man, Sam had had enough of being asked to become the 'new age' husband his wife expected him to be and had removed himself to another part of their property, where he had started to build a new house. Whenever he came around — which was inevitable on account of their shared workload — and sat down for a cup of coffee, she started on him, presenting the truths that should matter to him, her personal convictions, her new religion. She always began gently, then became more and more insistent, finally shouting after him as he left.

June confided to me that Sam was impotent. On the few occasions they'd had sex these last few months, he hadn't been able to get it up, no matter what they did to arouse him. 'You can have him, Carla!' she taunted repeatedly, after each tirade of complaints.

So four months into my stay, I finally did, and managed to prove to my friend that her husband wasn't impotent at all. I found him to be sweet and spicy, like hot mulled wine.

Human nature being what it is, June's friendship turned to rage. She screamed like a banshee and gave me a week's notice to move out of my tiny cottage near the stream. But I shall always remember her for the kindness she showed me while my legs were so sore. I would never have dreamt of seducing Sam — and he would not have dreamt of being seduced — if she hadn't thrown the gauntlet at our feet.

I RENTED YET another house, this time in South Fremantle, right on the beach. It was a nuisance to not have my own house. I must have rented a dozen different places over the years; some I had to leave within weeks, even days, due to inquisitive and intolerant neighbours. It just wouldn't do to have an old lady peering from behind her curtains whenever someone went in and out of my home! I learned the hard way that flats were no good; even attached houses were risky.

I was also just not secretive enough. When I moved into my South Fremantle three-storeyed, strata-titled villa by the sea, together with Doreen, an artist girlfriend, and her actress daughter, Lara, I allowed the neighbour to help me bring the massage table down to the basement room. I wasn't to know that he slept right on the other side of the adjoining wall, away from his wife's upstairs bedroom! I wasn't all that busy with massage then, as I had enrolled as a student of psychology at Murdoch University. I just wanted to do enough work to keep us going financially.

It was mere days before the frustrated old man began his crusade to have me banished by the local council, after his malicious efforts with the owner — who was supportive of me — had come to zero. He called all the neighbours together to discuss 'the activities going on at No 4'. I was refused an opportunity to attend, although I wrote a congenial message to all the tenants of the row of attached houses reminding them that I was the only real authority on the activities. Not one person bothered to reply. My neighbours on the other side were a group of young people who partied a lot and often pissed over the railing of the front balcony, but that was not deemed a problem by the other tenants — not compared to the supposed evils that were being enacted inside my villa! The meeting resulted in a formal complaint being sent to Fremantle Council, which promptly ordered me to stop my work on the premises or face legal action.

I had to accept that morality often breeds prejudice, and that there is no man more moralistic than a frustrated old Baptist who prefers wet dreams and self-righteousness to a relief massage. We wrote all our neighbours a cheerful goodbye note and Doreen regaled the neighbourhood with Puccini's *Oh, My Beloved Father*, her favourite piece, at top volume, 'To show them we're educated artists, for God's sake. We're an *asset* to this community, not a nuisance!'

Doreen, her daughter and I parted company, and I moved to Subiaco. In my first week there I had a visit from the Vice Squad, courtesy of the letters sent them by my previous neighbours. They phoned first, the Chief of the Vice Squad posing as a customer responding to my advertisement. They were decent chaps, although unconcerned at the hot and cold sweats they provoked when I opened my door to their uniforms. After they had stuck their heads inside my massage room, where my certificate was hanging on the wall, they smiled their goodbyes. On the way out, the Chief said, 'Oh, by the way, we'd like you to come along and register as a sole operator, so we know who you are and don't have to bother you any more.'

So, that's what I did. In that dingy office full of indifferent-looking keepers of the law, my photo was taken for their records. 'If ever you leave the game, let us know and we will remove all your details,' said the young Vice Squad officer as I was leaving. If only I could really believe that! Since I wasn't breaking the law, there would be no criminal record, they kept reassuring me, but the whole affair brought my Chinese nun ideal down to a common denominator of *vice*, and that appalled me. I felt like the 'necessary evil' people refer to when they don't want to condemn my trade, but end up doing so anyway with those words. God's Callgirl was someone they would never appreciate — how could they? My silent tears ran into another crack in my beautiful vase ...

Back home, I looked in the mirror and noticed a change in my expression. My face had taken on a determined, cold and serious look, without the golden light I had often imagined I saw around my reflection. I looked every bit of my forty-five years just then. I was shocked and, looking deeper into myself, found that I was disturbed on a number of fronts. I had no other profession to fall back on (except teaching, which didn't suit me). My use-by date was coming up — in the sex industry, you have to have the goods or you're dead wood. My hands were becoming slowly but surely ruined from being coated in oil so often, even if it was almond oil, and the muscles and veins that were beginning to stand out reminded me of my father's strong hands.

I thought about the clients I'd been attracting lately, like Ben, a little man who looked exactly like a gnome. It wasn't exactly work of the Goddess to be pulling on his reluctant pecker. His wrinkly body reminded me of a woollen garment that had been boiled hard, his mouth didn't quite close around his protruding teeth, and his ears were large, pointed and stood way out from his head. Ben did the rounds, not popular anywhere for long, and he understood and accepted that. More insistent than a cat, he was not put off for long with refusals, however rude.

Ben had a peculiarly annoying habit of twirling my nipples while he sat on the side of the massage table, legs dangling, lips smacking, as I worked his penis. Worked is the word — he had a hard time coming! That's all Ben wanted: no massage, no sex; just, apart from his exhausting relief, a brief kiss. He offered that puckered mouth and closed his eyes, waiting to touch skin so he could kiss it. How did I square this with the spiritual aspect of my work? Where was the energy exchange? Had I fallen into doing it just for the money?

That was a trap that could be hurtful in itself. 'I'll be back in the shake of a wombat's tail,' one new client said after his massage, explaining that his wallet was in the car. Do wombats have tails? Instinctively I went to the doorway, even though I wasn't exactly dressed for the casual eye of a neighbour or passer-by. As I watched, he hurriedly manoeuvred his car out of my driveway, bold as brass, and disappeared. The misery I suffered was agony — it wasn't just money I had lost, it was my dignity. This had never happened before! A larger crack threatened to undermine the integrity of my Chinese vase.

Thoughts I had never entertained before found their way into my mind and made an unwanted impact. I was forced to face the fact that I had absolutely no control over my clients' motivation, and many of them had formed hardened attitudes from contact with other masseuses and prostitutes. I particularly despaired of the silent, self-absorbed types, who couldn't distinguish between a divinely inspired caress and an indifferent slap on the buttocks.

I had to admit that most of my clients didn't fit my image of the travelling merchants on the Chinese vases! The men were simply themselves: they came for reasons they might or might not have been aware of, and they didn't often share them with me. The ideal I had adopted was one-sided. I could respect and give, but I couldn't count on real respect from every man that came into my room.

Something inside me changed with this realisation, and there was no going back. The pure enjoyment I used to know was no longer there. What I really began to detest was being touched up when I didn't want to be. To my chagrin and horror, this was happening more and more. A hand would wander from the guy lying prone on my table. He couldn't see my face so couldn't gauge whether I meant it when I brushed his hand aside. After a brief moment of acquiescence, the hand would slide up my leg again. He just wanted to feel up a fanny while being massaged, didn't ask permission and, worse, wouldn't take no for an answer. I kept squirming away from wandering hands as I massaged body after body. With clients I knew well, I usually wore nothing at all under a rather short skirt, but now I started wearing knickers under longer skirts to make it more difficult for invasive fingers. Never trousers — I should be able to be feminine and attractive in my massage room and still get respect!

It was a rude shock for me to discover that I only liked my clients when I believed they were playing my game. But in reality, I had been playing by myself! When I stopped playing ball, by refusing a request, spoken or unspoken, they'd sulk, disregard my wishes or just plain stay away. The strangest thing was that, up to now, they had actually been playing along very nicely. These 'travelling merchants' in need of female energy *did* go away feeling balanced and ecstatic. The only thing was, they didn't need a nun to do it! They just needed a straightforward whore, who never said 'enough' before their time was up and whose feelings didn't require their respect. After all, if she accepted their money she was at their service.

I wanted respect, but it was hopeless: most of the guys saw me as a commodity they had paid for. I came as part of a package — if I thought I was only selling massage, and could choose to give or withhold whatever else, I could think again. A pound of flesh — my flesh — was what they came for and the massage was just their thin excuse to get it.

I PICKED UP the phone to hear John, a real estate agent, wanting to bargain with me. Seemingly deprived of love, he was eager to bargain hard for everything else in his life, using the power of his wealth. He wanted only half an hour, he told me, revising the booking of a full hour that he had made earlier in the week, and he wasn't prepared to pay an hour's fee. It wasn't fair, but I changed my schedule to suit him. John then arrived half an hour earlier and wanted to talk. Not the sympathetic-ear kind of talk; he wanted to know what he was going to get for his money. He knew this was taking up my time, but it wasn't time that he was going to pay for.

John had always been a difficult client. I had given him too much to begin with, and when he found me pulling back, he naturally wanted to be sure that he'd get value for his money. What he didn't seem to realise is that people don't always put a price on what they have to give. What price goodwill? John's fear of getting less than he gave had already destroyed some of my generous goodwill.

Since I had agreed to see him, I had to make the most of it now. The vibrations coming off him as he strode into the massage room were like a distant scream from hell. I was wary and watched him with my arms crossed. But once in my room, I could see that this highly-strung, wily man with his Rolex watch, Pierre Cardin suit and $100 haircut, was just a person without anyone to take him to bed and love him. His loneliness had made him angry, although he believed he had his feelings under control.

'I'm gentle,' said John unexpectedly, hands held up with open palms towards me, trying to convince me with earnest hazel eyes. 'I'm not aggressive.' A man who isn't aggressive doesn't need to give assurances, but his words told me that his intentions were good.

John's dried-up soul had not forgotten what it was like to lie in a woman's arms. He ached for erotic affection. First of all, though, he wanted to indulge his fantasy of two people undressing one another — thankfully much easier than having my clothes ripped off, which was always a possibility with types like John. We faced each other to undress. John's erotic expectations made him fumble and the unbuttoning, usually easy to do, became difficult and almost comical. When it came to unhitching my bra, he couldn't manage it. I turned my back to him to make it easier. I had often fantasised about teaching guys how to do this blindfolded, in a flash, so that the magic of the moment wouldn't be lost. Not that the delay undermined John's libido — not a bit. Fumble, fumble, the bra was off and instantly John's greedy hands and body were on me. The man who had assured me he wasn't aggressive could barely stop himself from squeezing me to a pulp.

I stopped him immediately, stamping my feet, and he apologised, returning to the cool, collected businessman with the smiling hazel eyes. But it was quickly back to hard hands gripping, squeezing, grabbing, clutching. Was this John's idea of a passionate approach, or were his actions the barely controlled frenzy of desperate, angry need?

I spoke to him firmly, trying to get through to him what he should do. I didn't want to undermine him by telling him he was doing it wrong. 'I get turned on by gentleness, John!' My words had a positive effect. I could feel how important it was for his ego to believe that he had indeed turned me on — not only to prove his skills as a lover, but also because he would rather be with a woman who was receptive to him. He didn't want me to coolly play my role while privately despising him. Fair enough; but what kind of response did he imagine he'd get to his aggressive behaviour? And how did he figure that a masseuse or a prostitute would give him something for money that he couldn't get elsewhere?

In spite of his inability to turn a woman on, John still expected — no, demanded in his imperious way — a genuine response. I knew what he would be getting elsewhere around the traps. *How to fake an orgasm*, I had read in a women's magazine: *A smart woman knows how to keep her husband or partner happy.* The stunning cynicism had sent me reeling. How many women faked orgasm for the sake of their husband's ego, I wondered? What kind of 'smart' was that? What was left in a relationship when we were no longer honest? I honoured my clients by never faking an orgasm — at least, not until the very end of my career as a masseuse, when the game began to fall apart altogether.

On that day John was lucky: he had my sympathy. He was the very type of man who needed my services. Sex can soften the heart in men like John and make them decent for a time. But would the Chinese nuns have put up with his attitude? I sighed heavily, feeling certain that they would not. And so I tried to lay down some new rules. No more touching up when I didn't feel like it; and nothing beyond a relief massage for any man I didn't really like.

It became complicated. I found it difficult to remember what I had agreed to the previous time I'd seen each client. I started to keep files on my customers — what they were used to, what I had allowed, what I had refused, things to watch out for, etc — but when I spoke to a potential client on the phone I couldn't always consult my files and sometimes made appointments I later regretted. Too often, I hoped that a man might have changed miraculously since his last visit and would have different expectations. The truth was, I had trouble saying no. And the more I compromised myself, the less confident I felt each time I tacitly agreed to something I didn't want to do. A great uneasy feeling grew inside me.

I so wanted to be a decent woman in my own eyes. I felt shame when I didn't have the courage to break off a massage when a client insisted on touching me and I wasn't in the mood. Why is it so different now, I asked myself. Why was it all right for him to do this last week, but not now? I couldn't really blame the men for the change in my feelings. Nevertheless, it was important to me to lay down some rules, even if they were unacceptable to many of my clients.

I continued with my massage work, but I wouldn't do it nude and there was to be no sex, only a relief. In the dead of night, I promised myself that I would do no more relief massage either. I'd begun to believe that men who wanted sex or relief massage had miserable, inadequate relationships, and that I was making their alienation worse. My viewpoint could not have been more negative or one-sided. But come daylight, and my first appointment, and I reneged on my quixotic promise. For one thing, it's hard work doing straight massage for a full hour, only to be paid less for more effort. And it was extremely difficult to persuade my regulars to adjust to my new demands.

Joe listened attentively as he lay on my massage table, naked and vulnerable, ready for pleasure. He always enjoyed giving me a massage first and now it was his turn. It was hard to explain to his softly expectant eyes that intercourse was no longer on the menu. Joe was stunned; I could see that he couldn't understand. He was a sensitive lover. Having seduced me more than a year ago, he had a way of being totally present when he loved, a rare quality. Joe said nothing as I stumbled over my words and I too fell silent as I watched sadness cloud his face. I was grateful that he stayed, so I could give him my best massage as a gift.

There were genuine tears in his eyes when he turned over. I started to stroke his penis, but he stopped me. I realised that he wasn't about to try to change my mind; he just couldn't climax that way today. He reached out and caressed my face tenderly. Whatever I had given Joe in the past had been deeply appreciated; how could I have thought I was hurting him? How could I have got it so wrong? Here was a man who fulfilled every requirement a Chinese nun might think of, and I was knocking him back! I took off my top and hugged him, and he came as we hugged.

Bernard was another regular whom I had a heart-connection with. He drove a taxi and needed a good massage to counteract his long hours behind the wheel. Usually I went nude with him. When I suggested just a massage, Bernard refused humorously and tugged at my clothes. 'What's the matter with you?' he asked, incredulously. He lay down on the massage table and pulled me up on top of him playfully. 'We've done this before, you know, Carla, and it was very good.'

It was hopeless. I decided to go with it. I allowed him to take off my clothes and to thrill me with his hands. I give him his massage — my hands automatically going to the places that were tense and sore and needed attention. All the while, Bernard lay there quietly, not interrupting me. It was only his back that needed the massage; when I was done, he always turned over with a big smile, sat up and put me on top of his erect penis. With my feet braced on the table, he lifted me again and again. Waves of pleasure surged through us until we both came.

It was over. I felt flat as I dressed. I got busy with the things that had to be done: fetched Bernard a glass of water while he showered, put away the towels, rearranged the pillows. I wondered how he was feeling. When I met him in the hallway he looked great, a towel around his waist, a wicked smile around his lips. It wasn't any use: either I would have to refuse to see Bernard again, or continue having sex with him. Bernard wasn't only nice, he paid well, so it was a decision I kept deferring.

If I had been thinking clearly, I would have realised that several of my clients *did* fit the bill for my Chinese nun ideal. But there was something the pictures on the vase didn't tell me, an essential and very basic message that wasn't getting through: *When a Chinese nun doesn't feel up to it any more, for one reason or another, she quits!* But, like the pictures themselves, painted on the vase for ever, I didn't quit.

Instead, I kept *thinking*. And the more I thought, reasoned and pondered, the more I tired myself out.

Malcolm, a new client, broke down in sobs when I told him I didn't do sex. He apologised for his tears, but begged me to let him be inside me just once. 'I haven't been inside a woman for two years. I want to know if I'm still man enough,' he added, sombrely.

That last bit made sense to me, even if the rest was a manipulative tactic. Malcolm had brought a condom along, so instead of agreeing to intercourse, I offered to do fellatio, as long as he wore the condom. I instantly regretted it when I tasted the horrible spermicide and antiseptic, a dry astringent taste that stayed in my mouth for hours afterwards, even after several cups of tea, coffee, herbal tea and, finally, wine.

I gave up with the disgusting rubber and said, 'OK, we'll do it like you want.' (You win, because I should've known better!) I worked up his flaccidly disappointed penis with my hands till it became enthusiastic, and climbed on top of him. Poor Malcolm; he didn't really want to transgress my boundaries at all. After one stroke inside me, he gently lifted me away and came inside the condom. 'That's all I need,' he said. 'Now I feel complete.'

Most of my clients were decent men, agreeable, generous and genuine. There was nothing wrong with them or with what they wanted. The thing that was 'wrong' was that I wasn't used to respecting my own energy or the feelings of my body. And when I didn't respect myself, I felt bad. What I did didn't make me a bad woman; it just felt that way.

I found myself giving in to the pleasure of the erotic surge of sex again and again, only to feel more depleted than ever afterwards and disappointed in my lack of judgment and self-control. In the moments before orgasm, in the heat of lusty passion, I fooled myself into thinking that this time it would be different, that I'd still feel good when it was over. But the good feelings subsided very quickly. I didn't stop because I was addicted: addicted to sex, to the attention I was getting and to easy money. At the time, it was so difficult for me to feel all this completely.

I WAS CONSTANTLY petrified that my friends or acquaintances might find out that I did relief massage, and more. Consequently, I had few soul-baring conversations with anyone; in fact, my only confidant was my homosexual friend, Shane. He was a charming, artistic, intelligent, beautiful and tolerant young man, whose sole intention towards me was to support me. He came to my house to surprise me with his creative cooking, while his musical voice and sweet presence constantly lifted my spirits. With Shane, I could discuss almost anything. Almost. Even with him, I never discussed my deepest fear of being found out.

Apart from Shane, I developed a friendship with Ruth and Don, a couple who lived a few streets away. Again, we never discussed my lifestyle. I had started part-time teaching, to give the impression that this was my source of income. For two years we visited each other, and had many lively and funny philosophical discussions over dinners cooked by Ruth. My dark secret was my own, and seemed to take on more darkness over time.

There was one other secret I soon had to bear, a secret Don and I would equally share. The trouble began when Don told me he wanted to have sex with me. I looked into those large dark pools of his eyes and saw that our innocent sex jokes had turned into a fantasy for him. I knew that Ruth and Don were both virgins when they married, and neither had ever had another sexual partner. They had joked about taking on lovers, which made me hold my breath — in spite of the love and appreciation they obviously had for one another, this smoke might eventually uncover a fire. Ruth, for one, talked openly about how she'd taken a fancy to someone at work. But it was only something to laugh about; we always knew that her fantasy was going to stay just that.

I was severely taken aback by Don's request. Even though he was a dear friend, he was definitely not my type for a romantic fling and I'd never dreamed that he might feel otherwise. Was there something wrong with my sexual radar? I decided that, no, Don wasn't attracted to me, he just wanted to have sex with someone other than his wife, out of pure curiosity. I told him this, but to my surprise he didn't give up.

Finally *I* gave up one afternoon, thinking that the experience would fix him up for good: he would find out how boring sex could be without an emotional involvement. I agreed that he could come to my place. It was the strangest encounter I have ever experienced. Don's friendship reminded me of a gallant Roman warrior who would defend you to the end. Ruth, his wife, was like a queen to me, deserving the highest loyalty. Yet here we were, betraying her, but with no intention of hurting her.

Once naked and in bed, Don approached me with the straightforwardness he probably always brought to lovemaking with his wife. I made no particular effort to excite him; rather, I wanted to show him that it was the quality of the relationship that gives spice to sex, not a different body. I hoped that he would be as bored as I was. We had sex in the missionary position, and afterwards lay side by side on my bed, he on his back and me watching him. His face was turned to the ceiling, away from my eyes. Don chose not to confide in me what was going on inside his head, but he urged me to say nothing to Ruth. 'It would only hurt her, she wouldn't understand.'

I promised solemnly to keep our secret, but it was another burden to my fear of being found out. I knew that the world 'out there' would call me a strumpet, a whore, a *vice* girl. Someone who couldn't make a living doing something *decent*, who didn't know how to earn an income without selling her body. I believed in freedom, yet didn't have the courage of my convictions. In other words, *I was a fraud*.

THIS FEELING OF being a fraud, someone who was living a lie, became an intolerable torture. And so it was that one evening I attended a lecture by a famous psychologist from the USA, who proclaimed his wisdom on Jung's archetypes to a large audience. He looked like someone who might give me some insight into my suffering. I was determined to speak with him and patiently waited backstage until all the people had gone. He and his offsider, who had told him about my urgency, came in, sat down and waited to hear something extraordinary.

'So what is it?' asked Mr Famous, leaning forward, a hand on his knee, while his helper hooked an arm around the back of his chair.

'I feel like a fraud —'

I had barely managed to utter my dreadful confession when they both burst out laughing.

'Is that all?' Mr Famous exclaimed, getting up and moving away while my mouth hung open. Next moment they were both gone, laughing and talking about something else. I tried to process his response. What did he mean — that being a fraud was nothing to worry about? That everybody was a fraud and what else was new? That being a fraud was the easiest thing in the world to fix? I couldn't get it into my brain that it was a laughing matter. Was Mr Famous a fraud himself? That was one possible explanation, but not one I was willing to accept.

I remained as confused as ever, and turned to spirituality to try to find an answer. I investigated the Baha'i faith, transcendental meditation, raja yoga, delved into Indian religions, visited Buddhist monasteries. I avoided becoming involved with a guru — no Rajneesh, Sai Baba or Muktananda for me. Perhaps I thought these holy people would condemn me, or mesmerise me out of my unique path. It was scary enough to sit with a penetrating teacher such as Paul Lowe, once a devotee of Rajneesh. I definitely didn't want to be with anyone who could see straight through me and tell me I was a terrible person. No, I wanted to find a path that would tell me I was all right the way I was! Someone who could fix the poor, cracked vase inside me, who could take away my self-doubt and what I had started calling my self-sabotage, which was keeping me from being wealthy.

None of this was clear in my head at the time. If my thoughts had been clear, I would have heard myself say: *You are a slut and a sleaze and you don't deserve anything good.*

THE QUALITY OF my massage began to suffer. I wanted to get it over and done with, and I grew tired more easily. When I caught a glimpse of myself in the mirror, I was shocked to see how pale and unhappy I looked. It was so important for me to feel that I was doing some good with my work, but increasingly I couldn't find that inspiration. When the insidious suspicion that I might be doing harm instead of good grew, the term *vice girl* took on a new meaning. Slowly love changed to distaste.

The doubts that rankled my brain day and night developed into a veritable struggle between good and evil, threatening to unbalance me. I told myself not to be silly, and breathed deep sighs of relief when I felt good, but I couldn't keep at bay the conviction that the core of my being was rotten. The effort to live with my contradictions became a screaming nightmare. I had no one in whom to confide my despair, no one to offer me a healthier perspective, so I wrote out my confusion on paper, in frantic, disorderly notes. My journal filled up with bizarre and tortured ideas in my desperate attempts to gain some clarity.

I condemned myself for encouraging what I called 'men's alienated behaviour'. My guilt was intense. I couldn't see that my clients' motivation wasn't my business. I couldn't see that I was arrogant to believe that I could understand what they were thinking. What had happened to my initial conviction that my sexual contact with men would benefit them spiritually? Was I allowing myself to be intimidated by society's mores? That wouldn't have been possible unless there was some guilt lurking inside me, waiting to be triggered. But the guilt had been there long before I started my work. I had chosen a profession that would *prove* to me that I was guilty.

Sores grew on my feet and wouldn't heal. I tried antibiotics, mercurochrome, healing ointments, doctors, naturopaths — but the sores were relentless, the pus and pain signs that there was something vile in me that wanted to come out. I felt putrid with this excruciating dilemma rotting my soul. It was in this miserable state that I phoned Gaye, a specialist in rebirthing.

AWAKEN, DEAD PRINCESS

GAYE WELCOMED ME quietly into her apartment for my third session with her. Rebirthing is a process of connecting with the energies of early-life events through a particular way of breathing, then releasing them through the breath. What exactly was being released wasn't clear — apparently it didn't need to be — but the sessions left me feeling cleaner and lighter. Gaye was an experienced healer and a devotee of a revered Indian spiritual master, from whom she drew inspiration for her work. I trusted her.

As on my previous visits, I lay on a soft mattress on her parqueted floor. The room was warm, but as I followed her breathing instructions my body grew very cold. Gaye covered me up. Soon the breathwork began to open up channels of energy in my body that had been blocked by old fears. Coarse waves of energy began to pulsate through my legs and arms, feeling like raw electricity. This was normal, although uncomfortable, so I allowed it to happen and continued to breathe.

In an indefinable moment, my normal consciousness changed and I found myself waking as if in a coffin. My head was resting on a small firm cushion and I lay dressed in a long, plain, almost-white gown, the hem and sleeves trimmed with tiny embroidered flowers. I realised I had been buried there alive and immediately wanted to get out.

'What's happening?' asked Gaye, sensing that I had entered a visual domain.

'Stuck in a coffin,' I said in the flat voice of trance.

'Push against the lid,' she advised.

I did, with both hands and all my strength, but it was no use. 'The lid is made of stone and I can't move it,' I said hopelessly, and let my limp arms fall to my sides. I felt I had failed an important challenge. But years of experience had honed Gaye's intuition and she remained silent.

In the perplexed surrender that followed, something began to move in the silence. It was my own body, so I felt, rising up slowly, horizontally, from the coffin. It passed easily through the stone lid and, without opening my eyes, which were closed in death, I could see the little family chapel where the coffin rested on stone blocks. It was icy cold in that silent place of worship; the walls were moist with a dampness that had not lifted for years.

As I rose smoothly up to the span of the chapel ceiling, dark clouds gathered and I knew that I was on my way to hell, to meet the devil. Inexorably I rose towards the evil one, my arms folded over my chest, resigned to my dreadful fate.

What happened in the next few moments was the last thing I could have imagined. As I neared the mass of threatening clouds, arms shot forth like lightning in a storm to grab my floating body. I was instantly in the embrace of an unseen being who held me firmly. To my utter wonder and unspeakable delight, instead of being burned with devilish scorn I was enveloped in an unearthly bliss. All I felt was exquisitely pure love. Every cell of my body seemed permeated with joy and my body felt vibrantly alive, like never before. I was speechless, immovable, drowning in this bliss. There was no face, there were no words, only an overwhelming feeling of being held tenderly, merged with the one who was holding me.

My breathing stopped and conscious awareness vanished. I lay on Gaye's mattress, submerged in utter bliss, resting deep in original innocence; a blessed rest, lost to time and the sense of who I was as a physical being. My breath hung suspended for quite some time, until I heard Gaye's calm voice softly calling me back.

I smiled at her, but couldn't begin to speak of my experience. We were silent for a while. My breathing became regular and comfortable. Slowly my brain started to work again. What my experience had shown me was that so-called evil is somehow part of our existence. *How* it existed was not clear to me then. I felt, for that brief interlude, that in truth there was only love and no evil. Evil was a sort of upside-down love, that could be transformed entirely by understanding — an understanding that was not quite mine yet. Nevertheless, the contradiction that had been ravaging my soul had been relieved. For that time, I was good, only good.

Gaye's voice came into my relaxed state. I focused in on it, this voice that brought me back to the world. 'You now have to break away from all your evil friends.'

What did she mean by 'evil friends'? It didn't make sense to me. But I didn't ask any questions, just nodded my head, trusting that she knew what she was talking about. I didn't associate this with my massage clients — I had never told her about them. When the connection finally dawned on me a few days later, I became angry and shouted, 'No! The people who come to me are not evil! My work isn't evil! This doesn't make me evil!'

I didn't understand that I was being asked to drop all 'friends' who were a *bad influence* on me. Unfortunately, Gaye had used exactly the one word, 'evil', that would make me reject her suggestion. So, bad luck for me, I wasn't ready for this lesson.

Logically, I was right — my clients were not evil and I wasn't evil. But the work I was doing made me *feel* evil because my heart wasn't in it any more. I was going against my instinct, and so didn't have the necessary strength to rise above whatever negative energies came my way through close contact with my clients. What can be closer than sexual intercourse? This is not just physical contact, it entails psychic exchange. The psychic energies of each person tends to 'rub off' on the other. When I first began as God's Callgirl my energy was so strong, my intention so pure, that I could largely transform or discard whatever a client left with me. My positive attitude had brought out the best in my clients and in myself. But how could I expect to keep my own psychic energies intact when my motivation had been reduced to working for money and because I thought I was good for nothing else? Why couldn't I see that my level of compassion had dropped along with my enthusiasm, which caused me to become revolted by some of my clients?

Oh, if only I could have made such distinctions when I needed them. How could I have been so terribly obtuse? Well, it was perfectly easy, given my Catholic upbringing and my previous religious life. In the convent I had learned to equate low self-esteem with the virtue of humility. Worse, religion had taught me to be comfortable with suffering. These lessons ensured that I would deaden my sensitivity to the messages from my own body.

My sessions with Gaye did result in making me feel better about myself. I could once more feel loved for who I was, instead of pinning all my need for approval on success with my clients. The wounds in my feet healed. But whatever it was that had embraced me in those dark clouds was not going to let me off that lightly. If the message had not been clear enough, well, I would have to learn it bit by bit, through experience.

I CONTINUED WITH my massage work, and the struggle within me continued too. I felt as if I was addicted to sex, but what I was really addicted to was blocking my thoughts and feelings. I could not afford to investigate any further because of my deep-down belief in myself as evil, as belonging to the devil. I covered this up with my fervent desire for the opposite; the belief that I was really good, because my ideals were high.

When I felt fear, I reasoned with it. When I felt shame, I swallowed it down, again and again. Everything I discovered through therapy was subjected to the preservation of my hidden agenda. My newly-found conviction that I was *innocent* prevented me from feeling everything that was waiting to be felt. I was terrified to hear the cries from within.

Can we heal what we refuse to feel? Not in my experience. My shaky construct of my own innocence drifted away again. More than ever, I felt that I would die if my friends knew what I was doing for a living.

A new client who called himself Ray, an older man of about sixty, slim, educated and polite, came to me for a massage and asked for full oral sex. A blow job to the less polite. This sort of request had come up several times before, and although I had engaged in fellatio with gusto, I had always refused to go all the way and swallow. But because Ray was such a quiet, clean and well-mannered man and his penis wasn't too big, I agreed. This would be a new experience, I told myself — and it was. I was totally unprepared for the violent, uncontrolled reaction of my own body.

Ray watched helplessly as I ran to the basin and gagged and retched as the semen came into my mouth. He was so upset, but it had nothing to do with him. My body had remembered something my mind had long forgotten. It was a forceful reminder, and still I couldn't put the pieces together.

I TRIED TO change my career. For instance, I started up an introduction magazine — long before the local newspapers caught on to the idea. I worked hard, planning all the practical steps I knew were necessary for success. But although it seemed to others that I knew what I was doing, deep inside myself I was unable to truly envisage its success. There was something in me, like an authority with the power of veto, which made sure that nothing I planned would succeed. I sensed it, but had no idea how to address it. Eventually I called it by its name: self-sabotage; but daring to defy it proved absolutely useless.

Tentatively, I went for counselling sessions in what is known as voice dialogue. Each and every time, the child-voice talking to the therapist started to panic and choke, unable to breathe. Neither the therapist nor I could work out what this meant. We never moved beyond that point and I gave up the sessions. The same thing happened when I took up rebirthing again. Even a session in a warm bath, to simulate the warmth of the womb, came to a full stop with that stressful, choking breathing.

Inner child work was big at that time. The alternative magazines were full of it, and of phone numbers of practitioners. I decided to look one up. Alas, the woman blatantly tried to 'mother' me. In perfectly good faith, because she didn't know any better, she tried to make me identify myself as a child that was totally dependent on her. At the time, I couldn't verbalise the feelings that made me mistrust her approach, but they became clear to me one day when I was at her home and she answered the phone to a woman client, who, she later explained to me with pride, never did anything without first consulting her. The question arose: was this therapist just fulfilling her own needs?

I went on the learning trail again, attending lectures every time somebody came to town who seemed to be wise and had something new to offer. I signed on for seminars in motivation, changing beliefs, all that. Maybe the reasons for my troubles were somehow stuck in my muscles and the cells of my body, I thought. So I allowed a bully of a masseur to rolf my body until it was covered in bruises.

In order to overcome my fear, once and for ever, I walked on fire, on the longest strip of hot coals. Twice.

I needed a rest from all this. For some time, I had felt an urge to go south, away from the city. I had never equated this urge with anything spiritual, so had allowed the busyness of my life to override it. It was the summer of 1984. I was living in East Fremantle with my daughter Victoria and had just bought a roomy car. I'd never been further south than Pinjarra, which wasn't that far, but the call to get away was by now undeniable. I took Victoria over to Hal's and gave myself a week to find whatever was waiting for me. I packed the car so I could sleep in it along the way.

On that mysterious journey, which finally brought me to the little town where I would live for several years, I literally didn't move until

I felt clearly guided where to go next. I did not want to risk ending up in the wrong place by following my normal senses. I found myself in Bridgetown, sitting in a teashop, peering at a map and facing several possible directions, until it was clear to me that I should head towards Mount Barker. That afternoon, I climbed Bluff Knoll in the Stirling Ranges, creeping on my belly to the sheer edge, feeling weirdly afraid of plunging into the void below to join the wheeling and swooping birds.

I slept in my car at the base of the mountain, not leaving until it felt right, then drove to Albany, where I swam at Frenchmans Bay. The next evening I found myself parked on a ledge, overlooking the ocean. The moon was bright, but I slept well. It was getting hot towards noon the next day, but I was willing to stay put until it became clear that it was time to venture on.

Later that day, as I crossed the road after parking by the Denmark River, I was recognised by Mark, a man I had met in Perth. I was wearing very short French shorts and had a broad-brimmed hat pulled over my face as I headed to the deli for an ice-cream. As he passed me in his car, Mark couldn't see my face but recognised the legs he had admired recently at Swanbourne's nudist beach. His car stopped, reversed.

That evening, at his invitation, I attended an outdoor gathering under the full moon. I met a group of people sitting on straw bales around a campfire, dancing to the beat of drums, and felt immediately at home — as if they were friends I had known many lives ago. I decided to return to Denmark for a weekend once a month.

Six months later I moved there with my ten-year-old daughter Victoria, to a cottage a few kilometres out of town. It was a radical change, and would not be a bed of roses.

THE SMALL TOWN of Denmark — still without traffic lights — lies among lush green hills and is surrounded by waterways: the river, Wilson Inlet and the great Southern Ocean. The coastline is spectacular beyond belief with white sandy beaches and quiet, lucid pools where granite boulders break the huge ocean waves. The majestic karri trees, unique to this part of the world, filled the beautiful valley I lived in. The joy and light of that special place easily made up for the old and draughty wooden cottage Victoria and I lived in.

It was here that I met George, a man in whom I would finally find some of the characteristics of my father which I had managed to avoid in my previous relationships with James and Hal.

George was a soft-treading, softly spoken, broad-chested man who carried slightly too much weight for the size of his frame. He was only just taller than me, but carried himself very differently: where I walked upright and straight, he ambled in the most disarming way. George had an abundance of black curly hair, some of which grew into a neatly kept beard. He had a compulsion for cleanliness, although at times he showed an appalling sense of dress. He had been brought up by his part-Indian grandfather in the beautiful mountainous region of British Columbia. George was forty-four and I was forty-seven when he moved on to the farm I rented. He put his caravan in the shed not far from the house and used it as his bedroom.

My new sub-tenant had a habit of talking an awful lot and I found him tiresome until he became useful. I badly needed a man around the house, which dated back to 1945. George, it seemed, had the tools and the skills for any job. So far, so good.

One day, as I was washing the dishes after lunch, he casually remarked that if I ever needed a sexual partner, he was willing to be a surrogate lover if I wanted. A surrogate lover! I sniggered. I didn't see George as lover material — I knew of his predilection for dark beauties, preferably Asian ones, and his dislike of blondes. I was also three years older than him. In fact, I felt so sure of George's lack of interest in me that I felt free to walk around half naked in the heat, as if he were asexual. 'Surrogate lover' were not words to turn me on either; they suggested a cold, sordid compromise.

But George was one of those people who must never be underestimated. He had the patience of an American Indian. This had saved his life in Vietnam, when he had outmanoeuvred a VietCong guerilla in dense forest, knowing that whoever moved first was the dead man. George was disarmingly sweet when he wanted to be, and canny as any fox. His extremely lively and intelligent mind picked up and retained every bit of interesting and useful knowledge it could about the physical and psychological worlds of humans and animals. Knowledge, he knew, was power. I've seen him talk wild birds out of trees, coaxing them to sit on his shoulder or arm. He got on well with Victoria, who called him 'adopto-pop'.

George was a natural psychologist and his counselling skills have helped many confused souls. No one, however, could counsel George, whose sorrows and passions were too dark to be exposed and too difficult to handle. He had HD Thoreau's disdain for the 'good man' and carried with him an air of amoral superiority. He believed that most people were stupid, that he could tell them anything and they'd believe him. And it was true that he had a very convincing manner.

The people who became his friends in Denmark were not born yesterday and had a keen ear for bullshit. Eventually George became a more humble soul — but long after the time I was with him.

When George and I became lovers, I got to know him in an entirely different way. I quickly became enthralled by a magnetism I felt I had known before, perhaps in another life when the rascally Russian monk Rasputin was alive. The curious mix of cunning and innocence, the balming yet electrifying touch of the healer, the charisma of endless sexual energy was familiar to me. We were a perfect match in bed and I experienced lovemaking like never before. I opened up to George like a flower to the sun on a cold day.

I wasn't used to sleeping close to my partner, ever. George gradually taught me to stay in physical contact with him all night, snuggled up back to back. He used all the words of love, often in a charmingly child-like way, writing ingenuous messages on scraps of paper, accompanied by a carefully picked flower or two. And he said he only kissed people he loved. It was that one very special thing that made me believe he loved me, because I knew what he meant: kissing to me was private, personal and felt like more of a commitment than just having sex. I had rarely allowed my clients to kiss me. George's lips were full, soft and ever so willing, and his breath was sweet. I was never more seduced.

With George, I felt transported by a feeling of universal oneness, an ineffable completeness. I became lost in him. Before I knew it, I couldn't do without him.

After a year or so of this extraordinary liaison, George began to reject the attachment I had formed for him. He didn't have it in him to be direct, so he started making negative remarks about our lovemaking — or mine, to be precise. 'Why don't you ever come at the same time as I do?' he blustered. I was speechless, because I always did — couldn't he feel it? But his carping remark impressed itself so deeply upon me that I was no longer able to have a cervical orgasm with him. I didn't realise what he was up to; I believed that he was edging away from me because I was a poor lover.

He continued to alienate me in other ways. He wouldn't speak to me for weeks on end, keeping almost entirely to his caravan without an explanation, completely withdrawn into his shell. This sent me spinning into a frenzy of confusion and desire, which he simply ignored. Then he had sex with a visitor to our farm, a disciple of Rajneesh who later admitted that she had come with the specific intention of seducing George. She was dark-haired and sinuous and didn't have much trouble achieving her goal. George didn't ask my leave and he didn't explain; instead, he told me that he and I were not having a relationship and we were not 'an item'.

I was beside myself with incredulity and jealousy and suffered for months. I had no idea how to break the impasse, especially when he'd suddenly relent, throwing himself once more into energetic sexual embraces with me.

SUDDENLY, THE FARM was sold. This was heartbreaking for both of us; we had put so much energy and so much of my money into improving the place. We had six weeks to move out.

It was the ideal opportunity to break up our dysfunctional relationship, but George had heard of a nearby farmer who needed a couple to caretake his property, so we went for an interview. The place was idyllic and with the job came a newly built house. The trouble was that apart from the main bedroom with an en suite bathroom, promptly claimed by George, there was only a small spare bedroom.

'Would you live in this bedroom?' was George's direct question to me. I stood in the room; there was only space for a single bed. It had a lovely view, with the light coming in brightly through the window, but its very size suggested the subordination and submission that the power-hungry George would undoubtedly expect. 'No, of course not,' I replied, but my answer had been anticipated. The owner had been persuaded by George to provide me with a caravan and a few other extras to accommodate my needs. A soft light began to pervade my senses as the talking rolled on. I asked for a private interview with the farmer.

I could have ruined George's chances by simply telling the man that it wouldn't work out, but I didn't want to cheat George out of a job and his opportunity to be the lord of the manor. I simply persuaded the owner that George was an extremely capable man, who could easily manage my part of the job, as well as mend fences and deliver calves.

When the farmer consulted his wife, who had been hovering with cups of tea and biscuits, they agreed. I asked to break the news to George myself, as it was going to mean the break-up of our relationship.

George was piqued to have been left out of this conversation with the farmer, and curious and apprehensive as to its content. I made him wait till we were back at the farm and inside the house, before I told him about the favour I believed I had done him.

Nothing could have prepared me for his reaction. George flew into a rage such as I never expect to see again in any human. I can't remember his words, only his actions. He began to throw whatever was near him across the long rectangular living room. He started with ornaments — vases, bits of quartz rock, and pieces of wood gathered for their beautiful shapes — then the firewood, throwing with all the strength he could muster. The firewood went all over the lounge area, bouncing off the seats and walls, then he grabbed the dining chairs, dashing them against the floor before hurling them away. His fury was so immense that he finally ripped the door off its hinges, throwing it after everything else.

I sat at the far end of the room, my elbows propped on the oval jarrah table, my fists under my chin, watching this tornado in awed fascination, my heart pounding with adrenaline, and, it must be said, with growing satisfaction. It wasn't simply that I was finally having an effect on George the Quiet. It was an acknowledgement, deep inside me, that my decision had been right. This was a George I most definitely did not want to live with, under any circumstances!

For George — who says he can't even remember this occasion — his rage came from the bitter realisation that he had finally lost his power over me. The new job would have presented so many opportunities for him to control and humiliate me. Now they'd been taken away and, on top of that, he'd have to work harder! It never occurred to him to thank me for being considerate and not undermining his prospects.

As it turned out, George stayed in that job for four years. He decorated the house till it resembled an Indian cave, and contributed to protecting the environment by shooting kookaburras (intruders in Western Australia and predators of native birds) and luring feral cats to their death. Eventually, his desire to rule soured the relationship with his boss. I thank grace for the good fortune and common sense that was granted me the day I said goodbye to George. But his larger-than-life character had inevitably left its mark on me, as I was to discover.

I RETURNED TO Perth, where I met Persephone Arbour and joined her women's group. For the first time in my life, I learned to open up to women. I had never confided in my mother, who was there physically but never available to me emotionally; she even competed with me. Unconsciously, I had related to all women as I had related to my mother: I had never confided in any of them.

Persephone led the group skilfully, encouraging us to tell our stories and learn from our experiences. She injected a marvellous spirit of humour into those memorable evenings held at her home. I told the group about George, and learned about the concepts of co-dependency and self-esteem. I also told the women about my exploits as God's Callgirl. I was prepared for them to be appalled, but instead we all laughed a lot and together began the healing of the dreadful wounds of the recent past.

The laughter of my companions also helped me gain a new perspective on my previous sensual massage work. In this light, it seemed ordinarily OK again. What we did not touch on was the possibility that I had developed a certain disdain for men, based on the insidious belief that all they wanted was sex and that most were afraid of intimacy. This was a belief that had crept into my system without me even noticing it.

Although my contact with Persephone eventually grew more sporadic, she has stayed in my life and been an interested, compassionate witness to everything I was willing to share with her.

I HAD KEPT fond memories of my friends Don and Ruth, and one of the first things I did when I settled down in Perth again, and was teaching, was to invite them over for dinner. But they couldn't make it, not then nor the next week. Finally Don said he would come over to talk to me.

I hugged him cordially when he stepped onto my patio, but wondered at the stiffness of his body and his smile. 'A lemonade, Don?' He refused with an instant no and wave of his hand, but agreed to sit down in the pleasant shade of that hot afternoon. He got straight to the point, apparently deciding there was no time to waste on pleasantries.

'Carla,' he began, with head held high, 'Ruth and I will not be coming over for dinner, *ever*.' There was a pause while he eyed me sideways, perhaps to let this poisoned arrow sink in before his next shot. 'You are an evil person, Carla,' he said in even tones, as if he were a bishop or a judge. 'We pray for you, but we have decided to have nothing to do with you. You have an evil influence over people. This is the last time I will see you; neither of us will ever talk to you again.'

I was so shell-shocked that no thoughts would come, let alone the right words. I just couldn't believe what he was saying. Don didn't wait around for me to become coherent. 'Wait!' I yelled as he got to the gate, but still nothing had formulated in my brain that made any sense. One dreadful thought eventually became clear: Don had betrayed me — not only by telling his wife that we had had sex, but by blaming me instead of himself. I realised that judgment had been passed on me three whole years ago. They had said nothing to me then, and were not about to give me a chance to say anything in self-defence now. Even as I tried to speak, to convey my love to them, I felt the hopelessness of the situation. It had all happened so long ago. 'Give my love to Ruth!' I yelled, as Don let himself out and shut the gate.

I wrote a letter to them both, saying I loved them, that it was incredible that this misunderstanding had come between us. I received no reply. I sent flowers, but it was no use. I was so hurt that I confided in a mutual friend, who was a psychologist. 'What's all this about praying for me?' I asked, after she had listened carefully to my story. 'They weren't even religious.'

But Molly knew. She explained that Don and Ruth had become born-again Christians. She also made an astute observation. 'They probably needed a scapegoat after you left,' she said. 'It would have been easier to blame you and save their marriage, than to cause a rift by accepting that one of them might be responsible.'

I understood at last and it was easier to let them go. It was only after I'd lost my friends that I realised what they had meant to me: the only happy, normal couple in my life whom I had trusted. It would take me many years to find friends like that again.

IT WAS HAL who first suspected that there was something in my past that seriously needed healing. Hal and I were in frequent contact, even when I did not live with him, because of our daughter. When a therapist couple came to town who specialised in championing people who had suffered at the hands of adults when they were children, Hal urged me to go along and offered to pay the expenses.

Once signed up and present, it was a question of my speaking up, joining in. I watched participants fall in a heap on the floor, spontaneously screaming, and being embraced and comforted by John and Sue, who joined them there on the floor.

I decided to go for it and sat down on the lounge-room carpet, surrounded by several pairs of feet from participants lounging in chairs.

'Where are you?' The question came from John. To my surprise, I replied without hesitation: 'In the sandpit.'

'How old are you?' came John's second question.

'I'm two and a bit.'

'What are you doing there?'

'I'm sitting on sand ... it's coarse sand, wet ... my bottom is bare ... I like the grains of sand sticking on my hands and body.'

'Who else is there?' John continued.

'My dad; he is looking at me.'

'How does it feel when your dad looks at you?'

'It feels ... yucky.'

'Your father is looking at you and it feels yucky?' John's voice was full of indignation, making me feel safe to clearly recall what I had experienced back then, as a two year old. My father wasn't looking at my eyes, but staring at my bottom; his face was red and had a curiously stiff grimace. Yes, it felt yucky, very yucky.

John roared, 'How dare your father look at you like that?', and I began to cry, feeling both forlornly betrayed by my father's invasive staring and tenderly grateful for the supportive adults around me. Sue embraced me like a mother. It was so strange, to feel a mother's protective arms.

I felt a great deal lighter after that session, even though I felt bad that my father was a villain in everyone's eyes. They had called a spade a spade: there was no doubt in their minds — or mine, now — that my father had been leering at me, not just looking, and that it wasn't *right* of him to stare at my genitals like that.

That night, I had a dream. There weren't any pictures, but there were words that wanted to be remembered, urgently. I woke up early in the morning and wrote them down. I PROMISE TO FAIL AT EVERYTHING I DO, IF I AM ALLOWED TO LIVE, I wrote in capital letters. I wrote it several times, until it penetrated that this was literally a promise I had made at some time in my life. It was a very important clue, but what on earth was its context? *How* could I have made such a promise? *When* did I feel that my life was so threatened that I would make a deal like this? *Who* was the promise made to?

As I pondered, I remembered that feeling of self-sabotage which had made sure that nothing I tried to take me away from my massage career would ever succeed. When it came to crunch time, it always became 'clear' to me that none of my ventures would work, even when I employed outside expertise and no matter how many business courses I attended. I remembered what Robert Kyosaki had said during one of his brilliant Money and You workshops. He had looked at me directly and spoken very distinctly: 'Of course, for some it is too late.' I was in my early fifties then and desperately wanted to prove him wrong, yet I didn't trust myself to. My capacity for failure was uncanny, but somehow expected.

In one effort to get started in a new way of life, I enrolled for training in the so-called Efficiency Lessons, a graded series of sessions designed to empower people. I was so impressed when I experienced the Lessons for myself, that I invested a fair amount of money in becoming trained in administering them. I was doing really well; in fact, I seemed to have found a career for which I was superbly suited! Perhaps I was doing too well for some in the team. One, a woman psychologist, started asking questions about 'the credibility of the trainee facilitators'. It seemed that just about anyone with a presentable face could apply, she said. What were our qualifications? And then: did any of us have a police record?

We were required to detail our previous employment history. I decided to answer honestly: I had been a teacher, a bodyworker and also a prostitute; and yes, there was a time when my name and photograph were registered with the Vice Squad, so they would know my identity when they saw my advertisement. The record was scrapped when I left the prostitution business — I had called for confirmation and been told there was no record of me in their files — but that was not the point. An ex-prostitute was not the sort of person these people wanted on their staff, no matter how 'efficient' she was. The boss felt obliged to sack me. I left, fuming, blushing and feeling dreadfully ashamed.

This wouldn't have happened to just anybody. There was definitely a serious 'bug' in my system; a sabotage mechanism that matched the statement I remembered from my dream. The question was, what to do about it? A woman friend told me about regression therapy, which sounded as if it might help me to address the mystery.

Jan was a skilled therapist; she had a special gift for helping people to encounter memories of past lives and had given up a career as a successful businesswoman to do it. After I told her what I knew about my problem, she explained what we were aiming for: namely, to go into a past life which had a bearing on the dynamics that were still playing themselves out in this lifetime. Neither of us had any idea of what would transpire.

Jan went through her gentle induction as I sat on a comfortable couch in her living room. I closed my eyes in perfect relaxation ... relaxed ... relaxed ...

The first thing I became aware of was empty pale sky. A feeling of intense coldness came over me. Jan piled on the blankets as I shivered, but I could not get warm. Gradually the vision in my mind revealed the tops of pine trees ridging nearby hills, standing in deep snow. I saw myself then as a young American Indian woman of about fifteen, collapsed into a kneeling position, held by the snow, with blood flowing from my legs.

Then my eyes focused on two figures on horseback: one was a medicine man, the other my Sioux lover. The medicine man was the most powerful person in the tribe. No one contradicted him, especially the girls and women; they were not expected to have anything to do with tribal decisions. Yet this was exactly what I had done. I had the gift of being able to read minds and I could tell if someone was telling the truth or not. I had known that the medicine man was making up stories to build his influence and standing in the tribe. Rather than keep my own counsel, I had loudly accused him of lying, in the presence of the chief and all the elders.

I had broken a tribal custom by speaking out and I had undermined the medicine man's credibility. I should have known there would be retribution for this wild, impulsive action, but could never have envisaged my punishment: that I would be taken away from the camp and, once far away, that the hamstrings of my legs would be cut by my own lover, who was more bound to tribal loyalty than to his love for me. Unable to run away or return to the camp, I was left to die slowly in the snow, alone.

Softly, Jan asked me to look into the eyes of my lover, who sat on horseback, about to return to the village with the medicine man. I met his hard, self-righteous eyes and … oh! I was shocked to the heart to discover in him the eyes of my own father! As the life-blood flowed from my legs, I returned his look with an intense gaze. There was no love left in me then, and no pleading, no questions; there was only the overwhelming desire to punish him. And with all the intention I could muster, I cursed him.

How did the realisation come to me that this was how I had locked us both into lifetimes of conflict? I don't know. The thought just came that I would both love and hate this man, and he would love and hate me, until the cycle was somehow broken. I did not know that my curse would give him the power to crush me again and again.

It didn't matter to me whether my experience with Jan revealed a true story or not, whether reincarnation was true or not; the important thing was that these feelings about my father were being acknowledged, and that I had gained some sense of responsibility for the kind of relationship that had developed between us. Over time, the information gained through my work with Jan would bear fruit.

I continued my search for understanding by going to Byron Bay in New South Wales to do the Hoffman Process, which specifically dealt with father and mother issues. During all the angry pillow-bashing sessions, it puzzled me why I was driven to pulverise my father's imagined penis again and again and again. The penis would always restore itself and I would bash it to pieces again, until I was utterly exhausted and believed it must be done for since I was done for. In hindsight, it is a wonder that none of the therapists there picked up on this.

A curious part of this process included a spontaneous memory of the circumstances of my birth, with details my mother had forgotten until I later reminded her of them. I also understood the feelings of both my parents at my birth. Through the Hoffman Process, my perceptions of my father and mother were transformed from seeing them only as the people who brought me up, to sensitive human beings who were struggling along, doing their best.

During several quiet days on my own in a Byron Bay hotel, integrating what I had gone through in the Hoffman Process, the realisation came to me that it was the devil of my childhood religion with whom I had made my dreadful pact. I sat as if stunned while the implications became clearer. I had not wanted to die and risk going to hell — which meant I must have done something really bad to make me believe I *would* go to hell if I died. But what about confession — how was it that I did not believe God would forgive me for whatever it was I had done? Although I had been familiar with angels, always making room for them beside me when I was a child, I had turned to the devil and asked for *his* support. More than that: at some stage, I promised to fail at everything I really wanted to do in life, provided I was allowed to live! I was overwhelmed by these heinous thoughts, but relieved to have a clear strategy at last: *Exorcise this devil! Reverse this promise!*

First I went to Melbourne and told each of my parents face to face that I loved them. We all shed tears of joy.

BACK ONCE MORE in Perth, I parted with fabulous sums of money for all sorts of reprogramming techniques, including one very special and extremely expensive session in neurolinguistic programming, which purported to clear everything for all time. NLP works very well in many instances, but shouldn't be over-rated. If positive thinking works at all, it should have worked for me, but alas, it didn't.

I had several sessions with hypnotists, to no avail. Oh, dear. But I wouldn't give up; the urge to keep *fighting* this thing drove me on. Almost blindly.

I took on a full-time teaching job after my stay in Byron Bay, but became so tired of it, so thoroughly burnt out, that one day, when a semi-trailer came speeding through a red light, I didn't care whether it ran over me or not. It missed me by the merest hair's breadth.

I stopped teaching at the end of the semester but, rather than return to massage work, I moved back to Denmark for six months, living in a cabin on my friend Mark's property, making a little money from giving the Efficiency Lessons there. The environment was great for my health and morale, but the money inevitably ran out — especially when I had to give up my inexpensively rented little cabin — and so I returned to Perth and to what was easier: relief massage.

My break in the country had refreshed me and I felt enthused again. So here I was, back again at my old job in spite of everything, working during Victoria's school hours.

'I don't understand it,' said a new client, turning to me as he was preparing to leave. 'You look so innocent!'

'I *am* innocent!' was my swift reply. 'There's nothing wrong with what I do.'

I smiled at him, but his puzzled expression remained as he disappeared out the front door. I felt a key turning in my belly, telling me once again that all wasn't perfectly well.

I came home one day and pressed the button on the answering machine to retrieve my messages. Ravel's 'Pavane for a Dead Princess' filled my hallway. I let the measured, doleful music go on for a full half hour. There was no mystery to this: instead of putting a blank tape into my machine before I left, I had unwittingly inserted this haunting melody. Was it pure coincidence that I had chosen this particular tape, which I had forgotten to label when I recorded the music from the radio?

I thought of the princess in the stone coffin, waking to find herself buried alive, and my hair stood on end. Fuzzily, I saw myself as a woman of grace, dead to her real identity and living in an underworld. Wasn't it like living in an underworld to feel inferior to friends who had 'normal' jobs? I definitely did not want to tell them what I did for a living, and got in a real sweat that some people might guess.

I felt — and sometimes looked — a mess. I was waiting for a train at the city terminal one day, when I noticed a woman glance at me, then draw in a horrified breath and turn away, covering her eyes. Furtively I checked my appearance: my blouse was poking untidily out of my skirt, my sleeves and cuffs weren't too clean and, worst of all, the colours I wore clashed. My hat was perched on my head at a silly angle. Suddenly I saw it all as an expression of my inner discord. Tall, thin women like me don't get away with untidiness as easily as others; we stand out too much. The woman's reaction probably had nothing to do with me, but at the time I was ready to believe that I had horrified her.

I FINALLY CAME across someone I thought could help me with exorcising my devil: Rimmie, a sympathetic, charismatic shaman. He had special powers, using drumming to move energy and help people break through their most stubborn problems. He had performed some exorcisms in his past — that made him a *must*!

After familiarising himself with my story, he told me that what I had to do was call up my devil, visualise him and tell him to piss off. I sat down on a cushion on his floor, while he sat on a chair with his drum. I no longer believed in the devil as a Catholic reality; rather I saw it as an energy in my body with devilish characteristics: destructive, seductive, lying in every possible way. Even so, I knew I'd be able to visualise this energy as the devil I knew from my religious upbringing to fit the framework for this exorcism. I was apprehensive but wanted desperately to give it a go.

Rimmie started with a soft drum roll, taking it louder, then softer again, humming along like a honeybee and soon sending me into a dream-like state.

The devil appeared to me in a forest, where I was sitting against the smooth trunk of a large karri tree. As instructed, I described it to Rimmie. 'Breathe in the strength of the tree,' Rimmie coaxed me gently, drumming softly and persistently. 'Now, stand up and look him in the face.'

The shaman's drum grew a little louder. I breathed in the strength of the tree and, keeping my eye on the devil, used the tree's trunk to support my back as I eased up to a standing position. The devil waited patiently, smoke pluming from his evil nostrils as he parted blackish curling lips in a vile smile. His eyes gleamed wickedly, as if enjoying this game of 'Kill me if you can'; they reminded me uncannily of my father's.

But he wasn't my father, was he? He was the devil, and could be exorcised with the help of my therapist. My shaman friend was wetting his lips now, ready to utter the words which would surely liberate me from this beast.

'Tell him to be gone now!' he said authoritatively, interspersing his words with decisive beats on the drum. 'Tell him that he has been with you long enough and now it's time for him to go — he's no longer needed in your life.' Rattle, rattle, boom, boom!

A moment of hesitation on my part.

'The pact that you made with him as a child is over! Tear it up!' he yelled.

I gathered courage with the rhythm of the drum and words formed in my brain. I took deep breaths as I faced the monster. It was all malevolent grin, menacing me with piercing eyes that were sharp enough to cut through any Dutch courage. I faltered, but got through the performance with credible assertiveness. 'Begone, evil thing!' I shouted, my lips held tight to stop them from trembling. 'I renounce my pact with you! I am no longer afraid to die! I deserve to succeed at everything I do!'

I fell silent. The therapist slowed his drumming and waited for my breathing to slow down too. 'What happened?' he enquired, leaning towards me in eager anticipation.

'The devil laughed,' I said lamely. 'He ran away through the forest, laughing loudly.'

Needless to say, this failed attempt only reinforced my belief that whatever it was that had me in its grip was invincible. If there was something stronger, I hadn't found it yet.

But there *was* something stronger, and eventually *it* would find *me*, when I had given up looking desperately in all the wrong places.

THE VASE SHATTERS

IN 1993, MY father turned eighty. He was ill from cancer that was devouring his bowel at a ferocious rate. It was thought that he would not live very much longer, so I flew over to stay at my sister Liesbet's house, to be at his side. My two other sisters also flew in, Berta from Fremantle and Teresa from Canberra. We didn't want our father to die in a hospital.

Only six months before, he had hesitantly confided to me in his kitchen that he was suffering pain in his abdomen. He had groaned with the weight in his bowels and I should have suspected that something was really wrong at the time. My father rarely let on that he was in pain and his groan had been more than a complaint — it sounded like a ship sinking into the deep.

It was so strange that he was to die before our mother. She had been in a nursing home for a whole year already, and he had been dreaming of the time he would be free, when he was no longer required to pick her up and wheel her around on her twice-weekly outings. It had been a painful decision to admit our mother to a nursing home. She had begged us with tears not to leave her in that place with the awful smells, the crowded conditions that meant she had to eat her meals on her lap for want of a dining room, and where corpses were carried out the back door so nobody would notice anyone had died in there, where there was nothing else to do. It was no wonder that her response to this environment was to become introspective, then senile — a deterioration increased by the medications she took for pain. And yet she was still physically robust, while her husband had only weeks to live.

The four of us made a roster and tended our father day and night. His strength left him measurably every day; he watched this with incredulity. He had undergone an operation, but it had been too late: the cancer had spread upwards and into his lungs. Knowing that his time was limited, he had travelled to his beloved Germany for the last time, to say goodbye to family members there. He had to cut the visit short because of pain; he wryly remarked that he had flown back first class without being able to touch the free whisky.

He would test out his still-strong legs and arms, shaking his head with disbelief, but soon he had to rely on a walking stick, then a walking frame, to get his trembling body around. It was awesome to watch the man who had once terrorised us, now become dependent on us, like a baby.

It was so difficult for him. It was a while before he had the courage to ask us to clean his dentures, and let us see his shrunken face without them. The time came when he couldn't wipe himself after letting go his evil-smelling faeces. His skin had become softer than a baby's, so paper-thin that he begged for gentleness as he stood there. Yet he would eat lots of food, as if this would somehow return his strength. In the end, we told him gently that the doctor had said he should only eat when really hungry. 'What goes in has to come out again, so there's no point,' the doctor had said. My father silently considered this and acted on it immediately. From then on, only the ration provided passed his lips; he asked for nothing more. His acquiescence moved me deeply. It was a sign that he had accepted he was dying.

It was one of my father's last remaining pleasures to leave his bed at two every afternoon and install himself in front of the television to watch 'Days of Our Lives'. For countless years, he and my mother had been spellbound by these beautiful, greedy men and women who reliably betrayed each other, year in, year out. I had the miserable bad luck, once, to arrive from the airport on one of my visits from Western Australia while my parents were watching their favourite show. The front door wasn't locked, so I went in, announcing my arrival in a loud and cheery voice. No one came to greet me. I found them in the living room, their faces riveted to the demon screen. Without speaking, my father beckoned me imperiously to come in and sit down on the couch. My mother acknowledged my presence with a half glance as I crossed the path of her vision, without actually moving her head or meeting my eyes, her face contorted into an apologetic smile. I had arrived at crunch time for one of the characters. At last, they sighed deeply and I knew that it would soon be over and we'd have a cup of tea.

My father continued his addiction to the lives of those dreadful sham males and bitchy women. We sat with him to keep him company, taking a risk that the sticky soap opera might rub off on us. About ten days before he died, he suddenly shook his head, uttered a loud, 'Tch! Tch!' through loosening false teeth, and wondered out loud how anyone could watch such awful stuff. 'It's disgusting what those people do to each other,' he said, as if he had been asked for his opinion and this was his first ever review of the show. 'How can they put on terrible shows like that!' He got up to hobble back to his bed. We looked at each other open-mouthed at this sudden sign of sane disillusionment. Was our father becoming enlightened?

We four sisters shared a cup of tea in the kitchen while our father slept and discussed whether his frequent anger might have contributed to his physical condition. We could not accept that cancer can strike people for no reason. His outdoor lifestyle had been very healthy. Perhaps the destruction of his life-long efforts in the convent gardens had eaten away at him? Maybe our mother's constant belittling of him had finally taken its toll? He had endured it so long and so bitterly. And his diet hadn't been too good. He had been a closet chocaholic ever since he gave up smoking ten years previously.

No one can really know what causes an illness, but I felt, rightly or wrongly, that the unresolved secrets and conflicts of the past had played the most important part. Our father had never finished any relationship business: he lived in unresolved conflict with every member of his large family, and with several other people in his life, such as Mother Albion. There were many skeletons in my father's past, which might have taken up residence in his gut, to wreak their terrible havoc there.

I hoped so much during those last weeks that my father would open his heart to us, tell us the things he regretted having done, ask our forgiveness and die in utter bliss surrounded by his broken-hearted family.

He came close on two occasions: the first when we were sitting outside under a tree in dappled shade. I read while he sat silently musing to himself. 'I've told Father Ben everything,' he said to me after a while. 'And that makes it all right now, doesn't it?'

Father Ben had heard my father's confessions for many years, but the 'doesn't it?' expressed a lurking doubt. I could see a tension in his face that wasn't caused only by physical pain. I took my chances then and said, 'Only *you* know if everything's all right, Pa, or if you need to fix up anything with people as well as with God.' I dared not be more explicit. My father laboured under the impression that no one in the family knew his secrets.

He knitted his brows. He had to constantly confirm to himself that the Big Boss, as he called his Catholic God, had it all stitched up for him, in spite of his inner turmoil. And to the Big Boss he surrendered himself, like a good boy willing to accept anything from a stern father who knows best. He accepted his suffering as a punishment: the Big Boss was doing this to him for his own good. He repeatedly requested that no one should give him any medicines which might speed up his dying; he wanted his obedience to be absolute. When I finally administered the morphine by drip, he said he was frightened of being 'bumped off' and would only believe the word of the visiting nurse about his medication.

'I am peaceful,' he said suddenly, the next time we were both sitting outside again, enjoying the fresh air. I sat a little distance apart from him with my book. Chit-chat was not appropriate and he had rejected my offer of reading aloud to him. He was absorbing as best he could the queer fact of his dying, and the knowledge that he would be gone before his wife, after all.

I replied, 'I know you are peaceful, Pa, but I wish you could also be *happy*.'

He looked extremely pensive at that, but I went back to my book. He piped up again to ask, 'How do you know I'm not happy, Carla?'

It was then that I let him down. I felt the deep import of his question, but didn't give myself time to absorb it or do him justice with my reply. Instead I fended him off in a way I later regretted more than I can say.

'*You* know if you're happy or not, Dad,' I spluttered, then allowed my mind to blank out, unable to receive the sudden gift of his trust. It had been my cue and I had muffed it. I forgot to call on my own God or summon an angel to help me at that time. In the hour of his greatest need, or perhaps at a brief moment of unusual potential, I wasn't there for him. Even when he repeated his question, I gave him the same inadequate answer, poor man.

Still, there was an unexpected change in my father. Two nuns, old friends through long association, came to visit him and when they came out of the sick room one of them relayed an important message to me. It was Sister Victoire, our oldest friend, who had been charged to tell me that he was 'sorry for being so hard on Carla'. My heart almost stopped, my mouth gaped open.

I went in to see him shortly afterwards, when they had left. My father did not even look into my eyes, simply said in self-justification, 'You were always so wilful, Carla,' and turned his head. Did he remember then the absolute terror he had instilled in me in order to crush me into silence about his own wicked actions? He had apologised for being 'so hard', but not directly to me. I was breathless, nevertheless: it was the best he could do. It told me that his extraordinary violence had weighed on him, and he was sorry.

The great secret of his other demeanours had been for the priest's ears only and would not be discussed with the people he had hurt. It was too much to expect him to break his heart right open; even the knowledge of his impending death wasn't going to breach his reticence. I cried inside, for both of us. What does it take, if leaving the body, the planet and your family for ever, doesn't break down resistance? But in those last remaining days, he was loving and tender to all of us, giving us embraces which touched our hearts very deeply. He was showing love, and we could feel the realness of it. And yet he wouldn't die a totally happy man, choosing instead to cling to his faith, which promised total forgiveness through confession to a priest, and daring his God to be true to him.

MY MOTHER, MORE lucid during those extraordinary days than on many a previous occasion, asked to be brought to her dying husband's side. She was dressed and groomed by a kindly nurse who had taken a special interest in her welfare. A taxi designed for wheelchairs brought her the few kilometres, and I wheeled her into the spacious room where her husband — who had gloated that he would make the most of life after she had gone — lay propped up on a small mountain of pillows. His eyes showed deep pleasure at this gesture from the woman who had always claimed to know better than him in any situation. She was now so frail and yet still assertive. Her cheeks were flushed, her eyes intense, her face animated by an inner light as she approached him. I placed her wheelchair close to the bed, following her unspoken directions, and quietly left the room. I turned just before I closed the door and was transfixed by what I saw.

My mother's thin arm lay on his bed, her wasted twisted hand in his big bony one, and they were simply looking at each other, in wordless love. The light around them was almost visible; it shone with utter delight and passion from the eyes of my father, whose transfigured face I was able to see. The miracle of their love filled the room with a tangible vibrancy. Both of them were facing their impending final parting, and there was no room for anything else now but the utter truth of their love.

I understood in a flash how they had loved each other all their lives, truly loved each other deeply, even as they fought, betrayed, hated and belittled each other. Many people who had watched them, like me, had said, 'Why don't you go your own ways, for God's sake!' But in those sacred moments of grace, they forgave each other utterly and were wedded again, this time as true lovers, not out for themselves but there to give their all at last. I realised that it had been mistaken of me to judge anything that had gone on between them in the past — only they knew how much of it was exactly what they had wanted.

IN SPITE OF our rostered vigil, our father was alone when he breathed his last at four o'clock in the morning after our mother's visit. None of us had slept much that night. We were in the kitchen, having a cup of tea, when we sensed more than heard his gasp, and ran in to see his pitifully gaping open mouth, no longer able to suck in air. It was crying out to heaven. My father's spirit had begun the journey out of his body to freedom.

Luckily, there were at least four hours before the undertakers came to take him away — time enough for my brothers to see him briefly for the last time. I wanted to leave him undisturbed as long as possible, to allow his spirit to completely leave the body, but my sisters — more troubled by death — insisted on the body's speedy removal.

The undertakers arrived. It was a Sunday — and so early that the two young men, dressed in neat black suits, had not fully recovered from their Saturday night out. They were silent and respectful, concentrating as precisely on their job as they could, aware that I was watching their every move. The stretcher, covered with an open plastic body bag, was placed beside the bed and they heaved the grotesque but oh so familiar form onto it.

It was absolutely strange to me that my father, still dressed in his pyjamas, did nothing to stop this indignity. His still-supple and very tall body sagged in the middle and his arms and hands, no longer controlled by any consciousness, fell down either side. It was the sight of his strong, now lifeless hands that moved me most, no longer able to assert themselves in this world, finally useless. The undertakers tucked them into the black plastic bag, which they then zipped over his face.

'Will the family want to see the body?' we were asked. We said no; all of us had seen him. For the moment, we had forgotten about our mother. My father's body was spared the disturbance of being embalmed, which meant being disembowelled, but the undertakers were not pleased when my mother insisted on seeing her dead husband a full day later. They managed a surprisingly pleasing presentation nevertheless, dressing my father in his best suit.

After the undertakers had left that Sunday morning, we all sat together, stunned in spite of the long expectation of our father's death. I was about to learn something new about myself. For an unacknowledged part of me, my father's death was a moment of triumph, because I was still alive. In spite of the years of therapy — which had indeed transformed most of my sorrow, anger and fear into compassion for my parents — there was a tiny bitter corner where a spider lived. And she was about to unload her venom.

'I wonder how much money he left after all he spent on prostitutes. The funny thing is, we all knew about it anyway,' I added.

The words drifted into silent space. My sisters were too dazed to answer. But my comments weren't really aimed at my sisters; they were meant for the spirit I knew was hovering in the vicinity. In that moment when my father's spirit might have been utterly vulnerable, I gave him this treacherous spider-woman's bite because I was bitterly angry that he hadn't found it in himself to be totally open with me. Everything had been kept under the carpet right to the very last. And religion had given him the means to do this with impunity.

As soon as the words were out, I was pulled up by the impact of having said them. In the atmosphere around us, I could feel the chaotic emotional response of my dead father. I felt ill, realising that my revenge would have its own bitter consequences. The dead are helpless, after all, in our hands.

Deep sorrow enveloped my heart. I wept for a long time after that, not only for the loss of my father but for the cruel way I had chosen to take my revenge on him. I begged his forgiveness in the darkness of the nights following; then, finally, had the conversation I'd always wished I'd had with him in life, pouring out my pain, telling him how it had been for me. I forgave him then, really and truly. I had wanted him to be open towards me, but how open had I been towards him? He had always done his best, and in his dying days he had surpassed himself magnificently. It had been *my* mistake to think I knew better and that he should have gone further.

I did not stay for my father's funeral. It was the middle of the Melbourne football season, which made it impossible to change my flight without having to pay extra for a first-class ticket. The main work had been done, as far as I was concerned, and I could not face the awful sentimentality of the religious ceremony that would accompany the burial.

As it happened, it rained and rained on the day of the funeral and everyone got so wet that it was impossible to distinguish tears from the streaks of rain on their faces. A little under a year later, the same thing happened when my mother was buried beside him, in the same patch of mud. I heard all about both occasions, back in Western Australia. Sadly, I missed out on the opportunities of being intimately present with the other members of my family. *I couldn't have endured it*, I told myself. What did I really know about what my father needed to heal? It was I who needed to continue to heal myself.

NOTHING COULD EVER be the same again.

I used my increasing spare time to write about my family history, which was becoming an important process for me, and to keep a daily journal of what was going on inside me. I did just enough massage work to keep myself alive.

As before, I compromised in my work. Not as before, I faked an orgasm. I remember that moment as the nadir of my career. Bernard, my client, could feel the difference and he imitated the sounds I'd made to indicate that he knew I'd faked it. I had the very bad grace to deny it.

Unpleasant things began to happen. They weren't really new occurrences, but now they were right in my face, bothering me like they never did before. After I placed an advertisement, a competitor who wanted to do some damage would get a bogus client to phone and not hang up, keeping my line busy and preventing other callers from getting through. Working alone, I had limited capacity to compete with other individuals — let alone with brothels — but nevertheless I had to put up with this sort of harassment.

One day, when two clients who eventually did get through on the phone failed to turn up for their appointments, I decided I might as well go shopping. As I backed out of my driveway, I discovered a car parked right near the entrance, just out of sight of the house. I surprised the guy at the steering wheel, who was holding a camera, and then I understood. The opposition, whoever they were, had placed this vehicle near my house, making it obvious to all approaching customers that they were being watched and photographed. All my appointments were ruined. Privacy is so important and the lack of it can scare off potential clients for good.

The quality of client phone calls dropped to a new low. Guys would phone just to have a chat while they masturbated, hanging up the moment they came and leaving me completely in the lurch — a sickening experience. This sort of thing had happened in the good times too — you had to expect it in this business — but the undisguised truth of it hit home now: it was demeaning and infuriating.

On one sorry day, I had several fumingly obscene calls from a stranger. When, finally, I picked up the phone and blew a whistle into it, with no idea who was receiving the ear-splitting blast, I realised I was going mad. I was fed up too with having my phone tapped;

I recognised the tell-tale signs and hated it. In short, I became aware of all the things I had put up with for the sake of this career.

I lost my enthusiasm in spades and it started to show in my face. I was never any good at hiding my real feelings. One day I opened my door to a new client. Instead of coming in, he backed off with the excuse of needing to park his car somewhere else in the shade. He never came back. This was so demoralising, it felt like a brick in my stomach. It could have been deliberately staged as another blow from the competition, but I didn't believe so. My face just didn't radiate joy and confidence any more. I know I can be downright ugly when I scowl.

It was time to admit there was no longer any fun in it for me. God's Callgirl was dead. I didn't know exactly what had happened to kill her off, but as my belief in myself dropped, so, uncannily, did the quality of my clients. But immediately I had the thought that it was time to leave my profession, along came the opposing voices telling me I couldn't afford to give it up, that it was the only thing left to me now. The thought filled me with fear.

I threw myself into healing sessions once again, with increasing desperation. I attended weekend retreats, therapy courses, workshops, including Landmark Education's Forum and two more of their courses — looking for the insights that would heal me. I spent all the money I'd ever saved, keeping almost nothing for the future. These courses were so useful in their own way, but they couldn't do much for me — I was really only grasping at straws. I remained confused, suffering constantly from the effects of psychic dross transferred in sexual massage, especially when it included intercourse, although I allowed that rarely now. I no longer had the resilience I'd enjoyed when I was buoyed by a spiritual motive for my work and filled with a playful curiosity. Now my job was dragging me down. I had become tired and spent. A restless cauldron bubbled deep inside me, terrifying me with its potential to kill. A full two years had passed since I'd completed the Hoffman Process and uncovered my childhood pact with the devil. But this fear inside — terror of I didn't know *what* — was intense, and no therapist was able to help me understand it.

Until I met Jessie.

JESSIE WAS A streetwise sex counsellor — she had literally been brought up on the streets of New York City. I told her everything about my story that seemed to be relevant: the choking in therapy, my hopelessness. I happened to mention that my early sex education had amounted to the wisdom: 'kissing makes you pregnant'.

'How so, kissing makes you pregnant?' she asked me matter-of-factly.

Knowing that it wouldn't look too good to a streetwise woman, I still confessed: 'I believed that kissing excited the guy's passion so his semen would travel down your throat.'

'Did the nuns tell you that's what happens? That the semen going down your throat would get you pregnant?'

'No, they didn't. I just thought that. It seemed natural.'

'Why would you come to a conclusion like that if you'd never had the experience of it?'

Jessie's question sent my mind reeling. I sat there, in a wicker chair on her verandah, and that instant I knew the truth. My father's oral sexual abuse of me as a child was now suddenly so obvious! I was grateful to be sitting in a chair so I couldn't fall down. My head was in a dreadful spin. I also had the queer realisation that I had *always* known this! I had always known it somewhere, but I hadn't wanted to admit what my father had done. It had been crucial to protect the image of my father as a good man who loved me, his first, special daughter. I had hidden from myself that my father had not loved me enough to protect me; instead, he had been the one to violate me. He had been a devil to me. That knowledge had been far too painful.

Tears came to my eyes, but there was more to realise. A powerful reason for denying the truth was that I hadn't wanted to admit having been in collusion with him, a *partner* in his vile crimes. Oh God — I had wanted to *protect* my father. I loved him! It wasn't just my shame, but my great *love* for my father that had kept me too afraid to see the truth.

Jessie arrived back on her patio. Time had passed and I hadn't noticed it. I paid Jessie her hefty fee and left, wanting to put my head down somewhere, go to sleep, perhaps die.

I woke later that day with a certain clarity in my head. Pieces of the puzzle had clunked into place like great big keys fitting in their slots. My pact with the devil unravelled: 'the devil' I'd had to contend with was originally my *father*. As a child being abused in the night, when reality was mixed with dreams, I couldn't distinguish that. The abuse had been so overwhelming, had felt so bad and made me choke so much, that every time it happened I believed I would die a bad girl and go to hell. So I had prayed to the devil of my childhood faith to be saved from death. From death by choking, first of all. *Please, daddy, please daddy-devil, don't choke me to death.*

The whole picture became clear to me. I now knew that my belief in myself as totally evil had been embedded in me since my father had tried to shut me up by throttling and kicking me. The resulting guilt and shame I lived with made me feel unworthy of succeeding in anything that was important to me as I grew older, which was why I believed that I owed it to the devil, or the evil in me, to fail.

The devil in me .... Even at the time of this realisation, I did not fully apprehend that I was literally possessed. The energy I had directed towards the devil as a child did not leave me when I grew out of my religion. It had become a living entity in my body and seemed to have a will of its own. It was the possessing devil who sabotaged all my efforts to succeed in life, in order to confuse me and make me think ever worse of myself; who had sabotaged every effort I made to heal myself and thereby expose him.

I WOULD NOT immediately integrate all I had discovered at Jessie's; in fact, it seemed ages before everything I now understood sat comfortably with me. The wheels turned incredibly slowly, as if through treacle. It was one thing to understand with my mind; quite another to heal the emotional patterns that had dug deep grooves in my subconscious. My emotions were like elastic bands tied to my brain; I tried to change them and they would snap back, terrified of the unfamiliar, the unknown. To my horror, I found I was dogged by my shame as much as ever and by a terrible lack of self-confidence. I was a wreck. The only difference between understanding and not understanding was that now I saw myself confirmed as my father's reject. I felt that my father had ruined my life and I was sitting in the rubble. Forlornly, I went for more counselling.

'Will I ever be normal?' I asked the sexual abuse therapist in her city office. She was a busy government employee and couldn't offer me another session for three months. She looked shocked at my question: sitting before her was an elegantly dressed woman with no confidence that she could succeed in anything. My cheeks burned to read her reaction and to hear what she had to say.

'You've been abused in every way,' she said, leaning towards me across her desk. 'Abused physically, sexually, emotionally and mentally. You will heal if you go through the process I've described for you.' Then she added a remarkable thing. 'Or you will have to take up a spiritual path.'

And so I left, and bought myself a teddy bear as instructed and ate lollies for my inner child till I was sick. I bought the recommended book, *The Courage To Heal*, and gave the little girl inside me a voice by writing her words with my left hand. I imagined holding her and comforting her with gentle words. It helped immensely. I felt the child rise up from the ground where she had been crawling around in the darkness of fear, cowering in the coal shed that she had never felt free to leave. How long would it be before she would feel really safe again?

I continued this wonderful healing intensively for several weeks, delighted to have regular conversations with me as a little girl. Whenever I forgot, I found her hurt by my neglect; then I had to make it up to her. It was so important that she learned to trust my word.

Meanwhile, the therapist's words about taking up a spiritual path intrigued me. I asked myself what she might have meant by that. Meditation, religion? If so, what religion? Or was it living under a spiritual mentor? Perhaps we don't have choices, merely inspired thoughts leading us to actions which provide more lessons. In any case, Master Adi Da came to mind (known as Bubba Free John in Los Angeles in the early 1970s). I remembered how, when I first read a book about his life, the feeling in my heart was so radiant that I had looked down at my chest, even inside my T-shirt, to search for the light I felt so brightly. I hadn't been able to put the book down, hooked on the feelings and sensations that came to me as I read. Now I started seriously to wonder about this master who could so affect people from afar.

I began to attend weekly Adi Da gatherings, held in Fremantle by a devotee who had spent some time with her guru. And so I set out upon the perilous journey of those mesmerised by their master — a spiritual path for the innocent, the sincere, the brave, the confused and the foolish. I bought books and tapes, went on retreats and started to meditate twice a day. I felt Divine Love once more, as I had experienced it in the convent, only this time much more tangibly and strongly. Master Da's writings also inspired me: no one, it seemed, understood human nature and the ego better than he did. Master Da wrote many books, producing them at a prodigious rate, and we were supposed to buy them all.

MY WAY OF life as a masseuse continued, haltingly. Only direct interference from 'the hand of God' would finally end it. That hand manifested decisively and mercifully in the summer of 1994, although at the time I did not appreciate it. It turned my garden, and soon my life, completely upside down.

I looked out of the windows of my cosy house in Hilton, near Fremantle, and gazed at the ruins of my garden. I had chosen this place for its large garden and supposed long-term rental prospects.

I lived there alone, my daughter Victoria having elected to live with her father when she turned fifteen. Now, barely eight months on, the large block had been divided into three lots and fences were going up on either side of me. The single, prized tree, a shady oak, soon found itself on the other side of a newly erected fence. New septic tanks were being installed in the back of each yard.

The man operating the digging machine was sympathetic, but he couldn't help overturning the herbs, flowers and vegetable plots, the carefully rejuvenated hibiscus and veronica bushes. In the space of an afternoon, I found myself sitting in a house in a sandpit, angry and helpless to stop this destruction of all my plans for a peaceful life.

As if symbolic of not knowing where to go next, I cracked the big toe of my right foot on my bedpost. There! I was forced to stop working. My kind neighbours, Elsie and Bert, brought me soup and buttered bread and cheerful chatter. Bert had been like a kind father to me since I moved in. I first met him when I answered an unexpected knock at the front door: toolbox in hand, he wondered if I had any odd jobs that wanted doing. He helped me break into my house when I had left the keys inside, by removing tiles from the roof above the laundry.

Next I developed a very sore back. I couldn't walk straight and couldn't even think of doing massage. For a full week, I'd dragged myself around on crutches because of my toe; now I spent another week in agony because of my back.

During that second week, I was taken care of by one of my clients. He was a special angel who often came around to take me out for lunch or to the chiropractor, and he even did the shopping for me. I allowed Rob to help me out of bed one day, when I found it difficult to move. 'Rather you than me,' he quipped, grinning. It was a wonder to me that he would bother to come again after seeing me like this.

Rob was married, wealthy, and his business, whatever it was, had put him in touch with people in the justice system — police, detectives of all kinds, judges. He'd also had many experiences of massage parlours and brothels. I asked him questions while we sat having a beer with our restaurant lunch, but he was coy about satisfying my curiosity as to what was happening on the scene. He wanted to reassure me that it wasn't worth knowing about. 'Eat up, Carla. Take care of yourself.'

When I recovered from my sore back and broken toe, I told Rob I'd only do straight massage for him — I had really lost the energy for anything more. Rob took it in his stride. He could get the rest elsewhere, he told me.

My body had healed but I still had no idea where to go next.

The phone rang just as Elsie from next door arrived with some scones. To my utter surprise it was State Housing with an offer of a unit in Denmark for me. Three months earlier, a woman acquaintance had said to me, almost in passing, 'Get your name down with State Housing, Carla.' I'd laughed. 'What would they be able to do for me? I'm not a single mum or an invalid.' But she said it again, 'Just get your name registered with them.' So I'd gone down to their office.

Unbeknown to me, a group of units was being built in Denmark for the over fifties at that very time, and I was one of only two people who had applied for single accommodation. Bert suggested we go have a look — and he and Elsie absolutely approved of what they saw. A new unit! Space for developing a nice garden on all sides! It was a place I could retire to and securely stay for the rest of my life. This was an offer out of the blue that I could not refuse.

I moved in two weeks later. My whole world had taken a 180-degree turn while I was hardly looking. The hand of God had picked me up and dropped me down again decisively. It was none too soon.

IN THOSE LAST days before I left the city, I had some loose ends to tie up. I phoned some of my clients who had entrusted me with their number to say goodbye.

I wanted to say a special goodbye to Guy, quite a handsome young man who had developed a crush on me. He was a travelling jewellery rep and sometimes I'd reduce my fee by taking a good-looking ring or a pendant. Guy was tall with a perfect body and good manners. He lacked confidence in himself as a sexual being, and that was his problem, for he had a healthy sexual appetite. In my dealings with him I always found him polite, amiable, appreciative and attentive — in short, what any girl might dream of — yet he didn't have a girlfriend.

Guy and I had wondrous sex, once we got to know each other well. I enjoyed his young, muscular body, his smooth skin, clean breath and hair. Guy was always careful and brought his own condoms. The previous time I had seen him, I'd praised him for his good looks and charm and told him that if he wanted a girlfriend he wouldn't have any trouble finding one. He had listened to me with bated breath. Where on earth, I thought to myself, did a person like Guy get such a bad image of himself as a lover?

Guy had left me his mobile phone number, to contact him 'in case you have a free spot for me', so I rang him for the last time, saying I wanted a piece of jewellery as a present for a friend. When he came round, instead of leading him to my massage room with the soft pink light and seductive music, I took him to my brightly lit lounge room. He opened his display case and placed it on my lap, and it was then that he had the opportunity to see me in the ordinary light of day, without make-up, cheeks pale from present pain and past lack of sleep, hair lank for the same reasons. When I'm in pain, I can manage to look my age. From downcast eyes, I saw his startled reaction.

I looked at him and asked, 'Have you got a girlfriend now, Guy?' When he mumbled 'Yes,' I asked if she was nice. He nodded, looking all the while less comfortable. 'Well, then, Guy, you'll be a happy man, won't you?' I said, as I handed him back his case. 'I don't need anything today, and I will soon be leaving the city.'

I noticed his utter relief as I closed the door behind him. That wasn't too hard after all, I told myself. Closing the door, I noticed a bright little packet on the floor. In his nervous haste to get out of the house, Guy had accidentally dropped his condoms from his trouser pocket. They were flashy, the best anyone could buy, but I knew he wouldn't be back for them. I smiled and wished him well from the bottom of my heart.

Who should phone me the very next day, but Mephistopheles in the shape of a charming Asian woman who had become my friend during our days together as volunteers for the Money and You presentations. Susie and I met for lunch and she told me her new plan. She wanted to start her own massage trade in a house she'd just bought in the Perth business district, and she asked me to be in charge of it!

'You have experience and will make the girls do it right,' she explained. 'You will train them well in massage, and the place will keep to the rules — no drugs, just massage.'

I blushed that she thought so highly of me, but the temptation of a good income while having it relatively easy — no direct involvement in the massage work — was only fleeting. Every bone in my body told me that this would be a backward step for me; I was finally ready to leave my lifestyle, for good. I refused with my thanks, sold Susie my massage table, gave her my stack of towels and wished her well with her plans. She found a suitable manageress, made the money she was after and, in the end, sold the parlour for a good price.

IT WAS BLISS to be in Denmark again, now in my new little home. I delighted in the company of humorous, loving and honest friends. The Chinese vase that had inspired me so many years ago had completely shattered and I now had space to find peace among the shards. Yet I was soon to make another grand mistake, this time in the name of doing the right thing.

Some of my Denmark friends were devotees of Master Da and so I continued my studies and devotional practices as part of a small group. Devotees are constantly reminded to live in continual remembrance of their Master. I had put up a picture of him on a little altar and one on nearly every wall of my house. The pull towards Master Da grew so strong, that a year later, after attending a week's retreat in the picturesque countryside near Melbourne, I wanted to vow my perpetual allegiance to him. This time, I convinced myself, I was vowing myself to the ultimate cause, to a life of complete surrender that would lead to true spiritual realisation — including giving up more than twenty per cent of my income. I needed a Master; no one can do this great task on their own, I was told.

Before I was allowed to make my vow, I was asked to clean up my act regarding sexual matters. *Sexual relations are to be reserved for an emotionally committed relationship* — a major tenet that was to be taken seriously if I chose this path. At the time I was celibate but, as fate would have it, still in contact with a client because he happened to live in Denmark. Jack had lost no time in looking me up after I arrived. News of a fresh arrival travels fast in a little town! To me, Jack was like the salt of the earth: he was so innocent, so good, hard-working, simple and wholesome. When he first came to my door in Perth, he was wearing a fresh checked shirt, his newest baggy pants, his cleanest boots and a felt hat cocked to one side on his balding head, which he politely removed when he spoke to me. He was shy, with a disarming smile and a voice that was soft from cancer of the oesophagus, which was in remission.

Dealing with Jack was a simple and loving affair. He just longed for female company. He had married a young woman many years ago, who had tried to run off with a lot of his money soon afterwards. Even though he loved women and looked at them adoringly, he didn't really understand them and had no clue of what to do with them. I gave him the loving contact he looked for. He was content to be massaged and very happy to lie in my arms. He said he didn't like sexual intercourse, or to have his penis massaged to orgasm very often, because it made him feel tired afterwards. What he wanted was closeness and being touched, to relieve his loneliness.

I tried to explain all this as best I could to the devotees of Master Da who were in charge of my spiritual development. My contact with Jack was the only one that could be classed as sexual. It was complicated by the fact that Jack paid me. Jack also looked after me by lending me his car when mine broke down, and made me generous gifts of the apricots that flourished on the trees in his backyard. We cared for each other and I was committed to making him feel good. Could my relationship with Jack possibly fit their 'emotionally committed' tenet?

Of course not. It may have been a relationship between a loving prostitute and a loving man, but it couldn't possibly meet with their approval. I had to renounce this relationship before being allowed to make my vow to Master Adi Da. This moment of decision was an acid test for me: could I know for *myself* what was right and what was wrong? But hadn't I *felt* right many times before and later discovered I'd made a mistake? Shouldn't I now trust my new Master, or his representatives?

I took the vows. Once again, as in my convent days, I was willing to ignore the hurt I felt inside in favour of a higher purpose. I accepted the judgment of my supposed betters that my motives were impure, because Jack paid me. All this because I wanted to think of myself as a spiritual person. I was paying a high price for a new self-image.

To my lasting regret, I refused to see Jack the way I used to. I tried to explain to his bewildered large brown eyes behind the heavy-rimmed glasses, but the poor man couldn't understand at all and he suffered. He embraced me one last time, his innocent lips trembling against mine, his soft voice echoing in both our chests. I left Jack to his loneliness and his confusion. His cancer returned and he died a few months later in hospital, without my being there for him.

Jack's death was a turning point for me. No one, not the most spiritual master on earth, not the freshest sage from heaven, nor any god at all, had the right, ever, to tell me what is true for me. Dear Jack —

he served a higher purpose in my life by teaching me such a valuable lesson. During that sad time, I began to regain respect for my own inner truth.

I WITHDREW FROM Master Da. Strange to say, that caused me tremendous anguish. I felt that by going it alone again I was possibly giving away my last opportunity to completely surrender to the Divine, that I was losing connection with a special stream of grace. I didn't want to break a vow I had taken in all seriousness, all over again. And I took it to heart when I was told that Master Da felt each defection with terrible sorrow, deeply wounded at the rejection of the gift of himself.

To love Master Da was probably a great blessing. To leave him was an even greater one, because by doing so I was choosing one value above all: to be true to my inner self. The transcendence of fearful ego-self begins by no longer doubting the inner self. Maybe that was the purpose of Master Da in my life: to lead me to choose inner truth above any magnificent promise of liberation. I wasn't sure that I was doing the right thing; all my spiritually involved friends counselled me against my decision. Doubts racked my conscience as I removed all the photographs of Adi Da from my walls but, by some grace, I was not to be derailed again.

My shoulders were killing me, carrying my anguish about leaving Master Da and the guilt of my betrayal of Jack. I could have cried with pain and was desperate to feel better. So when I heard of Tom, an exceptional healer who had come down to Denmark from Perth for a few days, I went to see him.

The moment Tom lightly touched my torso as I lay prone on his treatment table, I felt a soothing sensation. Tears welled up; I hadn't felt the bliss of free-flowing energy in my body for so long. Tom's simple, momentary touch on my neck and on the vertebrae of my back let me know what I'd been missing: this feeling was like love for myself, acceptance of myself.

I had been so aware of my failures; for example, my failure as a devotee to follow even the simplest instructions regarding diet. Every time I made a cup of tea, I felt guilty. Every time I ate butter or eggs, honey, or worse, chocolates, even, God forbid, a cappuccino! My days had been preoccupied with whether I was getting it right, and I hardly ever did.

'So,' Tom said rather loudly, apparently reading my thoughts, 'you've been through a monumental battle. And it's all been kept on the inside!'

Very perceptive, I thought and was reminded of a psychic who had recently said much the same to me: 'You've fought tremendous battles and you've not succumbed.'

'You are a beautiful soul.' Tom dropped the words gently onto the table where I was lying. 'Why don't you show on the outside how you are on the inside?' That made me blink, the implication being that I wasn't much to look at for starters. Tom went on calmly, 'Your soul has a very fast and fine vibration. It's not like most souls, so no one has ever seen you. It's not that they don't want to; it's simply not possible for most people truly to see you, because you're out of their range of vision. All your life you have not been seen.'

I felt like crying a bucketful then, from happiness at being seen at least by Tom. He did not mention a devil.

'You are a very, very gentle soul,' Tom said quietly, as his fingers continued to rest lightly on my body. He went on to explain something about soul. 'Soul and mind are different,' he said. 'They each have a different vibration. The mind patterns are not trained properly in your case. They can be retrained. My job,' he added, 'is to help people like you to know who you are.'

I felt deeply reassured and affirmed by Tom's words. It was good to hear for the first time in months that I wasn't the failure I believed myself to be. Tom wasn't trying to charm me. When I said, 'It's a lonely existence, not being seen,' he chipped in immediately. 'No,' he said firmly, 'not really. That's only an emotional requirement. Once you relinquish the wish for fulfilment through the emotions, you find yourself with God and can be happy all the time. You will never feel alone.'

I'm glad I wrote down his words afterwards, since at the time they sounded like a very important truth, but I couldn't imagine how to 'relinquish the wish for fulfilment through the emotions'. That gift would come later, and then Tom's words would make wondrous sense.

As I lay there, my thoughts returned to Tom's words: *to truly know who you are*. But how do you *do* that?

Tom's gift was to read minds; he heard my thoughts and said, 'It's not about figuring it out. You have a great sensitivity — but also a strong intellect, so your mind gets in the way by wanting to *know* everything. You need to feel from the *inside* how to express your true self.'

Energies in my body seemed to be rearranging themselves under Tom's hands. A great feeling of being loved came over me, reminiscent of other times of grace, sweetly relaxing and healing the pain in my shoulders, neck and back

'Why are you so critical of yourself?' Tom broke in again, touching on a central issue. 'You assess yourself all the time.'

Tom was referring to the severe parental voice inside me that never left me in peace. Apart from the parental voice, there also seemed to be a judge, a sort of Reverend Mother in legal attire, and the all-seeing critical eye of God that I grew up with. I had been keeping the wrong kind of company all right! Had Gaye been referring to my own internal critics when she had admonished me to 'say goodbye to all your evil friends'? I doubt it! But if that had been the case, it would have been so accurate.

Tears of gratitude, relief and joy welled up. I found myself simply accepting myself as I was and it felt like coming out of a prison. So *this* was my starting point: self-acceptance! I was no wiser or more spiritual than this, and didn't need to be. This was reality! I couldn't wait to get on with life. I thanked Tom. What a blessing to have him come into my life when I needed him so desperately.

When I talked to a friend about my decision to retract my recent vows, he sensed my regret at what others called my disloyalty and he replied calmly, 'Carla, you only made those vows to yourself.' Again it came home to me, with the utmost relief, that the only truth I needed to surrender to was the truth I felt in my own heart. All outside references only detracted from that sweet union with the ever-present Divine in the depths of my own being.

Nothing is either good or bad but thinking makes it so, wrote Shakespeare. In my sessions with Gaye, several years ago now, I had had my first experience of this. Evil had turned out to be all-embracing love. Back then I had been too immature to really appreciate this extraordinary gift. Now I was beginning to savour this awesome truth.

YOU ASKED FOR IT, CARLA

IT WAS 1994. I would soon turn fifty-seven, and had just learned the first real lesson of my life: self-acceptance. I pondered with astonishment why it had taken me so long to understand this simple thing. The religion of my childhood, with its constant emphasis on sin, punishment, guilt and humiliation, had hidden the concept in some closet, or buried it beneath the floorboards, somewhere it would be hardest to find. How would the Catholic hierarchy control its subjects without the great power of guilt? If Catholics did not feel the constant need for forgiveness, for approval of 'the Father', would they go to church as often, or at all? Would they go to confession; would they continue to grant special status and respect to those who preach what is right and wrong (mostly what is wrong); and, most importantly, would they continue to give the money that keeps the machine going?

It was easy to blame it on my religion. Some fault lay with me too: I just hadn't been prepared to be honest. I had been too afraid to face the truth. And now that I was beginning to face it, what was the big deal? I can say from personal experience that honesty is the best exorcism there is.

I also saw that there was no real spiritual life without honesty. All that squirming about being good enough for God, for others or for my own inflated self-image — it had nothing to do with spirituality. I felt as if I'd been lifted out of a minefield, which I had mistaken for a path, and placed onto a new and strange way, to which my eyes and legs had not yet grown accustomed.

The past had made a very deep impact and required a lot of undoing. My new-found freedom was only a beginning. Deep-rutted patterns were being reformed, and it would take time and more experiences, not always pleasant ones, to turn God's Callgirl into simply God's Girl.

DENMARK TREATED ME well, even if the only paying work around seemed to be cleaning and a bit of gardening. The government stepped in and had me trained for six months in office skills. I continued to search in vain for real employment for another three years, after which, according to Social Security, I officially became a pensioner. A polite way of telling you that you're now getting too old and you might as well take a back seat.

I used my new computer skills to write about my experiences. Life was pleasurable — meeting friends for shared dinners, for dances, gatherings on the beach and in the coffee shop. I experienced the wonder and bliss of growing into an ordinary human being, a member of a community. And then it became time for a little explicit learning. If I thought I'd pretty well got my emotional self together by now and could start trading on my new self-image to impress my friends, then I could think again. The disaster that happened on my sixtieth birthday was all my own doing.

I wanted to entertain my friends with a performance. I wrote a script and called it my Sister Act. A nun (me) enters the stage on her knees, hauling a cross on her shoulders. Resisting temptation from a horny priest, she gradually transforms herself from a prissy suffering nun into a woman who tells risqué jokes and sings endearing songs. Finally, dancing to the music from *The Stripper*, she sheds pieces of her habit, flinging them into the audience, and ends up in a black lacy bra and tiny matching panties. She then runs to the embrace of the priest she had formerly rejected.

The subtext was that I would impress my friends as a truly liberated woman, free of sexual hang-ups and free of fear. I wanted them to think I was funny, titillating, slinky and still in pretty good shape. If only I had *acknowledged* this hidden agenda to somebody, or at least to myself! Even more hidden was my desire for a little fame and recognition, to 'be somebody' — this was something I definitely didn't want to admit. I was going to wow my friends with my new evolved self. Unfortunately, since it was only a cooked-up self, as is any supposed new, improved self, I was a sitting duck for my inner censor.

The evening progressed in a lovely mellow mood. About thirty of my friends turned up, bringing delicious food to share. There was a quiet hum of excitement in the air, a delicious blend of the pleasure of being together — chatting, laughing, embracing, admiring — and the enjoyment of shared food and drink, all in the beautiful setting built by my friends Mark and Ray high on the banks of Wilson Inlet in Denmark. I was happy to notice how at ease I felt; my performance was going to slay them!

It was only when my friend Claire was helping me into my nun's habit, that panic began to invade me. I swallowed hard, breathing deeply to quieten it down, but I was completely thrown. I remembered to let the fear come (accept it!), and it would die down. When the fear didn't go away in a hurry, my old strategy of trying to control it immediately came to the fore. No way would I allow myself to go on stage panting with fear and ask my friends to please wait until I'd gained my composure! That would not have been such a bad thing — it might have been the very *best* thing — but my hidden agenda got the better of me.

My embarrassment and discomfort were compounded when my nervousness got worse instead of better after my dramatic entrance. I ploughed on, straining my voice the way I had when I had to sing in front of my class in primary school, and getting very hot under my black habit. My friends were an appreciative audience nevertheless; they loved the silliness and my hilarious impromptu dancing.

At some stage, something took over that had nothing to do with my conscious will. I just enjoyed myself; singing, strutting and stripping with abandon, panting from the effort afterwards, supporting myself with one elbow on the mantelpiece while my friends clapped and laughed and wolf-whistled.

The morning after, however, my self-criticism was sharp and awful. I recognised my old enemy of self-sabotage — would the horror-pattern *ever* let go of me? I was a prisoner again and I felt it keenly. That old devil who laughed at me in the shaman's forest must surely have been satisfied. I sensed him glowering at me for thinking that I could ever be free of him. How it hurt!

I talked about it to my friend Jill. A friend can change one's perspective completely and Jill did so in no time at all. 'How about simply accepting that you had a hidden agenda? Just accepting dear old you for having these secret ambitions? We all have them, you know, and for the spiritual ones the ambition is to hide the fact that we have any ambitions!'

Her response took my breath away and immediately brought me peace. What a relief! There was no need to be anything special at all; I just needed to be ever so gentle with myself and accept myself truly, in spite of everything I perceived as faults, right down to the last little bit. I was lucky to have friends who had realised this long ago and now lived a life of simple sanity.

What else was there to do now but be compassionate with myself? I was beginning to feel that maybe I was no better or worse than anyone else in the world; that given the right circumstances, I too could take the path of a criminal, a lying, cheating bastard, murderer or sadist. I felt the seeds of all these possibilities in me and it sobered me. Paradoxically, maybe because it was the simple truth, the thought also gave me peace. I would always be an imperfect human, full of all sorts of illusions — except the illusion that hating myself was going to save me. I did not articulate it, but the truth is, I was taming my devil. I had discovered the one thing that makes it impossible for evil to live long in anybody: true and consistent self-acceptance, which is the work of unconditional love.

WHEN THE STUDENT is ready, the teacher will appear, so they say. In November of 1998 Isaac Shapiro came to town. Isaac — swarthy, sexy, hefty (he loved food!) and wonderfully *simple* — had woken up to who he was as a spiritual being. It was a pleasure to be in his company. He made himself available for questions and his patience was never-ending as he gently guided others to their true self.

I sat in the audience of a hundred or so and felt a pull to go up and speak with Isaac. However, I grew so hot with fear of speaking up in public that for days I couldn't find the courage. Then, finally, I found myself picking my way among the crowd to the front.

I sat next to him, with a microphone in my hand. My heart was galloping at a hundred miles an hour and wouldn't come to rest. Eyes riveted on Isaac, my vision blurred, I was about to speak when Isaac stopped me.

'Tell me what you are feeling,' he said.

'Fear,' I replied.

'Well,' said Isaac, 'that's an idea you have in your mind, a label for what you are feeling. Tell me what are the *sensations* in your body?'

I checked, moving my focus from my mind. The adrenaline that had been pouring through my veins was finding a pleasant plateau all by itself. 'I feel a warm sort of glow,' I said, which produced some laughter in the audience.

'So this is what you have been afraid of,' Isaac said, 'a warm sort of glow!' He chuckled, and looked at me steadily.

I nodded, not thinking all that clearly in that moment, feeling very warm indeed and probably sporting glowing cheeks. I prepared to go back to my seat again, but Isaac stopped me with a request. 'Please would you sing a song?' he asked, smiling mischievously but indicating that it was merely a request, not an expectation.

Immediately, the song I had bellowed out in class as a six year old, mortally afraid that I'd be seen as a wicked child, came to mind. Still under the influence of raw adrenaline, I sang '*Daar bij die molen*', not too melodiously but with a smile. At the end, I received a generous round of applause. 'Stay with yourself,' said Isaac, before I left his side. In the instant he said those words, I lost consciousness. I entered a space like deep sleep, where I had the experience of thinking nothing. Nothing at all — a peaceful and vast no-thingness. It seemed to last for only a fraction of a second as I met Isaac's steady eyes and his words went deep inside, like a present on a silk cushion laid on my heart. *Stay with yourself.* I knew these words contained the secret of happiness. I thanked him haltingly, he nodded in recognition, and I returned to my seat in the audience.

Apart from his words, Isaac had given me something else. In that moment of no-thingness, I had gone home to essential Self. For something so simple, this is hard to describe. From that place I retained a feeling, different from emotion, of myself as pure being. It was a deep understanding, or an understanding of the Deep in which we live. I felt myself, this Carla, grow up. I sat in quiet bliss, gratitude welling up in me for this tremendous gift.

Back home, I remembered more of Isaac's words, spoken to someone else. *Feelings are impersonal.* I realised with amazement that the feelings of shame, worthlessness and dread which I had owned as if they were exclusively mine, and lived by as the basic truth of me, were not even my own feelings! I had inherited them, most probably from my parents, who had learned them from their parents, from society, the church and so on. I had no control over these thoughts as a child, and still had no control over them as an adult.

I stayed with these realisations for a while, going back into the past and experiencing the familiar painful feelings starting to shake loose, then snap back, clinging to my skull for dear life. I had given them fifty-four years of life and they were not ready to die just like that. But Isaac had taught me the ultimate reason for self-acceptance: staying with myself, my true self. Acceptance of even the most difficult feelings and thoughts was a way of being with myself.

It was simple science. Self-rejection was a way of losing myself. Self-acceptance was a way of regaining myself.

ON 23 DECEMBER 1998, barely a month after Isaac's visit, I was knocked off my bicycle by a speeding truck on one of Denmark's narrow roads. The driver didn't stop.

I was hospitalised with a compound fracture of my right arm. The duty surgeon did not seem at all pleased to be assigned this case, so close to Christmas. He had his head in his hands as he sat there, both of us waiting for the operation to begin. He looked up and came over to me, to whisper fiercely in my ear, 'My job is to tidy you up and sew you up. It isn't to make you look pretty. If you want to look pretty, get yourself a plastic surgeon!'

The duty surgeon did a butcher's job of patching up my broken arm. Contrary to what he told me before the operation, he did not insert a metal support for the splintered bones, and his cuts and stitching were very rough. Afterwards, acute bursitis in my elbow prevented me lying down, and I suffered from a severe negative reaction to morphine, not discovered for two whole days. I was going crazy with pain and constant retching. Every time I closed my eyes I saw the letter M dancing in front of them. There were myriads of them and they refused to go away. Finally I asked myself what these Ms meant. The answer came immediately: M was for madness. I was going mad with pain, the wrong medication, an inability to keep down food or drink, and lack of sleep.

To my visitors who came on Christmas Day, I was a pitiful sight. Louis, my chiropractor, took one look at me and knew what I needed. The dear man, he reminded me of something I already knew but had forgotten in the midst of my distress: *Accept what is happening without resistance*. 'Breathe, Carla,' he said. 'Conscious breathing takes you out of your head and into your heart.'

And so, as I breathed in I accepted what was happening, and as I breathed out I continually surrendered to the mystery of why.

I accepted whatever was ahead of me and I sank into peace. 'What is surrender?' I had asked Persephone and her friends. For years I had wondered what true surrender might be. Here was the opportunity of a lifetime to better understand! Once again, it was about self-acceptance, bringing me to new depths of myself. The letter M changed to M for meditation.

Back in my own home, I learned to accept the incredible kindness of many friends who came with food and treats and offers of all kinds of help. I learned another meaning for M — the magic that happens when one surrenders.

It was impossible to receive so much love and stay the same. I mellowed in many ways — another 'M'.

I SPENT LONG periods in utter solitude and silence as my arm mended. I couldn't watch TV because it hurt my eyes; for the same reason, I couldn't read for long. Nor could I write. The strange feeling came over me that I lived in a void, like a shadow. Did I live in this void all the time, utterly alone, with people only thinly present? And was my ordinary activity just to fill this silent void with lots of distractions? I was afraid this might be true.

I played some light, sweet music, dreading the sudden snap back to empty silence at the end. I programmed the recorder to repeat the tape on a loop, thus stalling the end. Was I playing out the whole of my life this way? What was I trying to stall? The idea of annihilation, of disappearing as if I had never existed? I felt the inevitability of death all around me, as if I were existing in a world that had already died.

I didn't want this strange feeling, so I filled up the void with some rich chocolate cake someone had brought me from the coffee shop. I felt bad afterwards, yet also better somehow. I realised I had desensitised myself by over-eating. I no longer felt the inevitable death of my body so keenly. *None of us is going anywhere and none of us will stay here* — the voice from the void echoed through the silence. My neck, arm and hand hurt badly.

If I couldn't sink into the bliss of just being, maybe I should get laid, I thought. It had been years now! But there was no one to go to bed with, only memories surrounding me. I wanted a flesh-and-blood person who could see me, put real arms around me. Then I would have the illusion that I was not alone, after all. *The arms would let go of you*, the voice butted in. *He would go — to the bathroom, or to sleep. He would retreat into the nothingness at night, or into the mists of doingness by day.*

Weird thoughts. I was worried that ideas of suicide might come next. But by some grace, I realised that my musings weren't all negative; they were an invitation to understand something deeper than ordinary life. I called on unseen friends to help me — angels, anyone out there. At an indefinable moment, my feelings changed. I became willing to face death, and in that moment of willingness I entered a new freedom.

Life had brought me to an even deeper appreciation of the profound acceptance of 'what is'. I saw that it was the same as self-acceptance, because there is really nothing else out there. What is apparently out there is always, only, my self. This is not something I can really explain. It will only make sense to those who already know it.

There was now no suffering, just an incredible feeling of being able to enjoy whatever the moment brought, breath to breath, heartbeat to heartbeat, painful moment to painful moment. Success no longer had anything to do with having money, or a career, or being appreciated. Success was to live this moment in gratitude.

TO SPEED UP the healing of my broken arm, my daughter Caroline wanted me to see a powerful South American healer who was visiting Perth. I resisted for a long time, mainly because he charged a phenomenal amount of money which I could hardly afford. Caroline offered to pay for me if I didn't get my money's worth and, in the end, I agreed to a session.

I stood before Victor explaining the reason for my appointment. He ignored my arm and looked into my eyes. He was a stocky, dark man with unmistakable charisma and loads of optimism. Within a few seconds, he told me that for most of my life my spirit had been partly out of my body. He drew a picture, showing the outline of a spirit body hanging out to one side of my own body; it was in terrible fright and wanting to depart, attached only by the umbilical cord. I listened attentively — this made sense to me, in spite of my new-found peacefulness.

I looked around me, noticing with disdain the large cross in the room with lights all over it, the picture of the Virgin Mary — all the trappings of religion, and the Catholic religion at that!

Victor asked three women trainees to come and look at me. They described symptoms that confirmed his opinion, including having piercing eyes that made other people feel uncomfortable. This really made me sit up and listen. I had become aware that people sometimes tried to figure out what they saw in my eyes. They seemed to think I glared at them, and I found myself screwing up my eyes to make them appear softer. When I wanted to avoid other people's gaze, I had developed the disconcerting habit of looking straight past them.

I was asked to stand before the illuminated cross and ask for divine help. I closed my eyes and complied, ready for whatever was about to happen.

Victor then asked me to lie down on a large bench, helped by the three women, and he began a ritual to bring my spirit back into my body. He called out loud to my spirit and asked me to shout, 'I AM HERE!' as he slapped the soles of my feet very hard. I whimpered at the pain in my feet, but shouted as he'd asked, while the women prayed. Suddenly, he called out, 'In the name of God, I command you to go in!' and slapped my feet one last time. A loud, involuntarily cry came out of my mouth — and I felt my spirit enter.

I was helped off the bench and Victor watched me as I walked up and down. I felt renewed, simple, child-like. Not extraordinary, but completely ordinary. I understood, perhaps for the first time, what it was like just to be a human being, fully 'here'. It was a soft and simple joy. I felt a gentle confidence and natural grace as I walked, and gratitude towards Victor, the man who had brought my spirit back into my body.

He had succeeded in remedying something I'd had no idea of. I had been frightened out of my body at the age of six and had got used to it. It was remarkable to feel at peace with my whole self again. I breathed more easily and felt, at a profound level, that I had joined the human race. It was a special moment.

No mention was ever made of my arm, but it healed remarkably well after a second operation from one of the best surgeons in town.

RADICAL INNOCENCE

IT WAS AUGUST 1999 and I sat in my Dutch friend's backyard, having arrived at her house in Breda, Holland, via France, Belgium and London. I explained to her that I was broke, but had my return ticket.

I had responded to a strong inspiration to do a certification training course in what is called The Work with a woman called Byron Katie, and had put down a deposit without having the means to pay the rest. I trusted that things would come together for me somehow. I had the prospect of a compensation pay-out coming to me as a result of my road accident, so wasn't being entirely foolish. The trouble was that no bank or lending institution, nor one friend in Denmark, had been able to lend me a single cent against this pay-out which did not have a firm figure or date. Nevertheless, I organised as much as possible by using up all my available credit. At the very last minute, two dear friends in Perth lent me the airfare I needed.

'Do you think I'm crazy?' I asked my friend. Julia, a feisty woman of eighty, burst into laughter. No, she didn't think I was stupid; instead, she admired my intrepidness and offered on the spot to contribute two thousand guilders, enough to cover my fortnight's accommodation at the course with a bit over. I was also extremely welcome to be her guest and she wanted to spoil me at her expense. What a relief! Julia was a wealthy woman with a big heart and we got on very well indeed, enjoying each other's company.

I breathed in the balmy summer air in her backyard, so refined compared to the roughly scented air of Australia. I was back in my own country again, for the first time in forty-nine years. Only twenty minutes away by train was the town of my birth, Tilburg. I felt as if I was in a story book, one with a lot of bright, friendly pictures.

The course was due to start soon and so I made my way to Heeze, to Kappellerput, an old Jesuit monastery converted into a convention centre with room for about a hundred guests. When I originally booked, they emailed back that there was no room left in the course. I responded that I was coming anyway, and two days later heard that the course had proved so popular that Katie had decided to take on as many as the centre could accommodate.

The Work of Byron Katie began a few years after Katie's own awakening. Katie, a nicely rounded woman in her fifties, has known what it is to feel unloved and unworthy, what it is to hate and be filled with anger, grief, sadness and despair, how it feels to not function well enough to look after oneself. Simply by grace, she woke up one morning to realise it was stories that had held her bound. She has never believed a single story since.

Jesus said, 'Knowing the truth will set you free.' How often have we heard this and equated truth with one belief or another? Real truth doesn't have to be believed in because it sits deep in the heart.

The first part of The Work involves writing. 'My father ruined my life,' I began. I loved my father, and had forgiven him, but it was true that he had ruined my life; this was a 'fact' I had come to terms with. In answer to the question from my facilitator, 'Is it true that your father ruined your life?', I maintained that it was obvious, an irreversible fact. Wasn't my whole life since proof of the fact? 'I can look at how I deal with this fact, but I can't deny it,' I maintained.

'Who would you be without the thought that your father ruined your life?'

The question stopped me in my tracks. My mind went blank and I suddenly felt very tired; I wanted to opt out, faint, do anything rather than face the thought that I could live without this idea. It was a big effort to focus my mind again, to investigate and answer the question.

For four whole days I couldn't see that this was my *interpretation* of what had happened to me and how my life had evolved. As a result of this story, I had become used to the belief that I was a victim of abuse. A recovered or recovering victim, thank you very much, but still a victim. Moreover, if I couldn't blame my father, who was there to blame instead? *I* certainly wasn't going to take the blame for ruining my life!

On the fifth day, light dawned gently. It wasn't a matter of apportioning blame. What if there was *no one* to blame? What if my father and I had just done the best we could in our lives, given the level of maturity we had? What was I gaining from insisting that my father had ruined my life? Finally I was ready to give up my status as victim, so prized by part of me. The desire to blame others and avoid responsibility must be a deep psychic undertow that pulls us away from a larger truth.

I sought out the person who had started the process with me, four days ago. In answer to her question of who I would be without this thought, I finally replied, 'I'd just feel plain happy. I'd feel normal, just me, with a whole life, just like everybody else.'

My father instilled in me the belief that I was bad. The most profound thing about The Work is what is called the turn-around. When I turned this around, I found that I had called *myself* bad many more times than my father ever did. However innocently, I had been perpetuating a story. I turned *everything* around and then I had the truth that set me free. 'My life was ruined' became 'My life has been *blessed*!'

And that was a truth so deeply felt that I wept with joy.

A YOUNG MAN called Brett went up to do a piece with Katie because he felt ashamed of his father's profession: he ran a brothel. This stirred up similar feelings of shame in me.

Katie had no problem with prostitutes and their work. She said that these women provided a much-needed service, and the prostitutes of Amsterdam did it with style. Their bedrooms, even the doorways where they displayed themselves, were every bit as sacred as churches. She challenged us to believe otherwise; if we did, we were to investigate our beliefs.

Katie's naive idealism made me feel angry. Was she really unaware of the dirty, sleazy side of the game? The drugs, degradation, violence, subterfuge, pretence and lust for money? How could she blithely describe prostitutes as 'women providing a necessary service' as if they were check-out chicks?

In spite of all I heard Katie say, in spite of all my previous experiences, there still lurked at my core a belief that I was guilty. Had I not ignored so many clues to stop? Had I not gone against every insight and continued until I just couldn't go on any more? I thought that if Katie knew how *I* had been a whore, she'd soon drop her Mary Poppins attitude.

I struggled with this for a while before confiding in one of the staff. 'I feel shame and I don't have the courage to face it with Katie.'

'Good,' she said, 'by telling me, you've made a start.' And I felt she would support me when I requested to work with Katie.

In a hushed voice I barely recognised as my own, I asked if I could come up. Once seated beside Katie, looking into those clear blue eyes, I explained why I was worse than a normal prostitute and unforgiven by God or nature. I told her that I had become addicted to the lifestyle and that I had prostituted myself just for money, going against what I really wanted to do. I had betrayed myself.

'Did you do the best you could?' Her simple question reverberated around the room via her microphone.

My answer was just as simple, and nothing but the plain truth. 'Yes, I did.'

'So what's the problem?'

A delicious feeling of relief washed over me. What a to-do about nothing! What amazing knots we get ourselves into, all unnecessarily. Still, there was something I wanted to mention in particular, it had weighed so heavily on me.

'I alienated men by what I did, Katie. I feel that the men who came to me weren't capable of a normal relationship, and I made it worse for them by reinforcing their alienation. They often had guilty feelings and I reinforced their guilt ...' My words trailed off as I studied Katie's face.

'If those men were really as isolated as you think they were, it seems to me that you offered them something they needed and couldn't get anywhere else. And who are you to judge these men, and who are you to say what path they should be on?' Then with her typical directness, she almost shouted, 'How do you know that what you did was *right*? Because you did it. We do what we do, until we don't.'

My self-imposed guilt trip, based on a lifetime of learned shame, was demolished in ten minutes flat. I managed a hoarsely whispered thanks and I went back to sit among the others, enveloped in a sense of peace I had never experienced before. I felt cleansed — not in the Christian sense, as when a sin has been forgiven, but cleansed of illusions and lies. I knew without a shadow of a doubt that I was innocent and always had been, even when I thought I was betraying my inner truth. I was just like everyone else: everyone does the best they can, based on present wisdom or ignorance, otherwise they would be doing it differently. I could grant this understanding to others now that I had learned it myself, especially to my parents.

It surely is the ultimate gift of grace to return to original innocence and know yourself to be nothing but good, uncontaminated in your heart, no matter what your mental and emotional patterns might be. Now I had some brilliant tools for finding the truth in moments of self-criticism, as well as criticism of others.

What I had thought of as my real self when I was a child, a nun and a prostitute was the bad, guilty part of me. Because I had given my 'bad self' so much credence, it grew out of all proportions, and even came to have a life of its own — a sub-personality, a sort of devil. Every self-condemning thought gave this bad-self devil in me the energy it needed to stay alive. How extraordinary to discover myself to be radically innocent, a still and timeless being of grace.

.

MY KIND FRIEND Julia and I went cycling together in the glorious countryside, fragrant with herbs and wildflowers. She showed me the rough sandy beaches, and we sat by canals, rivers, dykes and lakes, and visited quaint villages and farms. In childhood, my circumference had been so limited; I had never even seen the sea. I felt privileged to be so royally treated by Julia. She took me to one of the few spots in Holland where you couldn't hear the traffic: the undulating expanse of natural grasslands called the Veluwe. Quietly we lay in the grass, so thankful for the beauty around us.

Then came the time for me to go exploring on my own. I boarded a train and went to Tilburg. I didn't expect to recognise much of the place after forty-nine years, but I was in for a surprise.

Along the route from the railway station — those familiar streets I had so often walked with my brothers and sisters — I crossed the large square where our annual *Kermis* or fair used to be held, and entered the cathedral where my parents were married. Suddenly the church bells rang out, the same bells my parents had heard as they walked down that aisle. I was deeply moved as I remembered their difficult lives together started here, in this very church, with so much love and courage.

I walked on to the house that had been my home. It had a new facade, not an improvement on the old one. I knocked on the door and the owner answered. I explained as best I could that this was my old home from long ago, that I had come all the way from Australia, and he let me sit in his lounge room while he busied himself in the kitchen. My seat was next to the window where I had lain as a child, sick with scarlet fever. I looked out over the little backyard: it seemed impossibly tiny, yet it was the same brick-walled space that had held our swing and monkeybar. There were the three doors: to the kitchen, the coal shed and the toilet.

I asked if I could walk around, and the owner said yes, leaving me to wander in silence.

The coal shed had been incorporated into the house as a neat laundry and toilet. The original thunderbox was a doorless and floorless space; no one had bothered to beautify it in any way. Where there was once a laneway at the back and a vegetable garden with a lilac tree and summerhouse, the owner had opted for a covered garage and a large games room. It is a great luxury to have undercover parking and any extra space in Holland.

I went back inside. In the nicely painted kitchen, I noticed the original wooden slats on the walls. The door leading to the cellar was now just a cupboard under the stairs. People no longer needed damp cellars since the invention of the refrigerator. Just opposite the front door was the narrow carpeted staircase leading to the bedrooms. I did not ask to go upstairs.

Memories crowded in, but I felt nothing but joy — joy for having been born, for having lived here, for all my experiences. The past no longer had a bitter hold on me. Instead I had only memories, thoughts in the moment, stories — and this was the miracle of The Work I had done with Byron Katie a week before.

WHERE NEXT BUT across the channel to England? In England was Alice, my ancient love, whose image had never left me. We had maintained sporadic contact over the years; now I was to take up her offer of staying with her 'should you ever come to the UK'. Well, I was coming, ready or not!

In my nervousness to catch the right train I missed it and had to wait for several hours to catch the next one. I phoned Alice: it was all right, she'd be there to meet me at the train station. 'Don't worry about going to Trafalgar Square as we'd arranged,' she said. 'That'll make it too late.' I breathed a sigh of relief. Having missed a train, I could do without the possibility of missing a bus as well.

The train rumbled straight across England's broad girth from London to Manchester. I alighted. No Alice. I walked towards the exit, then I saw her: a matronly figure running up the ramp to meet me.

'I've been so afraid I'd made you wait!' Alice was in a bustling mood. I looked at her, expecting a return gaze that would tell me she recognised me as the person who once was extremely fond of her, who had now come to her senses, but still had a very special regard for her. Alice extended her hand, then embraced me without our faces ever touching. My face reached out for hers, to plant a kiss on her cheek, but her firm grip and her quick talking prevented me.

Alice was full of questions about my trip. She smiled widely and I noticed a flush in her cheeks. Alice was nervous! I answered as well as I could, taking in her presence, as she was doing mine.

Her mouth was still red, all without lipstick, and her smile still wide and perfect. Her green eyes were still oh, so steady as they took you in. She had grown older and wiser, meaning cynical of life in general, of politicians and young women in particular. Alice was very pleased to be living in England rather than in any part of Ireland, thank you very much. Her wild side longed for the west coast of Ireland, but her practical side enjoyed what her lifestyle in England had to offer.

Her pleasant little home had an upstairs, and Alice showed me to her tiny sewing room where a narrow iron camp bed awaited me. 'The visitor's room,' she explained, 'is at present taken up by Sister Bridget.'

'What, Sister Bridget, the Irish historian I used to know at Stella Maris?'

It was one and the same. Now in her eighties, she often came to visit Alice, even though Alice had left the order. Sister Bridget was still loyal to the FCJs and I would not hear one word of complaint from her, nor any news that might be taken for gossip.

How was it that a person as colourfully critical of just about anything in the world as Alice was could continue to go to church every day? The Alice I saw was essentially still a nun, cardigan and all. She cared nothing about her looks and looked positively frumpy.

Alice resisted reading any part of my book, including the chapter about herself. Maybe she will never read it. I realised that not much of the past would be discussed between us. Nor would we ask each other personal questions. The only thing of importance to her, it seemed, was to treat me well as her guest. She shared her knowledge of the history of the area and drove me around until I felt confident enough to take the buses. It was only when she learned that the nuns at Broadstairs would not allow me to visit them that her rebelliousness came to the fore. Alice took me to meet an old FCJ friend who was living in stately retirement in a four-storeyed mansion not far away.

Alice knew how to reach Sister Mary's room on the top floor without anyone seeing us. I was introduced to Sister Mary — whose name I have changed here because she wished to remain anonymous — an old, wispy nun whose hair was nevertheless still a natural brown and whose pleasure it was to read books endlessly, judging from all the volumes lying around. She was unsteady on her feet so remained seated during our visit.

In spite of her age, Sister Mary had all of her wits about her. She sized me up suspiciously and I sensed an inner battle going on while she decided whether she could trust me. Finally, she decided to open up and tell me her story. She was hesitant at first, not knowing exactly how this information would be used, but in that precious half an hour Sister Mary gave me a bigger picture of the Mother General who had had such a large influence on my life, and the lives of many others.

Sister Mary had known her for a great many years. 'She was quite a character long before she was made a General,' she said with feeling. 'Margaret Winchester was the superior of a Canadian convent before she came to Broadstairs, and she was known for the bizarre treatment of her nuns. For instance, she made them all sleep on the floor instead of in beds.'

That sounded exactly like the person I had known. I tried to imagine the heroism of the nuns under her command; not so much for sleeping on the floor, as for being able to endure the continual stream of surprises she would have cooked up for them to test their obedience and humility. I said, 'Margaret Winchester seemed not quite sane to me.'

Sister Mary did not like this critical assessment of the General and proceeded to explain the underlying cause for the outrageous behaviour for which Margaret Winchester was remembered. 'During the war,' explained Sister Mary, 'as a superior residing at Broadstairs she was extremely concerned about the welfare of all the people in the various buildings there. She became hysterically nervous at every air attack, and when an incendiary bomb fell on the village at Broadstairs she thought it had fallen on the novitiate. The shock affected her mentally.'

Aha, I thought, by the time I met her, the General had been 'mentally affected' for at least sixteen years! Why hadn't this stopped her from being elected as a Superior General three years after the war, in 1948?

'She was an impressive figure,' said Sister Mary, as if guessing my thoughts. I agreed. But kept it to myself that Hitler, too, had been called 'impressive'.

Sister Mary moved on to what had inspired her, as a much younger nun, to take action against her own Mother General. 'During Madame Winchester's rule, she encouraged the already existing custom of nuns reporting on each other, until it grew like a killer vine in the order. Even nuns merely suspected of breaking a rule were reported. The General seemed to have an obsession with strict discipline and knowing exactly who was behaving in a way not entirely approved of. The nasty custom grew to political proportions: those who toed the line were rewarded with positions of power; those who did not were humiliated and demoted.'

I noted all this down as fast as I could — something Sister Mary did not like, I noticed, but the details were too important to trust to memory. Sister Mary wanted me to understand that she only acted after the General had really gone too far.

'She abruptly ordered Sister Helen, who was the principal of a large secondary school in England, to close down her school. The order came after all the staff had been hired and all the students enrolled for the coming school year. Sister Helen was a loyal nun, but also blessed with a good dose of common sense. She decided that enough was enough, and it was time to take this matter to a higher authority, namely the Bishop of London. This sort of thing had never been done before, and it was a political manoeuvre definitely not envisaged by the General, who then had no option but to let her keep her school.'

Sister Mary looked at Alice, who was sitting to one side with hands folded in her lap. Alice nodded: yes, this was how she remembered it also, and yes, Sister Mary, do go on.

'However,' Sister Mary continued, 'by taking the extraordinary step of going over her superior's head, Sister Helen had sparked off a war of intrigue inside the order. There were those who became more vocal about having Madame Winchester removed, most of them from her previous communities in Canada. [And, of course, Sister Mary, who managed to put aside her shyness and scruples to speak up.] Margaret Winchester played her cards by removing her nearest rivals to distant outposts, but it was no good. Nothing but her resignation would save the order from further misuse of power, and this is exactly what happened, in 1967.'

I scribbled away, my mind reeling at this riveting stuff that we in Australia had been blissfully unaware of. It seemed I had not been singled out for abominable treatment by the General, and I had been far from alone in my judgments about convent life in the early 1960s. To Sister Mary, however, the 1960s were the years of the great decline of the order and its demise as a significant force in Catholic society. The changes sparked a veritable exodus, but Sister Mary was anxious to impress upon me that this had not been her wish, that nothing she did had been intended to undermine the order. Most religious orders had to cope with similar defections.

What Sister Mary told me next made me smile wryly. Now that it was 1999, three decades on from the events she was describing, the evidence of all this turmoil — letters, diaries and documents which had been stored in archives at the archbishop's palace — should be available for public perusal. But they weren't. The FCJ nuns, afraid for the order's reputation and the people implicated, had persuaded the archbishop to keep them secret for another twenty years, by which time the key players would surely be dead.

Well, I thought, this action speaks for itself. I had no need, or desire, to look at any of those documents. I expect that the order will be finished before the twenty years are up. Once there were thousands of FCJs. Now there are less than two hundred, and most of them are elderly.

I thanked Sister Mary for confiding in me, but I could see that she wasn't quite sure that she had been wise.

I TOOK A bus to Sedgley Park. When I told Alice I was going, she reacted as though I was merely visiting a museum. 'I think Sedgley Park is a police academy now,' she said. It was, in the care of a person who appreciates the history of the place and is taking great care to preserve most of the buildings and the grounds as they originally appeared.

I rang ahead and an officer was assigned to show me around. He could not have guessed what I felt as I walked those corridors once more and was shown into the old music and history rooms, various lecture rooms, common rooms, the gymnasium and the chapel. We even went up the old oak staircase, still winding gracefully to the second floor, where the rooms had been converted into offices. I glimpsed the narrow wooden staircase that used to lead to our attic dormitories; now the attic was a storage area out of bounds. Our old refectory had been transformed into a private area for the officers.

Once my guide felt sure I had regained my awareness of the lie of the land, he let me wander by myself. I felt like a ghost returning;

neither nun nor student. The whole place looked like a giant, empty stage set for the drama that had played itself out when I was there. I walked through the corridors to that spot where the drains were blocked during the flood and I'd taken off my bonnet to go underwater. I grinned with pleasure as I saw in my mind the horrified faces of my lecturers.

The greatest gem in that place was still the chapel with its marble and wood and superb acoustics. I climbed the winding set of stairs to the loft, the oak creaking under my feet. I found the old organ still there, her worn-out bellows testimony to the sweet music conjured out of her over the years. I touched her reverently, a corpse without any breath left in her, but precious all the same. In that chapel loft, I felt ecstatic with gratitude. What a privilege to return to where I had once felt so broken, and now to feel so free! Outside in the gracefully sloping grounds once more, I kissed the leaves of the rhododendrons and thanked them for the part they too had played in my drama.

I sat down on a familiar wooden bench and gazed at the front of the complex; its religious architectural imprints were still visible in the shape of crosses on the walls. I recognised the windows of the library, tall trees still nearby. Thirty-four years didn't seem such a long time; back then, who could have guessed that the administration would be changed so soon? The bricks and mortar of Sedgley Park were still intact, but not a single nun was left.

Before I left, I had lunch in the mess and for the first time understood what it might have been like to be a lay student there, enjoying a meal with friends, talking to those close by, not obliged to be silent like we nuns were. I left Sedgley Park with a full heart, glad that so much had been preserved among all the things that had changed.

Back at Alice's home, I tried to tell her what I'd experienced, but quickly saw that Sedgley represented a past she no longer had any interest in. Instead, I relaxed into the strange and delicious feeling of being close at last to the object of my once-vehement obsession, and focused on appreciating her for who she really was: a woman full of strengths and apprehensions, like all of us, but with a charm that will always be uniquely hers. Her eyes are darker now, but still lively, and her smile as wide and generous as ever when she forgets the cynicism she feels towards the world.

Alice and I never did manage to speak frankly about the past. For years I felt keenly the sorrow of inflicting a wrongness upon her and myself, but now I am at peace. Although I don't know whether Alice agrees, I believe that neither of us were 'wronged', that we both chose our roles in that particular play.

WITH SOME FINANCIAL help from Alice, I flew to Dublin and took a bus west to Limerick to see my old friend, Sister Antoinette. Surprisingly, the taxi driver did not know the address, so I had a chance to wander around, asking for directions. Once upon a time, there would not have been a soul who didn't know where Laurel Hill Convent was.

When I knocked at the door, I received a right royal welcome. The convent's superior, Sister Catherine, and a bevy of ancient nuns, all nearing or topping eighty, came crowding around. They were full of gentle curiosity and pleasure at this interruption to their daily routine, and full of blessings for the visitor who had come from so far away to see their beloved Antoinette.

I was shown to Sister Antoinette's small room. She was ninety now and frail, but her memory was excellent. Her sweet smile was the same, lighting up her eyes behind the glasses, and we chatted and laughed until she was tired out. She couldn't believe that I had come all this way to see her. I apologised for being out of contact for so long, and let her know again and again during my three-day stay how much she had meant to me.

Each day I spent as much time as I could with her, leaving her to rest when she needed to. Antoinette rocked gently in her chair as we talked. She showed me photos of her community celebrating her fifty years of convent life, then sixty, and we reminisced about how it used to be, back in Benalla, with her reminding me of things I had forgotten. But Antoinette had grown tired after sixty-five years as a nun and ninety as a human being; she could no longer read, write letters or watch television. At times we just sat together, our eyes meeting in silence, and I felt glad to the depths of my soul for this meeting.

Back in Australia, I received a reply to the card I sent her for Christmas: Sister Antoinette had died peacefully not long after our reunion. God bless her sweet, kind soul.

GOD'S GIRL

BACK HOME IN my cosy unit in Denmark, I made time to be quiet and consider what I had learned on my travels. I felt I had come 'home' in more ways than one. I was happy, finally, to be with myself. It is a satisfying thing, to go to hell and back and end up at home laughing because you carried *home* with you all the way and didn't know it!

Now that I knew I truly loved my parents, I understood for the first time that they had truly loved me. It must have been hard for them, especially my mother, that I lived so far away and shared so little of my life with them, but she had accepted me the way I was and hadn't pushed me or interfered by complaining or giving me advice. What is that but unconditional love? And my father — how he had loved! Thinking himself inadequate — like so many men who were humiliated as children by their parents — he compensated by being strong. It has taken me all these years to feel the tenderness with which he made our toys for us, the pleasure he took in watching us play with them, and his anxiety to be the best man he could be. The torture of his guilt only grew because of his silence. He paid so very dearly for this.

In the grounds near Grange Hill, a monument with a plaque was erected to the memory of my father, the gardener of Genazzano. It was unveiled by the chairman of the college board on 22 August

1998. My father deserved this late recognition of his creative and passionate dedication to the beautification of the convent grounds and the many years of service he gave to the nuns at Genazzano. I wasn't there for the dedication ceremony, but attending family members were deeply moved.

The FCJ society, once so prominent in several countries, is in a steep decline. Most of the remaining nuns pray for a miraculous survival of the order. They live in a world of their own, and God bless them. The few relatively younger nuns have spread themselves all over the world in the hope of recruiting new members from countries like Indonesia, the Philippines and Romania. There are still some astute girls who are willing to combine their love of God with the opportunity for an education by entering the convent.

Both Sister Anna and Sister Benedict quit the order a few years after me. Anna married and had a son before she disappeared from my life. I met up with Benedict after her departure; she was suffering deep grief about having left. Here was someone who was truly a nun at heart, but whose convent had fallen short of being a genuine home. She died of cancer many years ago.

Vaucluse, where I endured my secondary education even as I enjoyed the congenial buildings and grounds, has been closed down for lack of pupils. There are no FCJ nuns teaching at Benalla and the small community has left the convent to live in a nearby house. In Australia it is rare to find any nuns still living in a convent community; most live alone in flats, some in houses. The hospice for the elderly at Genazzano will soon close because of the lack of trained FCJ nurses and declining numbers.

Sister Kevin is still one of the family's old favourites. I recently enjoyed a long friendly telephone conversation with the feisty ninety year old who now suffers from lung pains. She told me some of the history of Genazzano: how the pioneer nuns had struggled, and how welcome my sister Liesbet and I were when we came to help with the laundry and the ironing to lighten her tremendous workload. To Liesbet she confided once that, 'If we had listened to Carla, and had been kinder towards her and more understanding, then I think she would still be with us.' I thank Sister Kevin for her kind words, but I believe that everything happened the way it was supposed to.

When I was in Melbourne recently for Liesbet's sixtieth birthday, my youngest sister Teresa and I decided to go and have a look at Genazzano convent — late at night, so we wouldn't bump into any nuns, students or caretakers. All the gates were locked, but we scaled the walls where we knew they weren't so high and sauntered around in the moonlight, reminiscing about the past and identifying where things used to be in our time. It was a strange lifetime ago now.

When I left the order, my whip was the only thing nobody asked me to return, so I still have that inelegant memento of a severe and judgmental life — a very strong, cotton-twined and plaited whip, discoloured from years of vigorous use. I found out from Anna that she only ever used hers desultorily, unimpressed by the macabre process. I doubled up with laughter to see her re-enactment of her half-hearted pretence at beating herself.

It never occurred to me in the convent, but I am sure that Jesus had a sense of humour. Wouldn't a true spiritual teacher want to help those who had lost their sense of humour to regain it? I finally came across a print of Jesus laughing heartily. He was holding a cup of wine in a toast. *For Christ's Sake*, read the caption. For Christ's sake remember that human enjoyment of life is at one with spirituality! I treasured that picture until it fell to pieces from being put up on so many different walls in rented houses.

NOW THAT I am wiser, it is easy to look back and see why many of the therapies I tried didn't work for me. I was at an impossible starting-point as long as I thought of myself as fatally flawed, in dire need of fixing. All therapy could do was try to lay down some more positive beliefs on top of that mess. How can the mind heal the mind when the mind is the problem in the first place? With every attempt to fix my mind, I was also telling it that it was wrong and that I was rejecting it!

Self-acceptance, on the other hand, warts and all, is the action of the true self. People ask me how they can be more present; because they have heard of the power of being in the present; well, I always say that whenever I accept myself, there is more of my true self present. The radical understanding that made all the difference to me was that at core I am an eternal being, never tarnished, never broken, never lost. How can a devil continue to live in a person who no longer doubts her own goodness?

I have spent a fortune in my desperate attempts to get rid of a self that I didn't believe good enough. If I'd been fearlessly, relentlessly honest from the very start, I would have discovered my true self, the one that is at peace naturally. But how could I be honest when I believed my core to be rotten? Who can say what I should and shouldn't have done? We can only do what we are ready for; one little step at a time until our legs get stronger. In the words of Byron Katie: 'We do what we do until we don't.'

The one thing the ego-devils do not like is disclosure: simple, honest communication about what is going on. Telling your misgivings to a friend, or just to yourself, can remove the mystique, the danger. That is what I tend to do these days, and I turn my stories around ceaselessly.

I have been celibate for a long time, redressing the balance, I guess. It has been my challenge, even if I didn't recognise it until recently, to be thoroughly happy as a single woman. To find my worth without a man; to find my beloved in my self and everything around me. However, as a relationship could be fun and a rich ground for *living* love, I feel myself opening to the possibility of a special intimacy. It's a bit of a wild statement since I can't be sure if anything works in the sexual department any more! I am a blooming, fit and healthy woman, still appearing at parties showing off my stunning legs and weird outfits, but now entering the wise old crone stage of my life. My most real and intimate relationship is with myself. Intimacy with myself is precious and sweet, and it comes from being totally honest with myself, compassionate and tender. A lover would now taste my contentment, not my lust.

I enjoy being with people, animals and especially children. I take great delight in my two grandchildren, Victoria's son and daughter. Victoria has become a strongly protective mother, imposing the strict boundaries she never had herself. Her practical nature makes her turn up her eyes to heaven sometimes when she encounters me. Her life is a private thing and, like my mother did, I now let her learn her lessons her own way. Whenever I do come in with a suggestion, I get reminded that I am interfering and judging. She is a great teacher.

My other daughter, Caroline, is a musician. She has deep spiritual understanding and our communications are frank and sweet. Having a very tender heart, she says she never wants to have children because they take so much loving and caring and can get hurt so easily and, it seems to her, so inevitably. Victoria's children adore her.

James, my ex-husband, never remarried and lives happily in his house near Fremantle in Western Australia. He is still a generous, kind, typically Taurean man, with such strong ideas of how relationships should work that he believes no woman would ever enter one with him, and he may be right. His favourite book is *The Tao of Pooh*; he has a great love for children and is one of my friends.

When Hal got married, I helped my family members get ready for the wedding. With all my heart I wanted him to be happy and understood about not being invited. Our friendship is a given, although we hardly ever talk.

My friend George is a Denmark identity. For the last few years he has suffered from very bad health and a lot of pain. He has complained endlessly whilst staying patiently alive, to my amazement. Sometime in the past he thanked me for the chance to be his own boss after we left the valley. He is now more interested in helping others, offering to do practical jobs for the financially challenged. It was he who put up the fencing for my chookyard, banging six-inch nails into two-by-fours with the back of an axe.

Occasionally I have contact with some of my former clients. One came to spend three days with me and had the best holiday of his life, he said, because he was so peaceful in my little house. He shared my bed and behaved himself perfectly, although he admitted to taking a sleeping pill to make sure. It felt good to receive his friendship without expectations. Ex-clients phone me now and again, some send a card on Valentine's Day, and recently, on a shopping trip to Perth, one stopped me to ask if I was still available. I was pleased to be remembered and explained that I am now a grandmother, which didn't even make him blink. Not so long ago I received an offer from a would-be lover, to be well taken care of if I'd 'go with him', as he put it. He was youngish and very lonely, but I couldn't summon a scrap of interest in making him feel better. I have nothing left of my previous high illusions.

I agree with Deepak Chopra that 'only intimacy with the Self will bring about true healing'. I have compassion for myself now, which means that I am free to feel whatever comes up to be felt, to learn greater self-acceptance and be ever freer.

Isaac Shapiro's words, 'Be with yourself', take on a new meaning daily. As I told him when I met him again, 'being with myself' is the source of my dignity, my peace, my sense of humour about myself and all of life. Other people who have not doubted themselves might take this for granted, but for me it was a tremendous gift.

I COULD HAVE saved myself a lot of pain if I'd known before I started on my adult life journey what would work and what wouldn't. I might not have felt the need to become a nun, only to leave after my twenties were gone. I might not have become a prostitute and experienced the bitterness of loveless sex and the self-betrayal in subterfuge. I might have found my way home straightaway and not played the game of emotional snakes and ladders. But who can live beyond their evolution? And what would have happened to this story?

Life gave me exactly what I needed, all of the time. I am so lucky to have heard the call to wake up to my true self. What a *blessed* life! My misunderstandings were just that: I fell for a lie. And I thought I was dealing with the devil! Oh well, don't we all make mistakes?

When I started off on my fantasy of the Chinese nun, I was following the call of my soul. When I listened to that urgent message from my inner spirit to go south (and find Denmark) and was so careful to move only when it felt right, I was following that call. What else is that but doing God's will? I always followed the call of God *as best I could*. Fear prevented me from doing it better, until it didn't. Now I am simply God's girl. For ever.

POSTSCRIPT TO MY FATHER

I so adored you as a child,
And you so ignored me,
Then abused me,
And yet made for me a host of marvellous toys
And taught me how to fly kites,
How things grow,
And how beautiful is a spider web in the dewy morning sunlight.
You hit me hard when I irritated you;
I was such an impractical child,
And very, very wilful.
To hide your ugly side, your wickedness,
You throttled me into silence
Preferring a terrified, confused, bewildered child
To one who might talk about your own terrible actions.
Cancer took away your strength
And much of your arrogance.
You even apologised,
Though not to me directly,
In those days when life ebbed away so fast.
And then you died.
They came to take away your body;
Hands limp beside you.

If I had insulted you,
Those hands could no longer hit me or anyone.
Mouth gaping to the sky, pathetic,
No longer able to say,
'Sorry, Carla.'
Instead, it had said 'I love you',
With heart overflowing into burning eyes.
And now you are with God,
A God who does not judge;
Now you understand.
Now I understand.
You did the best you could,
And you loved.
You loved,
You abused,
You hated,
You hit,
You were engulfed by guilt.
You never outgrew your childhood griefs,
You worked hard,
You judged, defended, and finally became sick.
You are dead now,
And it is all right.
All right that you loved the best way you knew how,
And that it fell short of my expectations.
It's all right.
You are my special angel now.
I thank you, Beloved Dad.

ACKNOWLEDGEMENTS

FIRST OF ALL, I want to acknowledge the mysterious grace that has spurred this book along until it was finally completed. Over the years, this gracious urge has persevered whenever I thought it was too hard or when I tried to persuade myself that there was no need to continue.

In 1992, an anonymous benefactor arranged for me to have a laptop computer. I was not only very touched by this gesture, but in accepting it I also took on the challenge of one day finishing the book. This was the first of a long list of miraculous encouragements which were all necessary as my life continued through many inner changes and different motivations for writing.

I want to thank my friend, erstwhile counsellor and women's group leader, Persephone Arbour, for writing the foreword to this book and for inspiring me simply by being who she is.

My friend Yosi Collins sent me her old computer when I couldn't afford to keep paying for repairs to the laptop. My lack of computer knowledge has meant that I have often been dependent on assistance, but somehow this has always been provided, often completely free of charge. I count Murray Fairbanks and Bill and Rose McMullen among my most generous computer angels. Lynn Tulipan, a distant friend I hadn't spoken to for years, came to visit from Karratha one week and used her skills to type many pages of longhand onto my computer, then disappeared as suddenly as she had come. Thank you, Lynn.

Even the government stepped in inadvertently by providing a computer training course, ostensibly to retrain me for the workforce, but as all my applications for jobs were faithfully knocked back there was nothing for it but to put my new skills to use by continuing to write.

I thank Craig Chappelle from the bottom of my heart for reading the first draft for me (when the pages weren't even numbered) simply by way of friendship and giving me feedback without demolishing my confidence. English is not my first language and in prose this is often unconsciously evident in some strange twists of grammar! Don Eade, for several years the caretaker at Susannah Kathryn Pritchard's Writing Centre in Darlington, fortuitously came to live in Denmark and did me the favour of familiarising me with presentation protocol.

Another friend, Kumara, also a published author, provided the feedback of a reader with fresh eyes and many thoughtful suggestions.

I received unexpected help from an FCJ nun I met in England, who wishes to remain anonymous. This book became enriched as a result of her frankness and trust, and I thank her.

Books I have found useful in confirming certain dates in my chronicle include *These Women*, a historical account of the Mercy order, and *The Sisters Faithful Companions of Jesus in Australia*, the latter by Sister M Clare O'Connor, FCJ.

Sally Haigh took on the task of copy editor for my first draft, and she has done more than that. She is a veritable healer of the written word. I thank her for the unflagging attention and skill she has brought to the task and her willingness to give the manuscript the extra time it needed as it evolved beyond her original brief.

The professional advice of Tanya Marwood and Andrew Burke, both well known in Western Australia, helped shape my book to its present format.

I can't speak highly enough of the professionalism of the staff at HarperCollins. It has been an uplifting process to work with Nicola

O'Shea and see the manuscript improve through her superb editing skills. I thank Alison Urquhart for her true encouragement and for her patience and kindness in answering all my queries and acting on my behalf.

I sought occasional guidance from a woman who has a reputation for channelling higher wisdom, and spontaneously the topic of the book would arise. The message, 'Finish it; it will be successful', always came up, so I had the feeling I was on a mission from God. I thank the unknown friends who inspired her, and the other unknown, unseen friends who gave me guidance.

What of the many characters in this book, who all played their parts so well? From my heart I thank my parents, the FCJ nuns, my ex-partners, my two daughters, and the several people involved in my healing processes. And of course I particularly thank all the men who were once my clients. What would I have written without them?

I thank my friends in the little town of Denmark where I live for having faithfully reflected back to me the ultimate truth of One Loving Presence.

CARLA VAN RAAY